PRESIDENTIAL LEADERSHIP, ILLNESS, AND DECISION MAKING

This book examines the impact of medical and psychological illness on foreign policy decision making. Illness provides specific, predictable, and recognizable shifts in attention, time perspective, cognitive capacity, judgment, and emotion, which systematically affect impaired leaders. In particular, this book discusses the ways in which processes related to aging, physical and psychological illness, and addiction influence decision making. This book provides detailed analysis of the cases of four American presidents. Woodrow Wilson's October 1919 stroke affected his behavior during the Senate fight over ratifying the League of Nations. Franklin Roosevelt's severe coronary disease influenced his decisions concerning the conduct of war in the Pacific, from 1943 to 1945 in particular. John Kennedy's illnesses and treatments altered his behavior at the 1961 Vienna conference with Soviet premier Nikita Khrushchev. And Richard Nixon's psychological impairments biased his decisions regarding the covert bombing of Cambodia in 1969–1970.

Rose McDermott is Associate Professor of Political Science at the University of California, Santa Barbara. Professor McDermott's main area of research revolves around political psychology in international relations. She is the author of *Risk Taking in International Relations: Prospect Theory in American Foreign Policy* (1998) and *Political Psychology in International Relations* (2004). She is also coeditor of *Measuring Identity: A Guide for Social Scientists*. Professor McDermott has held fellowships at the John M. Olin Institute for Strategic Studies and the Women and Public Policy Program, both at Harvard University.

PRESIDENTIAL LEADERSHIP, ILLNESS, AND DECISION MAKING

ROSE MCDERMOTT

University of California, Santa Barbara

CAMBRIDGE
UNIVERSITY PRESS

CAMBRIDGE UNIVERSITY PRESS
Cambridge, New York, Melbourne, Madrid, Cape Town, Singapore,
São Paulo, Delhi

Cambridge University Press
32 Avenue of the Americas, New York, NY 10013-2473, USA

www.cambridge.org
Information on this title: www.cambridge.org/9780521882729

First published 2008

Printed in the United States of America

A catalog record for this publication is available from the British Library.

Library of Congress Cataloging in Publication Data

McDermott, Rose, 1962–
Presidential leadership, illness, and decision making / Rose McDermott.
p. cm.
Includes bibliographical references and index.
ISBN 978-0-521-88272-9 (hardback) – ISBN 978-0-521-70924-8 (pbk.)
1. Presidents – United States – Health.   2. Presidents – Succession –
United States.   3. Presidents – United States – Decision making.   I. Title.
JK609.M124   2007
352.23'6 – dc22   2007011717

ISBN   978-0-521-88272-9 hardback
ISBN   978-0-521-70924-8 paperback

Dedicated with heartfelt appreciation to
the best doctors in the world
for each saving my life in their own way.

They prove every day that the practice of medicine is both
art *and* science.

Iris Ascher, M.D.

Lyle Rausch, M.D.

Patricia Rogers, M.D.

Susan Sorensen, M.D.

Contents

Acknowledgments

I am delighted to have the opportunity to thank several individuals for particularly critical help during the research and writing of this book. Professor Robert Jervis encouraged me to undertake this project at the beginning. He also provided careful feedback and useful suggestions on the Nixon chapter. I am very grateful for his continuing inspiration, advice, support, and guidance. I would also like to express my appreciation to Fred Greenstein and Peter Katzenstein for continuing support and encouragement. Alexander and Juliette George were extremely generous in their help with the Wilson chapter. Juliette George in particular offered me access to extensive research materials and generously read more than one version of that chapter. I benefited greatly from several long telephone conversations on the topic with her. Several stimulating lunches with Walter LaFeber also helped crystallize my thinking on Wilson. Robert Gilbert read the entire manuscript and offered very constructive advice throughout. The book is much improved for his input, and I am very grateful for his kindness.

I remain deeply indebted to Dr. Robert Hopkins for everything he did to help bring this manuscript to fruition. Without his help, I would not have been able to access the Medical Archives at the John F. Kennedy Presidential Library, Boston. Dr. Hopkins generously offered several days of his time to help me read through the archives. Importantly, he helped me understand and interpret the meaning of the vast medical information available in those files. In addition, Dr. Hopkins brought his copies of the standard medical textbooks in use since the 1930s for me to examine in order to get a proper sense of the medical care available in each time period. He read the Kennedy chapter several times and the entire manuscript once. I am so very grateful to Dr. Hopkins for all his help and assistance. Stephen Plotkin and Deborah Leff provided a warm welcome and support during my time at the Kennedy library. At the Seely Mudd Library at Princeton University, Daniel Linke provided a great deal of assistance and information during my investigations of Woodrow Wilson's presidency. Farzeen Nasri and Manouchehr Ganji were very helpful concerning the case of the shah of Iran; I am very grateful for their time and assistance. Terry Sullivan, Paul Quirk, Bruce Miroff, and Martha Joynt Kumar provided assistance through the Presidency Research section list-serve of the American Political Science Association. I would also like to thank Florence Sanchez for her always cheerful and flawless help. Patrick Endress remained the world's most perfect research assistant throughout. All errors that remain are my own.

While I was writing this book, I was very fortunate to have the opportunity to get to know Leda Cosmides and John Tooby. They, and the community they have created, have provided me with tremendous intellectual challenge, growth, and stimulation. I am especially grateful to Stephen Rosen for his early and continuing support of this project, and for the funding I received from Andrew Marshall in the Office of Net Assessment of the Department of Defense.

I wish to thank Lew Bateman at Cambridge University Press for all his help and support in bringing this book to life. I also thank my husband, Jonathan Cowden, for his encouragement, help, and patience. The first summer I spent writing this book, I stayed with my mother in order to benefit from the vast resources of Stanford University's Green Library, including its depository of government documents. As always, I remain profoundly indebted to her for her material and emotional support. Words are clearly inadequate to express the extent of my debt and gratitude. I simply would not have been able to be me without her.

The final summer I spent revising this book proved to be the last I was able to share with our beloved German Shepherd, Demian. Late into each night, he would lie quietly beside me offering the remarkable constancy of his unconditional love, support, and acceptance. I feel very blessed to have had the privilege of sharing my life with such a magnificent dog. He provided an incredible model of approaching each day with joy and happiness, no matter what my ills or troubles.

ONE

INTRODUCTION

After the September 11, 2001, terrorist attacks on the United States, many Americans wondered why groups such as Al-Qaeda might hate America so much. Yet even violent and horrific acts often originate in real or perceived events that provide context, if not justification. American involvement in Middle Eastern politics has a long and often conflicted history. One such turning point in American foreign policy toward Arabic countries in the Middle East has received relatively little attention. The opportunities that the United States squandered with Egyptian leader Gamal Abdel Nasser prior to the Suez Crisis in 1956 appear even more tragic because decisions made then resulted, at least in part, from President Eisenhower's heart attack in September 1955, which forced him to turn over much of the responsibility for policy in the region to Secretary of State John Foster Dulles. Dulles's more intransigent views on the situation then held sway over subsequent Eisenhower administration policy.

When the United Nations separated Palestine into two separate states, one Jewish and one Arab, in November 1947, the Arab states remained antagonistic to the Zionists in their midst. On May 10, 1948, members of the Arab League, including Egypt, Jordan, Lebanon, Saudi Arabia, and Syria, were crushed in their invasion of the Jewish state by the much smaller Israeli military. Nonetheless, this defeat did not force the Arab states to recognize Israel. Egypt's Nasser believed that he needed more arms in order to launch an effective assault on Israel. To obtain these weapons, he signed an arms deal with Czechoslovakia in September 1955. This raised concern within the American government that Egypt was falling further under communist influence. This perception was strengthened when Nasser moved his recognition of China from the nationalist group of Chiang Kai-shek to the communist government headed by Mao.[1]

But September 1955 proved to be a tumultuous time for President Dwight Eisenhower as well. At this time, Eisenhower was ostensibly vacationing outside Denver, Colorado. On September 23, after a breakfast of ham, eggs, and sausage, he had driven more than eighty miles to do some work. Later, he played eighteen holes of golf, stopped for a hamburger lunch, and then played another nine holes of golf. During his golf, Eisenhower became angry over repeated interruptions from phone calls from John Foster Dulles that never seemed to go through properly. After eating lamb for dinner, he awoke in the middle of the night complaining of chest pains and his wife, Mamie, called Dr. Howard McC. Snyder to come treat him. The following morning, a cardiologist from the local Fitzsimons Army Hospital, Dr. Pollock, arrived and diagnosed that Ike had suffered a heart attack. He was then taken to the hospital. While he continued to recover fairly well, Eisenhower did not return to Washington, D.C., until November 11, 1955. In the interim, various officials traveled to Colorado to keep him apprised of national policy.[2]

During this critical period of time, American policy toward the Middle East fell largely under the purview and control of Secretary Dulles. Following the Egyptian arms deal with Czechoslovakia, Dulles made an offer to help Nasser fund his project to build the Aswan Dam on the lower Nile River. Nasser considered this project critical for Egyptian economic development. Dulles, calculating that Nasser would have difficulty paying for both the arms and the dam, had World Bank president Eugene Black go to Cairo to strike a deal for the bank, the United States, and Great Britain to help fund the $1.3 billion project. This offer was made on December 16, 1955. Nasser then wrote to the United States requesting certain conditions for the plan to move forward. Some of these conditions proved unacceptable to the United States; in addition, the Egyptians continued to build up their military forces using Soviet equipment. The Americans believed that this action would make it difficult for the Egyptians to have sufficient resources left over to contribute their part to the construction of the dam.

In addition, Dulles became embroiled in various debates on Capitol Hill, buffeted by those who wanted the United States to supply arms to the Israelis to balance the Egyptian buildup of military forces, supporters of the nationalist Chinese, and southern congressmen who did not want competition to American cotton coming from Egyptian fields. Dulles proved uninterested in surmounting this opposition to push forward with the plan to fund the dam. While his reasons remain somewhat shrouded, it appears that Dulles did not like Nasser and felt that the Egyptian leader was trying to blackmail the United States. He apparently believed that if America fell prey to such threats, it would send the wrong message to allies and enemies alike. After Eisenhower left the choice to him, Dulles decided against helping Nasser. On July 19, 1956, the U.S. government summarily withdrew its offer of help. The following week, Nasser nationalized the Suez Canal, claiming he needed the proceeds to help fund the cost of the dam.

Dulles made three critical errors of judgment in this period that might have been at least somewhat alleviated if he had not had such a free hand. First, he believed that if he withdrew the offer to help fund the dam, Nasser would lose ground politically in the region. To the contrary, when Nasser nationalized the canal, he became a hero to the Arab nations. Second, Dulles believed that the Soviets would not be willing or able to supplant American support. When the Soviets sided with Arab nations against Israel, France, and Britain in the ensuing Suez Crisis, their influence became heightened, not diminished. Finally, the timing of Dulles's announcement could not have been worse. The withdrawal of support took place just as the Egyptian foreign minister came to the United States to talk about the project, while Nasser remained in prominent public meetings with Yugoslavian leader Tito and Indian leader Nehru.[3]

Dulles's predispositions clearly had more impact than they might have otherwise because of Eisenhower's absence from the scene. Some scholars suggest that Eisenhower's heart attack was not as problematic as it might otherwise have been because there were no pressing crises.[4] Others note that Eisenhower's team approach to government similarly reduced the consequences of his absence from active participation.[5] But Eisenhower's military background and his skill in delegating authority, which by and large worked well to allow his government to function in his absence, also allowed certain actors like Dulles to make important decisions largely independently. While Eisenhower remained convalescing in late 1955, Dulles took his place front and center in the construction of American foreign policy toward the Middle East. Further, his most powerful and ardent opponent within the administration, Special Assistant for Cold War Strategy Nelson Rockefeller, who had been appointed by Eisenhower in 1954, resigned in December 1955, after being unable to see the president between the time Ike was stricken and early December.

In the end, Robert Gilbert provides the most eloquent summary of Dulles' impact: "The emergence of John Foster Dulles as essentially the sole architect of U.S. foreign policy during the President's convalescence had major ramifications. The most serious was that it contributed to a major upheaval in the Middle East and to a serious degeneration in the relationship between the United States and its allies – developments that might never have occurred if Eisenhower had not been ill at the time."[6]

Significantly, perhaps because of his military background, which made death such a constant companion, perhaps because of his own personal battles with illness, Eisenhower was the first president to push for a formal plan to handle instances of presidential disability and impairment. In recognizing the reality this book seeks to detail, Eisenhower instigated work that resulted in the Twenty-fifth Amendment to the U.S. Constitution.

ILLNESS AND RATIONALITY

Everyone gets sick. And everyone dies. Even powerful leaders suffer from physical limitations. But because their limitations can compromise the health and welfare of all those under their leadership, the consequences of their illnesses have an impact far beyond themselves. Their mistakes, miscalculations, or inactions can place more than their own lives at risk, and in this way their diseases matter more than those which afflict less influential individuals. Secrecy perpetuated in an attempt to hold onto political power can exacerbate this dynamic. This book seeks to examine, in depth, the impact of physical and psychological illness on the foreign policy decision making of several important American presidents in the twentieth century as well as the impact of foreign leaders' health on the decision making of American presidents.

When most people conjure up pictures in their minds of disabled or impaired leaders, the most evocative images remain quite dramatic: Adolf Hitler's hysterically tyrannical outrages; John Kennedy's recoiling after getting shot in the head while his wife attempts to climb out of the back of the car in her perfect pink suit; Ronald Reagan's split-second reaction as he is shoved into his limousine by a secret service agent after being shot by John Hinckley in a perverted attempt to impress actress Jodie Foster. What connects these divergent images and makes them memorable is their dramatic nature; however, disabilities or impairments that result from illness are less noticeable and can even be concealed. Certainly no leader who is unstable or ill could reach the heights of power in this age of aggressive investigative journalism. Or could they? And how would we know? Even when impairments remain subtle, they can still exert a decisive effect on decision making. And when side effects result from treatment itself, they can alter judgment as well. In addition, the stress of a powerful leader's job alone can lead to self-induced, if transient, effects on judgment. Crisis can add time pressure to any underlying weaknesses. And the abuse of alcohol and other substances can exacerbate such effects. The important point, from the perspective of the public in a representative democracy, lies in transparency. It is one thing for voters to knowingly choose an ill candidate over a healthy one for policy reasons; it is quite another to vote for an ill man believing he is well.

Many still dominant models in the political science and international relations scholarly literature continue to assume that individuals and their differences do not matter because state-level behavior is really controlled by forces beyond the individual, such as the relative power of nations. Even more common arguments suggest that all leaders act in similar ways to rationally maximize their interests.[7] Many leading models of rational choice decision making in political science argue that decisions are usually guided by the rationality and self-interest of leaders. These rational choice models revolve largely around notions of strategic leadership, which is capable of engaging in sophisticated and prospective cost-benefit analysis. Most of these theories assume that leaders make rational decisions and actions based on their available choices in order to maximize the probability of achieving their most desired outcome. Such models have difficulty accounting for the behavior of individuals who appear to defy such calculated choice and action, whether motivated by emotion, illness, or some other factor. For example, someone who is ill, and thus has a foreshortened sense of his expected life-span, may not discount the future in the same way that a healthy person might and may violate some of the maxims of standard rational choice assumptions and behaviors. As Crispell and Gomez write, "the concept that an undetected sickness in a powerful man can alter the course of history falls within the realm of irrational politics."[8] The more general aversion to seemingly irrational forces represents part of the reason that political science still lacks "a general theory relating health to political events."[9]

But this perspective is not the only one that is useful in understanding leadership and foreign policy decision making, and many others have long argued for the wisdom and viability of individual analysis. In examining the impact of illness on leadership, I argue against a predominantly rational characterization of leadership under these circumstances. Most people close to decision makers readily realize that leaders are prone to suffer from physical and mental limitations and illnesses that can, at least on occasion, render their decisions seemingly irrational or suboptimal. Leaders who are mentally or physically ill, old, or addicted to drugs or alcohol can easily make bad, even irrational decisions, whether intentionally or not. Strategic models of rational behavior thus fail to capture much of the complexity, nuance, and reality of real-world decision makers and their environments once leaders fall ill. A rational choice theorist might argue than an impaired leader would not gain power in a democracy and that his disabilities would prevent him from obtaining elective office in a competitive system. However, history obviously contests this assertion, as does the reality that some leaders achieve power by force, others do not become ill until after they have attained the highest office, and still others can afford to buy their way into power without having to be concerned about authentic competition.

I do not argue that medical and psychological factors are the *only* influences on decision making. Similarly, my discussion here is circumscribed to the impact of illness on decision making; I do not systematically address the influence of other factors that may exert irrational forces on leaders. Such factors are not deterministic in nature, and other political, material, and structural forces are important in describing, explaining, and predicting the outcome of decisions in international affairs. However, individual-level factors, especially those related to illness, have received less attention than they perhaps deserve, given their prevalence, in the literature in political science, leadership, and foreign policy decision making. Examining this topic can prove challenging, because most leaders possess clear incentives not to appear weak or ill for fear of being exploited or overthrown. And yet illness and disability appear to exert at least some influence on some leaders at critical junctions. In addition, having some knowledge of the medical and psychological strengths and weaknesses of foreign leaders might help American leaders anticipate and more readily and appropriately respond to leadership crises or transitions in other countries. Forewarning provides the best mechanism for America to protect its national security interests. For example, Osama bin Laden reportedly suffers from kidney ailments. Ways to track him or undermine his strength might include following or interdicting shipments of expensive dialysis materials or kidney medicines in remote parts of Pakistan or Afghanistan.

My goal here is to explore systematically some areas of decision making where possibilities for optimal rational decision making become restricted, almost by definition. In this effort, I hope to build on the pathbreaking work of authors such as Hugh L'Etang, Jerrold Post and Robert Robins, Robert Gilbert, and Bert Park, who have noted the importance of illness in leadership analysis to illuminate its impact on seminal foreign policy decisions within specific presidential contexts.[10] In applying and extending the discussion of leadership impairment to the realm of American foreign policy, I seek to extricate those aspects of human decision-making behavior which might be idiosyncratically physical, emotional, or psychological in origin. This facilitates subsequent investigation into those arenas of foreign policy making where political and psychological motives intertwine. By focusing on psychological and characterological factors in presidential leadership, it becomes possible to examine political factors through a uniquely personal and physical lens.

Impairments, by their very definition and nature, often manifest in unpredictable, idiosyncratic, and irrational ways. The impact of illness on decision making can appear to be similarly random, and yet is likely not. In human evolutionary history, people have encountered illness in many iterations; as such, humans have developed strategies that help maximize the possibilities for survival in the face of this challenge. Although such mechanisms may prove adaptive for successfully overcoming many illnesses, they may not necessarily facilitate high-level decision making on unrelated matters while ill. And yet, by and large, specific illnesses present well-defined and predictable symptoms, pharmaceuticals produce predictable clusters of side effects, and age-related declines occur in certain progressive, if intermittent, domains. Recognizing the categories of impairment can allow individuals and institutions to begin to make structural accommodations for the detection, treatment, and succession problems involved when leadership impairment arises.

THEORETICAL APPROACHES TO THE IMPACT OF ILLNESS ON LEADERSHIP

The necessarily idiosyncratic nature of disease has limited our ability to generalize about the impact of illness on leadership. In addition, how disease might affect policy outcomes depends on the individual, the specific disease, and the political and historical contexts of the time, as well as on the institutions in place to handle such an eventuality. Nonetheless, certain regularities have come to the fore, most notably presented in the work by Jerrold Post and Robert Robins.[11] These authors suggest that illness can play a decisive role in policy outcomes, but these effects often remain subtle, intermittent, and hard to uncover at the time. They also note that a leader's advisers, supporters, and family members can make matters much worse by attempting to protect the leader and keep his illness secret. Advisers often want to retain their own personal political power, which is tied to that of the leader, and thus seek to protect and preserve the leader's image of health and power. Patients and family members may go doctor shopping, seeking the best in medical care for the ill leader, while inadvertently precipitating clashes between the competing physicians. In addition, the demands of secrecy may tie the hands of competent medical personnel and prevent the delivery of optimal care, which may require a team-based approach involving more people than the leader or his family will allow. In some regime types, advisers and physicians may fear for their lives if their leader is deposed as a result of weakness, either real or imagined.

Further, the leader's personality can decisively influence the impact of his illness on policy, depending on whether he favors a more hands-on approach or tends to delegate more power and authority to others. Finally, the specific disease can determine the extent and nature of a leader's incapacitation. Some illnesses can be easier to manage, be more likely to prove fatal, or require treatment that exerts a greater effect than others. Some diseases, such as common cardiovascular disease, can slowly affect brain function over time and thus manifest only intermittently, which might allow careful advisers to show a leader only at his best, even if just for a few hours a day.

These important theoretical insights provided by Post and Robins prove true in this current study as well. Their conclusions remain crucial to understanding and appreciating the impact of illness on political leadership. Importantly, the similarities they mention may vary with regime type as well. In democracies, for example, a greater degree of freedom of the press may make it harder for leaders to hide their illnesses, while simultaneously raising the stakes for keeping it secret. In politics, no one wants to present himself as a weak leader; however, in democracies it may be easier to delegate important decisions to other leaders and branches of government if tragedy occurs. In a more authoritarian structure, the impact of a leader's incapacity may prove more devastating for the day-to-day running of the government.

ILLNESS AS AN ADAPTIVE, DOMAIN-SPECIFIC, CONTENT-LADEN PROGRAM

Modifications in functioning, taken as a collective, can be viewed as an adaptive program that holds important consequences for judgment and decision making in leadership contexts. Because illness presents a repeated evolutionary challenge, people have had many opportunities to evolve strategies for maximizing their likelihood of survival under such circumstances. These strategies remain instinctual; the affected individual does not need to engage these processes consciously and is often unaware of their operation. Nonetheless, such dynamic processes work to ensure that sufficient energy and resources are devoted to healing, even at the cost of less immediately important threats to the organism, such as abstract decision making about non-illness-related events and activities. The afflicted individual may not wish to be impaired in this way but may not be able to help it; sick people may prove no more able to control their emotional responses than they do their immune system during times of illness, precisely because all necessary and available resources will be recruited by the physical body to promote healing and maximize chances for the survival of the whole organism.

Evolutionary psychology provides an approach to human behavior and decision making that examines those functional, adaptive aspects of the human cognitive architecture which evolved in response to repeated problems encountered by hunter-gatherer ancestors. Designed by natural selection to address these repeated challenges, evolutionary approaches posit that the human mind contains numerous content-laden, domain-specific programs. In other words, humans are not born tabula rasa, subject to learning and socialization on a blank slate. Rather, humans are born with functionally specialized processes for handling specific problems encountered by their ancestors, including physical challenges such as

8

vision stability across changing light conditions and regulation of bodily mechanisms such as breathing and respiration, as well as more complex social behaviors such as foraging for food, avoiding predators, and finding mates. As Cosmides and Tooby describe, these processes are brought to bear under

> conditions, contingencies, situations or event types that recurred innumerable times in hominid evolutionary history. Repeated encounters with each type of situation selected for adaptations that guided information processing, behavior, and the body adaptively through a cluster of conditions, demands and contingencies that characterized that particular class of situation. This can be accomplished by engineering superordinate programs, each of which jointly mobilizes a subset of the psychological architecture's other programs in a particular configuration. Each configuration should be selected to deploy computational and physiological mechanisms in a way that, when averaged over individuals and generations, would have led to the most fitness-promoting subsequent lifetime outcome, given that ancestral situation type.
>
> This coordinated adjustment and entrainment of mechanisms constitute a *mode of operation for the entire psychological architecture.*[12]

In other words, the human cognitive architecture, here understood to incorporate not just thoughts but also feelings and other physiological processes in an integrated manner, evolved to respond to challenges repeatedly faced by our ancestors. Illness presented one of those repeated challenges whose successful resolution affected both fitness and survival.

Illness can entrain a cluster of responses that coalesce to produce a notable and predictable impact on the manner in which an ill leader rules. The effects can display a wide range of dimensions; for example, serious illness may limit a person's attentional abilities, emotional resilience, and cognitive capacities. These restrictions in functioning produce particular biases in the focus that a leader brings to his job. Specifically, illness works as a cognitive program that enhances internal focus, restricts time horizon, weakens cognitive capacity, affects perceptions of value and utility, restricts emotional resilience, and induces emotional lability. Although I briefly discuss each point in turn here, it is important to note in the following analysis that all these factors work in concert to color the lens through which sick leaders see themselves, their work, and the external world.

Internal Focus

Some political leaders may rise to their position of power because they have obtained specialized knowledge of particular areas of government or politics or garnered political favor through their personal charisma and skill. Rarely, however, does someone reach the pinnacle of power without maintaining an extensive focus on the external world of politics and important political actors.

Illness breaks this set. Illness by definition forces a person to focus on his internal world in a way in which political leaders, in particular, may never have had to previously.[13] The illness itself, whether through pain, impairment, fatigue, nausea, or simply the time involved in seeking help and obtaining treatment, demands that a leader's attention be drawn inward. A great deal of mental time, energy, and attention must now be devoted to the illness, its symptoms, its prognosis, its treatment, and its political impact. If a leader wishes to keep the illness secret, additional time and energy must be spent on hiding the illness and its effects from others. If the illness is fatal, existential and legacy concerns may preoccupy the person as well. He may become much more religious, for example.

Given that all humans have limited time, energy, and emotional and physical reserves, resources devoted differentially to one cause will inevitably remain unavailable for other purposes, however important they may otherwise remain. But serious illness will not take second place; it demands primary focus. Therefore, however important particular projects or goals may have been to a leader before the illness took center stage, everything else reverts backstage in the wake of a serious disease. Work may be neglected or delegated to others. But the inevitable result is that the leader will have less overall resources available to devote to his job in the face of illness, pain, and treatment.

Foreshortened Time Horizon

Time perspective represents an important variable in the way individuals relate to their sense of past, present, and future. As such, time perspective constitutes a fundamental representation of the way individuals construct their sense of time, history, and legacy. Some people remain preoccupied with the past, others manage to stay focused in the present, while still others concentrate on the future. This subjective focus in time can reliably exert a powerful influence on many aspects of human behavior, including educational achievement, risky driving, tendency for delinquency and substance abuse, various health dimensions such as likelihood to engage in preventive care, and mate choice.[14] Notably, many successful people tend to be future oriented, learning to plan and delay gratification in order to achieve their future goals, and many leaders would fall into this future-oriented category. Although often stressed in time management and certain religious traditions such as Buddhism, shifting from a future to a more present-oriented time perspective has been shown to encourage more risky behavior.

Illness itself forces a more present-time orientation on its victim. In the face of incipient illness, time is of the essence. Life seems shorter. There is too much to accomplish with too little time to do it. Sick people cannot defer treatment if they want to have a chance of recovery. Moreover, treatment may at least delay the appearance of the ravages of illness, which could have important political implications. In the wake of illness, men who had been future oriented are forced to focus on the present. No longer can they defer or avoid things they do not want to do because of their power and influence. No longer can they overcome the effects of illness simply because they confront important and timely policy decisions simultaneously.

Further, Post and Robins note that many leaders develop a greater sense of urgency in the face of a diagnosis with a fatal illness.[15] Rational decision makers often discount their sense of the future, such that the value of rewards that become available at different points of time in the future is denigrated.[16] Rewards in the future are less certain, and therefore typically deemed less attractive. As a result, they need to be more desirable in order to overcome the natural preference for immediate rewards.

Obviously, a leader's sense of the future can change if he believes that his life-span will be inadvertently and unexpectedly foreshortened. His sense of the future becomes more limited. The importance of his historical legacy becomes heightened and more salient, while simultaneously seeming more difficult to achieve in the remaining time in a weakened state. For example, when the shah of Iran began his so-called White Revolution to bring about a long-term program of modernization in his country, he believed that he had several decades to accomplish his goals. When he was diagnosed with cancer, his timetable noticeably quickened; at least some of the radical religious opposition he encountered in pursing this program resulted from the social dislocation and upheaval precipitated by a pattern of rapid modernization and secularization. Ironically, the shah had originally understood the importance of slow and steady change in order to achieve widespread societal acceptance, but his illness forced him to reevaluate this plan, to his ultimate detriment.

Lessened Capacity

Illness diminishes a leader's sheer physical, psychological, and often cognitive ability to work as hard as he might have been able to do previously. As a result, fewer resources remain available for processing information and making decisions. Optimal decision making requires full attention and the ability to bring to bear as much information about the situation as possible. Some people from the start possess more inherent resources and abilities in this regard than others and thus can manage better in the face of diminished capacity. But, regardless of skill and experience, sickness limits the previous ability of any leader to exert his full capacity in making important and influential decisions that can affect millions in both economic and military terms. The leader spends more time and energy dealing with the symptoms and consequences of his illness, undergoing treatment, and possibly ensuring secrecy. More time and energy must also be devoted to doctors and less, by consequence, to advisers and political demands. And more psychic energy becomes consumed with anxiety, depression, fatigue, and thoughts of death. Pain, in and of itself, can be incredibly draining and debilitating, even when the prospects for recovery appear positive overall.

In addition, many medications used in the treatment of various ailments can induce direct compromises in cognitive functioning. A leader undergoing treatment may simply possesses fewer resources for handling the crises of the day. Equally significant, such an impaired person may find less importance and interest in such events while he is fighting for his life.

Judgmental Alterations in Perceptions of Value and Utility

Any serious illness will weaken a person's physical and cognitive resistance to stress. Stress represents a complicated political and psychological phenomenon. Some leaders thrive on political crisis; others become paralyzed in the face of it. Stress and illness also exert a reciprocal and cyclical interrelationship. Stress causes illness, but illness itself also causes stress. It is not simply that a sick person may not be able to fight off other infections as quickly and easily as they might in a healthy state. An ill person also worries about his health, its impact on his family and job, and its likely course. All of a sudden, things that once seemed important appear trivial by comparison with the prospect of death. In the context of illness, other values shift as well. Events that may once have felt like a waste of time, such as spending time with loved ones, become precious and crucial means of coping. Other events, previously viewed as crucial, lose their importance or interest for an ill leader.

In this way, illness mediates the interpretation of all other information, biasing the individual's sense of its value. In this way, Irving Janis referred to illness as an "interpreter" that translates and influences, for better or worse, the value and importance of all other information which a leader processes.[17] In this context, illness serves to shift judgment and perception in such a way as to affect the assessment of utility, the assignment of personal meaning, and the allocation of restricted time, energy, and mental and physical resources.

Emotional Lability

Illness can affect emotional resiliency, both directly and indirectly. Directly, particular illnesses may cause emotional disturbances because of either the symptoms they produce or the effects of drugs that are used to treat them. But indirect effects remain equally significant and often counterintuitive.

Serious or fatal illnesses can often induce depression and other negative psychological effects. People who feel ill may become scared about facing death or be rendered tired and sick by the medication or treatment program. Such individuals will experience great difficulty summoning emotional resources beyond their immediate medical needs. It is not surprising when chronically ill people become depressed or anxious about their symptoms, their condition, their future, or their prospects for recovery. But the implications of such a mood shift can have profound political consequences. Depression itself, independent of the symptoms of any given illness, causes disturbances in sleep, appetite, energy, mood, and motivation.[18] The professional and political consequences of such impairments remain myriad and transparent. This psychically imposed paralysis can prove quite efficient because it does the most to maximize the person's chances of recovering by ensuring that all available resources are directed toward healing. When this withdrawal persists after illness abates or emerges in the absence of physical disease, the symptoms of depression can prove particularly debilitating on their own.

Less obviously, leaders who suffer from serious physical and psychological impairments often manifest remarkable and unusual compassion for others who suffer from ill health or its economic consequences. In this study, both Franklin Roosevelt and John Kennedy remain notable in this regard. Franklin Roosevelt's affliction with polio, in particular, lessened his tendency toward arrogance and produced a remarkable empathy for those who suffered from a wide variety of economic and physical perils. Even his wife commented on the importance of his limitation for his understanding of those in need. The initiation of many of his New Deal programs can be viewed in this light. In addition to supporting small, local programs designed to help others with polio, such as his own spa at Warm Springs, Georgia, Roosevelt created a vast governmental safety net for those who fell on hard times for a variety of reasons as a result of the Great Depression. John Kennedy did not create the same extent of social programs that Roosevelt did, but his example served to emphasize physical fitness in schools, among other places, and the death of his young son, Patrick, inspired the subsequent development of the medical discipline of neonatology, a creation responsible for saving the lives of countless premature infants.

Summary

Because serious illness can exert such a profound influence on so many areas of human functioning, it should not be surprising that it can similarly impact political leadership abilities as well. Serious disease, and the treatment often required to manage it, can affect a leader's attention span, emotional stability, and cognitive abilities in major ways. The demands of illness allow no other possibility. Sometimes these limitations will be evident, but, more often than not, many effects can be successfully hidden from public view by advisers and family members.

The impact of illness on leadership can thus influence a leader's decision-making abilities in decisive and somewhat predictable ways. Attention becomes focused inward. Time horizons shorten, urgency increases, and a sense of the importance of historical legacy heightens. Cognitive and physical capacities diminish. Perceptions of value shift and relocate. Leaders may become both more depressed personally and more aware of the influence of their social and health policies on those who suffer. Taken together, this syndrome of illness functions as a kind of physical and psychological bias that influences the style and effectiveness of political leadership.

In this book, I explore the extent to which particular leaders' political performances may have been impacted by their health problems. I argue that health issues present one of many inputs in assessing leadership performance and quality. Other inputs – such as the extent, quality, and kind of political support or one's intelligence, motivation and goals, and worldview – provide similar factors by which it might be possible to measure leadership performance and skill.[19] In the health domain, some medical issues and concerns exert more of an impact than others. Mental or neurological illness presents a much greater threat to reasonable decision making than a broken leg or an infection might. In this book, I argue that health issues interact with particular *other political* concerns to produce especially destructive outcomes under specific circumstances.

At the extreme, impairment proves largely uninteresting politically because an exceptional limitation would be widely acknowledged and accepted, as when a leader lies on his deathbed following an assassination attempt. However, subtle impacts of health on cognitive performance can emerge as more nuanced and influential than expected, and thus more interesting than might appear obvious at first glance. When do health constraints begin to cause problems, and when do they pass unnoticed? Health problems may limit performance in making various decisions in unexpected or unacknowledged but nonetheless powerful ways, including situations in which a leader must make a choice between equally bad or unattractive options, cases in which premature cognitive closure can precipitate unnecessary conflict or intransigence, examples where mental or physical resources and endurance are overtaxed, and instances where powerful social or emotional forces pull for consensus in order to demonstrate loyalty, solidarity, or commitment to an important value. In addition, even subtle impairments can affect attention, memory, or judgment about what a leader perceives to constitute an important problem, how he allocates his mental and physical resources, which events in memory remain salient as relevant and instructive analogies for current problems, and how choices are made. Impaired leaders may have less resilience and shorter attention spans than their unimpaired peers, and these limitations might encourage the systematic biases in performance noted previously under specific political conditions.[20] These situations are most likely to occur when the leader has a wide range of freedom of action with a great deal of power, as is often the case during foreign policy crises in particular.

Because an impaired leader, by definition, suffers from a medical or psychological problem in a political context, the decision to remove such a person from office must remain both a political and a medical issue. A leader should be well and competent enough to make reasonable decisions. However, it often requires a medical doctor to diagnose illness and political actors to determine if the impairment is great enough to prohibit service. Neither doctors nor politicians are themselves sufficiently skilled to render such a determination alone. As Post and Robins insightfully note in arguing that leadership can prove harmful to a leader's health, "to submit to optimal medical treatment could be politically fatal, but not to submit to optimal medical treatment could be personally fatal."[21]

POLITICAL RAMIFICATIONS

Whereas any discussion of the impact of medical and psychological illness on foreign policy decision making must revolve around medical information, diagnosis, and treatment in exploring impairment, any examination of its impact on policy must evaluate the political context within which impaired leaders operate. Leaders do not operate in isolation. Their abilities and limitations interact with specific political environments, which can either exacerbate or ameliorate the effect of their disability on policy decisions and outcomes.

Post and Robins provide the most comprehensive outline of the systematic ways in which personality, politics, and illness can interact.[22] First, they note the importance of the nature of the illness and how it manifests itself. So, for example, a broken leg will not impair a leader's decision-making capacity in the way that a stroke would. Similarly, sudden changes in behavior following a stroke might prove much more dramatic and difficult to conceal than the slow, insidious, intermittent onset of Alzheimer's disease.

Second, how difficult a disease is to hide can affect the extent to which it is disclosed. In earlier days the press was more restrained in reporting certain conditions; few reporters ever photographed Roosevelt in his wheelchair, for example. However, even now some diseases would be easier to conceal than others. Any illness that presented obvious cognitive effects and limitations would be more difficult to conceal from the public than illnesses with less obvious, if no less serious, mental limitations, such as creeping senility or progressive substance abuse.

Third, the effect of drugs, either illicit or not, and alcohol can exert particular effects on leadership performance as well. While a little alcohol may be required for many diplomatic social exchanges, too much can severely impair decision-making abilities. Fourth, the medical and ethical challenges of providing medical care to important leaders can compromise the quality of their care, as well as affect the political consequences of it.

Fifth, both age and illness can affect leadership performance and success. Post and Robins note that this reality interacts with the personality and style of the leader to either potentiate or circumvent the impact of these factors on political decisions and behavior. For example, a leader who accepts his increasing infirmity or limitations with equanimity can make reasonable accommodations and still remain effective while in office. On the other hand, a leader who refuses to accept such realities may rail against them in ways that precipitate international conflict. This can happen, for instance, if a leader feels that his time is limited, and he has not accomplished everything he wanted to achieve, and therefore takes tremendous risks in order to meet this own goals before he is deposed or dies.

Finally, the relationship between the nature of the illness and the kind of political system in which it occurs can influence the quality of treatment, the outcome of policy, and the issue of succession. Illness in a democracy may be hidden as in an autocracy, but the impact of this illness on policy outcomes can change depending on how much control a leader has over policy, what rules for succession exist in a particular political context, and how much the illness and its treatment distract the leader from his professional responsibilities.

Several implications of these interactions deserve consideration. First, medical information remains important not just for leaders who are suffering and for those under their influence. Medical information and intelligence also matter greatly as an important part of foreign policy intelligence. Carter's policy toward the shah of Iran would most likely have been altered had he had timely and accurate information on the true state of the shah's health. Because he did not find out until very late that the shah was ill, and because the information about the necessary treatment the shah required was incorrect, whether by accident or design, Carter felt pushed by humanitarian concerns to admit the shah into the country in 1979. This act led directly to the seizure of the American Embassy and American hostages in Tehran. Needless to say, seeking to obtain accurate and adequate medical information on foreign leaders should become a priority in military and defense intelligence communities.

Second, the interaction of personality, illness, and politics can exert a profound effect on the nature of foreign policy decisions and actions. Impaired leaders, at least under certain circumstances, may make different and more suboptimal choices than their unimpaired peers would or than they might have made when well. Also, impaired leaders may still make better choices than their unimpaired peers. Coming face to face with illness and death may give such individuals a particular sensitivity for the suffering of others, which their unimpaired brethren do not share. In addition, an impaired leader may simply remain a superior politician to whatever healthy alternatives may be available.

Conclusions

Having outlined some of the major issues and controversies surrounding presidential health and impairment, I discuss in the next chapter the specific impact of aging, physical and psychological illness, and addiction on decision making. The chapter considers what is known about the impact of certain illnesses, such as heart disease, on cognitive capacity and reviews the most common side effects of typical drug treatments for such ailments. Then I investigate the likely implications of such conditions and treatments for the specific decisions and actions of particular leaders.

The bulk of the book will provide a detailed analysis of four American presidents who were impaired, and the impact of their conditions on specific foreign policy decisions during their tenure. Chapter 3 examines the impact of Wilson's psychological intransigence and October 1919 stroke on his behavior during the Senate fight over the consent to ratify the League of Nations, as well as his psychological and neurological limitations. Chapter 4 addresses the impact of Roosevelt's severe coronary artery disease on his decisions and actions during the last two and a half years of the Second World War. Particular attention is paid to his decisions surrounding the conduct of the war in the Pacific. Many observers have argued that Roosevelt gave away too much to Stalin at the Yalta conference in 1945 as a result of his illness, whereas others claim that even Roosevelt at his best would have been too constrained by the political and military situation to have been able to wrest any more from Stalin than he was able to do at the time. The contrast in Roosevelt's decision-making skills and abilities and actions at various times illustrates nicely the intermittent nature of cognitive impairment in cases of coronary artery disease. Next, Chapter 5 analyzes the impact of John Kennedy's various drug treatments, including the use of steroids for treatment of his Addison's disease, and narcotics and amphetamines for back pain, on his behavior with Khrushchev during the Vienna conference in 1961. Chapter 6 examines Richard Nixon's psychological character and how it may have affected his conduct in the Vietnam War, especially his decisions regarding the covert bombing of Cambodia in 1969–1970. The next chapter discusses the implications of these issues and findings for determinations of presidential competence and disability. In particular, the Twenty-fifth Amendment and other suggestions for ensuring presidential competence are discussed. Some concluding thoughts on the care of presidents complete this book. In addition, an appendix on the use and misuse of medical intelligence in assessing foreign leadership provides an extensive examination of the case of the shah of Iran and the impact of his hidden illness on U.S. foreign policy decision making during the Carter administration. This appendix emphasizes the importance of collecting accurate medical intelligence on foreign leaders to support American presidential foreign policy decision making more effectively.

Unlike many other areas of life, wealth, power, and status cannot mitigate the occurrence or ravages of disease on those afflicted. Powerful leaders are not exempted from illness by virtue of their position or its influence. But unlike the impact of personal illness and death on a less powerful or influential individual, a leader's illness and demise can affect the lives of many others in decisive ways. Understanding the cluster of effects that afflicts such leadership provides one step in the direction of encouraging an informed and attentive citizenry, which, in a democracy, can seek institutionally to minimize the negative impacts of illness on foreign policy.

TWO

AGING, ILLNESS, AND ADDICTION

Illness raises the specter of unpredictable choice and action. Leaders who are impaired by physical or psychological illness or unduly affected by drugs and medication rarely remain as stable or predictable as those who are not. The prospect of disabled leaders arouses fear, anger, and anxiety in many observers and constituents as they contemplate the loss of stability, security, or predictability in their nation's future.

This public discomfort can produce different outcomes. On the one hand, voters often appear loath to vote for candidates who had past serious illnesses, even if they appear to be "cured" at the time of the campaign. This occurred in 1972 with the revelation of vice-presidential candidate Tom Eagleton's past bouts with depression and his treatment with electroshock therapy. McGovern was forced to pull Eagleton off the ticket in the wake of the public furor, thus leading to accusations of lack of judgment on McGovern's part for selecting Eagleton. Politically and perhaps medically, McGovern may have been justified in his choice, but the public wanted a chief executive who, they believed, could stand up to the inherent stresses of the job without undue vulnerability. Despite the fact that Eagleton had experienced his depression many years prior with no subsequent recurrences, about 30 percent of people who suffer major depression do not always respond well to medication.[1] This outcome was also fueled by high levels of public stigma, as well as ignorance, surrounding mental illness, along with a deep-seated and widespread belief that people who suffer from mental illness in whatever form do not really ever get better. In fact, Eagleton was reelected to the Senate by those constituents who knew and trusted him most, and he continued to have a successful political career without subsequent psychological impairment.

Of course, this also highlights the difference in public perception based on an official's position. While the public may be happy to vest confidence in a legislator with a history of serious mental illness, they may remain understandably reluctant to give ultimate control of the nuclear "football" to such a man. This episode highlights the enormous, and often unfounded, public fear that psychological illness in particular precipitates. Possibly, as education increases, public attitudes can begin to change slowly. By 1990, for example, the fact that Florida senator Lawton Chiles had taken Prozac did not prevent him from being elected governor, despite his opponent's attempt to use this information against him.[2]

Because serious consequences can result from a mentally ill leader, the public should be concerned about such impairments. Many psychological illnesses, however, remain highly treatable, with success rates, depending on the condition, of upwards of 90 percent. But treatment requires the person being able to acknowledge and seek help without fear of political suicide. As long as mental illness continues to be devastatingly stigmatized, leaders who suffer from serious depression and other mental illness will be driven to hide their conditions, remain untreated, and thus ironically become much more likely to exert a negative impact on their decision making without others necessarily being aware of this dynamic. Eagleton, who received treatment, did not commit suicide. By contrast, both British Lord Castlereagh, foreign secretary and leader of the House of Commons in the government of Lord Liverpool in the post-Napoleonic era, and James Forrestal, secretary of the navy during the Second World War, and America's first secretary of defense, neither of whom received proper treatment, committed suicide.

Another example of public reaction to an ostensibly "cured" illness occurred in the case of Paul Tsongas's 1992 bid for the presidency. Despite claims that his lymphoma was cured, the public did not seem to trust that he would not fall ill again. After a series of primary losses, Tsongas was forced to pull out of the race for financial reasons. As it turned out, he and his doctors did hide a recurrence of his cancer from the public during the campaign. In this case, the public proved right. In fact, Tsongas began chemotherapy on the day that he would have been inaugurated and later died of his preexisting condition during the time he would have been in power had he been elected.

The second way in which the public may react to anxiety about the health of its leaders involves denial. Especially if a leader's illness is insidious in onset, intermittent in occurrence, and not mentally debilitating, such as congestive heart disease, loyal staffers may be able to help him hide the severity of his impairment from outsiders. When this occurs, the public, and even the press, may not pursue the case as aggressively as they might follow, for example, a case of sexual indiscretion. The era also affects the extent to which these cover-ups are possible. Roosevelt's impairments, for example, were hidden from the press and the public quite successfully; the press was even complicit in hiding his paralysis from public view in a way unimaginable today. Reagan's aides were able to downplay the severity of his mental compromise. For example, in a 1982 visit, Reagan toasted the people of Bolivia while he was in Brazil, appeared confused about who was fighting whom in Latin America, and was even known to call his dog by the wrong name.[3] Vice President Cheney and his doctors withheld important information about medications that he was taking.

So what impairments and disabilities produce the most anxiety in the general population? Are they the illnesses that should raise such concerns? Would a more educated public react differently, appropriately demanding more information in cases where such concern merits attention, while also accepting some other illnesses that currently remain more frightening to the public than incapacitating to the leader?

This chapter seeks to outline some of the ways in which leaders can become incapacitated while in office. One of the central tasks involved in assessing disability revolves around establishing a baseline for relative impairment. Obviously, there can be many reasons and causes for suboptimal decision making, some relating to luck, timing, or skill. How and when can impairment be distinguished from these other alternative explanations for decisions, behaviors, and outcomes? Previous unrelated medical and psychological research has already helped establish some well-respected parameters for normal physical and psychological functioning. If previous medical or psychological literature has suggested that certain cognitive or behavioral sequelae result from particular illnesses or medications, and the leader is known to suffer from a particular precipitating condition or manifests expected symptomatology, we can gain confidence in arguing that the leader's impairments followed from the particular condition or treatment, just as it would in any other person.

Through a comparison between established baselines and leader decisions and actions, we can develop a richer understanding of historical cases where aging, illness, or addiction have critically affected a leader. The investigation here of four presidents' impairments, treatments, and consequences for specific foreign policy decisions, as well as the effect of one foreign leader's medical illness on U.S. foreign policy, can help establish decision rules and procedures for handling future cases of a leader's illness or impairment. Impaired leadership is a dynamic, multifaceted, and complex issue. Knowing more is not always enough; greater sophistication in interpreting what to do with medical and psychological information and knowing what information matters is the key to greater understanding and more responsible solutions. To be clear, all three types of problems – aging, illness, and addiction – produce the shifts in internal focus, foreshortened time horizon, lessened capacity, judgmental alterations in perceptions of value and utility, and emotional lability discussed in the previous chapter.

SELF-SELECTION

Leaders often seek their fate, as do their followers. Especially in a democratic system, individuals often put themselves forward for election. They run for a variety of reasons, but it seems obvious that at least some of those who seek political power do so because they are especially interested in power for its own sake. In and of itself, this particular incentive structure predisposes certain types of people to seek positions of political leadership. For example, shy and retiring types who do not want private aspects of their lives investigated and judged may choose not to run, even though they may be immensely qualified for the actual tasks of office. Narcissists, on the other hand, only too eager to obtain evidence of their superiority, might seek out elected office at a disproportionate rate, regardless of their qualifications. Yet voters can choose only among existing options; they cannot support candidates who refuse to run for office.

Robins's work on the relationship between psychopathology and political leadership remains limited to cases of psychological deviancy, not physical impairment.[4] While much of his discussion on the origins of madness lies beyond the scope of this work, Robins raises some insightful issues about the relationship between larger societal forces and psychopathology in leadership, as well as the relationship between mental illness and political power more broadly. Drawing heavily on work in anthropology, Robins argues that times of great societal upheavals produce a disproportionate number of deviant people, including more pathological leaders. An obvious example of this occurrence lies in Adolf Hitler's rise to power. Although many authors have pointed to various psychological problems which appear to have plagued Hitler, few argue that his pathologies were severe enough to compromise his leadership abilities, at least until the very end of the war. Hitler may have demonstrated paranoid and narcissistic tendencies, and these personality problems were likely exacerbated by substance abuse of various kinds, but the paranoid elements of his world view found ardent admirers among many ordinary Germans, who were angry and frustrated by the devastation wrought on Germany by the First World War and the harsh terms of the Treaty of Versailles.[5] As Post so eloquently writes in his review of Redlich's book, Hitler's political paranoia represented "the fit between a malignant leader and wounded followers."[6] A particular mix between leader and followers establishes and maintains pathological leaders in positions of power. In other words, part of the success of deviant leaders lies in the transferential lock they create with their followers, who seek the biased view of the world they present.

A similar argument can be made with regard to regime types; for example, those that rely on repression and other means of violence to maintain societal control enhance the likelihood that certain types of psychopathology emerge in leadership circles. Paranoid leaders may garner the support of a populace that feels vulnerable and threatened. Totalitarian regimes can succeed when the public finds the economic and social costs of freedom too high to bear, such as in ethnically fractionated societies like Yugoslavia and Iraq. Democratic systems, while they may weed out some of the intellectually and politically weaker candidates, do not prevent powerful narcissists from obtaining office; the reverse seems the case because it often takes someone with a grandiose self-image to make it through the brutal campaign process.

Robins makes a compelling case that "it may be that certain forms of madness, like other traits, are most likely to be seen where they help their holder to achieve power than where they do not."[7] He argues that in some cases it can prove difficult, especially at the outset, to distinguish between an extreme charisma and various forms of mental illness. Again, a political leader like Hitler comes to mind. In retrospect, his psychological problems may seem clear, if not specific, and yet he was enormously successful in gaining the trust and support of the German population prior to the Second World War; indeed, after losing the April 10, 1932, presidential election to Paul von Hindenburg, Hitler was appointed chancellor in 1933. Everyone who knew him commented on his tremendous charisma; the line between his appeal and his pathology remained very fine, at least in the early days of his power. Similar cases have been known to occur. For example, manics in an expansive phase can often exert very strong persuasive powers through their charm, wit, and optimistic visions for the future.* They can also be charismatic and effective at getting people to do what they want.

Robins concentrates his analysis on three facets of the relationship between pathology and leadership: recruitment, retention, and removal. Many types of mental illness prevent people from attaining political power; serious illness can often prevent individuals from being organized enough, or functional enough, to effectively run for office. However, Robins argues that certain types of mental illness benefit particular people

---

* I am reminded here of a former patient at a Veterans Administration hospital who during a two-hour leave once convinced the local Winnebago dealership to deliver 24 Winnebagos COD to the VA the following Monday. The salesman remained convinced that the RVs were going to a rich, athletic doctor despite being told the buyer was a patient on the locked ward.

who are trying to attain power. Paranoid and hallucinatory behavior, in particular, seems to help leaders achieve power because leaders seized by such visions and beliefs can appear particularly compelling and persuasive. Paranoia can energize a movement and provide clear guidelines for action, especially under obvious external instances of threat, such as an attack. In this case, a leader can direct his paranoia toward a vulnerable group whose existence may appear to pose some kind of economic or social threat. Hitler's scapegoating of the Jews, for instance, allowed ordinary Germans to blame the Jews for all their economic and social ills, while benefiting from the wealth that could be forcefully extracted from them. Hallucinatory behavior can also, in certain circumstances, offer a blueprint for action. The classic positive case of an effective leader aided by visions remains Joan of Arc.

Once in office, a pathological leader, like any other, needs to maintain his power. In this situation, a deviant leader may remain in power if his followers share his particular pathology for their own various reasons. Again, because Hitler's followers shared in his anti-Semitism to a greater or lesser degree, they could share in his paranoia about Jews without questioning his overall judgment. Pathological leaders may also stay in power if their odd behavior remains limited in time or place, so that it is not evident to most people most of the time, or remains encapsulated to a particular topic, event, or group. Particularly in times of great social upheaval or stress, deviant behavior can prove useful in helping to structure new types of social exchange or interactions. Sometimes eccentric behavior can serve a leader well, especially if it conforms with general societal biases and proves useful against an external enemy, as sometimes a ruthless or aberrant style might. Thomas Schelling's notion of the "rationality of irrationality" whereby a leader might force opponents into concessions by making them believe he is crazy, and thus capable of taking inordinate risks, falls under this category.[8]

A pathological leader can sometimes remain in office by asserting repressive control. When others challenge his leadership, he can jail or kill them and remain in power through fear and domination. Stalin provides an excellent example of just such a leader. In addition, a deviant leader can stay in power if those surrounding him manage to take control and serve in his stead. They might do this to retain their own political power, to impede a political rival, or to maintain the leader's rule for reasons of personal loyalty or fear. Sometimes pathological leaders are removed from office, either through established procedures or through violence and overthrow.

Yet sometimes it can also prove difficult to distinguish the effects of mental illness from the effects of ordinary stress, such as that which might easily accompany a job of international pressure and importance. Mental illness remains a severe stigma in society. Some forms of mental illness present more of an impediment to successful leadership than others; severe depression, such as that experienced by Calvin Coolidge upon the death of his son, can render a leader essentially unresponsive.[9] Coping with the effects of mental illness in a leader can prove extremely challenging, especially as it is often insidious in onset and intermittent or cyclical in its manifestation.

AGING

Aging presents a particular challenge for stable, healthy leadership because most world leaders are in late middle or old age by the time they ascend to power, or remain in power until older ages.[10] It typically requires decades to rise in political rank and to achieve the kind of experience and support necessary to make a bid for power. Advanced age is by no means a disability in and of itself. However, increasing age is associated with an increased incidence of such ailments as arteriosclerosis, cancer, stroke, and end-stage alcoholism.[11] In addition, the treatments for such ailments, including various pharmaceutical regimens, carry their own supplemental risks to the elderly, especially with regard to distorted judgment.

Thus, aging really presents a double-edged sword in leadership. On the one hand, older leaders often prove unusually effective and insightful, bringing a unique and extensive history of experience and understanding to their job. On the other hand, older people tend to suffer disproportionately from certain particularly debilitating types of diseases. The naturally occurring and unavoidable consequences of age therefore threaten powerful leaders in particular, because they tend to be drawn from the more experienced, and thus older, ranks of leadership. Although older leaders may lack the energy and vitality of younger ones, they often more than compensate for this deficit of stamina with increased experience, wisdom, and perspective. The problem arises when aging leaders begin to fade, through some combination of stress, illness, or medication.

One aspect of aging that appears to be universal in manifestation is decreasing energy and stamina. This factor, more than illness, may prove decisive in choosing a leader. In the election of a new pope in 2005, for instance, cardinals over the age of eighty remained ineligible to vote or run for the office. While this age-related restriction may result partly from the desire of church leaders to avoid choosing a new leader too often, it also reflects some concern that men over eighty may not have the endurance of a younger man in responding to the demands of office. Interestingly, the cardinals elected the seventy-eight-year-old Cardinal Ratzinger as pope. Perhaps the church elders did not want another long papacy following the extended reign of John Paul II, which could occur with the election of a younger pope, but perhaps too they valued the extensive experience and wisdom that comes with age. Or perhaps they simply wanted someone with assured conservative credentials, more likely to be found in the ranks of the older clergy. Ratzinger had demonstrated his conservative proclivities as head of the Congregation for the Doctrine of the Faith, a post that he held under Pope John XXIII.

Second, age exerts a differential impact of stress on older people. However, some leaders, regardless of age, thrive on stress, and even go out of their way to seek out the stimulation inherent in stressful situations.[12]

Stress produces an enhanced effect on older people, although individual differences provide a continuum of effects across the aging spectrum; everyone knows someone who remains sharp as a tack well past ninety, while others seem unable to function well beginning in their early sixties.* Robert Sapolsky, a biologist at Stanford, has studied the effects of stress on baboons in the Serengeti. He argues that aging itself can be understood as the progressive inability to deal effectively with stress.[13] Chronic stress can affect anyone negatively regardless of age. It can predispose people to cancer, lead to heart disease, and cause suppression of the immune system. At any age, heightened stress can impact people's performance in negative ways; but this decline occurs much more rapidly with age. In other words, in many ways older people function as well as younger people, unless additional stress comes into play, whether in the form of even minor illness, time pressure, a novel or rapidly shifting environment, or even physical exercise. When such stress occurs, older people do not function as well as they once did, or as well as their younger counterparts might.

Counterintuitively, older people tend to exhibit too much, not too little, of a physiological response when confronted with stressful situations. In other words, they secrete more stress hormones even when they are not stressed. They have a hard time turning off the relevant stress-related hormones after the stress is no longer present. These stress-related hormones include epinephrine, norepinephrine, and glucosteroids. When these hormones exist in the absence of a stressor, as appears more commonly in the elderly, they can compromise the immune system and make the person more vulnerable to various secondary illnesses, just as people who take steroids to control asthma may suffer from cataracts and other side effects of the medication. For example, Sapolsky demonstrated that higher levels of glucosteroids, found in elderly rats, made tumors grow almost twice as fast as in young rats, who have a lower baseline level of such hormones.

---

* Aging used to refer to people starting in their mid-sixties. Current gerontology refers to "old" as someone in their late seventies and beyond. Even then people are divided into groups of the "young old" between seventy-five and eighty-five and "old old" after eighty-five or so, even though many people function very well into their nineties.

Such elevated hormones also tend to elevate blood pressure, a coronary risk factor found much more commonly in older individuals.

To make the effect of stress on age even more complex, recent research indicates that not all kinds of stress exert the same kind of impact on human biology. Some kinds of stress, such as sleep deprivations, loud noise, bright light, and heavy workloads, produce catecholamines, including adrenaline, to help the person respond quickly and cope effectively with the increased pressures. But stress associated with uncertainty and a lack of predictability in the environment releases an altogether different set of hormones, corticosteroids, such as cortisol. And elevated cortisol levels, regardless of age, impair learning and memory and cause weight gain, among other things.[14]

A third major concern related to aging derives from the impact of age alone on certain cognitive processes.[15] The problem, of course, lies partly in deciding what exactly constitutes "aging." Some younger people in their fifties or even forties can start to suffer from the effects of cerebral degeneration brought about by arteriosclerosis, whereas people well into their nineties or even beyond can operate with great mental clarity. However, once arteriosclerosis begins to degrade cognitive functioning, the pattern of progress typically becomes increasingly severe over time.

Bert Park has suggested criteria for the impact of aging on the brain, in increasing order of impairment:

(1) Loss of recall and recent memory; (2) the inability to make up one's mind while delegating decision making to others; (3) the proclivity to become set in one's ways – to become, if you will, a caricature of oneself; and (4) a restricted ability to abstract, thereby returning to well-remembered themes or anecdotes when faced with unfamiliar material or circumstances. As the process accelerates, the individual begins to perceive gray issues in black and white terms. Even then, intellectual deterioration does not necessarily follow a steadily progressive course. Good days alternate with the bad, reflected in the universal observation that the elderly perform better in structured situations.[16]

Park's fourth criterion poses special problems for an aging leader. The ability to think abstractly, to assimilate and interpret new data or novel situations quickly, to draw creative conclusions, and to seek innovative solutions to a crisis forms the foundation of effective leadership. As this skill diminishes, a leader's ability to perform effectively and efficiently can become compromised.

These effects become even more pronounced in the elderly following anesthesia, as would be required in the event of any necessary surgical procedure. Anesthesia represents a special case because its effects can produce profound and persistent deficits in cognitive abilities. The medical term for this impairment is postoperative cognitive dementia. Many factors appear to contribute to its occurrence in elderly patients following surgery. Age remains a major exacerbating condition. Other factors include decreased preoperative cognitive functioning, overall general level of health, and intraoperative events.[17]

In earlier studies, researchers discovered that elderly people suffer profound mental impairments, including memory loss, cognitive impairment, and difficulty finding words for up to six weeks following surgery.[18] As a result elderly patients undergoing anesthesia are routinely instructed to refrain from any important decision making for at least a week following the administration of anesthesia.[19] Thus, Reagan's making important decisions concerning the Iran-Contra scandal from his hospital bed may have been pure folly; on the other hand, it may simply have been politics that were too clever by half because such decision making could always be plausibly denied if it did not work out as planned, as in fact occurred when Attorney General Edwin Meese claimed during the Irangate hearings that Reagan may have approved the illegal shipments of arms to Iran when his judgment was compromised as a result of his surgery and postoperative medications. Reagan gave three different answers to the Tower Commission inquiries about his role in Iran-Contra. In his first two answers, he indicated that he had approved what was done. Only in his third answer did Reagan admit that he did not remember making this decision, and it was both reasonable to assume that his memory may have been compromised by anesthesia and medication and politically expedient to excuse his participation in such illicit activity.[20]

More recent studies have expanded medical understanding of the impact of anesthesia on the elderly in particular. Cognitive side effects of anesthesia include a delayed recovery of cognitive functioning following surgery.[21] In patients older than sixty, 19.7 percent manifest symptoms of cognitive dysfunction seven days after surgery; 14.3 percent remain impaired after three months.[22] Further studies conducted specifically with cardiac surgery patients produce similar results. In one study, patients were assessed using a wide battery of common neuropsychological tests between three and ten days after surgery. They found a significant decline in six specific areas of functioning in more than 66 percent of patients. These limitations encompassed concentration of attention, immediate verbal memory, psychomotor speed, visual construction tasks, and verbal skill deficits.[23] An additional study reported that more than 40 percent of spouses still notice some sort of cognitive deficit in their mates twelve months after coronary bypass surgery, especially in the realm of short-term memory. These problems were serious enough to lead to altered interpersonal relationships between spouses.

Age produces an impact on the brain independent of any effects of anesthesia. Park's categorization of the effects of aging on the brain dovetail nicely with the features that Post describes as the psychological manifestation of hardening of the arteries, or arteriosclerosis, a common characteristic of coronary artery disease especially prevalent in the elderly.[24] These factors include rigidity of thought, especially the increasing inability of a person to think abstractly. Such individuals come to rely more and more on concrete, rigid, structured, familiar patterns or thinking and response. Impairment of intellect and judgment can affect concentration, memory, and decision making. Emotional lability increases as people become less able to control their emotions; emotions often become more mixed as well, such as when crying and laughter become not far removed in terms of time or stimulus, often co-occurring, as when elderly people may smile through their tears when recalling a fond memory from the past; this tendency can be witnessed in small children whose brains have not fully developed yet as well.

Further, as Park noted in his description of the more general effects of aging on the brain, a person's earlier personality characteristics become exaggerated. If a person was a little angry, they may now become belligerent and even aggressive; if they were suspicious, they are now paranoid; if they were good and loving and kind, they become saintly. However, good days alternate with bad. Sometimes decline can precipitate quickly, other times more slowly. For purposes of assessment when arteriosclerosis is suspected, medical personnel prefer to observe a person over several days at different times of the day to get a clear picture of the level of cognitive decline. Differential diagnosis can prove difficult because senility and depression often present in remarkably similar ways in the elderly in particular. One of the typical diagnostic differences relates to circadian rhythms; dementia often produces a "sundowner" syndrome where the person gets worse as the day wears on, while anyone who has ever been seriously depressed knows that the worst time of the day occurs upon arising, first thing in the morning. As Post writes, "If one can with some certainty diagnose cerebral arteriosclerosis, even though an individual apparently may be alert on a specific occasion, the other features already enumerated – in particular, decline in intellectual abilities and problems of judgment – are, nevertheless, operating."[25] Typically denial on the part of the patient accompanies the presence of disability. Apparent disregard for the loss of previous abilities sometimes goes by the French name *la belle indifférence*, literally translated as "the beautiful indifference," suggesting that those afflicted remain untroubled by their limitations.

Recent research indicates that the impact of aging on the brain produces effects that mimic those that result from damage to the hippocampus, the portion of the amygdala, where emotional processing often occurs, which appears responsible for transferring information into memory. Both aging and damage cause impairments in learning. Reductions in the number and regulation of various synaptic structures that connect neural cells in the hippocampus, resulting from age or injury, can impair the encoding of memory and enhance the erasure of memories, which in turn lead to various kinds of larger cognitive problems and deficits. In addition, deficits in the storage and retrieval of information, especially concerning the spatial organization of the environment, can also produce difficulties with learning and memory. At an extreme, such deficits help explain the common problem with wandering seen in patients with Alzheimer's disease, who often fail to find their way home even after living in the same place for years; but this problem can become evident even when a healthy older person moves to a new environment, or demonstrates difficulty in finding objects like keys and in locating new places. In a more abstract sense, difficulty in learning may help explain why leaders oftentimes overly rely on the historical analogies of their youth, which are overlearned and readily available for retrieval; such scenarios are familiar and accessible to them, and do not require new learning to recognize or implement.

ILLNESS

In addition to aging, physical and psychological illness can have a tremendous impact on leaders as well. Illness can take either a physical or a psychological form, although often these categorizations meld in the presentation of any given disease. For example, one of the common symptoms of Graves' disease, a disease of the thyroid gland that President George Herbert Walker Bush was diagnosed with in March 1991, is depression.[26] While most people think of depression as a primarily psychological illness, in many cases it can be brought on or maintained by various medical conditions or can follow as sequelae. For example, anyone who has experienced chronic or prolonged pain knows that depression can often accompany the physical experience as pain wears down energy, hope, and resilience over time.

Physical and psychological illnesses are not unusual among leaders, whose abilities are seriously impaired by them more often than the public may realize. Such problems are partly a function of age, partly a function of stress, and partly a function of being human. While in office, for example, several American presidents suffered from physical or psychological ailments: George Washington had an abscess on his thigh; Chester Arthur suffered from Bright's disease, a kidney ailment; Andrew Jackson had a bullet removed from his shoulder; and Grover Cleveland had two secret surgeries for cancer of the jaw in 1893. Woodrow Wilson had an incapacitating stroke in 1919, and his condition was kept secret throughout the rest of his term in office by his wife, Edith, and his physician, Admiral Cary T. Grayson. Franklin Roosevelt's heart disease was so serious that he died less than five months after his fourth election. Eisenhower suffered a heart attack, underwent surgery for ileitis (Crohn's disease), and had a stroke while in office. Kennedy suffered from Addison's disease and back pain, requiring constant treatment with medication that can cause cognitive side effects. In addition, he appears to have received amphetamine injections. In addition to his incipient Alzheimer's disease, Reagan was shot and had colon and prostate cancer surgery while in office.

While in office, President George Herbert Walker Bush's Graves' disease presented as atrial fibrillation. Once properly diagnosed, he received the standard radioactive iodine treatment, which required avoiding close contact with others for several days to limit radiation exposure. In January 1992 he had a bout with the flu during a state dinner in Japan. At the time, the oft-replayed picture of Bush slumping into the arms of Prime Minister Miyazawa was presented as a symbolic exposition of American dependence on the Japanese economy. President Clinton, while largely overtly robust during office, had to undergo surgery for a torn thigh muscle after a bad fall while on a visit to Florida in March 1997.

A wide variety of illness, both physical and psychological, can affect leaders while in power. In examining this issue, Hugh L'Etang conducted the first and most important work on the subject of impaired leadership.[27] In his book, L'Etang categorized the different types of illnesses and conditions that might impair a leader's ability to render effective judgments and decisions. These included problems associated with workaholics, mental illness, alcoholism and other forms of drug abuse, age, illness including diabetes, and what he termed "self-destructive aggression," which he saw as the way in which anger can negatively impact the functioning of a leader's heart and lungs. Most presciently, L'Etang wrote about the expense-account meal. The notion of the impact of diet and exercise on physical functioning has increased in importance over the past quarter century. Certainly, dining out frequently makes it harder to avoid the high-salt, high-fat diet that exacerbates heart conditions.

L'Etang was cautious in warning that the mere presence of these illnesses and conditions should not immediately lead to the conclusion that those afflicted are not fit for office. The existence of some kind of impairment does not automatically mean that the particular condition inevitably exerts a negative impact on judgment and decision making. Depending on the condition, the person, and the political context, illness may precipitate a debilitating effect on the leader. But there are other situations where a particular compromise may not prove deleterious to the leader's ability to render and execute careful and effective judgments and actions, as might be the case with many sexually transmitted diseases, for example.

L'Etang builds on previous work by psychiatrist Dr. Mottram Torre to argue that the best way to assess and evaluate the extent to which illness impacts leadership performance is to evaluate four essential leadership qualities, including vitality, mood, rationality, and intellectual capacity. If the illness impacts any one of these qualities severely, or if limitations in several areas add up to serious restrictions overall, then an impairment may limit the quality of leadership performance. If such occupational detriments do not occur in the wake of illness, then disability need not be diagnosed. In other words, particular illnesses may not necessarily impede a leader's ability to run a nation successfully if they do not exert a negative influence on the person's energy, stamina, mood, or cognitive abilities. Well-controlled diabetes, for example, might fall into this category of illness. Other conditions, while seemingly minor, may exert a more decisive impact on a leader's ability to render effective judgments and decisions; a hit on the head might cause such a problem, at least for a short period of time.

PHYSICAL ILLNESS

Issues of physical health can present in a wide variety of forms and duration. Accidents can occur, as with Clinton's fall. Temporary ailments can produce dramatic events, as was the case with President Bush's flu incident in Japan. Sudden incapacitation can occur any time an assassin makes an attempt on a leader's life. As Abrams details in his essay on the assassination attempt on Reagan, sudden incapacitation as a result of trauma can produce a whole series of psychological and physical consequences.[28] Trauma, such as that which a shooting would no doubt provoke, can cause depression, withdrawal, agitation, perplexity, emotional instability, and paranoia. Blood loss, which can be severe following an assassination attempt, as it was in Reagan's case, can produce agitation or mental confusion. Further, Abrams argues that surgery alone creates postoperative depression and anxiety in nearly 100 percent of patients, at least for a time.[29] Postoperative recovery can include periods of mental and perceptual disorientation. In addition, pain following surgery, or as a result of injury alone, can produce anxiety and irritability.

In Reagan's case, the anesthesia he was administered during surgery was thiopental, which can cause profound hangover effects and can also lead to overconfidence and slowed reaction time. Add to this the various medications that Reagan took for pain following surgery, including morphine, codeine, Demerol, and Valium, and mental compromise becomes readily assured. Morphine alone produces mental clouding and detachment, while valium has been shown to lead to impaired learning up to fifty hours following administration.[30]

Post argues that the illnesses that pose the greatest danger to public welfare are those which can go unrecognized for long periods of time before detection or obvious incapacitation occur.[31] Such diseases are typically categorized by their insidious slow onset, their initial subtle effects, and their fluctuating course, so that on some days the affected leader appears much better and stronger than on others. Alert advisers can schedule public appearances for an impaired leader on just those days and at those times when the leader appears to be at his best and strongest. Illnesses such as cancer, diabetes, heart disease, or Alzheimer's disease and other incapacitating dementias fall into this class and can slowly distort a leader's capacity without others being necessarily aware of a specific date of onset or a clear pattern of impairment. The form and onset of illness can impact the extent to which it might impair judgment and decision making, whether it can be hidden from the public, and how the leaders' physician might be involved in diagnosis, treatment, and even cover-up. Much of the potential for success in undertaking a medical cover-up depends on how many people know about the problem from the outset. If awareness remains limited to the inner circle, a cover-up is more likely to succeed. In some sense, the more overtly serious or traumatic the illness, injury, or disability, the more likely it is to be discovered, and thus the less likely it is to have an impact on public policy, because appropriate procedures can be put into place to treat the condition and make sure that responsible officials can assume the mantle of command either temporarily or permanently if such action becomes necessary. More subtle illnesses may have a different outcome. As Post notes,

> But it is the insidious illness, the subtle disability, not readily obvious, which in many ways is the most problematic for the political system. When the onset is gradual and the symptoms are fluctuant, the leader is unlikely to present an obvious or consistent public image of medical impairment even though the disability is evident to the inner circle. In such a circumstance, if the leader and his inner circle ignore how much the illness is compromising his decision making and effectiveness and carefully orchestrate his public appearances, the presence or degree of the disability can be significantly obscured. Such a situation can present a conscientious leadership circle with a choice between being loyal to the leader who may be temporarily ill and deceiving the public.[32]

PSYCHOLOGICAL ILLNESS

Psychological illnesses may present even more catastrophic consequences for the ability of a leader to make reasonable judgments and for a leader's nation to be well served. Many primarily physical ailments, independent of their physical effects, create psychological and cognitive side effects. For example, patients who suffer a heart attack often display symptoms of depression, anxiety, and insomnia in the wake of the attack. Further, more than half continue to manifest depression and other psychological problems up to four months after the attack. A third of patients report problems of fatigue, memory, concentration, emotional stability, and irritability for more than two years following their attack. In fact, heart disease alone appears to predict decline in intellectual ability and functioning.

Strokes can cause similar cognitive impairments, including depression, anxiety, emotional instability, and memory loss. Between 40 and 60 percent of patients remain cognitively or emotionally impaired following a stroke, while more than 25 percent suffer memory problems. Individuals with hypertension experience similar effects as well, including depression, anxiety, irritability, emotional instability, and shortened attention span. Oftentimes, these restrictions are accompanied by deficits in judgment; reduced speed in comprehension, thinking, and mental processing; and memory impairments.

Cancer can also produce cognitive sequelae. Depression, anxiety, and anger are common responses to cancer, and certain kinds of chemotherapy can lead to serious cognitive problems as well.[33] Medications can also induce or exacerbate these symptoms in people suffering primarily from physical ailments.

Yet mental illness can manifest on its own as well, independent of any physical precipitant. Under the category of mental illness can fall transitory illnesses like depression, which, if properly treated, can remit within a reasonable period of time in the majority of cases, as well as more persistent and severe disorders such as schizophrenia. But even in circumstances of transitory illness, clear cognitive impairments follow. Serious depression, for example, can induce a tendency to focus on more bottom-up information-processing styles, a greater propensity to focus on detail to the exclusion of larger issue concerns, preoccupation with fear and anxiety, and a literal, if temporary, lowering of IQ. The difficulty with such illnesses, of course, is that they can be neither predicted nor prevented. Calvin Coolidge was a vibrant and active politician prior to the death of his favorite son, sixteen-year-old Calvin Jr., in 1924; after the loss of his son, Coolidge fell into a serious and unremitting clinical depression that resulted in his complete disengagement from politics and political life.[34]

Most commonly, depression is characterized by at least five of the following symptoms: depressed mood; anhedonia, where the person feels nothing and does not care about anything; weight disturbances; sleep disturbances; psychomotor disturbances; fatigue; feelings of worthlessness or guilt; "diminished ability to think or concentrate, or indecisiveness, nearly every day"; and obsessions with death and suicide. According to the *Diagnostic and Statistical Manual of Mental Disorders*, many individuals with depression report "impaired ability to think, concentrate or make decisions. They may appear easily distracted or complain of memory difficulties. Those in intellectually demanding academic or occupational pursuits are often unable to function adequately even when they have mild concentration problems."[35]

These kinds of impairments can present severe, unmanageable constraints on a powerful political leader. In addition, psychological problems appear the least likely to become exposed to the public eye, especially because individuals make extreme attempts to hide these kinds of symptoms because of the social stigma associated with them and can do so with effort for short periods of time. As discussed earlier, Tom Eagleton was removed from McGovern's Democratic ticket in the 1972 presidential campaign because of revelations that he had suffered from depression, been hospitalized, and received electroshock treatment for this illness.

In addition, there are other pervasive and insidious psychological illnesses that may not be as transitory. Robins and Post argue that the political world presents the ideal screen upon which certain affected men and women can project their personality disorders. They argue that paranoia is the most common of the personality disorders to manifest itself in the political world, although it may appear to the casual observer at least that narcissism exists quite commonly as well. Robins and Post use paranoia to refer to a broad set of personality traits that are "characterized by guardedness, suspiciousness, hypersensitivity and isolation."[36] From a psychodynamic perspective, the grandiosity of paranoia represents an inadequate attempt to overcome deep-seated feelings of inadequacy that often begin in childhood as a result of parental neglect or abuse. No amount of external validation or success can serve to adequately fill the deep psychic void that such individuals experience at the center of their being.

At the extreme, paranoia represents a kind of pathological narcissism, because elements of both paranoid and narcissistic personality characteristics can feed off each other in the same person. After all, being surrounded by enemies or becoming the object of conspiracies and the obsession of adversaries places the paranoid person in the center of everyone's universe; persecution remains infinitely preferable to indifference. Self-absorption demands attention regardless of form or kind. Indeed, a person can suffer from both a narcissistic and a paranoid personality disorder simultaneously. Post discusses a "malignant narcissism," a syndrome that combines ambition and aggression with an absence of conscience and paranoia. Such a personality disorder becomes particularly dangerous, according to Post, because it can combine with, or produce, a destructive charismatic leadership style. Such leaders not only believe that the rules that apply to everyone else do not apply to them because they are so special but also go to extreme lengths to accomplish their goals because they cannot live with the possibility or consequences of failure. Post characterizes Saddam Hussein of Iraq, Kim Jong Il of North Korea, and Fidel Castro of Cuba as examples of such a personality structure.[37]

People afflicted with paranoid personality disorders tend to suspect without foundation that others are exploiting, harming, or deceiving them; remain preoccupied with doubts about the loyalty of others; appear reluctant to confide in others for fear of information being used against them; read demeaning or threatening messages into benign remarks and events; bear grudges or remain unforgiving; perceive attacks on their character and react with anger where others see no such attacks; and retain recurrent suspicions about a partner's fidelity. This disorder, which is more common in men than women, is often diagnosed when at least four of these characteristics are present.

Robins and Post find evidence for the pervasive presence of paranoia in a wide variety of world leaders, including Pol Pot, Idi Amin, Joseph Stalin, and Adolf Hitler.[38] As evidence for the manifestation of paranoia on the political stage, for example, they note that Stalin killed between 20 million and 40 million of his own people and officers in various purges throughout his reign. In Uganda, Idi Amin was responsible for the deaths of more than 375,000 of the 11.5 million inhabitants of his nation. Between 1971 and 1979, he consistently blamed others for the political troubles in his country and demonstrated incredible grandiosity. In Cambodia, Pol Pot was responsible for the deaths of more than 15 percent of the population between 1975 and 1979. His behavior resulted from his xenophobic hatred of everyone who was not Khmer Rouge, a predilection that existed simultaneously with his pathological idealization of all things Khmer.

C. Owen, a physician and prominent former politician in the British government, has also written about the relationship between political regime types and the development of paranoia in leaders. While it may be the case, as Robins suggested, that paranoid leaders are disproportionately attracted to, and often surprisingly effective in, positions of political power, it may also be the case that certain political environments or situations evoke, or even create, paranoia in otherwise normal leaders.[39] Owen eloquently describes how this process might take place:

> One of the questions most commonly asked by a concerned public about leaders committed to brutal politics is: are they mad? Hitler, Stalin, and more recently, Saddam Hussein, Milosevic, and Mugabe have often been described as being mad in popular newspapers, when in fact they were far from being certifiable. In part the very question reflects a wish of those who live within democracies to underplay the latent evil within society, and to forget or ignore the brutalizing effect on personality that stems from living within, let alone presiding over, a Communist or Fascist dictatorship, or an ethnically divided country such as Rhodesia or the former Yugoslavia. The longer a leader lasts in office in these regimes, the more their power stems not from popular consent but from imposition. National minorities within a divided country can give their leaders ethnic electoral support, but such leaders are vulnerable to coups or assassination. They tend to lead evermore secret lives, become out of touch with the people they lead and the reality of

the world around them, and develop paranoiac tendencies. In addition, such leaders almost always become corrupt.[40]

Such commentary points not only to the difficulty of distinguishing illness from evil but to the way in which the power of the situation can corrupt individuals over time as well; the torture of Iraqi prisoners by formerly ordinary American soldiers at Abu Ghraib prison provides a clear illustration of this phenomenon. A reciprocal relationship exists between a leader and his followers, and between a leader's style and his regime type. Certain regime types, such as those totalitarian or authoritarian structures that rely on repression for control, may unduly exacerbate particular personality characteristics, including paranoia, in their leaders. In turn, certain personalities may find it easier to successfully rule such regimes than their more institutionally constrained democratic counterparts.

But paranoia does not represent the only psychological condition that can pose severe consequences for world politics when leaders become afflicted. Narcissistic personality disorders appear commonly on the world stage as well. This disorder afflicts about 1 percent of the population and, like paranoia, is found more commonly in men, who constitute up to three-quarters of those affected. People suffering from a narcissist disorder might disproportionately self-select into positions of political power because of their need to believe that they are special and deserving of only the best and most of everything.

Narcissistic personality disorder is defined as a pattern of grandiosity, need for admiration, and lack of empathy. It manifests in at least five of the following ways: grandiose sense of self-importance; preoccupation with fantasies of unlimited power, success, brilliance, or beauty; belief that the person is special and can be understood by or associate with only other high-status people; desire for excessive admiration; a sense of entitlement; interpersonal exploitativeness; complete lack of empathy; enviousness; and arrogance. Post has argued, for example, that Saddam Hussein represents a prime example of this disorder on the world stage.[41] Post saw Hussein's disorder manifested in his destructive messianic ambition for unlimited power and in his absence of conscience, uncontrolled aggression, and paranoid outlook. Thus, analysis of leaders' personalities from a distance represents more than a mere academic enterprise. Implications drawn from such interpretations can suggest different, and often nonoverlapping, intervention strategies and policy responses.

ADDICTION

Addiction can take many forms in political leadership. The most common addiction is alcohol abuse. This occurs, at least in many, as the consequence of years of social drinking in political situations that becomes more severe in some over time. False allegations of alcoholism in Tom Eagleton, along with true reports of electroshock treatment for depression, contributed to his removal from the Democratic ticket in McGovern's 1972 presidential campaign. In 1989 Senator John Tower lost his nomination for secretary of defense in the Bush cabinet over concerns surrounding his alcoholism.[42] Senator Key Pittman, chair of the Senate Foreign Relations Committee during Franklin Roosevelt's presidency, provides perhaps the most dramatic example of the serious effects of alcoholism on performance in powerful office. Escalating alcoholism cycled with destructive behavior to bring about Pittman's ultimate downfall. He battled for his sixth term in 1940, becoming ill from alcohol six days before the election; despite his victory, he died five days later of alcohol abuse.[43] Congressman Wilbur Mills, Democrat of Arkansas from the late 1950s until the 1970s, also suffered from alcoholism; his career came to an end after he was found drunk early one morning, swimming in the reflecting pool on the Washington Mall with prominent stripper Fanny Fox.[44] Estes Kefauver, Democratic senator from Tennessee, was an early favorite for the 1956 presidential nomination, earning a vice-presidential slot on the Adlai Stevenson ticket, but he undermined his own effectiveness with his heavy drinking. He was pressured by his parents, who expected him to make up for an older brother who died tragically before his time, just like the young senator from Massachusetts, John Kennedy, who wrested the 1960 nomination from him.[45]

Alcohol is a central nervous system depressant and induces sleep. At low doses, imbibers often experience a lack of inhibition and gregariousness, but in larger doses, alcohol consumption can produce sleepiness, depression, and anger. Alcohol systematically impairs performance in a number of realms. It has negative effects on vision, slows reaction time, and decreases performance on a wide variety of judgment and motor tasks. In general, the more complex the task, the less alcohol it takes to begin to notice impairments in performance. Alcohol has a detrimental effect on memory, affecting both storage and retrieval but exerting a stronger influence on storage.[46] Older studies have reported a relationship between alcohol intake and increased levels of risk taking, recklessness, and aggression.[47]

An additional problem with alcohol arises when an alcoholic tries to quit. Alcohol is one of the few drugs that can kill an addicted person who attempts to quit suddenly and without medical support. While most people manifest only weaker signs of withdrawal, which nonetheless include nasty symptoms such as agitation, tremors, vomiting, nausea, sweating, and rapid heartbeat, some experience the more severe symptoms, including delirium tremens. Serious withdrawal symptoms can include confusion, disorientation, hallucinations, seizures, and death. Before modern treatment strategies were developed, about 37 percent of people experiencing alcohol withdrawal died. Current detoxification takes a person off alcohol through the use of cross-tolerant tranquilizers, such as Valium, whose dosage is then lowered slowly. The current rate of death resulting from withdrawal holds at about 2 percent.[48]

Other central nervous system depressants that can be abused include tranquilizers, such as barbiturates and benzodiazepines, opiates, and pain killers. The effects of barbiturates and benzodiazepines are similar, although barbiturates remain much more lethal at lower dosages. Barbiturates lower respiration and blood pressure; like alcohol, their rapid withdrawal has the capacity to kill. Benzodiazepines, such as Valium, on the other hand, typically do not have effects outside the central nervous system, although they do appear to have some muscle relaxant properties that operate through the brain. They rarely kill except in large doses and in combination with other drugs, such as alcohol. Reagan's national security adviser Robert "Bud" McFarlane discovered this when he tried to kill himself on February 9, 1987, following the Iran-Contra scandal, by swallowing numerous Valium; he was admitted to Bethesda Naval Hospital to sleep it off and emerged none the worse for wear, with the possible exception of the assault on his pride. Valium is typically prescribed for anxiety and sometimes for insomnia. Interestingly, its anxiolytic effects do not seem to occur in people without anxiety. Low doses of benzodiazepines appear to exert little influence on motor performance. However, they do appear to reduce the ability to learn new information, both visual and verbal, by as much as 66 percent. Duration of impairment depends on the particular drug taken; barbiturates have a shorter impact than benzodiazepines because of their briefer half-life in the body. The duration of learning effects from benzodiazepines can be twenty-four hours or more. Significantly, the user typically will not recognize any drug-induced learning impairment that might occur.[49]

Withdrawal from benzodiazepines produces less severe effects than alcohol withdrawal, depending on dosage and length of use: it can produce agitation, depression, insomnia, stomach pain, and seizures. Even with a tapered withdrawal, symptoms usually last about two weeks and include such ailments as anxiety, sleep problems, difficulty with loud noises and bright lights, weight loss, and numbness or tingling.

There appear to be two types of withdrawal processes from benzodiazepines. The first type of benzodiazepines, called sedative hypnotics, cause tremors, delirium, cramps, and possible convulsions in those using high dosages for at least a month. These drugs, including Halcyon, are typically prescribed as sleeping pills. The second kind, low-dose withdrawal, happens in those who have been taking low doses for more than six months. Symptoms here can include anxiety; panic; irregular heartbeat and high blood pressure; problems with memory, concentration, perception, and loud noises and bright lights; and a sense of derealization. These symptoms appear to come in ten-day cycles and can last as long as a year. People addicted to high doses for longer than six months may experience both types of withdrawal. About 15 to 44 percent of people who withdraw from recommended doses may experience some withdrawal symptoms.[50]

The final class of sedative drugs that might easily be abused includes opiates like heroin, morphine, and the new drug of choice, OxyContin. Opiates are typically used in medicine for the relief of pain. People abuse opiates to relieve depression and anxiety and induce euphoria. People can even become addicted after a single session. When first used, their most typical side effects include nausea and vomiting, resulting from stimulation of the brain's chemoreceptor trigger zone. The body usually becomes tolerant to these effects after a single dose. Performance slows a bit, but this occurs more in the psychomotor than in the cognitive realm. Characteristic later side effects of opiates include tiny pupils, constipation, and immensely lowered sex drive. Although heroin can cause a prototypical nod, or sleepiness, shortly after ingestion, heroin actually induces insomnia and other sleeping problems over the long term.

Although the pleasant effects of the drug may last for only thirty to sixty minutes, the letdown can prove quite agitating. Over time, the addiction causes activity and social interaction to decrease and aggressiveness and isolation to increase. More importantly, addicts quickly develop a tolerance to the positive effects of the drug, so that they maintain their use merely to hold off the withdrawal effects more than to induce any euphoria. Opiate withdrawal, while incredibly painful and difficult, is almost never lethal in the way that alcohol or barbiturate withdrawal can be.

Heroin withdrawal, for example, progresses along an extremely predictable path, starting six to twelve hours after the last use, and ending by seventy-two hours after use. The user begins withdrawal with restlessness, agitation, yawning, chills, goose bumps, and nausea. After a second phase involving eight to twelve hours of a form of deep sleep called yen sleep, the addict awakens to cramps, vomiting, diarrhea, twitching, and sweating.[51] Severity of withdrawal symptoms depends on how much of what drug an addict was abusing. Less potent drugs taken at lower levels produce less severe withdrawal symptoms. Withdrawal can be stopped almost instantly by injection or consumption of any opiate, including methadone.

Significantly, people who are in pain, or other chronic users of opiates, appear not to manifest many of the cognitive impairments typically associated with opiate use. Opiates in the body really look like "smart drugs" in action. If there is pain, the pain is typically reduced, though not necessarily eliminated, with few or no side effects, even at reasonably high doses. Most difficulties with opiate abuse derive either from the legal and financial problems resulting from addiction or from the medical problems that result from unclean methods of injection, as when dirty needles infect addicts with HIV, hepatitis, or other illnesses. If there is no pain, the typical effects of addiction and withdrawal are easy to witness.

Amphetamines are central nervous system stimulants. They cause an increase in heart rate and blood pressure. They also cause a dilation of the blood vessels and airways in the lungs. In fact, amphetamines were developed as a treatment for asthma, because they proved so quick and effective at opening constricted air pathways to the lungs. Use of amphetamines can produce several unpleasant results, including headache, dry mouth, stomach problems, and extreme weight loss. Heavy use or overdose of amphetamines can cause dizziness, confusion, tremors, hallucinations, problems with heart rhythm, and panic. Convulsions and coma occur in overdose conditions as well.

The main effect of using amphetamines is that they tend to make people feel good, at least initially. The effects of amphetamines and cocaine are extremely similar and, in the case of intravenous use, identical. Amphetamine use at high doses, or with intravenous or intranasal induction, produces strong positive rushes. High-dose users almost always characterize these feelings in strongly sexual terms. Even with lower doses of amphetamine usage, mood improves, energy increases, and, in many cases, the person feels as if he has a clear mind and a strong motivation to get things done. Depression often occurs when the user comes down off the drug, and tolerance to its positive effects occurs extremely rapidly, often after even a single use.

Amphetamines do appear to improve performance on certain tasks. They increase visual skill and endurance and diminish the effects of fatigue on performance, especially in tasks that require prolonged or diligent attention. Many of the studies demonstrating some of the positive effects of amphetamine use on performance were conducted by various militaries during the Second World War. Positive effects were especially noted for pilots, who did not show any diminution in performance over time as a result of fatigue with the help of relatively low doses (five milligrams) of amphetamines. Some researchers have argued, however, that these effects appear limited to overlearned tasks, while they may actually impair performance under conditions requiring flexible and creative thinking.[52] For competitive athletes, amphetamines do appear to improve the performance time over their best nondrug event times by about 1 percent, a difference that can prove critical, even definitive, at world-class levels of running, biking, or other physical sports.

Amphetamines, however, can cause some serious side effects over time. The person tends to have an increased sense of well-being, alertness, and energy. But tolerance quickly develops and then more and more of the drug is needed to achieve the same effect. The risk of toxic responses at these higher doses becomes very real. When this occurs, addicts demonstrate impaired judgment, becoming increasingly grandiose and euphoric, overoptimistic, and less cautious and more impulsive in their actions. Impairments that appear to be characteristic in stimulant addicts include deficits in cognition, motivation, insight, and attention. Addicts show emotional instability, impulsivity, aggressiveness, and depression.[53] Those who have used large amounts for long periods develop stereotyped behaviors, referred to as punding, where they repetitively perform some ritual, meaningless task, like washing their hands or crossing and uncrossing their legs, for long periods of time.[54] Such behavior might appear evident, for example, in someone who can't stop rearranging items on the top of his desk. In high dosages, amphetamines can induce a form of psychosis – amphetamine psychosis – that is indistinguishable from any other form of psychosis in presentation. The symptoms include hallucinations, delusions, hostility, and violence. Oftentimes, paranoia is present as well. Users who develop psychotic episodes often report feeling the experience of bugs crawling under their skin. A cocaine user might call these cocaine bugs; an amphetamine user typically refers to these as crank bugs.[55]

Amphetamine withdrawal often potentiates depression and fatigue. This can occur as soon as a half hour following administration of the drug. Addicts who have used a high dosage of the drug for a long time can precipitate severe depression from drug withdrawal, including suicidal ideation or attempts.

Evidence of amphetamines abuse by British prime minister Anthony Eden during the Suez Crisis in 1956 explains a lot of his seemingly bizarre behavior at the time.[56] Close advisers and observers noted his frenzied, panicked style, as well as his isolation, paranoia, and inability to sleep. He became irritable and argumentative. More severe reactions to high doses of amphetamines include talking too much or too fast, lack of emotional control, hyperactivity, hypervigilance, suspiciousness, aggressiveness, and hostility, which remain consistent with the reports of Eden's behavior by his friends. High doses of amphetamines over time can provoke confusion, delusions, hallucinations, and paranoia. When Eden's doctor cut him off for fear of an overdose, Eden collapsed in the middle of the crisis and had to be sent to the Caribbean with the public excuse that he was suffering from a fever related to the reemergence of a bout of malaria. Fever, in fact, is a classic symptom of abrupt withdrawal from amphetamine abuse.

One of the notable things about the use of these illegal substances by leaders is that most often their doctor is their supplier.[57] The doctor, over a long period of personal and intimate contact, often develops a personal loyalty to the leader. In some countries a doctor who does not offer what is demanded may be killed. In the American cases, problems occur more often when the doctor is not well trained in substance abuse or not properly supervised by others. While personal physicians remain crucial for the timely care for a sick or impaired leader, such doctors can easily err on the side of personal loyalty, perhaps even unknowingly facilitating their patient's addiction, thus compromising the care of their patient and possibly betraying the national welfare in the process. This happened, for example, when the Capitol doctor, Freeman Cary, prescribed inappropriate medications to at least two powerful U.S. leaders. In one case, Cary misdiagnosed Senator John East of North Carolina's symptoms of depression, anxiety, and insomnia. Cary prescribed sleeping pills and tranquilizers to which East became addicted. East later used these prescription drugs to commit suicide in June 1986. In reality, East suffered from hypothyroidism.[58]

This same physician was responsible for overprescribing Placidyl, a sleeping pill, to Supreme Court Justice William Rehnquist before he ascended to the Court. Sleeping pills are rarely recommended for more than two weeks of regular use because of the high potential for addiction. Only recently has one sleep drug, Lunesta, been approved for long-term use. Rehnquist took this drug in excess of recommended dosage under this doctor's care for more than nine years and had to go through treatment for withdrawal in 1981. Later, his addiction became an issue in the Senate hearing on his Supreme Court confirmation.[59]

Presidents and other leaders can be affected by prescription medications that are given in service of other medical conditions, but which may have powerful cognitive side effects as well. Steroids present particular problems because they are commonly used to treat so many ailments, from asthma to pain resulting from inflammation, and yet can produce such extreme mood effects. To some extent, as Post and Robins note, every drug also creates its own disease.[60]

Some leaders manage to be aware of, and eschew, such drugs and their effects. In the most heroic example, John Foster Dulles, who was dying of extremely painful stomach cancer, refused any pain medication because he was concerned that it would interfere unduly with his job as secretary of state under Eisenhower. In another example, Lady Bird Johnson admitted that one of the reasons she did not want her husband Lyndon Johnson to run for president in 1968 following one heart attack was because she was afraid that his tendency to refuse medication that might affect him mentally would harm his health and cause another heart attack.[61] Less extreme measures than those taken by John Foster Dulles have also been taken by others in an attempt to prevent cognitive deficits as a result of medication. Clinton, for example, underwent only local anesthesia during the surgery to repair his injured thigh in 1997 and was given only antiinflammatories for pain, in order to stay conscious and avoid a transfer of power to Vice President Gore during his ordeal. Yet, extreme chronic pain can produce its own mental limitations and effects as well, so a balance must be achieved between illness and treatment effects. One recent study, for example, showed that people suffering from a physical illness showed a deficit in verbal IQ. This effect was not otherwise explained by the presence of depression, cognitive load, or medication.[62]

CONCLUSIONS

Aging, illness, and addiction can affect a given leader's judgment and decision-making abilities. How these conditions affected particular leaders within the context of specific foreign policy contexts will be the subject of the remainder of this book. Leaders will be presented in chronological order. In each case, a leader and his relevant illness will be discussed, followed by an examination of a particular foreign policy decision that was assumed or appeared to have been at least partially affected by that leader's impairments. These leaders present a sample of the kind of medical and psychological conditions that can affect leaders in systematic and predictable ways by significantly impairing their ability to make optimal judgments, at least in the foreign policy arena.

THREE

THE EXACERBATION OF PERSONALITY: WOODROW WILSON

B y any measure, Woodrow Wilson was a remarkable man of tower-
ing intellect, rhetoric, wit, and accomplishment. Before becoming
the twenty-eighth president of the United States, he was a successful professor of political science, president of Princeton University, and
an active governor of the state of New Jersey. Wilson's achievements as
president mark him as one of the most influential in the country's history;
moreover, Wilson's ideals in support of self-determination, sovereignty,
and human rights have continued to instruct and direct American foreign
policy in decisive ways through the remainder of his century and beyond.
And yet, in common wisdom, Wilson often seems most closely associated with his greatest defeat, the failure of his beloved League of Nations
covenant to win approval in the U.S. Senate. Both ironic and clichéd, it
nonetheless proves true that Wilson's character possessed the seeds of his
own destructive tragedy. Yet the loss of his goals proves no less dramatic
or devastating because of their source.

Psychobiographical studies of great men often lean toward a discussion of what was wrong with the person. Earlier biographies, and those
without psychological bent, commonly seek to note the laudatory aspects
of an individual's life, providing a model for the reader to strive toward
in one's own life. But perhaps because of intrinsic aspects of the psychoanalytic models that dominate psychobiographical studies or some
unconscious inclination on the part of such authors, many such studies focus on an individual's failings,[1] which may explain why they have
fallen out of favor. This perspective appears particularly problematic
in examining a man such as Woodrow Wilson, whose skill at his best
could rarely be surpassed. Nonetheless, under particular circumstances

and, after October 1919, in the wake of a major stroke, his capacities became compromised by the interaction of his physical illness, his prior personality, and his social and political environment. It is impossible to understand how Wilson's actions contributed to the defeat of the treaty he held most dear without an appreciation of how all the elements intertwined a such a way as to lead to Wilson's inevitable failure. From this perspective, this chapter seeks to explain Wilson's psychological and physical history within the specific political context in which he operated. In so doing, while emphasis inescapably falls on Wilson's limitations, the analysis is not meant to detract from his noteworthy skills and accomplishments; the following case chapters of Franklin Roosevelt, John F. Kennedy, and Richard Nixon should be read in such a light as well.

To begin at the end, the second half of Woodrow Wilson's second term as president presents perhaps the most extreme example of medical cover-up in American history. During his last eighteen months in office, from October 1919 until March 1921, Wilson was an invalid, unable to move his left arm and leg, disinterested in work, isolated by his wife from the outside world, and struggling with his responsibilities and limitations. During this time, Edith Bolling Galt, Wilson's second wife, with the acquiescence of his doctor, Cary T. Grayson, essentially ran, or in many cases failed to run, the U.S. government in his stead. Many departments within the U.S. government continued to operate as usual with little or no direction from above. But others, most notably the State Department headed by Robert Lansing, needed more executive leadership and decision making than they received. In many cases, things simply did not get done. Some bills passed through presidential inaction, and other pressing matters never received any presidential leadership whatsoever. Mrs. Wilson screened all the information her husband received, and it remains unclear what she did and did not actually show him. Often pressing political issues that did generate a response came back with her childish handwriting in the margins, ostensibly reflecting the president's opinion. Problems emerged because Mrs. Wilson's singular concern remained her husband's health, not the welfare of the country. As one prominent study of Mrs. Wilson concluded,

> She was never interested in politics except where it affected her personally...Personal rather than political convictions were the motivating force behind the decisions she made. Rarely did she act in accordance with what might be best for the country. She left those issues in which she had no personal interest to her husband's more competent political advisors....The result was not that Mrs. Wilson ran the White House like a president, but rather that she ran it inefficiently and with a primary concern for the welfare of her husband.[2]

But run it she did. Edith Wilson herself later commented about her activities: "I don't know why you men make such a fuss. I had no trouble running the country when Woody was ill."

The president's failure to exercise adequate leadership over the country for the rest of his term was hidden from the public with great care by his wife and physician. As Grayson recalled, Edith stood "like a stone wall between the sickroom and officials."[3] But Mrs. Wilson justified her actions as merely following the doctor's orders, claiming that "It is always an excitement for one who is ill to see people. The physicians said that if I could convey messages from cabinet members and others to the President, he would escape the nervous drain audiences with his officials would entail."[4] Yet the problems confronting the country at the time were not trivial. Given the tumultuous times at the end of the First World War, with many pressing national and international concerns, Wilson's disability fell at a critical juncture in American domestic, diplomatic, and foreign policy history. Wilson's story contains tragic elements because his absence from power led not only to the defeat of the League of Nations. The loss of his previously high level of effective engagement in government at all levels also deprived the country of any number of positive outcomes in various areas that undoubtedly would have occurred had Wilson been in full possession of his faculties. As Hugh L'Etang wrote, "It was not so much that the machinery of government was halted, that documents could not be signed, that Ambassadors could not be met, that officials could not be appointed or even discharged; it is that Wilson, isolated by his intimates and handicapped by increasing obstinacy, mental deterioration and failure of judgment, destroyed any hope of attaining even some of the objectives for which he had ruined his health."[5]

Serious domestic problems ran rampant. Inflation was atmospheric, with prices running 102 percent higher than their 1914 levels. Recession loomed, unemployment was high, and race riots and labor strikes emerged in various places as well. A steel workers' strike in September 1920 resulted in the death of eighteen strikers when federal forces were called in; early on, Wilson had tried to convince the head of United States Steel to meet some of the worker's demands, but after his stroke, his administration did nothing to defend the strikers. U.S. Steel turned tough, and without government intervention on their behalf, the workers called off their strike in January. A second strike among the coal workers proved similarly problematic. Despite high postwar inflation, these workers had not received any wage increases after the war. When John Lewis came in as the new president of the United Mine Workers of America, he supported their requests for fewer hours and wage increases of up to 60 percent. Lewis called a strike for November. In this instance, Wilson's personal secretary, Joseph Tumulty, acting in his name, intervened with Attorney

General Mitchell Palmer and Secretary of Labor William Wilson to settle the strike in favor of the workers.

Further, a Red scare consumed the nation, when communist parties formed in 1919 and a general strike was called by the Industrial Workers of the World in Seattle. The precursor to the Federal Bureau of Investigation, the Bureau of Investigation, uncovered a plan to assassinate prominent individuals. When Congress failed to act on this information, Attorney General Palmer sent out federal agents to arrest 4,000 people on the night of January 2, 1920, on suspicion of harboring communist sympathies. And national paroxysms of self-reflective moralism surrounding alcohol use and Prohibition were soon to engage the country.

The irony is that these serious domestic problems were not even on Wilson's radar screen. Even pressing problems in foreign affairs received little of Wilson's attention, including a fight with Britain over shipping, difficult relations with Mexico, and the recognition of the new country of Costa Rica. What Wilson did care about was the most important issue facing the country in foreign affairs, namely the questions surrounding ratification of the Treaty of Versailles and the Covenant of the League of Nations ending World War I. In these areas, many scholars claim that Wilson's impairment impacted his foreign policy profoundly. In particular, Link and Weinstein argue that his inability to manage this legislation and his unwillingness to compromise led to his cherished League of Nations Covenant being rejected by the Republican-dominated Senate.[6] However, all such arguments rest on the counterfactual assumption that a vital Wilson would have proved willing to compromise with Senator Henry Cabot Lodge and other Senate Republicans over the reservations they desired in the League of Nations Covenant.

As Alexander and Juliette George and others have argued, even a healthy Wilson may have been unwilling to engage in such a compromise. Even a strong Wilson, entrapped by his psychological propensities to reject compromise, may have doomed the treaty to failure. However, a healthy Wilson may have been in a better position to garner the necessary supplementary political support to push the treaty through. Ironically, Wilson did appear to compromise in part by offering certain "interpretations" just prior to his major stroke, which he later rescinded, ordering members of his own Democratic Party to vote against the league treaty in the Senate to prevent its passage with "reservations" of which he did not approve. Thus, all arguments suggesting that Wilson's physical ailments alone doomed the treaty to failure rest on an unknowable assumption about a healthy Wilson's willingness to compromise on principles that were critically important to him; given both his lifetime and recent history, it is not at all clear that such compromise would have been in the offing.[7]

WILSON'S PERSONAL BACKGROUND

Wilson was born in Virginia in 1856. Much of his youth was influenced by the devastation wrought by the Civil War, and the deprivations inherent in the Reconstruction-era South. As a child, he stuttered. He did not learn to read until he was eleven years old, much to his father's constant anger and annoyance. Weinstein argues that Wilson suffered from dyslexia, but the Georges view Wilson's late development as symbolic of his passive resentment toward his authoritarian father, for whom learning was critically important. Their argument gains credence from the fact that almost all developmental dyslexics remain plagued by prototypical writing errors, especially poor spelling, features that never characterized Wilson's writing.[8] By any measure, Wilson's sheer will in overcoming these early educational deficits to become a noted political science professor and president of Princeton University, as well as one of the century's greatest orators, is nothing short of remarkable.

Wilson originally trained as a lawyer but was an abject failure in his chosen profession. Following his early and intense interests in constitutions, Wilson attended Johns Hopkins and was awarded a degree in political science. He went on to become a professor of political science, first at Bryn Mawr, then at Wesleyan, and finally at his beloved undergraduate alma mater, Princeton. In 1885 he wrote a classic book entitled *Congressional Government*, based on his dissertation, which became a standard reference for many years. Following the publication of his second well-received book, *The State*, in 1889, he was offered a professorship at Princeton University. He went on to become president of Princeton. He was also named president of the American Political Science Association. His early tenure as president of Princeton was marked by considerable success, especially in his ability to promote academic achievement over social status as the measure for success in college by instituting the preceptorial system. He resigned in 1910 following a difficult fight with his former friend and ally, Dean West, over the construction of a quadrangle system at Princeton, designed to overthrow the ancient and exclusionary eating clubs and replace them with a system of residential education, along the lines developed by Yale slightly later, after receiving a grant from Edward Harkness. In Princeton's case, the eating clubs remained, and still remain, too powerful to eliminate. Wilson also failed in his attempt to integrate the new graduate buildings into the center of campus. Wilson went on to be elected governor of New Jersey and then president of the United States in 1912.

In his first term as president of the United States, Wilson achieved a number of truly impressive accomplishments. During his first year, the Sixty-third Congress was the most productive in history up until that point. Under Wilson's leadership, Congress passed a great deal of important and influential legislation, including the Underwood-Simmons tariff revision, the Glass-Owen banking and currency reform legislation, and the Clayton Antitrust Act, designed to address problems related to trusts and monopolies. In addition, Wilson succeeded in passing the bill establishing the Federal Trade Commission. He initiated another series of important domestic legislation during the final year of his first term. This progressive legislation included federal regulatory and welfare mechanisms, such as direct aid to farmers and protective labor laws. Wilson's most extensive biographer, Arthur Link, who edited the multivolume *Papers of Woodrow Wilson*, argued that no president in history had been as productive as Wilson in creating such a large body of domestic legislation in the period prior to American entry into World War I.

In view of the tremendous energy and dedication that such accomplishments must have demanded, Wilson's physical collapse in the later part of his presidency seems especially tragic. There exists no doubt that a healthy Wilson would have been more engaged, for good or bad, in the discussions surrounding the passage of the Treaty of Versailles in the Senate in late 1919 and early 1920. The heart of this treaty, to Wilson's mind, was his own brainchild, the League of Nations proposal. Again, one can argue that the league treaty would have passed had Wilson remained healthy and engaged in the process. For evidence of this claim, Wilson presented four "interpretations" of the treaty, which he gave to his Senate representative, Gilbert Hitchcock, just prior to going on a western tour. After his stroke, when Hitchcock obtained a series of new "reservations" that were close to Wilson's original "interpretations," an isolated Wilson refused to compromise. However, it remains unclear how willing Wilson was to accept the interpretations he put forward as part of a final treaty ratification, or how much they might have represented opening gambits whose purpose was to frame the debate in a manner more consistent with his own position than that of the Republican irreconcilables.

After reviewing the debate over what really happened to Wilson, and its effect on his political behavior, this chapter will outline the basis for arguments concerning Wilson's physical and psychological limitations, and explore how his various dynamics affected the debate and ultimate failure of the League of Nations in the U.S. Senate.

DEBATE

Woodrow Wilson presents one of the most complex and fascinating cases of presidential disability in history. Wilson had suffered from a series of lifelong problems with various physical ailments, mostly psychosomatic in origin, with increasing incidences of real illnesses superimposed over time; these illnesses likely resulted, at least in part, from uncontrolled hypertension. In early 1919 he suffered from a series of ailments while in Paris, including a case of what appears to have been influenza. Wilson's most severe physical impairment came about in the wake of his first, and only agreed-upon, major stroke, following a speaking tour in the western states in late September 1919; the stroke occurred on October 2. After this event, he never fully recovered complete movement of his left arm or leg or his former level of mental activity. He did, however, have a partial return to cognitive functioning following a viral infection in late January 1920, after which he was able to do some work.

The exact nature of Wilson's health problems has been a source of controversy. One salvo in the battle was presented by Sigmund Freud and William Bullitt, who argued that Wilson suffered from neurotic conditions that impaired him throughout his life.[9] They portrayed Wilson as a man driven by unconscious and inconsistent desires. They found the source of much of his unhappiness in his early unrequited love for, and broken relationship with, his cousin Hattie. Their psychobiography of Wilson, which did not come out until after his death, has not been well received. Bullitt, one of the young liberals who worked for the State Department early in the twentieth century, remained a wealthy friend of Colonel House, Wilson's close friend and adviser. He held a long-standing grudge against Wilson for snubbing him after he tried to open diplomatic talks with Lenin at the end of World War I. Bullitt was one of three diplomats who resigned in protest over the terms of the Treaty of Versailles, which they believed were too punitive toward Germany. In September 1919, just before Wilson's major stroke, Bullitt testified before the Senate, repeating negative comments about the treaty made to him by Secretary of State Lansing. Importantly, Lansing did not believe that the league was as important as the peace treaty; further, he had opposed some of Wilson's fourteen points as vague and too impractical to implement. At this point, Bullitt began his earnest opposition to Wilson.

Thus, his interpretation of the source of Wilson's troubles needs to be treated with a healthy degree of skepticism, because Bullitt has good reason to hold a biased opinion against Wilson. Further, because the book was apparently written quite late in Freud's life, many question the true extent of his intellectual involvement with this project. In a review of the book in the *New York Review* in 1967, Erik Erikson posited, based on the language, that Freud had written only the introduction. Erikson suggested that Freud, like many Europeans, had been disappointed by Wilson's actions in Paris and was distrustful of Wilson's religious motives. In particular, Freud noted that Wilson's image, "as it rose above the horizons of Europeans, was from the beginning, unsympathetic." As Wilson's involvement increased, "the more severely we suffered from the consequences of his intrusion into our destiny." In particular, Freud remained deeply suspect of the intrusion of religion into American civil life, what Freud referred to as "Christian science applied to politics." He considered such self-righteous hypocrisy inconsistent with the insights of science necessary to make progress in the real world. He likened Wilson to a doctor "who wishes to restore the eyesight of a patient but does not know the construction of the eye, and has neglected to learn the necessary methods of operation."[10] Moreover, Erikson also intimates that Freud's collaboration with Bullitt was inspired more by his gratitude to Bullitt for getting him out of Vienna to London in 1938 than by any true intellectual association.[11]

Nonetheless, the notion that Wilson may have suffered from some psychological limitations has a clear basis in evidence. Alexander and Juliette George offered a well-respected and meticulous psychodynamic interpretation of Wilson's behavior.[12] Perhaps the best-known and most influential psychobiography ever written, *Woodrow Wilson and Colonel House*, presents a careful psychodynamic tracing of President Wilson's life and political career.[13] In particular, the Georges argue that, as a child, Wilson felt frustrated and angry being at the mercy of his perfectionist and authoritarian father, a Presbyterian minister. They suggest that Wilson's failure to read until he was eleven was a clear sign of his emotional trouble in general, and his stubbornness in particular. In later work, their argument gains credence from letters and interviews that documented the Wilsons' harsh parenting strategies toward their other son, known as Josie, a man who never managed to overcome his resistance to education and failed to succeed in a way that would make his father proud.[14]

The Georges posit that Wilson's chronically low self-esteem and his repressed anger toward his father resulted in a self-defeating pattern of behavior destined to repeat itself throughout his life. Many analysts refer to this kind of behavior as repetition compulsion; individuals seek out ways to repeat powerful psychological situations until they master them, which they often prove unable to do. This insight undergirds the aphorism, "when you are a hammer, everything looks like a nail"; in this model, people represent little more than an experience waiting for a particular event that triggers their underlying dynamic issue. In Wilson's case, he could not tolerate any compromise with powerful male authority figures because such a situation reminded him of his relationship with his father. Although he was never able to stand up to his real father, exhibiting an overtly sycophantic approach to him in his letters, he nonetheless managed to transfer the rage he felt toward his father and project it onto other men who he believed were trying to thwart his will. On many occasions, Wilson was able to defy the authority of other men who tried to make him submit to their will, although he failed in two significant cases with Dean West at Princeton and Senator Henry Cabot Lodge in the Senate. Notably, as the Georges write, both men "resembled Wilson's father in important respects: Lodge had a mordant wit. Both men were strong, erudite, of notable facility with the English language and of patrician (not to say condescending) bearing."[15]

The Georges trace Wilson's career from before his time as president of Princeton, including his failed attempt to install the undergraduate residential college quadrangle plan that he advocated against Dean West's opposition, through to his failure to secure Senate confirmation for his own League of Nations proposal against Senator Henry Cabot Lodge. In both cases, Wilson lost his battle of wills, and many would say that these losses resulted at least in part from his own intransigence. The Georges demonstrate how Wilson compensated for his low self-esteem with a compensatory drive for power, which led him to achieve many political successes. In this way, they seek to test Harold Lasswell's hypothesis concerning Political Man, which has at least two important component elements. First, Lasswell argued that scholars might locate the source of a politician's behavior in the way in which a leader displaces his private needs onto public objects and then rationalizes these acts in terms of the larger public good or interest.[16] Second, Lasswell suggested that such men may seek power compulsively as a means to compensate for feelings of low self-esteem. In this way, personal insecurities can generate public and political instability. Using this insight in combination with careful archival work across the whole of Wilson's life, the Georges conclude:

> Our theory is that Wilson felt overwhelmed as a child, that his brave attempts to preserve his selfhood through such coping strategies as refusing to learn and taking refuge in the world of his imagination did not suffice. Further, we believe the facts suggest that "Tommy" harbored perfectly natural resentments the very existence of which were too fearful to admit even to himself let alone express to his formidable father or his sympathetic but very proper and very vulnerable mother who early became inordinately dependent on him.
>
> This hypothesis is supported by the data which indicate that in later life Wilson felt beset by a painful excess of explosive emotion the nature of which he recoiled from examining.[17]

This dynamic played itself out throughout Wilson's life in selectively defined but clearly triggered interactions, which reminded him of his earlier vulnerability at the hands of his father. Note the contingent nature of this process. If Wilson felt competent to handle an issue, and no one disputed his authority, he could act in completely cool, dispassionate, brilliant, and effective ways. But when his self-esteem was pricked or his authority was called into question in a particular way that reminded him of his father, Wilson became predictably belligerent and intransigent, even to the point of risking the substance of an issue, to prove his power and authority, which for him often took the form of moral imperative and approbation. This process occurred with both Dean West at Princeton and Henry Cabot Lodge in the Senate in remarkably similar psychological dynamics. In such circumstances, Wilson not only sought to succeed to prove his father's predictions of his failure and weakness incorrect through personal skill and victory, but he also felt compelled, even encouraged, to vent his spleen on those who questioned his authority in a way in which he was never able to directly challenge his father:

> In certain situations in his public career, Woodrow Wilson's self-defeating stubbornness and unwillingness to defer (or at least make expedient gestures of deference) to men whose cooperation was essential to the accomplishment of his goals were irrational behaviors that arose from underlying low self-estimates against which he had constantly to struggle. We tried to show that for Wilson, carving out a sphere of competence in public life and striving for high achievement were means of overcoming feelings of unimportance, of moral inferiority, of weakness, of mediocrity, of intellectual inadequacy.[18]

In sum, when Wilson proved unable to tolerate frustrations of his personal will, he refused to compromise, especially with powerful male authority figures, in ways that ultimately led to his notable defeats, both at Princeton and as president of the United States.

The Georges' interpretation of Wilson generated a vociferous debate among those who sought to place Wilson's character in a more positive light. In particular, Arthur Link, the editor of the Wilson papers, and Dr. Edwin Weinstein, advocated a more hagiographic view of Wilson. Whatever intransigence, stubbornness, or belligerence that Wilson demonstrated, in this view, resulted not from any psychological neuroses but rather from physiological illness caused by strokes. Weinstein, Anderson, and Link argue that the source of Wilson's difficulties was not psychological but rather physical in nature.[19] They trace the crises in Wilson's careers to a series of strokes that they claim began as early as 1896 and continued until the one that caused his death in 1924. The stroke in 1896 ostensibly caused weakness if not paralysis in his right hand and arm, and a stroke in 1906 led to almost complete blindness in his left eye.

Subsequent scholarly debate surrounding the putative source of Wilson's intransigence in the face of the League of Nations proposal and his failure to compromise with Henry Cabot Lodge over the final form has tended to differ along these lines.[20] Dr. Weinstein and Arthur Link argued that Wilson's recurring strokes precipitated many fractures in Wilson's personality that others witnessed.[21] The Georges, along with physicians including the ophthalmologist Dr. Michael Marmor and the psychiatrist Dr. Jerrold Post, argue that the evidence does not support the notion of Wilson having had any stroke before the massive one he sustained on October 2, 1919.[22] They suggest that the original episode Weinstein and Link mention in 1896 could have been little more than "writer's cramp" and that the most serious episode in 1906, which left Wilson partially blind in his left eye for the rest of his life, resulted from a local retinal hemorrhage and not a stroke.

Given the vast amount of physical writing Wilson did, literally hundreds of pages a month, it is not implausible that at least some of the early symptoms of pain, numbness, and tingling in his writing arm could have resulted from a form of carpal tunnel syndrome or peripheral nerve entrapment. But debate on this issue, as so many others, remains clouded in controversy. Dr. Jerrold Post wrote that after consulting five medical experts in neurology and psychiatry and orthopedics, none found evidence of a stroke on the basis of Wilson's 1896 symptoms persuasive. His consultants suggested that such symptoms as reported by Wilson and his friends and family were more consistent with a musculoskeletal problem, such as carpal tunnel syndrome or a diseased cervical disk.[23] The editors of the Wilson papers, led by Arthur Link, disagreed with this interpretation, denying the likelihood of cervical disease or carpal tunnel in favor of their previous stroke hypothesis.[24]

In disputes surrounding Wilson's eye problem, Dr. Michael Marmor, for one, argues that the event that precipitated Wilson's blindness in 1906 was more likely a retinal hemorrhage than the stroke that Link and Weinstein believed it to be.[25] Marmor, an ophthalmologist at the Stanford Medical Center, adds the important point that "[f]irst, many types of disease of incapacity – not necessarily stroke – may account for an emotional or psychological response. Second, diffuse vascular disease and aging may intensify pre-existing beliefs and personality traits, even when cognitive powers remain intact."[26]

In his writing on the subject, Dr. Bert Park presented yet another alternative explanation for Wilson's symptoms that attempted to find commonalities and unite the psychological and physical positions more closely. While falling more on the side of the Weinstein-Link hypothesis, at least partly because Link served as a strong mentor, Park differs concerning the particular nature of the disability that affected Wilson. Finding some compelling arguments and value in the alternative positions presented by Drs. Marmor and Post, Park notes that all parties agree to the existence of hypertension in Wilson as early as 1906, when Wilson saw ophthalmologist Dr. George de Schweinitz for the burst blood vessel in his eye. While the original records were destroyed by de Schweinitz's medical partner, Dr. Alexander Fewell, Dr. Weinstein obtained some information on them from the man who took over Fewell's practice, Dr. Edward Gifford. Gifford claimed that Fewell read Wilson's record to him and discussed it with him before destroying it. According to Gifford, the record documented that Wilson suffered from "very high blood pressure" and that his retinas showed changes consistent with that diagnosis. After seeing de Schweinitz, Wilson visited an internist, Dr. Albert Stengel, who recommended rest. Wilson took his advice, canceled all his impending duties, and spent the summer in Britain.[27] There, he visited the Royal Infirmary in Edinburgh on August 31 and used one of the few blood pressure machines then available in the world. Dr. Boyd confirmed hypertension at that time; Wilson was even given medication to treat it, although no truly effective antihypertensive drugs existed at that time.[28] Park speculates that the medication that Wilson was most likely administered would have included either sodium nitrate or sodium iodide, treatments advocated at that time for hypertension, which are essentially ineffective.[29]

Park argues that uncontrolled hypertension would produce exactly the kind of retinal hemorrhage that de Schweinitz apparently witnessed in 1906. Park suggested that such a condition could prompt the occurrence of small strokes, or so-called lacunar infarcts, leading to what is now commonly referred to as multiinfarct dementia.[30] While not as large as the major artery occlusion posited by Weinstein to have caused Wilson's character deterioration, these "little strokes" can still account for transient cognitive impairments, including problems with memory, judgment, abstract thinking, and emotional stability. However, these subclinical events often produce no observable effect until a number of them have accumulated or the underlying hypertensive condition precipitates a more major cardiovascular event. Park argues that Wilson's hypertension, evidenced as early as 1906, led to a series of these small-vessel lacunar infarcts. In his view, accumulation of these infarcts led to "mild but progressive dementia."[31] And, as all agree, Wilson sustained a large-vessel stroke, caused by an atherosclerotic occlusion of the right side of the brain, in October 1919.

Thus, Park suggests, premature aging of Wilson's nervous system, brought about by uncontrolled hypertension, along with some atherosclerosis, contributed to Wilson's dementia. By dementia, Park means some loss of intellectual or cognitive function brought about by an organic disease process, such as uncontrolled hypertension. Park states that the criteria for establishing the diagnosis of dementia or organic brain syndrome "include (1) cognitive changes that interfere with occupational or social obligations; (2) memory impairment; and (3) impaired abstract thinking, faulty judgment, and behavioral aberrations."[32] Park argues that Wilson manifested all of these symptoms subsequent to his massive stroke in October 1919.

Evaluation

A problem in weighing several different hypotheses about the causes of Wilson's impairments is that much of the medical information has been lost or destroyed. Apparently, none of Wilson's doctors wanted to take the chance of hurting his reputation; clearly, he inspired great loyalty and fondness on the part of his associates. Notably, the records of both Wilson's neurologist, Francis Dercum, and his ophthalmologist, George de Schweinitz, were destroyed.[33] The only surviving record of Dercum's examinations exists in the Grayson papers.[34] While some of Cary Grayson's diary has been made public, and he wrote his own memoir about his life treating President Wilson, some papers remain solely in the possession of the Grayson family. More importantly, many of the notes in Grayson's diary appear vague by current medical standards, although not necessarily so by the standards of the day, and it can often prove challenging to know just exactly how to translate some of his medical characterizations into current diagnoses.

In addition, in seeking to explain any one person's behavior or his impact on a particular event, it is important not to fall prey to too much medical reductionism.[35] Many things, including health, can affect a person's performance. Even a skillful, resourceful, and charismatic political leader cannot control the outcome of an event that involves other influential people or countries. Here Marmor's comment about the many medical and other sources that can precipitate a given response points to an important consideration in all psychobiography: multiple independent causation. It is unlikely that any single cause can be used to explain as large and complex a phenomenon as the impact of Wilson's health on his performance or the failure of the League of Nations covenant to pass in the Senate, and there are many political as well as interpersonal dynamics to consider.

But attributing some causality to Wilson's final uncontested stroke would not necessarily invalidate at least some of the Georges' argument about the primary emotional and psychological nature of Wilson's character. Most victims of stroke experience personality shifts that represent an exacerbation of the person's previous personality. Dr. Bert Park cites a particularly telling passage from psychiatrist Dr. Lawrence Kolb on how this process works as people age or encounter some kind of organic brain disorder or dementia: "Altruistic sentiments are usually lost early, while egotistic, selfish ones are intensified.... As the patient with mild organic brain syndrome becomes aware of the gradual impairment of his capacities, there is at first an intensification of already existing character defenses.... *He becomes more like himself.*"[36]

Thus, even if Wilson did suffer from strokes, big or little, numerous or single, the behavioral effect would still be to exaggerate those aspects of his earlier character and personality. If such was the case, then the Georges' analysis of Wilson's character becomes especially salient and important in seeking to understand the way in which any organic mental events might have produced particular behavioral changes.[37]

Much of what is at stake in these kinds of debates over the character of particular subjects is their place and stature in history. Biographers often become invested in, and identified with, their subjects and may not want any seemingly pejorative interpretations to go unchallenged; this was likely the case with Link's position on Wilson. Conversely, certain authors may have a particular ax to grind with their subject; such motivation inspired Bullitt's biography of Wilson, at least in part. The unstated and unchallenged assumption in the debates between the Georges and Link, in particular, is that for Wilson to have suffered a physical ailment like a stroke is somehow preferable to his having suffered an emotional one, like low self-esteem and self-defeating behavioral patterns. The stigma attached to mental health interpretations and explanations by some may reflect the times in which they were written, although popular attitudes toward mental illness are hardly more sophisticated now. But this argument seems unlikely; political interpretations still assume that a leader is somehow less responsible for a physical than a psychological ailment, and that assignment of blame is more appropriate in the latter than in the former category. Political ramifications for physical illness also remain less severe than for mental impairment, the implicit notion being that the former is somehow not as bad as the latter overall.

Psychological Perspective

Alternative psychological explanations exist for Wilson's symptomatology, at least prior to his devastating stroke in October 1919. Throughout his life, Wilson's times of bad health were closely correlated with his emotional unhappiness, high level of stress, or having too many demands on his time. Even his early symptoms of pain and weakness in his arm could have been psychosomatic in origin. Wilson grew up with a strongly moral outlook and identified as a devout Presbyterian. Psychological weakness represented moral failure and, as such, could not be admitted or allowed. Yet there is some evidence that Wilson may have had an affair with Mary Hurlburt Peck, an unhappily remarried widow he met while taking a rest cure in the Caribbean in 1907, and whose acquaintance he renewed in 1908. Over the course of the following seven years, until Wilson married his second wife, he enjoyed a rich correspondence with Mrs. Peck.[38] Wilson, traveling by himself, was lonely and hit it off with this woman he met through mutual friends. Wilson's attachment to Mrs. Peck caused some kind of subsequent rupture with his first wife, Ellen. No correspondence remains from the seven months following Wilson's 1908 return from Bermuda, a notable omission given the weight of subsequent correspondence. Further, Wilson left for the summer in England without Ellen, who had accompanied him the year before. In one notable letter home during that time, Wilson writes Ellen:

I never in my life longed for *you*, my sweet, sweet darling, as I do now or realized more entirely all that you mean to me, everything that sustains and enriches life. You have only to believe in and trust me, darling, and *all* will come right, what you do not understand included. I know my heart now, if ever I did, *and it belongs to you*. God give you the gracious strength to be patient with me! "Emotional love" – ah dearest, that was a cutting and cruel judgment and utterly false; but as natural as false; but I never blamed you or wondered at it. I only understood – only saw the thing as you see it and as it is *not*, and suffered, am suffering still, ah, how deeply![39]

Whether Wilson actually cheated, or only formed an emotional bond with Mrs. Peck, is less important in some sense than the obvious pain his action caused his beloved wife, for which he experienced intense guilt and responsibility. In the last year of her life, Ellen Wilson told Dr. Grayson that the "Peck" affair was the only unhappiness her husband had ever caused her, taking care to note that there was nothing wrong in it.[40] Wilson carried sufficient guilt about this event that he again suffered severely when he felt forced to confess it to Edith Bolling Galt prior to their wedding. In that instance, Wilson's son-in-law, Secretary of the Treasury McAdoo, and Colonel House had heard rumors that Mrs. Peck might sell her personal letters from him to his political enemies. In an effort to forestall the wedding for a bit, so as to appear more seemly following the death of Wilson's first wife, McAdoo lied and told Wilson that he had received an anonymous letter to this effect. Wilson confessed to Edith Galt, who forgave him, but never forgave House, whom she suspected of instigating the plot to postpone her marriage.[41] The morning after his confession to Edith Galt, he wrote her in a telling, completely characteristic manner: "I have tried, ah, *how* I have tried to expiate folly by disinterested service and honorable, self-forgetful, devoted love, and it has availed only to lead the loveliest, sweetest woman in all the world, for whom I would joyfully give my life, to mortification and dismay."[42]

In someone with Wilson's history of psychosomatic illness during times of stress, somatic symptoms such as the "neuritis" he complained of in his hand could easily have resulted from the guilt he experienced about having the affair, particularly in the period of 1907–1908 when his behavior most clearly caused his wife, Ellen, pain. Recall that at this time neurological patterns were not common knowledge, and such "glove parasthesias" were not at all uncommon in "hysterical" personalities or in individuals understood to be sensitive or easily excitable by nature, as was Wilson.

While the evidence for this psychosomatic claim is mostly circumstantial, and by no means does it represent the only or even main cause for various forms of "neuritis," both Wilson's and Peck's letters are unusually affectionate, even for a man given to overly sentimental language in his personal writings in general. In the archives, there are subsequent records and documents demonstrating that he paid $15,000 to purchase a home for her and her son in New York in 1915.[43] Certainly in the early 1900s, buying a house for an unrelated woman was not common or lacking in meaning for a socially respected man. His attachment to Mrs. Peck was strong and authentic, regardless of whether or not it ever turned sexual. Yet no one can read Wilson's voluminously elegant and eloquent letters to his wife, Ellen, without recognizing how desperately and devotedly he loved her. Recall also that Wilson came from a strongly moralistic and Presbyterian upbringing, where he would feel guilt and shame over cheating on his wife, even if only in his heart, or causing her unnecessary anguish. Moreover, as noted previously, his father was one who taught Wilson that physical illness results from moral weakness. Thus, if Wilson felt that he had been morally weak, it would not be psychodynamically inconsistent for him to manifest that shame, guilt, and weakness in psychosomatic physical symptoms, such as weakness, tingling, and numbness in his right hand and arm.

Wilson was subject to fits of deep and severe depression, evidenced most clearly in his response to the death of his beloved wife. When Ellen died of a kidney ailment, Bright's disease, in 1914, Wilson complained of thought and memory problems common in depression or complicated bereavement patterns. Grayson here may have inadvertently made Wilson's grief worse by holding back the severity of Ellen's illness from Wilson; at the time, Grayson did not want to hurt Wilson any more than he was already suffering from his wife's illness. Even with the events of the First World War, Wilson commented that he had a hard time focusing on external events after losing his loved one: he commented that "the affairs of state were no substitute for the intimacy of a loved one."[44] At the time, he wrote to one of Ellen's friends that "God has stricken me almost beyond what I can bear."[45] After noticing problems with his thinking and memory processes, Wilson even told his friend Colonel House that "he was unfit to be President because he could not think straight."[46] He said he felt that his life was over and he wished that someone would kill him.[47] Years later, after his major stroke and long after he had married Edith, Wilson would awaken in the middle of the night and "he would pick up the search light and turn it toward a picture of Mrs. Ellen Wilson.... This was not done a few times but literally hundreds of times. It was a routine matter with him."[48]

Wilson's uncharacteristically aggressive foreign policy move to invade Mexico and seize a customhouse at Veracruz occurred during this period of grief. From a psychological perspective, it is easy to posit that Wilson's anger at Mexico was at least partly a reaction to or transfer of his anger and grief over the illness and death of his wife. Wilson had disapproved of General Vitoriano Huerta's policies since the beginning. Wilson feared that Huerta supported British oil interests in the region that were in competition with American companies. At the time, U.S. investment in Mexico reached $2 billion, and Americans owned 43 percent of the property values. Wilson refused to recognize Huerta's government, after he seized power by killing the previous dictator, Francisco Madero, who had himself only recently overthrown the previous longtime dictator Porfirio Diaz. Wilson demanded that Mexico hold democratic elections acceptable to the United States. Wilson then made several unsuccessful covert attempts to unseat the Mexican dictator.

During the time surrounding Ellen's illness and death, Wilson took an unusually aggressive action and, using the arrest of 7 American soldiers as a pretext, ordered the invasion of Mexico, which led to the deaths of 19 American soldiers and more than 300 Mexicans. Huerta broke off diplomatic relations with the United States, which prompted Wilson to immediately mobilize another American unit along the border with Texas. This action appeared to unite the Mexican factions and almost precipitated a war. However, Wilson then appeared overcome by the deaths of the American soldiers and the recklessness of his original decision and reversed his previous policy.[49]

Wilson's mood appears to have improved only upon meeting and marrying his second wife, Edith Bolling Galt. Dr. Grayson introduced them in what appears, at least in retrospect, as a form of therapy. Edith Galt could not have been more different from Ellen Axson. Ellen supported Wilson's many friendships, especially with other women, because she instinctively understood his insatiable need for love and approval. Ellen even considered Woodrow's social life to be her responsibility: "Since he has married someone who is not gay, I must provide him with friends who are."[50] Ellen's last conscious thought was of Wilson. Just before she died, she pulled Dr. Grayson close to her and said, "Doctor, if I go away, promise me that you will take good care of Woodrow."[51] Edith was an entirely different kind of woman, who was much more possessive of Wilson's attentions and affections. Edith precipitated Wilson's rupture with almost all his friends and associates. Her influence appears to have proved a crucial factor in Wilson's break with his closest adviser, Colonel House, and probably aided in distancing Wilson from both his secretary Joseph Tumulty and Secretary of State Lansing as well.[52] In addition, far from being the sweet, retiring, loving, and devoted wife that Ellen had been, Edith emerged as a strong force to be reckoned with in her own right. When Wilson became incapacitated, she did not hesitate to protect her husband, screening him from all the people and problems that she believed might upset him. In truth, this process almost certainly exacerbated and prolonged the extent of his impairment, because it is now well known that patients who are kept socially isolated do much worse than those who are kept emotionally engaged and stimulated following strokes. Had Ellen survived, Wilson's own health outcomes would have been decidedly improved.

Physical Perspective

Weinstein argues that between 1906 and 1920 Wilson suffered at least six medical episodes that he argues were minor or major strokes.[53] The problem is that Weinstein constructs this evidence with very few contemporary documents remaining, none of which prior to 1919 unequivocally support his contention. First, many standard tests and measures that would be part of a normal patient chart nowadays would not have been possible in Wilson's days. There were few blood pressure machines. No technologically sophisticated diagnostic tools like magnetic resonance imaging or computed tomographic scans to determine the source of a brain problem were available, nor were neurological tests done to determine mental capacity. Second, most medical records and reports of examinations appear to have been systematically destroyed by Wilson's doctors and consultants, with the exception of the diaries and memoir of Cary Grayson. As discussed previously, Wilson's ophthalmologist, George de Schweinitz, left his records to his partner, Alexander Fewell, who destroyed all of de Schweinitz's records in the 1950s. The only record that remains is the memory of Dr. Gifford, who took over Fewell's practice in 1961 and who discussed Wilson's case with Fewell based on de Schweinitz's record. Gifford confirmed that de Schweinitz found Wilson to have very high blood pressure, as well as retinal hemorrhages and scarring consistent with that diagnosis. Wilson's consulting internist, Alfred Stengel, left his records to his son, who subsequently burned them. And the consulting neurologist, the well-respected Francis Dercum, decreed that all his patient files be destroyed upon his death.[54] It is very interesting to note how many respected and notable physicians who treated Wilson went out of their way to destroy their records of him.

What remains are Cary Grayson's diaries and some observations made by intimate friends and associates, along with reports of medical conclusions by others. The problem here becomes interesting because Arthur Link was unwilling to show Grayson's diaries to anyone during his lifetime. Now that he is dead, it is possible to read some of these diaries at Seely Mudd Library at Princeton University, where Link worked, and to which he left his papers. The Princeton library does not have the complete diaries. Grayson's diary from the early years remains with his descendants, who have been reluctant to release it to scholars, probably because a great deal of the scholarly literature has been very critical of Dr. Grayson's treatment of Wilson and his participation in the cover-up of the severity of Wilson's last stroke. The record indicates that the decision to hide Wilson's condition lay primarily in Mrs. Edith Wilson's hands. Dr. Grayson even prepared an explicit memo on the severity of the president's condition in preparation for an expected congressional investigation, but he never released it. As the editors of the papers describe Dr. Grayson's remaining memorandum, they note that it "makes one important fact clear – that Mrs. Wilson did veto the divulgence of the fact that Wilson had suffered a stroke and that Grayson, acting in conformity with her wishes, decided to fall back on what he called general statements."[55] Supporting evidence for this claim can be found in Ike Hoover's draft memoir of the president's illness, where he writes that:

> Tumulty tried so hard to get to the President during all this time of months but he was kept away as if he was a leper. No doubt, Grayson would have let him in for they sort of worked together but Mrs. Wilson would not do so and so Grayson could not insist. Not for a minute for the truth of the matter was, that Grayson himself did not have much to say in affairs. He could reach Mrs. Wilson but dare not go beyond. He could get one to see Mrs. Wilson but there his influence stopped. He was blamed for a lot he didn't do along that line for the truth of the matter was that in affairs of that kind, Grayson's status was not so high with Mrs. Wilson, especially in view of the fact that she knew he was working in a measure with Tumulty.[56]

Grayson's treatment of Wilson, and his complicity in hiding the severity of Wilson's illness from the nation, remains a very complicated issue. Some have argued that Grayson was not a competent physician.[57] Grayson attended the College of William and Mary and then received his medical degree in gynecology in one year at the University of the South. Continuing his medical training with the Medical Corps of the U.S. Navy after graduation, he became the assistant White House physician under President Theodore Roosevelt and, after him, President William Taft. Grayson was picked by Wilson as his physician after he intervened quickly to sew up a cut on Wilson's sister's forehead after she slipped at his inauguration; Grayson was present in his professional capacity as President Taft's physician. Grayson also had good social connections by marriage; he was related to Presley Marion Rixey, the surgeon general of the navy.[58]

Those who argue that Grayson did not represent an optimal choice for Wilson's physician claim that Grayson, a startlingly handsome man, was chosen for his social charms and marital connections more than his medical skills, and he did become a close personal friend of Wilson. Both men were from Virginia and enjoyed telling stories. They appreciated each other's conversational skills and abilities, especially in the early years. They appear to have had a father-son relationship, because Wilson had no sons of his own, and Grayson's father was dead.

Grayson served as a skilled, devoted, compassionate, and caring physician to Wilson his whole life and kept his pledge to Ellen to look after Woodrow even after he left the presidency. As noted, Grayson prepared an honest report, along with Dr. Dercum, on Wilson's condition in mid-October 1919. According to both doctors, Edith Wilson prohibited this statement from ever being issued. Both Dr. Dercum and Dr. Grayson apparently felt that medical ethics demanded that they defer to Wilson's wife's preferences. When Secretary of State Robert Lansing came to see Tumulty to ask him to certify to the president's disability so that Vice President Thomas Marshall might act in his stead until Wilson's health returned, Tumulty replied emotionally that he would never acknowledge such a thing. When Grayson walked into the room, Tumulty apparently said that Grayson would not certify such disability either. Link argues that the best evidence indicates that Grayson simply remained silent on the issue.[59]

When Lansing called a cabinet meeting on October 6 to consider whether Marshall should take over as president during Wilson's infirmity, Grayson apparently told the cabinet that Wilson's condition was improving but that no real work should be brought before him at the moment because it would prove too stressful. He went on to indicate that Wilson wanted to know why the cabinet meeting was being held and did not approve of this activity in his absence.[60] Wilson later took his revenge on the disloyalty he perceived in Lansing by firing him in February 1920, although the record indicates that Wilson was on the verge of firing him just prior to his major stroke, upon hearing of Bullitt's testimony regarding Lansing's negative characterization of the league before the Senate.[61]

Grayson did his best by Wilson. By some accounts, Grayson even persuaded Wilson to resign in January 1920 for his health but was overridden again by Mrs. Wilson, and the president deferred to her wishes as well.[62] Mrs. Wilson believed, based on a conversation with Dr. Dercum, that if Wilson were forced out of his job, his mood would collapse and his condition would deteriorate, and she did not want to take any such chance. She recalled, after all the relevant players had died, that when she asked Dr. Dercum if her husband would be better off resigning, Dercum replied, "For Mr. Wilson to resign would have a bad effect on the country, and a serious effect on our patient. He has staked his life and made his promise to the world to do all in his power to get the Treaty ratified and make the League of Nations complete. If he resigns, his greatest incentive to recovery is gone; and as his mind is clear as crystal he can still do more even with a maimed body than anyone else."[63] Further, it is also possible that Mrs. Wilson simply did not want to move out of the White House, especially given how ill Wilson remained, and how much help was available to him as long as he was president; this institutional support no doubt made her life much easier in caring for a gravely ill man. Grayson provided a somewhat different description of the events surrounding Wilson's consideration of resignation, however. Grayson reported a middle-of-the-night conversation he had with Wilson where Wilson asked him if he should resign in rather suicidal language. Grayson dissuaded him, and, according to Grayson, Wilson apparently never broached the subject again. While it may be impossible to know exactly what happened, both Wilson and Grayson appeared to have been aware of the full severity of Wilson's compromise at that moment in time.

Although some may argue that Grayson did not provide Wilson with adequate medical care, there were very few medications available to treat the problems from which Wilson suffered. Grayson did what he could, availing himself of good common sense and the best medical knowledge available at the time, encouraging a good diet, exercise, rest, and adequate sleep. He called in the leading experts of the day to consult. De Schweinitz was a prominent ophthalmologist, and Dercum was probably the leading neurologist in the country at the time. Grayson's devotion and loyalty to Wilson stands beyond reproach. When Wilson died on February 3, 1924, Grayson was the last one to leave the coffin; he remained in Washington after Wilson left office simply to treat him and stopped practicing medicine altogether after Wilson's death. He ran the American Red Cross for a while before retiring to build a very successful and still functioning horse breeding farm in Virginia, which is still run by his descendants.

Others argue that Grayson betrayed his country by participating in the cover-up of Wilson's illness, although some of that responsibility also lies with Wilson's cabinet officers and the Republican opposition. But the fact remains that, as a physician, which was his primary responsibility, Grayson never betrayed his patient or his patient's welfare, at least to the best of his ability. From the perspective of standard medical ethics, he met his obligations for confidentiality and care that were first and foremost to his patient. In this way, this case calls attention to the ethical dilemma of a presidential physician: are his central responsibilities only to his patient, or does he remain accountable to the nation as well? Can a physician simultaneously maximize both goals? The cover-up was instigated and maintained primarily by Mrs. Wilson, who firmly believed that any threat to her husband's power and status would be detrimental to his health and her welfare. With the exception of Lansing, who more than most needed the executive direction that was lacking, Wilson's cabinet appointees remained very loyal and probably did not want to lose their jobs by throwing their boss out of office. But at this time, Wilson was too sick to fire anyone, including the disloyal Lansing.

Further, the Republican opposition never challenged the president's ability to serve; despite a very heavy political battle, Henry Cabot Lodge, for instance, never once called for Wilson's resignation or removal. Rather, Lodge knew and understood Wilson's personality. To the extent that Wilson's stroke served to exacerbate his premorbid personality, Lodge's predictions of Wilson were only strengthened and verified by subsequent events. Lodge accurately judged Wilson as one who would refuse to accept even mild reservations rather than compromise, despite the fact that

Wilson had previously written out his own interpretations, which were similar to Lodge's reservations. Lodge correctly surmised that if he added just such reservations to the treaty, Wilson would refuse to accept them, thus ensuring the defeat of the treaty overall. Lodge's strategy worked brilliantly, and no one could blame Lodge for the treaty's failure.[64] Further, the Republican opposition knew that as long as Wilson remained infirm, and the country continued to deteriorate, the public would tire of all the economic and social fallout from the war, and the Republicans would win the presidency in 1920. The Republicans did just that when Warren Harding won the presidency over James Fox and his vice-presidential candidate, the young Franklin Delano Roosevelt.

The real question then is to how to interpret Grayson's diaries in order to obtain the most accurate information about Wilson's health. Some claim that Grayson did not know or understand what was really wrong with the president;[65] but many of these people also admit that Grayson openly expressed his fears for the president's health to close friends and, in one instance, to the cabinet inquiring into his health. In that case, Grayson simultaneously claimed that the president was fine but that the stress of knowing that the cabinet was meeting without him could kill him. The confusion can be understood through the lens of Grayson's extreme loyalty and confidentiality to Wilson. Obviously, Wilson was not a well man. Medical textbooks at the time documented the difference between neurasthenia and stroke, and any competent doctor at the time would have known this difference. Certainly the noted neurologists that Grayson consulted about Wilson's condition knew this.[66] And recall that Grayson had also seen Wilson through many psychosomatic complaints, and so he knew that the president's constitution was particularly vulnerable to negative emotions. He did not want to do anything to hurt his patient, even if that meant compromising the level of leadership in the country.

Why does any of this matter? There are two important reasons why Grayson's behavior during Wilson's most serious illness is worthy of discussion. First, a great deal of attention has been paid to the role of the president's personal physician, and how that position places a physician at the uncomfortable interface of doctor-patient confidentiality and the public's right to know about the disability of its leaders. Currently, it falls upon the president's doctor, at least in part, to determine if the president is sufficiently impaired to invoke the Twenty-fifth Amendment, but such a constitutional provision did not exist in Wilson's time. And it is not clear what his cabinet and doctor would have done at the time, even if the Twenty-fifth Amendment had been in effect. Again, the personal physician may feel loath to display any ostensible disloyalty toward his or her patient.

The only one to call for Wilson's resignation was Secretary of State Robert Lansing, who had done his best during the president's illness to keep the government together and running.[67] During the five and a half months following the president's stroke, the cabinet met twenty-one times in sessions called and run by Lansing. These meetings were supposed to have been reported to Wilson. But when Lansing asked if the president should step down in favor of Vice President Marshall, both Tumulty and Grayson refused to declare Wilson incapacitated. Tumulty told Lansing directly, "You may rest assured that while Woodrow Wilson is lying in the White House on the board of his back I will not be party to ousting him. He has been too kind, too loyal, and too wonderful to me to receive such treatment at my hands."[68]

When Wilson gradually returned to doing some work beginning in February 1920, he fired Lansing, ostensibly for holding cabinet meetings without his knowledge, but more obviously for demonstrating disloyalty by calling for Wilson's resignation earlier the previous year. In addition, this situation was complicated by Wilson's disagreement with Lansing over the proper handling of the continuing crisis with Mexico. In the fall, several events in Mexico had once again strained relations with the United States. First, the Mexican government began to seize oil wells of companies who had not obtained permits to drill, including American companies. Second, an American consul, William Jenkins, was ostensibly kidnapped. It turned out that Jenkins probably engineered his own abduction as a way to pressure America into doing more to protect American citizens in Mexico. When he refused to post bail, Lansing sent strong letters to Mexico demanding his release, or threatening war. Expecting Wilson to provide no direction on the matter, Lansing handled the matter on his own. When the Senate found out about Lansing's failure to consult Wilson on a matter that might lead to war, it gave the Senate the excuse it needed to go see Wilson directly, ostensibly to confer with the president on the matter, but in reality to check on his physical health and condition. At this meeting, Wilson was raised in bed, the windows were drawn so that light was low, his useless left arm hidden under the blankets. As each senator entered the room, his name was whispered to Wilson so that he could greet him personally. The deception succeeded because no one asked him any detailed or difficult questions during the brief meeting. Later, through a message, Wilson ordered Lansing to back down and not go to war with Mexico.[69]

The second reason that Grayson's behavior deserves attention lies in the critical nature of his diaries, the only remaining contemporary medical records available. Are we to trust them? When Grayson reports indigestion, do we believe that it was simply that, or are we to assume that even in his private diaries he was protecting Wilson for posterity and indigestion really means stroke, as Weinstein suggests so often was the case? One of the most noteworthy aspects of this investigation into Grayson's diaries is that most of the secondary literature relies on Link's argument in the Wilson papers that Wilson suffered a series of strokes going back at least to 1896. And yet all the references for these numerous reported strokes return to one of three footnotes in the Wilson papers edited by Link where Link asserts, *despite the contemporary medical memos indicating more minor complaints*, that certain events were really strokes. And yet nothing in the papers themselves actually states that there was a stroke before 1919. Link was motivated to preserve a positive image of Wilson, which in his mind required attributing all of Wilson's belligerence and intransigence to physical causes beyond Wilson's control.

What if Grayson was right? What if many of Wilson's earlier complaints were the result of a wide variety of stress-induced and psychosomatic illnesses that were not entirely rooted in early cardiovascular disease? What if the devastating, incapacitating physical illness really did not fully manifest until 1919? What difference would that make? For one thing, such an interpretation would shed a different kind of light on Wilson's counterproductive behavior in the Paris Peace Conference and his early actions concerning the Senate League of Nations vote. For another, it would offer support for the Georges' interpretation that Wilson's behavior at Paris and afterward constituted little more than a continuation of Wilson's earlier character traits, which incorporated belligerence, intransigence, and an unwillingness to compromise with powerful male authority figures who reminded him of his father, such as Senator Lodge. Further, if Park's argument about the impact of long-term uncontrolled hypertension leading to presenile dementia holds weight as well, then his argument that such individuals become caricatures of their premorbid personalities adds further credence to the Georges' argument concerning the decisive impact played by Wilson's personality on the political defeat of the League of Nations treaty in the Senate.

In modern medicine, psychological ailments are understood to be of similar character to physical ones in that people who are mentally ill cannot always be held accountable for all their actions in the way a healthy person might be. In other words, psychological illness would not make Wilson a worse man or a less dedicated public servant, but rather one who was unduly taxed, and possibly crippled, by a job that stressed his psychological capacities beyond their limit.[70] After all, disability need not result from entirely one type of ailment or another; psychological and physical conditions intertwine and overlap. Strokes can serve to exacerbate previous personality characteristics.[71] So, in Wilson's later years, it should not be surprising to see an exaggeration of his premorbid personality, including increased intransigence, belligerence, and egocentricity.

In addition, after late 1919 in particular, evidence exists of the kind of cognitive and memory impairments that would be expected in any stroke victim, including signs of dementia. Wilson evidenced these limitations at least temporarily between October 1919 and February 1920. In the end, he was unable to use his previously formidable political skills to marshal his cherished League of Nations through the confirmation process. His memory appeared to falter even before the October stroke. For example, in his testimony before the Senate Foreign Relations Committee about the league on August 19, 1919, he made at least sixteen substantive errors in his three-hour testimony, something that was previously unheard of in Wilson, who used to prepare meticulously for public presentations.

Would these actions and mistakes have been enough to categorize Wilson as occupationally impaired? By any modern neuropsychological test, it would. One standard considers disability to be present when the person demonstrates an inability to shift thinking as the circumstances change, account for personal thoughts or actions, persevere in a task or goal to completion, grasp parts of a whole, learn from experience, accept what is and is not possible, and detach one's ego from interpersonal conflict. Park carefully documents that Wilson was not able to do any of these things following his attack in October 1919, and yet he remained in office until March 1921.[72]

In particular, it becomes evident to anyone who studies the historical record that Wilson's entire handling of the League of Nations vote was characterized primarily by his unwillingness to compromise, his inability to shift reflectively with the changing political circumstances, and the intensely personal nature of his fight with Senator Lodge over the treaty's ratification. Wilson even instructed members of his own party to vote against the league covenant if it had reservations attached. Wilson's behavior, representing exacerbations of his premorbid personality characteristics, led to the rejection of the treaty in the Senate.

WILSON'S HEALTH HISTORY

Wilson grew up under the stern Presbyterian beliefs of his minister father and may have shared the view that illness, like failure, was a sign of moral weakness, perhaps even sin. Wilson's further professional development appeared to support the dominant stereotypes of the time that academic or intellectual figures were necessarily physically sick, weak, and vulnerable by disposition.[73]

The future president appeared sickly and suffered from a host of psychosomatic ailments in his youth, mostly surrounding periods of emotional stress or turmoil. As soon as the stress remediated, the illness disappeared. For example, Wilson decided not to return to college at Davidson after his first year, claiming illness. Yet once he returned home, he seemed to be fine. More than anything, Wilson appeared to be suffering from homesickness and an inability to separate from his parents. Eventually, he matured and entered Princeton in 1875. While at Princeton, Wilson represented the epitome of good health for four years; not coincidentally, he appeared to be quite happy during these years.

Once he returned to attend law school at the University of Virginia, his old symptoms returned. He was conflicted about his career choice. He embarked on a time-consuming and ultimately futile courtship of his cousin Harriet Woodrow, spending so much time writing to her and visiting her that he almost got thrown out of law school for absenteeism. He took her rejection of him very hard. Once again, when he returned to law school for a second year, his symptoms returned until eventually his parents suggested he come home to convalesce. Soon, his symptoms miraculously disappeared. Again, when he set up his law practice after graduation in Atlanta, the old symptoms of stomach complaints returned, until he decided to give up the law, and entered graduate school in political science at Johns Hopkins in 1883.[74]

Two things are particularly notable about Wilson's health problems. First, they definitely came and went in relation to his level of emotional stress and turmoil. When he was feeling emotionally upset, he became plagued with a wide variety of physical complaints, mostly centering on stomach problems. For years, he used a pump daily to clean out his stomach. Yet as soon as he returned to a familiar and less stressful environment, like his childhood home, his symptoms cleared up quickly and completely. Such psychosomatic symptoms are not uncommon among those who suffer from depression and anxiety-related disorders. And illness that is psychosomatic in origin is no less real than illness created by a more observable physical malady. Thus, Wilson was clearly susceptible to experiencing physical ailments as a result of his psychological disturbances.

Second, at least some of Wilson's psychological disturbances appear to have been brought about by the intense nature of his self-criticism. He set enormously high goals for himself and became quickly and fiercely upset and disappointed if he failed to achieve them. Ironically, although it is common in clinical experience, he gained little satisfaction from success. While failure made him miserable, success seemed to make him no less anxious.

These points prove significant and interesting in light of the later physical ailments that Wilson experienced. No one would claim that Wilson did not experience some very real physical illnesses, but it is also important to note that from early on he had a history of expressing his psychological anxieties and depressions, of which he had many, through vague somatic complaints.

At this point in Wilson's medical history, opinions begin to diverge. The Weinstein and Park hypothesis argues for the onset of a series of strokes, either large or small, which began to affect Wilson's health and behavior. Others see the increasing manifestation of Wilson's earlier character deficits, including his noted stubbornness, obstinacy, and belligerence.

The first episode appears to have occurred in 1896 and involved his reported weakness and pain in his right arm. At this time, Wilson apparently began to manifest some personality exacerbations, becoming increasingly critical of others in particular. Weinstein argues that this event constituted the first of many strokes and finds evidence of subsequent strokes affecting his right arm and hand in 1904. Marmor and others characterize Wilson's symptoms at this time as resulting from some kind of peripheral nerve entrapment, as might occur as a result of inflammation from overuse, a possibility easily imagined given how much longhand writing Wilson did. Others suggest a different, albeit similarly localized condition – that Wilson's problems resulted from a cervical disc degeneration in the spine.

In May 1906 Wilson awoke almost completely blind in his left eye. Partial blindness remained with Wilson for the rest of his life and was exacerbated by additional left hemisphere blindness in both eyes subsequent to the massive stroke in 1919. Although Weinstein suggests that this blindness resulted from a cerebral incident, the medical evidence does not support this view. Wilson almost certainly sustained a localized retinal hemorrhage as a result of his uncontrolled hypertension.[75] Because the retina is the only part of the body where arteries can be inspected directly, Dr. de Schweinitz, one of the leading ophthalmologists of his day, was unlikely to miss the difference between a retinal hemorrhage and a stroke, even in 1906; indeed, he wrote a textbook on eye diseases that discussed just such a distinction that was published in that year.[76] At the time, de Schweinitz told Wilson that he had a blood clot in the eye. Dr. Gifford later confirmed this diagnosis, saying that de Schweinitz had found high blood pressure, retinal hemorrhage and scarring (exudates), and retinal spasms in Wilson at that time.[77] The episode more likely resulted from retinal hemorrhage as sequelae to uncontrolled blood pressure than from a larger stroke.

In addition, House reported that Grayson said that the president's kidneys were not functioning well in 1915, a common side effect of uncontrolled hypertension.[78] Along with these physical signs and symptoms, Wilson's friends and colleagues begin to note subtle changes in his personality, including increased rigidity and obstinacy. This self-defeating characteristic emerged in his inability to achieve his goals because of his own unwillingness to compromise. Early on, Wilson, as president of Princeton, achieved considerable success in convincing the board to move from a lectureship-style educational program to one involving preceptors working with small groups of students. This $2 billion dollar plan required the hiring of more than 50 new preceptors, who displaced many of the senior old-guard professors. With the support of the new preceptors, Wilson hoped to establish his new quadrangle plan. Many of the faculty strongly opposed this plan, however, and Dean Andrew West, a former friend of

Wilson, proved critical in pulling the plan down toward defeat. Wilson's inability to compromise led to the plan's inevitable failure, a pattern that was to repeat itself in his fight with Henry Cabot Lodge in the U.S. Senate over the ratification of the Treaty of Versailles and the covenant of the League of Nations. Similarly, Wilson had great early success as governor of New Jersey, instituting many effective progressive reforms in involving finance reform, workman's compensation, and the regulation of utilities. Given that the Democratic conservatives expected a less progressive candidate, Wilson's actions alienated many of those whose power and money had helped him get elected. But his reforms had by then made Wilson the new darling of the reform platform of the Democratic Party.

In 1913 Wilson reported a return of his left-sided pain and weakness, this time in his left shoulder. Again, Weinstein attributes this incident to another stroke. Park notes that the evidence does not necessarily support such a conclusion.[79] Dercum was called in and recommended the standard treatment for muscle soreness. It is highly unlikely that Dercum, one of the nation's leading stroke experts at the time, would have made such an incorrect diagnosis. His response supports the contention that this incident was not a stroke but the recurrence of a joint or muscle problem, perhaps bursitis.

Beginning toward the end of his first term as president of the United States, Wilson began suffering from frequent and blinding headaches. Typically such headaches result from tension or muscle stress, and given Wilson's prior proclivity toward hypochondriasis and psychosomatic illnesses, it may be impossible to identify the real source of the problem. However, Park and others suggest that these headaches resulted from high blood pressure; because of their increasing severity just prior to his major stroke in 1919, this diagnosis seems reasonable.

Beginning in late 1918, Wilson appeared to recognize that he was having memory problems, admitting to House that he often forgot the conclusions of a morning meeting by the afternoon and that his mind had become "leaky." He told another official that he felt he was becoming absent-minded. He required that officials submit written memos for meetings that he had with them, but he often forgot about them nonetheless.[80] Yet Wilson never considered not attending the Paris Peace Conference. He eschewed skilled and experienced diplomats in favor of his own personal intervention. Further, he isolated himself, refusing to seek or listen to advice from others, including Colonel House. He did not even maintain an adequate secretarial staff to keep notes that might have helped prod his weakened memory or alleviate the pressures on his sore arm.

Two illnesses afflicted Wilson during the course of the Paris Peace Conference that exerted permanent effects. On April 3, 1919, he became violently ill with coughing, fever, and diarrhea. At the time Grayson diagnosed this illness as influenza. At first, Weinstein saw this incident as yet another stroke, although the symptoms were not indicative of such a diagnosis, and he later backed away from his initial diagnosis.[81] For example, there appeared to be no weakness or muscle paralysis, but there was evidence of a viral infection. Park originally made the assumption that an infection, possibly complicated by encephalitis, may have led the president to experience delirium.[82] He, too, later backed away from his original analysis to argue that while delirium was possible, encephalitis was unlikely.[83] Delirium, which can be caused by high fever alone, causes abrupt problems with memory, thinking, attention, and even orientation.

That Wilson fell prey to influenza at this time would not seem unreasonable. Park notes that delirium brought about by transient viral infection can lead to permanent intellectual and emotional impairment when superimposed on someone already suffering from signs of dementia, brought on by chronic high blood pressure.[84] He reports that almost everyone who knew Wilson claimed he was never quite the same after his April illness in Paris. In particular, Herbert Hoover recalled that "prior to that time, he was incisive, quick to grasp essentials, unhesitating in conclusions and most willing to take advice from men he trusted." Afterward, Hoover simply found Wilson obstinate. Hoover speculated that Wilson's mind had lost its "resiliency."[85] White House usher Ike Hoover said that "one thing was certain: he was never the same after this little spell of illness."[86] Even Grayson wrote that Wilson's attack of influenza in Paris proved to be one of the contributory causes of his final breakdown.[87]

Link and others maintain that it is unlikely that Wilson suffered from the worldwide influenza pandemic during his illness in Paris. In one set of notes, a consulting expert claimed that the epidemic was over by April and that no one else Wilson knew had been ill, both factors making the flu an unlikely diagnosis; yet these authors continue to contend that Wilson suffered a small stroke at this time.[88] However, recent analysis provides compelling evidence that Grayson was right and Wilson fell into the flu's grasp. In John Barry's masterful book, *The Great Influenza*, he reports that more than 1,500 people died in Paris in March 1919 and that the *Journal of the American Medical Association* reported that "the epidemic has assumed grave proportions, not only in Paris." Further, Barry documents that Wilson's wife, her secretary, Ike Hoover, and Cary Grayson, all people who worked intimately with Wilson, became sick around this time. Even British leader Lloyd George and French leader Clemenceau seemed to have contracted mild cases of the flu. One young American aide, Douglas Frary, came down with the flu the same day as Wilson and died of it four days later at age twenty-five.[89]

After his return from Paris, Wilson began experiencing episodes of coughing, particularly at night, which Grayson referred to as asthmatic attacks. Park suggests that these attacks were not asthma, as modern science would recognize it, but rather early symptoms of heart failure, where the body coughs in order to help blood return to the heart when lying down. Grayson subsequently notes that Wilson often slept sitting up, which helped to diminish these attacks, providing some confirmation of Park's theory.

Of course, these events were quickly followed by the major stroke that Wilson sustained in October. Given widespread congressional disapproval for his League of Nations treaty, Wilson had decided, against Grayson's indication, that he had to carry his message about its importance to the people. He made a train trip to the western states in early September and gave more than thirty-two speeches in the following three weeks. Wilson continued to deteriorate both mentally and physically as the trip progressed. As the intensity of Wilson's headaches grew, he experienced double vision and memory losses. He even lost his place at times when giving his speeches. Finally, on September 25, in Pueblo, Colorado, Wilson all but collapsed. His condition worsened during the night, and finally Dr. Grayson and Mrs. Wilson convinced him to return to Washington. The train went straight through to the capital. Wilson disembarked from the train, walked to his waiting car, and appeared to wave to nonexistent crowds on the way back to the White House. The story of the phantom wave made the rounds and elicited concern from officials and private citizens alike. For the next few days, Wilson was seen taking his habitual drives and walks around Washington.

Then, on the morning of October 2, Wilson collapsed with his massive stroke, which apparently occurred from an occlusion of the right internal carotid artery, which supplies the side of the brain that largely controls the left side of the body.[90] Wilson became almost totally paralyzed on his left side. At the time, he almost died of uremic poisoning because of swelling in his prostate that blocked his urinary tract. In truth, despite some minor recovery after an apparent viral illness in February 1920, Wilson never regained his health in any meaningful way. Nevertheless, he managed to live a surprisingly long time for someone with such severe cerebrovascular disease. No one, for example, would have predicted at the time that he would outlive his presidential successor, Warren Harding. Wilson did not die until February 3, 1924.

The editor of the Wilson papers, Arthur Link, characterized Wilson as "partially disabled by hypertension and small strokes from July to October, 1919, totally disabled by a massive stroke from October 1919 to February 1920, and severely impaired physically and mentally from February to April 1920. Indeed, that impairment continued to a lessening degree until the end of Wilson's life – certainly to the end of his presidential term in March 1921."[91] He goes on to state that "Wilson was 98 percent disabled from 2 October to 15 December, 90 percent disabled from that time until 1 February, and probably 75–80 disabled for the rest of his term."[92] Yet, it is still possible that a disabled Wilson, with all he represented to the nation and the world, still provided a better symbol of leadership than Vice President Marshall.

IMPACT OF WILSON'S HEALTH ON THE LEAGUE OF NATIONS

Wilson's strategy for peace rested on his fourteen-point plan, which he presented to Congress in a speech on January 8, 1918. Wilson originally developed this plan in response and reaction to Lenin's call for revolution and an end to the war. Caught between the colonialism and secret treaties presented by his French and British allies, which he detested, and the communist threat posed by Lenin's new control over Russia, Wilson instead formulated and advocated a liberal vision for a postwar world based on self-determination, free trade, and a kind of world government, or league of nations, to arbitrate conflict without war.

Wilson's fourteen points included provisions to preclude secret treaties and to ensure freedom of the seas, free trade, disarmament, self-determination even in colonial regions, and a League of Nations to preserve political independence and territorial integrity for all states. Even before the conference, however, Wilson had already lost on a couple of his points. First, the British refused to accede to freedom of the seas. And Wilson himself had compromised one of the points involving Russian self-determination by insisting on maintaining U.S. forces there.

Nonetheless, Wilson sought to recreate the postwar world in line with his fourteen-point plan. Originally, Wilson had called together a group of experts called The Inquiry to help build a peace plan based on these points, but, increasingly isolated, he often ignored their advice.

From early on in the Paris Peace Conference, Wilson made some uncharacteristically counterproductive political choices and decisions. For starters, he seriously reduced the possibility of the resolution making it through the Senate without serious opposition by refusing to place a single Republican on the peace commissions. Further, Wilson believed his own participation to be so critical that he supplanted experienced diplomats from their rightful place at the negotiation table. Wilson's increasing isolation made him unwilling to seek, and unable to accept, any suggestions other than his own. Wilson expected that his own personal popularity with the people would win the day. In this way, he seriously miscalculated, as he had when he called for the U.S. midterm elections to be a referendum on the League of Nations; when the population returned gains for the Republicans, most likely because of salient domestic issues related to agriculture, Wilson was hurt and surprised, failing to understand how many other factors, such as local issues, influenced midterm elections. In the case of the Paris Peace Conference, Wilson failed to recognize the close connections forged during the war between the British and French in particular and to understand the devastating losses that produced a desire for vengeance on the part of the victors. The Europeans had lost 8 million soldiers and an additional 20 million civilians as a result of the war and its aftermath; the victims and their survivors demanded reparations from the Germans for instigating such suffering. America lost approximately 53,000 men in battle, with an additional 63,000 deaths from other causes, such as the flu. Wilson may have felt he should hold decisive moral sway in the peace negotiations. Yet the United States had hardly borne the bloody burden of the war, a fact that his European allies did not hesitate to remind him of.

Wilson did believe that he was on a personal moral crusade. He argued, "If I did not feel that I was the personal instrument of God I couldn't carry on." Lloyd George's characterization of the conference supported Wilson's self-presentation: "I think I did as well as might be expected, seated as I was between Jesus Christ and Napoleon Bonaparte," the latter a reference to French leader Clemenceau.[93]

Wilson achieved some notable successes early in his participation in the Paris Peace Conference. He managed to get the other powers to agree that the league would become an inseparable part of the peace treaty. Second, his idea for the covenant for the League of Nations was similarly accepted and approved. In addition, he managed to thwart a French plan to retain control over German military affairs, and a similar proposal to turn the league into a primarily military alliance. In the peace process, Wilson gained confidence from these early successes when the Smuts resolution was adopted, ensuring that the league covenant would take precedence over decisions about reparations and other issues.[94] Wilson felt this meant that the other parties agreed with him that the league was the most important part of the peace. Instead, Clemenceau and Lloyd George believed that they could trade their consent early on this issue for later concessions on the part of the American on issues more important to them, such as reparations.[95] In other words, Wilson's performance began at its best and then quickly deteriorated into much more counterproductive action, particularly following his serious illness in April.

Fairly quickly, the conference degenerated and progress stalled. Wilson remained obsessively focused on the league covenant to the exclusion of all else, while the French and British were preoccupied with the questions surrounding German reparations. As Park noted, such single-minded focus is common in cases of early dementia, where the person remains more comfortable dealing with familiar and well-known issues rather than novel ones that require the ability to learn new information, which can be particularly difficult for someone in this condition. Further, in such cases of dementia, an individual's premorbid personality becomes exacerbated in a way that in Wilson's case would serve to heighten his intransigence, especially on issues where he perceived himself to hold moral imprimatur.

Wilson left Paris on February 14, 1919, for a month in Washington. At this point, Henry Cabot Lodge made clear that the league as proposed was unacceptable because it failed to acknowledge the Monroe Doctrine. Wilson returned to Paris and insisted that the delegates accede to the Monroe Doctrine. In exchange, Wilson made a number of uncharacteristic concessions that weakened both his fourteen points and his moral leadership. In particular, he agreed to allow Japan to stay in Shantung, a former German colony. The Japanese had threatened to leave the league if they did not get what they wanted, and Wilson felt that it was more important to keep Japan involved than it was to uphold his point concerning self-determination. However, as Park notes, "on balance, the record simply does not sustain the suggestion that Wilson's compromised health necessarily translated into compromised decisions by the President during and immediately after the April illness."[96]

What remains particularly significant in the negotiation process is that the stalled talks took on new life when Wilson became ill and immediately thereafter. Some of the most important decisions were made in the period surrounding his influenza in April. From his sickbed, Wilson approved many proposals that he had previously rejected. He acceded to a German reparation plan devised by the French, which included no time or money limit; to a military provision in the league; to limiting the size of the German army; and to allowing the insertion of a German "war guilt clause" and a trial for the kaiser. Several of these concessions amounted to wholesale reversals of positions that Wilson had staunchly advocated for years up until two weeks prior. However, he never compromised on many issues that were central to his moral principles. He did not surrender the sovereignty of any German land to France, for example. Yet he did compromise on issues that prevented German postwar economic reconstruction and set the stage for the rise of Hitler and the onset of the Second World War. As Park indicates, "the evidence does not then conclusively support the hypothesis that illness played a major role in any of the alleged concessions Wilson made to the Allies during this period."[97]

When the Germans arrived for the peace talks on April 14, they expressed their objections to the settlement, and Wilson remained unmoved. Considering that the Germans had hoped that Wilson's idealism might allow the possibility of a fair peace prior to the end of the war, Wilson's refusal to reconsider elements of the treaty signaled his increased intransigence.

Once Wilson returned to the United States, he faced another brutal fight trying to get the treaty and its covenant ratified by the U.S. Senate. Specifically, Wilson sought approval for Article 1 of the treaty, the establishment of the League of Nations, but many members of Congress and the public did not want to be forced into involvement in foreign wars in which America had no real interest simply because of participation in the league. The main Senate concerns revolved around Article 10, which guaranteed political independence and protection against external aggression for all league members. Wilson considered this article to represent the "heart" of the treaty and would brook no opposition to it.

Because the Republicans had gained control of the Senate in the 1918 midterm elections, Henry Cabot Lodge became chairman of the Senate Foreign Relations Committee. At the time, there existed about sixteen "irreconcilable" isolationists in the Senate, under the leadership of men like Idaho senator William Borah and the influence of former president Theodore Roosevelt. These men agreed to oppose the treaty in whatever form it appeared. In addition, there were about forty-nine Republicans who supported ratification of the treaty as long as certain of their "reservations" were met. Wilson retained enough control over the remaining Democratic senators to order them to join the irreconcilables to defeat the treaty 55 to 39. However, public support for the league continued to grow, and Lodge himself began to move toward conciliation. However, once again Wilson refused to allow the Democrats to compromise, and on March 19, 1920, a second Senate vote on the league containing Lodge's reservations was 49 to 35 in favor of the league. However, this bill, in which twelve irreconcilables joined with twenty-three Wilsonian Democrats against the league with fifteen reservations attached, failed to reach the required two-thirds majority necessary for passage. Not until 1921 did the United States officially end its war with Germany by signing a separate peace accord.

In early August, some Senate reservationists offered a proposal with four main conditions, including the right of Congress to decide whether to go to war, the right to withdraw from the league with a two-year notice, the exclusion of certain domestic issues such as immigration and trade from league jurisdiction, and the recognition of the Monroe Doctrine. Wilson drafted similar but not identical "interpretations" at that time and sent them to his representative in Congress, the ranking minority member of the Senate Foreign Relations Committee, Gilbert Hitchcock. Rather than wait for a resolution, or attempt to rally support for the treaty and the league in the Senate, Wilson decided to take his case to the public and arranged for his ultimately devastating speaking tour of the West.

Wilson's trip ultimately cost him the remainder of his physical health. During Wilson's illness, Senate opposition to Article 10 of the treaty in particular strengthened. The Senate wanted assurance that America would go to war only with the joint approval of Congress and that ratification of the treaty would not go into effect until these conditions had been approved by at least three of the other four major powers. Wilson finally agreed to meet with Hitchcock on November 17 to strategize passage of the treaty. At that time, Wilson appeared to agree to the reservations he had suggested in early September before he left on his speaking tour. When Hitchcock sent his letter to the president through Mrs. Wilson, however, Wilson's dictated response refused the possibility of compromise. Whether she read this statement to him or what he might have replied is unknown. Link argues strongly that Mrs. Wilson served as a mere secretarial conduit between policy makers and President Wilson during his long illness. Link argues that Mrs. Wilson made only two errors where her husband was concerned.[98] First, she refused to allow the truthful statement by Grayson and Dercum to be issued; second, she vetoed Grayson's suggestion that Wilson resign his office. However, a great deal of other evidence indicates that Mrs. Wilson took a more active part than a mere secretary might and decided what information would be shown to Wilson. Park indicates that she may have even filled certain vacancies on her own. But there is no doubt that she actively screened what she showed to Wilson, making herself more than a mere conduit of information.[99]

As a result of Wilson's failure to compromise on these reservations, the Senate voted to defeat consent to ratification of the treaty on November 19. However, Lodge's reservationist proposal also failed to achieve the two-thirds majority required to win. Throughout this process, Wilson remained exceptionally isolated. In particular, Mrs. Wilson wanted to ensure that the severity of Wilson's illness be kept from public knowledge; however, he also was not able to receive new information or get a sense of what was really going on in the country or in the Senate. From this isolated viewpoint, Wilson devised a plan in June whereby he sought to challenge senators who had voted with Lodge to resign and then run for reelection. If they lost, it would ensure the passage of the treaty. If they won, he would resign. Amazingly, at the time, Wilson also began to make plans for the cabinet to staff his expected third term; this fact alone demonstrates a particular detachment from the political reality of the time.[100] Attorney General Palmer made clear that his resignation idea was not constitutionally tenable. Yet Wilson adamantly continued to believe that he enjoyed the support of the people. He even called for the election of 1920 to be a referendum on the league. Clearly, he had not learned his lesson from the similar strategy he had taken with the midterm elections in 1918 or from his thwarted speaking tour; in both cases, he failed to garner the support he desired.

Following the vote for defeat in November, Hitchcock and others tried to resurrect the treaty the following year. They met throughout January to try to reach a compromise with Lodge on Article 10. Tumulty drafted a letter accepting the reservations. The treaty could have passed at this point if Wilson had agreed to its provisions. However, an odd thing happened. Wilson came down with some kind of viral infection in late January. After he recovered from that illness, his condition in general seemed to improve somewhat. He now appeared to have both the energy and desire to take charge of the ratification vote once again. In late January, Wilson wrote to Hitchcock saying that he would not accept any reservations to Article 10. He then proceeded to fire Secretary of State Lansing, replacing him with a trustworthy friend, Bainbridge Colby.

Wilson issued a letter to Hitchcock on March 8 that doomed the passage of the treaty for good. He wrote: "I am sorry to say that the reservations that have come under my notice are almost without exception not inter- pretations of the articles to which it is proposed to attach them, but in effect, virtual nullification of those articles.... Militaristic ambitions and imperialistic policies are by no means dead, even in the councils of the nations whom we most trust and with whom we desire to be associated in this task of peace."[101] Obviously, the European allies were irate over this statement, and Wilson lost what little remained of his support in the Senate as a result of this letter as well. The defeat of the treaty on March 19 was assured by the publication of this letter. According to Arthur Link,

Wilson's letter to Hitchcock on 8 March 1920 had to be ranked among the most important documents in the history of the American presidency. Wilson had suffered much loss of mental power during the preceding year, but he was not insane. He was simply severely impaired, physically and mentally; that is, his stroke had stripped away his usual ability to perceive political realities, had exacerbated his tendency toward combativeness and intransigence, and caused him to see issues in terms of black and white and to go back to what he thought were first principles. For example: Compromise is dishonorable; it is better for the United States to stay out of the league if it could not be its unchallenged leader, and so on. To make the story sadder, it appears that Wilson thought that he was writing the first document in the coming presidential campaign in which he hoped to be the Democratic candidate.[102]

The Georges describe the flaws that led to Wilson's defeat in the Senate as characteristic of his behavior:

Wilson's behavior...after the stroke of October 1919 was entirely consis- tent with his behavior before it. Both before and after, ample warnings were conveyed to him of the all but inevitable consequences of his refusal at every turn to compromise. Both before and after the stroke he rejected these warn- ings. Friend and foe alike watched, fascinated...the awesome spectacle of Wilson's step by step repulsion of every opportunity – and there were many – to save the Treaty. The stroke seemed to modify his behavior not one whit.

To those who knew and loved him best, his refusal to compromise was a source of sorrow rather than surprise. A sense of some terrible inner logic to his self-defeating behavior, in terms of stable, persistent characteristics they had long since recognized.[103]

Perhaps just as sad, Wilson's inability to compromise on points he himself had accepted at an earlier time meant that Wilson sacrificed all the political values and beliefs for which he had put his life and health at risk.

CONCLUSIONS

Perhaps the greatest tragedy of Wilson's life revolves around its irony. Wilson risked his health to pursue his dream of a League of Nations that might be able to resolve conflicts peacefully without resorting to war. Yet, as a result of his original belligerent personality becoming exacerbated by a serious stroke, which compromised his memory, judgment, and attention, he was unable to achieve any of the goals that he sought most dearly.

Hugh L'Etang, in writing about Wilson, suggests that "Those who are driven by ambition, ideals or unrealized and undefined psychological tensions are often careless of rules and risk. The world would be poorer without men who defy the odds, and achieve the impossible; the world might be better off if these men did not regard waning mental and physical vigor as another challenge to be faced and conquered."[104] Wilson likely suffered from a common characteristic of many stroke victims, that of anosognosia, which is a kind of denial or unawareness of the presence or impact of serious limitations, including cognitive impairment or paralysis. Often, *la belle indifférence* can prove a blessing by preventing stroke victims from becoming overly frustrated or wistful about their prior level of functioning. While he might have been occasionally or somewhat aware of increasing limitations early in the process of his progressive dementia, Wilson did not understand the severity of his illness well enough to recognize that he could no longer adequately discharge the duties of president. After he suffered his stroke, his wife made all important decisions for him, including the one to remain in office and keep the severity of his condition secret. As she pointedly told Tumulty, "I am not thinking of the country now. I am thinking of my husband."[105] Wilson's incapacity was all but total between the period of October 1919 and February 1920 and fairly severe well past the end of his natural term in office until the end of his life in 1924.

Wilson's rigidity of thinking, his obstinacy in the face of challenges to his positions, and his single-minded devotion to the cause of the League of Nations brought about the reality he sought to prevent from the outset: the defeat of the treaty in the Senate. Many of these personality characteristics, which were present earlier in his life, became exacerbated as the result of his uncontrolled hypertension and later viral illnesses and stroke. The fact that these illnesses may have intensified his earlier characteristics makes the content of those character flaws even more meaningful and significant.

One's disability is judged relative to preexisting capacity. By any measure, Wilson was an enormously smart, skilled, energetic, devoted, and capable public servant for many years. Thus, part of the tragedy of what was lost lies in what could have been gained in its presence. Who knows what Wilson might have accomplished had adequate blood pressure medication existed in his day? In addition, Wilson's wife, although clearly with good intent, no doubt seriously prolonged and deepened Wilson's intellectual and emotional compromise following his massive stroke in October 1919 by refusing to allow Wilson to regain normal social contacts, in a way his former wife, Ellen, undoubtedly would have encouraged. Social isolation remains one of the greatest predictors of poor outcome in stroke patients.

Nonetheless, if Wilson's original personality had been different, the outcome of the events surrounding the ratification of the league might have shifted. In other words, although Wilson would still have been affected in memory, judgment, and other mental processes, his social interactions might have produced a different outcome. If his premorbid personality had been one of withdrawal in the face of conflict or one that sought cooperation, these characteristics might have been the ones to exert themselves more strongly in the wake of physical compromise secondary to dementia, delirium, or both. Yet it is precisely the self-defeating nature of his earlier personality characteristics that led to his downfall, as they became exacerbated by serious cognitive compromise. In this sense, Wilson fell victim to that greatest of tragedies: his own inherent character flaws.

FOUR

LEADING WHILE DYING: FRANKLIN DELANO ROOSEVELT, 1943–1945

Roosevelt's complex health problems offer the opportunity for two interesting comparisons of the impact of physical illness on political decision making. Roosevelt suffered from at least two major kinds of debilitating illness: polio and cardiovascular disease. The first, which paralyzed Roosevelt beginning in 1921, appeared to exert little, if any, impact on his decision-making skills and abilities. The second, consisting of congestive heart failure, hypertension, and hypertensive heart disease, seems to have exerted subtle, increasing, but typically transient effects on his cognitive skills and abilities over time. These effects began to exert some influence over his decision-making abilities beginning by late 1943.

Importantly, the impact of Roosevelt's health on his decision-making capacities proved inconsistent over time, in keeping with the nature of his ailment. In the majority of cases, including the conference at Yalta, where the effect of Roosevelt's health on his abilities has been most consistently scrutinized and criticized, Roosevelt's illness probably played no part in the outcomes he achieved. However, it appears likely that the increasing severity of Roosevelt's cardiovascular disease exerted some subtle, albeit profound, negative impacts on his judgments and behaviors at some earlier meetings and conferences. Specifically, Roosevelt's choice between General MacArthur's and Admiral Nimitz's plans concerning the future of the Pacific campaign, made in July 1944 in Hawaii, seemed affected, at least in part, by his decreasing energy, increasing detachment, and shortened attention span. In addition Roosevelt's early backing of the Morgenthau plan at the conference with Churchill in Québec in September 1944, concerning the treatment of Germany after the war, may also have

83

been influenced by his lack of attention in the face of severe fatigue and illness.

Ironically, the biggest impact of Roosevelt's illness on his decision making and behavior seems to have come not from sins of commission but rather from sins of omission. Problems swirling around Roosevelt in the last year and a half of his life may have worsened more from his inability to engage and concentrate, maneuver and manipulate, as he had during his first twelve years in office, than from bad decisions or mistakes he made. Because the decision-making apparatus he set up kept Roosevelt at the center, where he often was the only one aware of all the various strands of a problem, or where his personal relationship with particular people kept things in balance, his absence raised tremendous difficulties for his successor.

The biggest impact of his illness on the outcome of history was his death itself. Roosevelt died at sixty-three years of age in Warm Springs, Georgia, on April 12, 1945, as a result of a massive cerebral hemorrhage. As with Wilson, had Roosevelt lived, even in a diminished state, but especially in a healthy one, immediate postwar history would almost certainly have evolved quite differently. Roosevelt had a very different history and relationship with Soviet premier Stalin than Truman did, and Roosevelt left Truman ill-informed and ill-prepared to deal with the many pressing responsibilities that would be thrust upon him following Roosevelt's death. One can only speculate whether Roosevelt would have dropped the atomic bomb, whether the Cold War would have developed as it did, or whether the postwar peace would have looked the same.

The major health problem that beset Roosevelt developed slowly, manifested inconsistently, and remained hidden to most outside observers. Like Wilson before him, Roosevelt suffered from high blood pressure, a condition that does not present or evolve in the same way now as it did in the early parts of the twentieth century; "Roosevelt's clinical course was highly atypical of essential hypertension because of its late onset (at 54 years of age) and progression to a malignant phase."[1] Before the development of modern high blood pressure medication, the prognosis for patients with this condition remained poor: mean survival was 10.5 months, and no patient survived more than five years in one prominent study in 1939.[2] Thus, at the time, Roosevelt lived longer than average. Antihypertensive drugs, which first became widely available in 1949, would have materially benefited the health, vitality, and longevity of both Wilson and Roosevelt. By 1993, for example, the average survival of patients with accelerated hypertension was eighteen years.[3] Had such drugs been available in Roosevelt's time, even his doctor believed that they would have had a beneficial effect on Roosevelt's blood pressure, perhaps even forestalling his death for a period of time.[4] However, the fact that careful medical attention today might forestall such an illness now does not deny the severe impact of its consequences on Roosevelt's health and longevity at that time.

HEALTH CONDITIONS

Polio

Roosevelt suffered from two debilitating and troublesome health problems over the course of his life. The first, polio, rendered him paralyzed, initially from the chest down and later from the hips down, but did not, at least directly, lead to any serious compromises in his ability to serve as president. While polio restricted the president's physical mobility, it did not interfere with his intellectual or cognitive functioning. It probably did, however, contribute, at least indirectly, to the severity of his heart disease by precluding the kind of systematic exercise program that can often mitigate against arteriosclerosis.

Roosevelt was born on January 30, 1882. His mother had been given too much chloroform during labor, resulting in Franklin being born nearly dead. He had to be resuscitated and was not expected to live. Although he eventually survived, the chloroform apparently affected his mucous membranes in such a way as to leave him particularly susceptible to colds and sinus problems for the rest of his life.[5] Roosevelt, like Kennedy, was persistently ill throughout much of his younger life. In 1912 he contracted typhoid fever, in 1915 he suffered from appendicitis, and in 1918 he became infected with double pneumonia and severe influenza during the worldwide pandemic.[6]

He married his distant cousin Eleanor in 1905, and the marriage produced one daughter and five sons, one of whom died in infancy. His daughter, Anna, became his closest companion and played a decisive role in securing adequate medical treatment for Roosevelt later in life. Roosevelt began his political career by serving in the New York State Senate, where shortly after his first reelection he was tapped by President Wilson to serve as assistant secretary of the navy. It was around this time that Eleanor engaged the young and pretty Lucy Mercer as her secretary. Franklin's subsequent affair with Lucy had disastrous consequences in many areas of his life: it precipitated a permanent marital estrangement; it increased the interference of his mother in the marriage, who bullied Eleanor into staying to ensure her son's political future; it decisively affected his children's approach to both Franklin and Eleanor; and it cemented a life-long attachment. Lucy, then Mrs. Winthrop Rutherford, was the person staying with Roosevelt when he died, while Eleanor remained in Washington at the time. Anna encouraged her father's attachment to Lucy because she believed it made him happy; the fact that she had known about Lucy's presence at Franklin's death forged an even deeper estrangement between Eleanor and Anna after his death.

In 1920 Roosevelt earned the vice-presidential nomination under James Cox for the Democratic ticket for president. Although the Cox-Roosevelt ticket went down to defeat, Roosevelt emerged as a young man of promise to watch in political circles.[7]

The following summer, in 1921, while he was vacationing in Campobello, Maine, Roosevelt took a swim in the cold lake and later appeared to come down with a case of the flu. By the next day, he found it difficult to move his legs. Roosevelt had been stricken with polio. It took three doctors to get the diagnosis right. The first local physician thought he had a cold. Another physician, Dr. Keen, a prominent neurosurgeon who had operated on President Cleveland's jaw many years prior and had consulted on Wilson's case, was vacationing nearby and called in for a consult. He diagnosed Roosevelt as having a blood clot in his lower spinal cord, later upgrading his diagnosis to a lesion on his spinal cord when the paralysis did not improve. Eleanor Roosevelt wrote later to Roosevelt's brother that she was shocked at the $600 bill they received for Keen's magnificent misdiagnosis. Worse still, Keen prescribed deep massage, which Eleanor carefully administered in order to aid her husband. Unfortunately, these excruciatingly painful treatments served only to worsen the paralysis.[8] Finally, a third doctor, Dr. Lovett, was called in and properly diagnosed Roosevelt's condition as polio. Franklin was immediately rushed to the hospital, where he spent the following six weeks. After his release from the hospital, Roosevelt spent many further months recovering at the family's private estate in Hyde Park, New York.[9] This time of recovery proved very difficult for the entire family. Roosevelt's mother and wife remained in almost constant conflict concerning his proper care and treatment. Because the polio virus was not well understood at the time, and fear of infection remained high, Roosevelt's children were kept away from him, leading to great, and in some cases lasting, alienation.[10]

Roosevelt's illness, by interrupting his political career, may have inadvertently helped save it. As Robert Gilbert notes, Roosevelt was prevented from running to near certain defeat in the 1924 presidential campaign that elected Calvin Coolidge. Similarly, Roosevelt was not tempted to run against popular New York Governor Alfred Smith in 1922, thus positioning himself to become Smith's appointed successor in 1928 and the successful presidential candidate in 1932 against Herbert Hoover, whose administration appeared moribund.

Roosevelt's polio was widely hidden from public view for the remainder of his life. It is hard to imagine this being the case in this day and age of aggressive investigative journalism, but the press corps at the time remained complicit in hiding Roosevelt's disability from public view. He was almost never photographed below the waist, getting into or out of cars, being carried by bodyguards, or in his wheelchair.[11] If members of the press tried to press their luck, secret service agents simply seized the cameras and exposed the film.[12] Robert Ferrell notes that of the thirty-five thousand still photographs of Franklin Roosevelt in the Roosevelt Library, only two until quite recently show him in a wheelchair, and none show him being carried, lifted, or pushed.[13] Occasionally Roosevelt would be shown standing, while his leg braces were hidden from view. Roosevelt knew that he could not be portrayed as a crippled man before a public that craved a strong and vigorous leader to guide them out of a long period of economic depression. Roosevelt presented an image of someone who had conquered the effect of polio and could now walk. Most people alive during the Roosevelt years still claim that they had no idea until after he had died that he could not walk.

Although Roosevelt's polio caused complete physical paralysis below the hips, this illness did not exert any effect on Roosevelt's cognitive functioning. His judgment and decision-making abilities remained unaltered by this physical limitation at this point. That does not mean that his experience did not affect his self-image or character development. When asked what effect polio had had on her husband, Eleanor Roosevelt responded that "any person who has gone through great suffering is bound to have a greater sympathy (for) and understanding of the problems of mankind."[14] Roosevelt's secretary of labor, Frances Perkins, also believed that Roosevelt's impairment helped him politically, by making him more accessible.[15] As Post and Robins note, the history of a person's past illnesses and reactions to it need to be understood and appreciated in order to examine the impact of present illness on performance.[16]

As Gallagher writes, polio always exerts a profound impact on its victims; it transforms young people from vibrant and active members of society into physically dependent paralyzed individuals.[17] Their perspective on the world and their place in it can be dramatically affected. It often becomes the defining event of a person's life. Many others in Roosevelt's situation might have given up any hope for public life after contracting the virus. Gallagher writes that polio defined Roosevelt's subsequent response to all illness. Based on values he had learned in childhood, and hardened by the experience of his first few weeks with polio, Roosevelt developed certain responses to illness that would carry over into his later years. First, he never doubted that he would recover, even walk again. He refused to acknowledge anything negative or unpleasant. Denial became a way of life. He insisted on good cheer and would not allow negative emotions to enter the picture. He considered all subsequent challenges to be trivial in comparison to what he had already accomplished in overcoming his paralysis. He once remarked, "if you had spent two years in bed trying to wiggle your big toe, after that anything else would seem easy."[18] Imagine the confidence, fortitude, and courage such a statement implies;

all subsequent challenges might pale in comparison with such an ostensible victory of mind over body. It would not be surprising if Roosevelt similarly believed he could overcome other physical limitations he might encounter in life through sheer force of will.

Further, Roosevelt's experience with polio led to unanticipated character effects later in his life during the onset of congestive heart failure. He was used to overcoming illness and performing well in office despite his physical limitations. He had a well-entrenched habit of ignoring personal adversity. As Post and Robins write, his disability had "led him to incorporate leading despite impaired health as a core element of his political personality."[19] Roosevelt was able to use these well-established coping mechanisms to deal with the impact of a new disability on his behavior, including denial and will power. The largely successful mechanisms Roosevelt developed early on for handling polio did not change with the specific nature of his illness later in life. Although the nature and cognitive impact of the two illnesses differed, his response to them remained similar.

Although Roosevelt's polio may have affected him politically, psychologically, and physically, it did not compromise his abilities to exercise his duties as president from a mental or cognitive perspective. Robert Gilbert advances the novel argument that polio may have actually improved the president's political prospects, not only by improving the timing of his reentry into public life but also by moving Roosevelt farther to the left, making him more sensitive to human illness and pain, strengthening his character, improving his self-control, and mitigating some of his prior arrogance. Gilbert argues persuasively that these characteristics provide the defining achievements of Roosevelt's domestic policies: "Compassion and perseverance were the characteristics that, at least in part, led his administration to be judged one of the most successful in American history."[20]

Heart Disease

Heart disease presented an even more serious illness for Roosevelt toward the end of his political life than polio had at its outset. Probably beginning as early as 1937, Roosevelt suffered from high blood pressure, which eventually contributed to his coronary artery disease and final cerebral hemorrhage. The early signs and symptoms of high blood pressure are often nonexistent. Damage occurs silently before manifesting in various forms of end-stage organ disease. The cognitive compromises that affected Roosevelt as a result of his illness came on gradually, occurred intermittently, and exerted an impact only inconsistently, as is typical of this condition. Unlike Roosevelt's polio, however, his high blood pressure and heart disease did affect his cognitive abilities, at first intermittently but then increasingly from about December 1943 until his death in April 1945.

Most commentators and historians have focused on the Big Three conference at Yalta as presenting the clearest case for the impact of Roosevelt's health on his decision-making abilities. This supposition naturally results from the proximity of the conference to his death, the haggard pictures of Roosevelt taken at the conference itself, and the common criticism that Roosevelt made unnecessary concessions to Stalin at Yalta because he was in effect too weak or tired to fight him. Bert Park and Robert Ferrell in particular have presented meticulously thorough documentation in support of the argument that Roosevelt did not appear to have been cognitively compromised at the time of the conference.[21] The outcome of the conference actually supports this contention, because even a healthy Roosevelt may not have been able to wrest more concessions from Stalin than what the allegedly sick Roosevelt achieved, given the military situation on the ground in Europe at the time.

Roosevelt, however, may have been impaired by his illness in some significant ways during earlier decision-making episodes, most notably during his trip to Hawaii to plan the future of the Pacific War with General MacArthur and Admiral Nimitz in July 1944, and again at the Québec conference with Churchill in September 1944. The fact that he could have been more impaired sooner and less impaired later is not inconsistent with the transient and intermittent nature of the effect of arteriosclerosis on cognitive functioning.

Early in Roosevelt's lifetime, high blood pressure was not typically treated by the medical profession as a serious illness, at least partly because there was little that could be done to adjust it. Remarkable as it seems given the current medical obsession with detection, the increasingly stringent standards for acceptable levels, and recent advances in treatment, cardiology itself did not become a medical specialty until the 1920s. Besides rest and diet control, the only real treatment for high blood pressure at the time involved the use of phenobarbital, a barbiturate, which was used to help calm a person and thus lower his blood pressure. This kind of treatment works better for those whose underlying cause for high blood pressure is anxiety or stress than those for whom the underlying cause is physical or genetic. It does not address the underlying condition and exerts only temporary, if any, effect on the overall blood pressure rate. A standard medical text in 1931 stated that, "The treatment of hypertension itself is a difficult and almost hopeless task in the present state of our knowledge...the hypertension may be an important compensatory mechanism which should not be tampered with, even were it certain that we could control it."[22]

Once high blood pressure began to be treated as a more serious condition, various methods were used to determine what constituted ideal blood pressure. The first number, systolic, measures the maximum pressure of the heart when it contracts. The second number, diastolic, measures arterial pressure when the heart is at rest. Early on, medical science argued that the top, systolic, number should be 100 plus your age. Until very recently, anything under 140/90 was not considered to be serious. More recent guidelines encourage doctors to keep their patient's blood pressure under 120/80. By whatever standard might be employed, Roosevelt's blood pressure increased dramatically between 1935 when his reading recorded a pressure of 136/78 and 1937 when it had risen to 162/98. By 1944 Roosevelt's blood pressure was regularly running over 200 systolic and over 100 diastolic. By 1944 Roosevelt's doctor should have realized the severity of Roosevelt's medical condition. Dr. Bert Park, neurosurgeon and historian, quotes the statement of the standard medical text in 1944, *Cecil's Textbook of Medicine*, about high blood pressure: "In malignant hypertension, the systolic blood pressure is exceedingly high, 200 to 250 mm [millimeters], and the diastolic pressure is correspondingly elevated. Retinal hemorrhage . . . and congestive heart failure commonly complicate the clinical picture and cerebral vascular accidents are not infrequent. The condition is invariably fatal."[23] Wilson's retinal hemorrhage most likely resulted from high blood pressure.

Nonetheless, Roosevelt's primary physician, Admiral Ross McIntire, proved incompetent in his medical treatment of Roosevelt throughout the president's final illness. McIntire graduated from two medical schools, Willamette University and the University of Oregon in 1912. He joined the navy when the United States entered World War I. He became Roosevelt's physician, over Lieutenant Commander Joel Boone, the previous White House physician, through the intervention of Woodrow Wilson's physician, Dr. Cary Grayson. McIntire met Grayson while working in the Naval Dispensary in the early 1920s, where Grayson still worked so he could continue to care for Wilson in Washington, D.C. Grayson liked McIntire because they both shared the view that the president's health was private business and need not be disclosed to the public. Grayson also recommended the eye, ear, nose, and throat physician to Roosevelt because of Roosevelt's chronic sinus condition. During his association with Roosevelt and his administration, McIntire rose from the rank of lieutenant junior grade to vice admiral during World War II, although he did not serve in any combat duty. By 1938 he was appointed surgeon general. This job, which he held concomitantly with his job as physician to the president, brought with it supervisory capacity over 175,000 medical personnel, 52 hospitals, and 278 mobile units.[24] McIntire benefited, in terms of both money and status, as a result of his association with the president.

Roosevelt's really serious medical complications began after he returned from the Tehran conference of the Big Three in late 1943, exhausted and ill. Roosevelt had stopped in Egypt on his way to the conference to meet with Chiang Kai-shek and Churchill. In Tehran, agreement was reached about opening a second front in France in 1944 and dismembering Germany after the war. Upon returning from the conference, Roosevelt appeared to have a respiratory illness that would not go away. Roosevelt's daughter, Anna, became increasingly concerned, and by mid-March, she had approached McIntire to find out what was wrong with her father. Anna's intervention forced McIntire to consult a cardiologist, Dr. Howard Bruenn, who was in charge of the Electrocardiograph Department of the U.S. Medical Hospital in Bethesda, Maryland. Bruenn was a young and highly skilled cardiologist who graduated from Johns Hopkins Medical school in 1929 after studying with the leading specialists of the time.[25] He had been resident physician and a member of the faculty at Columbia Presbyterian Hospital in New York City prior to the war. McIntire outranked Bruenn, but, unlike McIntire, Bruenn had a preestablished career and reputation in medicine independent of the military. Like many others, Bruenn joined the navy following the Japanese attack on Pearl Harbor on December 7, 1941. Bruenn first consulted on Roosevelt's case on March 27, 1944. What he found horrified him. Although initially McIntire refused to give Bruenn his medical chart on Roosevelt's history,[26] Bruenn repeatedly insisted and eventually received McIntire's records. He saw that Roosevelt had suffered from severe iron deficiency anemia in May 1941, when his hemoglobin had been an extraordinarily low 4.5 grams per 100 milliliters (the normal range is 12 to 16 g/100 ml).[27] In later reports, Bruenn stated that Roosevelt's severe anemia dated from 1938 or 1939.[28] Anemia, among other symptoms, causes profound fatigue. It can also make a person more susceptible to contracting illness and hinder recovery. McIntire believed the anemia resulted from bleeding hemorrhoids, although it was not until Bruenn joined the case that the president was given iron supplements to counteract the anemia. Roosevelt responded well to this treatment. Although the anemia was severe enough to indicate the possibility of internal bleeding, no one appeared to look for any additional cause. Anemia remains important because it can exacerbate congestive heart failure by forcing the heart to work even harder to get adequate amounts of oxygen into the blood.[29]

Regardless, Bruenn's discoveries during the course of his examination revealed much more serious immediate concerns. Bruenn diagnosed the president as suffering from "hypertension, hypertensive heart disease, cardiac failure (left ventricular) and acute bronchitis."[30] He immediately recommended the following treatment plan: one to two weeks bed rest, digitalis, a restricted low-salt diet, codeine for the cough, sedation to ensure rest, and gradual weight loss. McIntire immediately rejected Bruenn's conclusions because of the enormous demands and time pressures on the president. At first, Roosevelt was told to rest and given codeine for his cough.

On March 29 McIntire brought in additional doctors for consultation on Bruenn's diagnosis and treatment. At that meeting, Bruenn suggested that Roosevelt needed to rest, cut down on his cigarette smoking, take phenobarbital (whose major side effects include sedation and impaired concentration), get a minimum of ten hours sleep each night, and begin a 2,600 calorie diet, among other things.

A further meeting was held on March 31 at which two honorary medical consultants to the navy were present, Dr. James Pallin, who became head of the American Medical Association, and Dr. Frank Lahey, who set up the Lahey Clinic in Boston. These doctors examined the president, and much discussion about proper treatment ensued. Lahey was concerned about Roosevelt's gastrointestinal tract, and Pallin, while agreeing with Bruenn's diagnosis, did not think Roosevelt's condition severe enough to warrant the use of digitalis, a powerful heart stimulant used in those suffering from cardiac failure that makes the heart more efficient so that it does not have to work as hard. Digitalis, while effective, does not constitute a cure for heart disease and also becomes less and less effective over time.[31] Bruenn argued stridently for his position, noting that Roosevelt's history and physical limitations all supported the use of digitalis. He told the other doctors that if his recommendations were not implemented, he would quit the case.[32] The other doctors finally agreed, and Bruenn instituted a digitalis regime for the president. Yet McIntire released a press statement at odds with the diagnosis, claiming that "the check-up is satisfactory. When we got through, we decided that for a man of sixty-two we have very little to argue about."[33] This comment represents a remarkable example of a medical cover-up with far-reaching consequences.

The positive results of the new regimen were immediate and dramatic. Roosevelt's condition improved substantially within a matter of days, vindicating the diagnosis and treatment plan advocated by Bruenn. From this point, Bruenn essentially took over the day-to-day treatment of Roosevelt until the time of FDR's death about a year later. However, McIntire remained the official public spokesman on Roosevelt's health and consistently pronounced him to be in good health and in good shape for a man of his age. Even after Roosevelt's death, McIntire continued to claim that Roosevelt had been in good health until his dying day and that FDR's final stroke had been a "bolt out of the blue." Further, McIntire ordered Bruenn not to tell Roosevelt or his family what he knew about the president's condition; however, a letter from Anna to her then husband, John Boettinger, during the Yalta conference, suggests that Bruenn had told her about the severity of her father's heart problem:

> Just between you and me, we are having to watch the OM [Old Man, meaning Roosevelt] very carefully from a physical standpoint. He gets all wound up, seems to thoroughly enjoy it all, but wants too many people around, and then

won't go to bed early enough. The result is that he doesn't sleep well. Ross and Bruenn are both worried because of the old "ticker" trouble – which, of course, no one knows about but those two and me. I am working closely with Ross and Bruenn, and using all my ingenuity and tact I can muster to try to separate the wheat from the chaff – to keep the unnecessary people out of OM's room and to steer the necessary one's [sic] in at the best times. This involves trying my best to keep abreast as much as possible of what is actually taking place at the Conf so that I will know who and who should not see OM. I have found out through Bruenn (who won't let me tell Ross that I know) that this "ticker" situation is far more serious than I ever knew. And, the biggest difficulty in handling the situation here is that we can, of course, tell no one of the "ticker" trouble. It's truly worrisome – and there's not a helava lot anyone can do about it. (Better tear off and destroy this paragraph.)[34]

Most of what is now known about Roosevelt's medical care and treatment in the last year of his life comes from a paper written by Dr. Bruenn, at the insistence of Anna Roosevelt, with her three brothers' permission, which was published in 1970. This is because the bulk of Roosevelt's medical file, like Wilson's, has been lost or destroyed. Bruenn recalls that the last time he saw it, he wrote a note concerning the circumstances of Roosevelt's death, returned the file to the safe where it was kept, and never saw it again. Numerous historians have tried to trace the file to no avail. At the time that Bruenn last returned the file, only three men had a key to the safe where the medical records were held. John Harper, head of the Naval Hospital, Robert Duncan, executive officer of the hospital, and Admiral McIntire all had keys. Most people, including Bruenn, speculate that McIntire destroyed the file in order to protect his own reputation concerning the severity of Roosevelt's illness and his inability to correctly diagnose or treat it. Of those with access to the file, only McIntire had any motivation to destroy the file. He may have done so to protect the president's privacy, or he may have done so to prevent others from criticizing his diagnosis and treatment of the president.

Given the severity of Roosevelt's condition in March 1944 when Bruenn entered the picture, it is likely that Roosevelt would not have lived out the year without Bruenn's intervention. More interesting from a counterfactual perspective is the possibility that if Bruenn had been brought into the case a year or so earlier, Roosevelt might have lived out 1945 or slightly beyond. For Bruenn, who thought that the major factor contributing to Roosevelt's cardiac failure was his high blood pressure, the real tragedy lay in the lack of adequate medication to reduce blood pressure, which was not available until shortly after Roosevelt's death. Bruenn argued that "unquestionably, it would have had a beneficial effect on his blood pressure, which was, presumably, the initiating factor in his final illness."[35] As with Wilson, adequate medication to reduce high blood pressure might easily have changed the course of history had Roosevelt been able to avail himself of it.

Nonetheless, Bruenn's intervention came at a critical time and added crucial months to the president's life. Bruenn supervised Roosevelt as the digitalis improved Roosevelt's cardiac function, his lungs cleared, his heart diminished in size, he lost weight, and he even managed to cut his cigarette use back to six a day.[36] Interestingly, Bruenn claims that Roosevelt never asked any questions about his medical care, or anything about the medication he was taking. McIntire claimed never to have discussed the president's condition with him. As late as 1990, Bruenn seemed surprised, even upset, that Roosevelt appeared not to know that he was a cardiologist.

Yet Ferrell reveals an interesting explanation for these factors.[37] On the basis of newly released diaries of the president's cousin, Margaret (Daisy) Suckley, Ferrell reveals that Roosevelt did know he had a blood pressure problem, most likely from his physical therapist, George Fox, who also took the president's blood pressure. Second, it is also clear that Roosevelt knew that Bruenn was a cardiologist. Daisy's diaries indicate that Roosevelt described Bruenn to her as "one of the best heart men."[38] How Roosevelt gained this knowledge is uncertain. McIntire may have told him, and Roosevelt, although ill, was never stupid. He knew he had been wheeled into an electrocardiograph unit for his original examination with Bruenn. He had his blood pressure taken every day, and Bruenn saw him almost every day and traveled with him. Daisy's diaries indicate that Roosevelt knew how sick he was. On May 5, 1944, she wrote about the president that "He said that he discovered that the doctors had not agreed together about what to tell him, so that he found out that they were not telling *him* the *whole* truth & that he was evidently more sick than they said!"[39]

This way of obtaining and using information was typical of Roosevelt's style in other areas of his political life as well. He remained at the center of many political issues, battles, and debates and often had different people working on different parts of a problem, sometimes even overlapping in the areas they had been assigned to cover. But Roosevelt remained the only one who had access to all the pieces of information in order to pull things together. Roosevelt may have had his own personal and political reasons for not making either McIntire or Bruenn or Anna aware of his knowledge concerning the severity of his illness. He may not have wanted them to know so that he could try to prevent them from curtailing his activities more than he desired. He may have felt he had no choice in the matter given war pressures and that he must do his job regardless of the personal consequences. He may have treated heart disease as he did polio, as yet another crippling illness that could be overcome through sheer will power and a certain amount of denial.

Bruenn did his best to take care of Roosevelt after he first examined him in March 1944. At various times, he administered phenobarbital to the president to help lower blood pressure and, on occasion, codeine for pain or cough. Codeine was used, for instance, following a gallbladder attack that Roosevelt experienced while vacationing at Hobcaw, Bernard Baruch's estate in South Carolina, in April 1944. Following this episode, Bruenn continued to travel with Roosevelt throughout the rest of the year, and the rest of FDR's life.

In July 1944 Roosevelt took a train to San Diego on his way to Hawaii. While on the train in San Diego, he accepted his fourth presidential nomination from the Democratic National Convention.

After his return to Washington, Roosevelt left for Québec, Canada, where he met with British prime minister Winston Churchill to plan the end of the war against Japan. During this conference, Bruenn noted even higher than usual blood pressure readings for Roosevelt.[40] At the time, he was on about one gram of digitalis a day and half a grain of phenobarbital three times a day. Following the election in November and the inauguration in January, Roosevelt left for his last big summit conference in Yalta with Churchill and Soviet premier Joseph Stalin. During this time, he was given some codeine for a cough from a cold he caught on the ship. His blood pressure remained unchanged, except for one incident following a hard day's discussion of the Polish question at Yalta, when Roosevelt manifested his only episode of pulsus alternans, a dangerous condition whereby each alternate heart beat pulses weaker, then stronger. This serious condition is caused by a combination of heart failure and high blood pressure. Rest was enforced, and his pulse returned to normal within a couple of days.

Shortly after his return, he took a trip to Warm Springs, Georgia, to prepare his speech for the opening of the United Nations in San Francisco later that summer and died there on April 12, 1945. On that day, Roosevelt woke with a slight headache and some stiffness in his neck, which Bruenn reported was relieved by a slight massage. Early in the afternoon, about 1:15, while seated as the subject of a portrait, he complained of a terrible headache and collapsed. Bruenn was called to his side and arrived within fifteen minutes. He recorded a pulse of 96 and a blood pressure of "well over" 300/190; the president had wet himself involuntarily. Bruenn administered papaverine and amylnitrate to relieve vasoconstriction. The president's blood pressure went down, but his right pupil became dilated. At 3:31, the president's breathing stopped, and, making every possible effort to save his life, Bruenn began artificial respiration, administered caffeine sodium benzoate intramuscularly, and shot adrenaline directly into Roosevelt's heart muscle. With no response, Bruenn pronounced him dead at 3:35.[41] Roosevelt's arteries were so clogged at the time of his death that the pump used to inject formaldehyde "strained and stopped."[42]

Dr. Bert Park has presented a thorough medical analysis of Roosevelt's condition in the last year or so of his life. Park argues persuasively that the president suffered from a combination of medical conditions, including congestive heart failure and chronic obstructive pulmonary disease (COPD) that together led to a condition of "secondary metabolic encephalopathy." Encephalopathy refers to interruptions in consciousness that can be brought about by physical states in the body or changes in the brain. Although Bruenn does not mention chronic obstructive pulmonary disease explicitly, he does mention the cyanotic blue cast of Roosevelt's lips and fingernail beds. Bruenn attributed this symptom to Roosevelt's heart disease and poor circulation. Park argues that Roosevelt likely suffered from COPD as a result of his longtime habit of cigarette smoking, a common effect of such a lifelong habit. Park notes that Roosevelt suffered from almost all of the classic symptoms of pulmonary induced encephalopathy, including a persistent cough, cyanosis, shortness of breath, headaches, tremors, and mental states of confusion, drowsiness, or inattention.

One of the early symptoms of secondary metabolic encephalopathy involves mental confusion. Park draws on the standard medical text on coma and stupor to explain that this condition is most commonly caused by "subacute chronic diffuse hypoxia of the brain."[43] This means that the brain does not receive enough oxygen, which can happen for a variety of reasons. The basic text, by Drs. Fred Plum and Jerome Posner, *Diagnosis of Stupor and Coma* (2007), points to four causal conditions for such hypoxia, all of which Roosevelt suffered from, according to Park. These conditions include severe anemia, congestive heart failure, pulmonary disease, and hypertensive encephalopathy. One of the reasons that hypertension causes such a serious compromise in heart health is precisely because it accelerates arteriosclerosis. Park references the standard medical text, *Cecil's Textbook of Medicine*, to quote that blood pressure of over 160/95 increases a person's risk of coronary heart disease by three times, congestive heart failure by four times, and stroke by seven times. Park also quotes from Plum and Posner that in cases of hypoxia "Judgment slips away early, and confusion, disorientation and lethargy emerge."[44] Park carefully notes, however, that this condition manifests intermittently, so that periods of competence can be punctured by periods of confusion. These tend to occur when one or more of the underlying causes worsens. So, for example, encephalopathy might occur when blood pressure surges or when anemia worsens.

According to Park, Roosevelt suffered from frequent, if brief, episodes of diminished consciousness during his last two years in office. His secretary, Grace Tully, expressed concern that Roosevelt appeared to fall asleep over his mail or during dictation with increasing frequency.[45] Other advisers commented on how Roosevelt would appear to fall into "reverie," sit with his mouth open, fall asleep during a conversation, or blank out in the middle of signing his name.[46] At Yalta, for example, James Byrnes wrote:

> I was disturbed by his appearance. I feared his illness was not entirely due to a cold and expressed this concern to Mrs. Boettinger [Anna Roosevelt]. She thought my opinion arose from observing him during the moving pictures.... She explained that, while looking at pictures, the President would have his mouth open because of his sinus trouble and that this made him look badly, but he was not really ill. Dr. McIntire also expressed the belief that the President's appearance was due to a combination of a sinus infection and a cold.[47]

Lord Moran, Winston Churchill's doctor, found Roosevelt's appearance at Yalta similarly unsettling:

> To a doctor's eye, ... the President appears to be a very sick man. He has all the symptoms of hardening of the arteries of the brain in an advanced stage.... I give him only a few months to live.... The day before we left England, I received a letter from Dr. Roger Lee of Boston [former President of the American College of Physicians and also the American Medical Association]. He wrote, "Roosevelt had heart failure eight months ago. There are, of course, degrees of congestive failure, but Roosevelt had enlargement of his liver and was puffy.... He was irascible and became very irritable if he had to concentrate his mind for long. If anything was brought up that wanted thinking out he would change the subject." ... The President no longer seems to the P.M. [Prime Minister Winston Churchill] to take an intelligent interest in the war; often he does not seem even to read the papers the P.M. gives him.[48]

William Rigdon, also present at the conference, commented on the same phenomenon: "Some of us noticed, but without concern, that his lower jaw often hung down as he watched the pictures."[49] The so-called open-mouth syndrome results from inadequate circulation of oxygen to the brain, a common occurrence in older people suffering from heart disease.[50] These occurrences speak to the kind of encephalopathy that Park describes. Intellectual impairment can accompany these episodes, and it appears that this happened to Roosevelt on occasion at least during his last year or two in office.

As the condition of encephalopathy worsens, other symptoms start to appear. As Plum and Posner write, "Initially the patient appears preoccupied or just uninterested.... As the disease progresses, drowsiness becomes more apparent.... This pattern of drowsiness preceding other changes is more characteristic of secondary metabolic encephalopathy."[51] They go on to write both that "[m]ost conscious patients with metabolic brain disease are confused.... Their abstract thinking is defective; they cannot concentrate well and cannot easily retain new information" and that "changes in mentation and awareness are the earliest and most reliable warnings of the more slowly developing varieties of metabolic encephalopathy.... Altered awareness is the first and most subtle index of brain dysfunction."[52]

Park also notes that many of these symptoms can be brought about by chronic obstructive pulmonary disease, either alone or in combination with hypertension. Park cites an article by Drs. Austen, Carmichael, and Adams describing the potential cognitive side effects of COPD in later stages:

> Impairment of consciousness was noted.... In each the principal complaint... was that the patients were extremely drowsy and often fell asleep while at work, while eating, or while in conversation.... They were also described as being forgetful, irritable and easily confused.... Many stimuli passed unheeded, and there was obvious difficulty in assimilating all the details of the situation.... A lack of ability to recall recent events and a failure to think quickly and coherently appeared to be the result of the inattention and reduced awareness.[53]

Roosevelt manifested many of these symptoms of secondary metabolic encephalopathy and chronic obstructive pulmonary disease in the last year of his life in particular. The episodes appeared transient and intermittent, which is consistent with the natural course and history of the condition. His condition would have been exacerbated during times of increased blood pressure. As a result, it becomes possible to trace the relationship between his health and his decisions at critical junctures; judgment should appear worse as the underlying conditions accelerate.

DECISIONS

Roosevelt was subject to intense pressures as president during the Second World War and had been subjected to incredible stress in both domestic and international relations as president for almost twelve years prior to the more serious collapse of his health in 1943. After 1943 he was subject to ever increasing political and military pressures concerning the conduct of the war and the creation of the postwar world system. Several of the decisions that Roosevelt made in his last year can be scrutinized for evidence of the impact of his chronic illness on his decision making. Yalta has presented the most common case to be analyzed from this perspective, at least partly because Roosevelt died so shortly after its completion. Ironically, Roosevelt appears to have performed adequately and appropriately at the time of that conference, even if some of the agreements reached there began to break down upon his return, and especially after his death. Yet Roosevelt cannot be held responsible, ultimately, for what occurred after his death, especially if he counted on being able to control the process as long as he was alive.

In at least two sets of decisions, however, Roosevelt's condition, particularly that aspect of it which Park characterizes as encephalopathy, impacted his decision making in negative ways: those made at the conference in Hawaii in July 1994 concerning the future direction of the war in the Pacific; and his endorsement of the harsh and vindictive Morgenthau plan for postwar Germany that Roosevelt pushed, against Churchill's inclination, at the conference in Québec in September of that same year.

In addition, Roosevelt's health may have also impacted a set of important domestic decisions that had foreign policy implications. Specifically, Roosevelt's decision to run for a fourth term as president and the larger Democratic Party decision to nominate Truman as his running mate deserve consideration for Roosevelt's uncharacteristic lack of interest and engagement.

Hawaii

In the summer of 1944, desperately needing rest, all the while trying to conduct the war in Europe, Roosevelt took a five-week trip by train and ship to meet in Hawaii with Admiral Chester Nimitz and General Douglas MacArthur.[54] Roosevelt's job at the Hawaii conference was to arbitrate between the two military leaders over the future strategy of the Pacific campaign. Hoping to vindicate himself, MacArthur had a personal stake in returning to the Philippines after his earlier defeat there by the Japanese. Nimitz and some members of the Joint Chiefs of Staff had become increasingly uncomfortable with MacArthur's plan to invade Japan via the Philippines and Okinawa. They preferred a strategy that would have skipped over the Philippines and approached Japan by way of Formosa, now Taiwan. They had notified Roosevelt of their consensus on this point prior to his departure.[55] Roosevelt met with MacArthur and Nimitz for two and a half hours on July 27, as each man presented his unique perspective on how to win the war in the Pacific – by any calculation, an inordinately short period of time to discuss such a complex and significant issue, especially after such a long and arduous journey to get there.

At the end of the meeting, Roosevelt decided to allow MacArthur to continue his island-hopping campaign through the Philippines and Okinawa from Australia to Japan. But, in a deeper sense, the result of the meeting was Roosevelt's abdication of a careful, thoughtful decision on the matter. The limited amount of time Roosevelt spent on such an important issue and the abruptness of his decision indicate his fatigue, if not his disinterest. From the start, and prior to the meeting, Roosevelt had favored Nimitz's plan to invade Japan via Formosa. As time wore on and lunchtime approached, the military leaders continued to argue their respective positions. Roosevelt abruptly stopped the discussion, suddenly reversing his earlier preference without explanation, and declared his support for the MacArthur position, thus ending the meeting. Unusually, he made this decision without further consultation with other military officers, including General George Marshall. Following the meeting, MacArthur presciently commented that "the President will be dead within the year."[56]

This decision led to the October 1944 MacArthur "I have returned" invasion by 200,000 American troops into the Philippines. Circumstances for the invasion were not propitious, and bad weather and stiff Japanese resistance led to the deaths of 100,000 Filipino civilians in the first month of the campaign, which included door-to-door fighting in the capital of Manila. As historian Carol Petillo commented, it was "one of the most destructive, albeit well-intentioned, armies of 'liberation' the world had ever seen."[57] Given strong Japanese resistance, the battles at Iwo Jima and Okinawa were among the war's most bloody. The fight for Okinawa cost more than 12,000 American lives alone. Walter LaFeber argues that such costly battles no doubt spurred Roosevelt to push Stalin to enter the war in the Pacific as quickly as possible at Yalta.[58] Robert Ferrell argues that this delay made the nuclear bombing of Japan a more attractive option than it might have been had the American invasion advanced more swiftly or with fewer American lives lost, as might have been the case if Nimitz's Formosa plan had been followed.[59]

While Bruenn did not keep records of Roosevelt's blood pressure during his trip to Hawaii in the diary that has survived, Roosevelt appears to have experienced some episodes of encephalopathy at this time. Staffer John Flynn's depiction of Roosevelt during this meeting remains particularly striking: "He faltered and paused, his eyes became glassy, and consciousness drifted from him. The man at his side nudged him, shook him a little, and pointed to the place in the manuscript where he broke off, and said, 'Here, Mr. President, is your place.'"[60] Park agrees that Roosevelt's behavior at the conference in Hawaii represents one of the instances where his illness affected his decision making for the worse. Roosevelt's fatigue, clouded consciousness, and inability to concentrate may have prevented him from taking the necessary time and investing the required energy to consider the argument from all sides, consult the appropriate people, and render a thoughtful and appropriate judgment, as he had done in the past with similar military decisions.

Ferrell finds even more sinister consequences from Roosevelt's failure to attend more carefully to the strategy for the war in the Pacific.[61] He indicts Roosevelt for his lack of attention to the situation in China. When nationalist leader Chiang Kai-shek refused to fight the Japanese due to his preoccupation with fighting the northern Chinese communist forces of Mao, Roosevelt dismissed the U.S. commander there, General Joseph ("Vinegar Joe") Stilwell, rather than confront Chiang more directly. Stilwell had never been a fan of Chiang, whom he once referred to as "an ignorant, illiterate, peasant son-of-a-bitch,"[62] but when he heard that Chiang had refused to fight against the Japanese after they had attacked Stilwell's forces, he went into Chiang's office and "hit the little bugger right in the solar plexus."[63] While Roosevelt might have wanted a more compliant and controlled officer in charge at the time, the Japanese attack on Stilwell's forces threatened the bomber bases in southern China that Roosevelt had hoped to use in the fight against the Japanese. A more interested and alert Roosevelt almost certainly would have fought harder either to bring Chiang into the fight against Japan or, failing that, to abandon support for him. Instead, when Chiang demanded that Stilwell be replaced, Roosevelt replaced him with Lieutenant General Albert Wedemeyer, who did not oppose Chiang's refusal to fight the Japanese. Further, Roosevelt made his friend Patrick Hurley, who knew nothing about China, his personal representative to Chiang's government and eventually offered unconditional support to that government at Hurley's encouragement. Ferrell argues that if Roosevelt had been able to devise a better strategy toward China and recognized the inherently corrupt nature of Chiang's regime, he might have also been able to prevent the communist takeover and the subsequent war in Korea. Under such a scenario, the United States might well have also proved more successful in fighting the Japanese in the Pacific, thus avoiding the need to drop two nuclear bombs on Japan in late 1945 in order to end the war.

Further, Ferrell charges that Roosevelt's lack of attention to Southeast Asia, and in particular his lack of engagement with Ho Chi Minh, who was seeking U.S. support against the French at the time, set up the future American war in Vietnam. Ho Chi Minh had learned all about self-determination and sovereignty from Woodrow Wilson when Ho served as one of the staffers at the Paris Peace Conference in 1919. As an anticolonialist himself, Roosevelt had shown some sympathy with this position and had supported anticolonial forces before, including the Indian opposition to British occupation. As Anthony Eden explained, "Roosevelt did not confine his dislike of colonialism to the British Empire alone, for it was a principle with him, not the less cherished for its possible advantages. He hoped that former colonial territories, once free of their masters, would become politically and economically dependent on the United States."[64]

Had Roosevelt been active enough to recognize and support the nationalist desires of Ho Chi Minh against French colonial oppression, rather than allow the French to deal with the problem in their own way, the American involvement in Vietnam might have been avoided. The situation in Southeast Asia remained delicate and complex, but Roosevelt at his best was a highly skilled diplomat. While it may be the case that, had he been well, he might have supported the Vietnamese against French imperial rule, it is also possible that even then Roosevelt might not have been able to pay adequate time and attention to the matter, given the sheer size and significance of the other issues that confronted him during the Second World War. However, no matter how sympathetic he may have been to such an ultimate goal, Roosevelt at the time was primarily, almost exclusively, focused on winning the war in Europe, not on helping the Vietnamese achieve self-determination. Roosevelt remained preoccupied, along with Churchill, on trying to keep DeGaulle in the fight for Europe; he would not have been able to side with Ho Chi Minh against the French and hope to succeed in his more central goal.

Québec

Roosevelt returned from Hawaii via Alaska and gave a speech to workers at the Naval Shipyard at Bremerton, Washington, on August 22, 1944. By this time, Roosevelt had lost a good deal of weight and his leg braces no longer fit him properly, offering little support. As a result, he had to brace himself against the lectern, using his upper body.[65] Although Roosevelt experienced severe chest pains, he managed to complete his speech. Afterward, Bruenn took an electrocardiogram and determined that there had been no damage to Roosevelt's heart, but nonetheless declared this to be the single incident of angina that he witnessed the president experience. In a later interview, Bruenn stated that this event was "proof positive that he had coronary disease, no question about it."[66] McIntire passed it off as muscle pain resulting from the wind.[67]

Roosevelt returned to Washington, where things returned to a relatively normal pace until the conference in Québec. By this time, Roosevelt was working less than four hours a day because of his fatigue and his need for rest due to his heart condition. Ferrell notes that Roosevelt was absent from the White House for 175 days in 1944, often at Warm Springs, Hyde Park, or Hobcaw, the South Carolina retreat owned by Bernard Baruch.

In September 1944 Roosevelt met with British prime minister Churchill in Québec to make a plan for postwar Germany. By this time, Roosevelt appears to have been persuaded by his good friend and secretary of the treasury, Henry Morgenthau, to adopt a "pastoral" plan for Germany in which the Allies would not only divide Germany among the postwar powers but also remove all industry and police the country. In many ways, the plan resembled the peace that the British and French had tried to impose on Germany following the First World War. Unlike the Treaty of Versailles, however, the plan did not call for any German war reparations. Churchill violently objected to the plan. He believed that a healthy postwar British economy depended on an economically strong Europe, including an economically integrated Germany. He submitted to Roosevelt's preference only when Roosevelt offered a $6.5 billion postwar credit to the financially strapped British government.

Once Roosevelt returned to Washington, both Secretary of State Hull and Secretary of War Stimpson expressed their surprise and horror at what the president had done. Hull, a Wilsonian liberal with deep beliefs about the importance of free and open trade for economic prosperity, told Roosevelt that a viable open economy depended on a strong Europe with a vibrant Germany at its center. Roosevelt indicated to Stimpson, Hull, and others that he had not remembered even signing the Morgenthau memo at Québec. Eventually, Roosevelt rescinded his support for the Morgenthau plan, saying he had "pulled a boner."[68] Stimpson records that Roosevelt claimed to be "frankly staggered...and said he had no idea how he could have initialed this."[69] He also declared that "it must have been done...without much thought."[70] Although pleased with Roosevelt's reversal, Churchill wondered if he had gone crazy.

Although no specific readings from July 1944 have survived, Bruenn's notes indicate that Roosevelt's blood pressure was running alarmingly high starting in April 1944, with readings in the 220/120 range not uncommon. Speech writer Robert Sherwood, seeing Roosevelt at this time, reported that he was "shocked by his appearance....I had heard that he had lost a lot of weight, but I was unprepared for the almost ravaged appearance of his face. He had his coat off and his shirt collar seemed several sizes too large for his emaciated neck."[71] On the second day of the conference in Québec, September 15, Bruenn records a blood pressure reading of 240/130, a dangerous level. On September 20 Bruenn reports that for the last few weeks, Roosevelt's pressure had been running in the 180/100 range. Such blood pressure ranges could induce the kind of encephalopathy that Park describes as contributing to cognitive impairments. The strategy Roosevelt embraced in his early acceptance of the Morgenthau plan relied on a trusted friend's assessment and required no new learning on his part. Quick reversal came in the wake of strong political indications that the position was not popular, the type of response that Roosevelt had spent his successful political life overlearning to obey.

Lord Moran, Churchill's physician, noted that Roosevelt appeared to have some mental impairments at Québec. The extent to which Roosevelt's support for the Morgenthau plan was influenced by his fatigue and encephalopathy at Québec is a hard call. Despite his frequent diversions into remembering his happy boyhood visit to Germany in 1891, Roosevelt had shown previous inclinations to impose a hard peace on Germany after the war.

Perhaps Roosevelt was unduly influenced by Morgenthau while in a tired and weakened state. As Ferrell accurately argues, Roosevelt was not a reader; long before his cardiac illness interceded, he preferred to learn from listening to, and talking with, a wide variety of people. His natural instincts in foreign policy did not appear to be as strong or as incisive as in domestic policy. Further, he often privileged military over political factors in making decisions concerning the conduct of the war and the outcome of the peace, which makes Roosevelt's behavior in Hawaii appear particularly odd.[72] Other trusted advisers who might have advocated against the Morgenthau plan were not available to Roosevelt at Québec. In particular, Roosevelt's close adviser Harry Hopkins was unable to attend because he was too ill to travel. Further, Roosevelt might have been too tired or disinterested because of his health to really care or to fight for a different outcome. As with the decision about the war in the Pacific, Roosevelt demonstrated a short attention span and limited energy in his ability to deal with the problems presented by postwar German reconstruction plans.

It is also possible that Roosevelt knew exactly what he was doing and that his support for the Morgenthau plan was entirely consistent with his previous statements and positions on the treatment of postwar Germany, including the preliminary plan supported by all Big Three leaders at the conference in Tehran in late 1943, which agreed that Germany should at least be dismembered after the war. Once Roosevelt returned and saw how unpopular his position was, he chose to disavow the plan rather than continue to support it. Those to whom he disavowed his knowledge of support for the plan, Hull and Stimpson, were the very advisers who had expressed shock at his endorsement of the plan. Out of habit or interest, he may have been concerned about his upcoming reelection in November.

Nonetheless, others who were not so involved with the development or advocacy of the plan also report that Roosevelt claimed not to have remembered signing the document. For a politically sophisticated actor such as Roosevelt, claiming he did not remember if such a fact were not true does not help him and would make him look as if he was losing his hold on political power, a lie that would have been extremely damaging to him. This consideration makes Roosevelt's memory loss claim appear particularly likely to be true. Bradley Smith wrote that "FDR claims not remembering having signed the Morgenthau memo."[73] And Rexford Tugwell claimed, "It is interesting that Franklin almost at once, but without any admission, abandoned the Morgenthau Plan.... At any rate, he proceeded to pretend that he knew nothing about it. Unfortunately, his initials were evidence to the contrary."[74]

The most convincing support for the notion that Roosevelt appears to have been impaired at the time of the Québec conference, and perhaps not fully attentive to the Morgenthau plan or its implications for the reconstruction of postwar Europe, lies in two observations. First, his blood pressure was extremely elevated during the conference itself. Because the exacerbation of encephalopathic episodes is precipitated by increased blood pressure, this is one time when such an event is clearly documented at the concomitant time of an atypically bad and odd decision. The second factor lies in the disastrous nature of the plan itself. It seems unlikely that, had Roosevelt really taken the time to carefully understand the plan and all its implications, he would have supported it. As much as he may have liked Morgenthau and desired retribution against the Germans after the war, he would have realized the potentially disastrous economic implications of such a plan for the postwar world economy. Roosevelt also understood the lessons of the imperfect peace that settled the First World War; punishment that proved unduly harsh on the vanquished could rise up to instigate further conflict later. After working hard, and almost failing, to bring the United States out of the Great Depression following the stock market crash of 1929, he would likely have remained especially sensitive to the economic implications of postwar plans for the American economy.

Yalta

Yalta represents the final meeting between the Big Three at the end of the Second World War. By the time of the next meeting in Potsdam in July 1945, Truman would be president of the United States. Many contentious issues were placed on the table at Yalta. Roosevelt remained consumed with two issues in particular. First, he sought to gain Russian agreement for a postwar international body, which was to become the United Nations, and, second, he was invested in securing Russian cooperation in the military campaign against Japan once the war in Europe against Germany had been won. Other issues that were discussed included the dismemberment, demilitarization, and reparations of Germany, and how to settle the question of Poland. After the war, many came to see Roosevelt as having "sold out" to the Russians at Yalta and, in particular, having given the Russians access to China. Ambassador Bullitt, for one, concluded: "Roosevelt, indeed, was more than tired. He was ill. Little was left of the physical and mental vigor that had been his when he entered the White House in 1933. Frequently he had difficulty in formulating his thoughts, and further difficulty in expressing them consecutively."[75]

Yet the reality is also that Roosevelt held a pretty bad military hand at Yalta and did his best to accomplish his main objectives at the conference, using what little moral and financial leverage he had to achieve his primary goals. In this he succeeded, although some of the agreements reached at Yalta broke down further after Roosevelt died. Proper blame for much of the collapse of these accords lies both with Stalin's failure to live up to his agreement concerning Poland and with Truman's later actions as president, and not so much where they have often been placed, on Roosevelt's doorstep, for agreeing to immoderate concessions at the time. Part of this criticism of Roosevelt may have resulted from his failure to mention the deal he made with the Soviets concerning their entry into the war against Japan in his address to Congress upon his return. Although he considers Roosevelt's actions in this regard to have been a mistake, Robert Gilbert correctly points out that Roosevelt may have wanted to keep this agreement secret to prevent a preemptive attack on the Russian eastern flank by the Japanese, an action that would have stalled the crucial campaign in Eastern Europe.[76]

Several individuals had expressed concern with Roosevelt's health even prior to Yalta. James Farley, former chairman of the Democratic National Committee, commented, "Cordell Hull and I agreed he was a very sick man ... and should not be called upon to make decisions regarding this country and the world."[77] There is no question that Roosevelt was a very sick man by the time of the Yalta conference in February 1945. The journey by sea, air, and car took a long time. Roosevelt's physicians were careful not to let his plane fly at more than 8,000 feet, for fear of the effects of altitude on his weakened heart. Because of this low altitude and the fact that the plane had to fly over Nazi-controlled territory in Greece, the plane was accompanied by a fighter detail. Because the plane held only twelve and was the only one with a fighter detail, all the high-level officials scrambled to get on board. Once they arrived in Crimea, the drive to Yalta took about five or six hours over very bad roads. The American party stayed at the Lavadia palace, built by the last Russian czar, Nicholas II, in 1912. The area had recently been under Nazi control, and the building was bereft of everything, including doorknobs and chandeliers. Senior officials had to share limited bathroom facilities. The building, including all the bedding, was infested with lice and other vermin. Advance teams went and sprayed the building with DDT prior to the president's arrival.[78] Admiral William Leahy later wrote that Churchill told Roosevelt, "If we had searched the whole world to find the worst meeting place, it would not have been as bad as the Crimea."[79]

Many at the conference did not think that Roosevelt looked well. Perhaps the most educated, prescient, and telling comments came from Lord Moran, Churchill's physician:

There was a good deal of talk after dinner about the conference at the President's house. Everyone seemed to agree that the President had gone to bits physically; they kept asking me what might be the cause. . . . It was not only his physical deterioration that had caught their attention. He intervened very little in the discussions, sitting with his mouth open. If he has sometimes been short of facts about the subject under discussion, his shrewdness has covered this up. Now, they say, the shrewdness is gone, and there is nothing left. I doubt, from what I have seen, whether he is fit for his job here.[80]

However, most other observers at the conference indicated that despite Roosevelt's physical decline, he proved able to rally himself to perform well in the crucial meetings. Charles Bohlen wrote:

> I was shocked by Roosevelt's physical appearance. His condition had deteriorated markedly in the less than two weeks since I had seen him. He was not only frail and desperately tired, he looked ill. I never saw Roosevelt look as bad as he did then. . . . I was relieved somewhat, however, to note that his illness did not affect his speech. . . . I saw enough of Roosevelt to conclude that while his physical state was not up to normal, his mental and psychological state was certainly not affected. He was lethargic, but when important moments arose, he was mentally sharp. Our leader was ill at Yalta . . . but he was effective.[81]

Edward Flynn noted, "The President's physical condition was far from good. I saw, though, that when the President reached the point where occasion required him to take part in the conferences, by supreme effort of will he became completely alive and alert to what was going on. But later in his bedroom I was shocked at the toll that had been taken by his years of labor."[82] Several participants went out of their way to mention Roosevelt's skill in spite of his illness. Anthony Eden, later prime minister of Britain, wrote, with some rancor, "I do not believe that the President's declining health altered his judgment. . . . Roosevelt found time to negotiate in secret, and without informing his British colleague or his Chinese ally, an agreement with Stalin to cover the Far East."[83] The special envoy to Churchill, W. Averill Harriman, testified to a Joint Senate Committee on Armed Services and Foreign Relations on August 17, 1951, about Roosevelt: "Unquestionably, he was not in good health and the long conference tired him. Nevertheless, for many months he had given much thought to the matters to be discussed and, in consultation with many officials of the Government, he had blocked out definite objectives that he had clearly in mind. He came to Yalta determined to do his utmost to achieve these objectives and he carried on the negotiations to this end with his usual skill and perception."[84] Secretary of State Edward Stettinius wrote:

> I always found him to be mentally alert and fully capable of dealing with each situation as it developed. . . . There was no briefing by the State Department. . . . Throughout this give-and-take, his mind functioned with clarity and conciseness, furnishing excellent proof that he was alert and in full command of his faculties. . . . The pace of the Conference was grueling and by this time the President naturally showed fatigue. However, he continued to explain the American position skillfully and distinctly, and he also served as a moderating influence when discussions became heated.[85]

Even James Byrnes, later secretary of state under President Truman, commenting that, "so far as I could see, the President had made little preparation for the Yalta conference. . . . I am sure the failure to study . . . while en route was due to the President's illness," nonetheless concluded, "I am sure that only President Roosevelt, with his intimate knowledge of the problems, could have handled the situation so well with so little preparation."[86] Robert Stuart, a young assistant secretary in the office of General Smith, Eisenhower's chief of staff, recalled meeting Roosevelt in Algiers following the Yalta conference: "To this day, I remember feeling a sense of shock and dismay. . . . He looked white as a sheet and was covered with perspiration. He appeared to have some difficulty focusing. . . . Yet even though he recovered after a few moments' delay and became his charming self . . . I was shocked by his appearance seeming both exhausted and sick."[87]

Yet Bruenn noted no changes in Roosevelt's heart or blood pressure during the conference, except for a particularly contentious day discussing the Polish question when Roosevelt did develop pulsus alternans, as discussed previously. In a later interview, Bruenn stated unequivocally that "clinically there was no evidence of strokes. His memory for both recent and past events was good. His behavior toward his friends and intimates was unchanged and his speech unaltered." He went on to argue that Roosevelt's health "did not impair his ability right until that final day."[88]

Although Roosevelt did not get what he wanted on every issue in Yalta, he did secure Soviet agreement on some of the issues that mattered most to him. He understood that Churchill and Stalin had made a previous accord in October 1944 in Moscow on how to divide their postwar influence in Europe. The Soviets took 90 percent influence in Rumania and 75 percent in Bulgaria and Hungary, and they gave the British 90 percent control in Greece. They agreed to split Yugoslavia 50–50. Roosevelt knew that he could do little to overturn this agreement. He remained very concerned, however, with his vision for a postwar United Nations. At Yalta, Roosevelt did get Stalin to agree to drop his request for a veto over procedural issues in the Security Council. Stalin did, however, demand three seats on the Council, one each for Ukraine and Belorussia, in addition to the one for the Soviet Union. In a brilliant stroke, Roosevelt countered that he might then ask for voting rights for all then forty-eight American states, at which point Stalin dropped this voting issue altogether.

Roosevelt was also desperate to gain cooperation from the Soviets in fighting the war against the Japanese. He possessed estimates that indicated that Soviet entry into the war against Japan could prevent 200,000 to 1 million American casualties. Roosevelt did manage to secure Russian agreement to enter the war against Japan three months after the war was over in Germany. In return, he offered several concessions to Stalin, including control over the Kuril Islands and the southern part of Sakhalin, a sphere of influence in Outer Mongolia, and special rights to the Chinese ports of Port Arthur and Dairen. The Soviets had some historical claim to the southern part of the Sakhalin Islands, which they had lost to the Japanese in the Russo-Japanese War; these islands were taken by force in 1904, while the Kuril islands had been given over by treaty. Although many Americans later claimed that Roosevelt sold China out to the Soviets, Roosevelt demanded that Stalin work with Chiang Kai-shek, not Mao, in reaching agreements over China. In this way, Roosevelt hoped to prevent the possibility of having to recognize the communist Chinese government as the legal one. He also understood that if Stalin's army were in place to fight against Japan, there was little he could do to prevent it from seizing the Japanese territory the Soviets wanted. Stalin did indeed enter the war a few days before Truman dropped the atomic bomb. Despite little effort in the war in the Pacific, the Soviets did claim the agreed-upon spoils of the conflict.

Much disagreement persisted at Yalta over Germany and Poland. While Roosevelt may have wanted greater freedom for the Poles, he also understood the military reality of the war, which was that Russian troops had overcome and occupied the disputed territory. The Soviets retained de facto control of the region. While Stalin agreed broadly to notions of free elections in Poland at Yalta, he assumed a different meaning for the phrase than either Churchill or Roosevelt. Upon his return to Washington, Roosevelt remained concerned about Stalin's activity in Poland. Churchill expressed similar concerns to Roosevelt and asked for his advice. In a note he wrote an hour before he died, Roosevelt replied to Churchill, "I would minimize the general Soviet problem as much as possible because these problems, in one form or another, seem to arise every day and most of them straighten out. . . . We must be firm, however, and our course thus far is correct."[89] Roosevelt believed that he and Churchill could keep Stalin in line and make sure he lived up to his word without overreacting to each issue along the way. From Warm Springs, however, Roosevelt did write Stalin a firm, even harsh, letter about the situation Churchill raised. The letter was set to be mailed the day Roosevelt died. As a result, it was never sent.[90] It might not be too far a stretch to consider that Roosevelt's dismay over the collapse of his agreements with Stalin at Yalta may have contributed to his final surge in blood pressure and consequent cerebral hemorrhage. There is also no doubt that his death shifted the outcome of the Polish question more toward Stalin's control as well.

Finally, on the issue of Germany, all three powers agreed to turn over some of Germany's territory to Poland. This boundary issue was not finally settled until 1970, whereby Poland retained some of Germany's pre-1939 territory. The powers agreed to divide up German territory into sectors, and Churchill won a place for France in that partition, against Roosevelt's and Stalin's inclination. The issue of reparations presented the greatest area of conflict. Stalin wanted $20 billion from Germany, with half going to the Soviets. Churchill did not approve, feeling that forcing high levels of German reparations would both harm the German economy, which was essential to a strong British economy, and set up conditions that might lead to another war, as the Treaty of Versailles had precipitated World War II. Roosevelt, as usual in the Big Three meetings, tried to mediate and agreed to general numbers, which were to be cemented later.

Many writers who have examined the impact of Roosevelt's health on his decisions at Yalta agree that his performance did not appear to be significantly impaired, given the political and military cards that he held at the time. His positions and decisions remained consistent with earlier positions he had held, and he was able to attain important concessions from the Soviets in the areas he cared about most, the United Nations and the war against Japan in the Pacific.

Sometimes people who suffer from transient and intermittent illness, such as Roosevelt did with encephalopathy, can rally when the situation demands it for relatively short periods of time. It appears that Roosevelt managed this sort of rally for most, if not all, of the critical meetings during the Yalta conference. Once the conference finished, however, Roosevelt began a more consistent and increasing decline. During the voyage back from Yalta, Roosevelt's close friend and adviser "Pa" Watson died. All reports indicate that Roosevelt took this death very hard, and Watson's loss made him sad and depressed. He apparently spent long hours by himself, staring out to sea. In making his speech to Congress concerning the conference, he remained seated, and for once he made reference to the uncomfortable weight of his leg braces in public: "I hope you will pardon me for the unusual posture of sitting down during the presentation of what I have to say, but I know you will realize it makes it a lot easier for me in not having to carry about ten pounds of steel around the bottom of my legs."[91] Close advisers who watched this presentation seemed universally horrified at his performance, which they felt uncharacteristically wandered into the tangential too often and for too long. However, by the time of his last press conference in March, before leaving on his final trip to Warm Springs, Georgia, many felt his performance seemed his best ever, again speaking to the intermittent nature of the effect of hypertensive heart disease on cognition.

Reelection

Although the bulk of this book is dedicated to an examination of the impact of illness on foreign policy decision making, in Roosevelt's case there are two sets of interrelated decisions that, although primarily domestic in nature, held enormous consequences for the future development of American foreign policy. These included Roosevelt's unprecedented decision to run for a fourth term as president and the Democratic Party imposition of Harry Truman as his running mate.

Various indications exist as to whether Roosevelt really wanted to run for a fourth term. Medically, he probably should not have run even for his third term. But leaving that issue aside, several people, including his doctor, Bruenn, believed that Roosevelt did not actually want to run for office a fourth time, but did not feel that he, or the country, had a choice. When interviewed in 1990, Bruenn summarized:

> I remember when the pressure was put on him to run for the fourth term. All those people around him depended on him for their jobs, for their reputations, everything. I'm not only talking about the secretaries but such people as Steve Early, the press secretary, everybody. The president was the center pole, no question about it. Hannegan, who was then Chairman of the Democratic National Committee, wanted the President to run. They all wanted him to run. And he wasn't particularly anxious to run.... He felt he had done his job. Not quite, that's true. He felt he had to complete the job but he knew he wasn't a 21-year-old either.... It took a certain amount of persuasion to convince him to run. It wasn't a "I want to be President for another 4 years" sort of thing.[92]

When asked who else might have run in his place, Bruenn responded that "there was nobody." Interestingly, even knowing better than anyone else the severity of Roosevelt's illness, Bruenn claimed that he would have supported Roosevelt's run, had he been asked:

> Should he or should he not have run for the fourth term? And I must say, in all honesty, if I had been asked what my opinion or judgment was, I would have been greatly swayed by the circumstances. Here we were in the middle of a great war which had been conducted fortunately or unfortunately on an almost personal basis between Stalin, Churchill and Roosevelt. I can say unquestionably that when Truman came in after the President's death, he had seen the President twice and knew nothing about what was going on. The President had a personal relationship with these others and I thought that was damn important.[93]

Others, such as Ferrell, insist that Roosevelt wanted to be president. According to Ferrell, the presidency represented a powerful convenience to Roosevelt, who was not an inordinately rich man (he had put two-thirds of his personal wealth into buying and developing the Warm Springs Foundation) and he needed a great deal of physical help to get through the day. As with Wilson, the office of the presidency offered a great deal of institutional and medical support for Roosevelt. Due to his estrangement from his wife and most of his children, except for Anna, who saw herself as a latter day Edith Bolling Galt Wilson, Roosevelt's life had little meaning or companionship outside politics. From this perspective, Roosevelt had every reason to run for a fourth term, especially given that he may have also felt he had a job to finish in ending the war, and making the peace, that no one else could accomplish as well, even given his physical limitations. Unusually, in this case, reality more than narcissism proved the culprit in such grandiosity. His wife, Eleanor, seemed to share this perspective as well. She indicated that, as long as he did what his doctor told him to do, "he could stand going on with his work."[94]

Of course, the question of whether Roosevelt wanted to run is different from the question of whether he should have run. His son James apparently never accepted the fact that Roosevelt's doctors allowed him to run for a fourth term, given how bad his health was at the time. He wrote, "I have never been reconciled to the fact that Father's physicians did not flatly forbid him to run."[95] He also claimed that "the fourth-term race in 1944 was my father's death warrant.... I realized with awful irrevocable certainty that we were going to lose him."[96]

But run Roosevelt did, and he won. He was nominated by the Democratic National Convention that was held in Chicago in the summer of 1944. Roosevelt went through on the train on his way to Hawaii via San Diego. He never got out of the train in Chicago, and he gave his acceptance speech from the train in San Diego. The pictures of his acceptance speech, along with rumors of his ill health, prompted his handlers to organize several campaign appearances throughout the country. The experience in New York was the most harrowing. Roosevelt rode in an open car through pouring rain waving at his constituents for more than four hours. Along the way, Roosevelt's car would pull into previously appointed heated garages where "Secret Service agents quickly lifted (him) from the car and stretched him out full length in blankets on the floor. They removed his clothes down to the skin. He was towelled dry and given a rub down. He was redressed in dry clothes, brandy was poured down his throat and he was lifted back into the car."[97]

In November, he won the election by the smallest of his four margins. His inauguration took place on the south portico of the White House and he gave the shortest inauguration address in history. He looked horrible. Woodrow Wilson's widow commented to Secretary of Labor Frances Perkins, "He looks exactly as my husband did when he went into his decline." Perkins admonished her, "Don't say that to another soul. He has a great and terrible job to do, and he's got to do it, even if it kills him."[98] Perkins herself had tried to quit, but been admonished by Roosevelt, "No, Frances, You can't go now. You mustn't put this on me now. I just can't be bothered now. I can't think of anyone else and I can't get used to anyone else. Not now! Do stay there and don't say anything. You are all right."[99] The campaign took a great deal out of Roosevelt, according to Secretary of State Stettinius: "I was concerned about the President ever since his inaugural address on the porch of the White House on January 20. That day he seemed to tremble all over. It was not just his hands that shook, but his whole body as well. . . . It seemed to me that some kind of deterioration in the President's health had taken place between the middle of December and the inauguration on January 20."[100] John Gunther concurred, "I was terrified when I saw the President's face. I felt certain he was going to die. . . . It was gray, gaunt and sagging, and the muscles controlling the lips seemed to have lost part of their function."[101]

Roosevelt positioned himself at the center of many issues in ways that meant that no one else had a complete picture of any particular strategy, issue, or event. Although he was working only a few hours a day, he had spent years developing working relationships with powerful leaders like Stalin and Churchill, and working on issues related to the conduct of the war. Was Roosevelt in 1944 as skilled and effective as Roosevelt in 1932? Absolutely not. Was four hours a day of Roosevelt in 1944 better than sixteen hours a day of Thomas Dewey might have been? This remains a harder call. Perhaps, perhaps not.

The complicating factor, of course, lay in Roosevelt's lack of interest in his vice president Harry Truman. As Bruenn notes, Roosevelt met with Truman only twice, and he told him virtually nothing about the running of the government, or the secret deals he had made with Churchill and Stalin about the postwar world. Roosevelt's 1940 running mate had been Henry Wallace, and Wallace believed that he would run again on the ticket in 1944. But Democratic party bosses, aware of Roosevelt's health problems and concerned that Roosevelt might not live through another term, did not feel that Wallace would make an appropriate president and threw their support behind Truman, without telling Roosevelt. Roosevelt himself equivocated, telling both Wallace and a White House assistant, former Senator James Byrnes of South Carolina, that he would support their candidacy for the vice presidency prior to the convention. Roosevelt continued to go back and forth, feeling that Byrnes was too ambitious, but knowing that Party leaders found Wallace too left wing. Party leaders made sure that Roosevelt got an earful about Wallace's limitations prior to the convention. Both men wanted the nomination because they believed that Roosevelt would not live out the next term; both saw the nomination as a short stepping-stone to the presidency itself. Roosevelt vacillated in his support right through the early days of the convention. Maybe partly due to his illness, he seemed not to be able to make up his mind. As a result, powerful Democratic leaders managed to orchestrate an overthrow of Wallace in favor of Truman.

When Roosevelt died, Truman came into power knowing virtually nothing about the running of the government, or foreign policy issues, aside from his own service in France during World War I. Many years later, in old age, Truman would tell writer Thomas Fleming about FDR: "He was the coldest man I ever met. He didn't give a damn personally for me or you or anyone else in the world as far as I could see. . . . But he was a great president. He brought this country into the twentieth century."[102] Truman's perception of Roosevelt's attitude toward him was right; Roosevelt did not care about him enough to even dislike him. And Roosevelt's failure to adequately inform Truman about the job made everything about the postwar transition much harder. As Ferrell writes, "Government under Roosevelt was so personal that only the nation's chief executive knew how it worked; Truman needed tutelage on how to deal with different constituencies and different advocates."[103] But Roosevelt never gave him any.

Ferrell suggests that part of the reason Roosevelt engaged in risky politics regarding his vice-presidential running mate was not merely that he was ill and disengaged, but also that he really believed that it did not matter because he would live out his fourth term. After all, he had lived with a chronic illness like polio without serious incident for years. He had a habit of denial when it came to personal illness; he believed, and knew from experience, that will power could overcome disability. Perhaps the most insightful analysis on this point comes from Richard Nixon: "But entering into this was Roosevelt's personality, his deep-set conviction that he was the whole cheese. He was, let's face it. This bolsters what I said previously, that I don't believe that it *ever* occurred to Roosevelt that he would die. He had been in the White House twelve years, and I suppose he figured he would have a fifth term. It never occurred to him that anybody else would be president."[104]

McIntire had specifically enjoined Commander Bruenn from informing Roosevelt or his family of the gravity of his health problems. Regardless of the reason, Roosevelt's failure to play a more active role in the determination of his vice-presidential running mate meant that he abrogated his responsibility in favor of party officials whose primary interests may not have been providing the most qualified candidate. Roosevelt similarly abdicated his responsibility in failing to prepare Truman adequately for the enormous job that faced him upon Roosevelt's death.

CONCLUSIONS

Roosevelt's medical condition and its impact on his decision making provides a very complex set of examples concerning the ways in which illness does, and does not, impact behavior in a meaningful way.

Roosevelt's early victimization by polio did not impair his cognitive functions but did set up a pattern for dealing with illness that remained with him the rest of his life. He would not accept failure, he denied the ability of illness to impact his behavior, he stayed positive, and he kept working. These habits and talents carried over into his response to the much more critical cardiovascular illness that affected him later in his life.

Beginning as early as 1937, Roosevelt began to suffer from high blood pressure. His condition was exacerbated by the fact that his paralysis discouraged him from serious cardiovascular exercise, and he sustained a heavy smoking habit through at least 1944. Over time, Roosevelt's medical condition worsened, and by 1944 he was diagnosed with hypertension and congestive heart failure. Along with his previously diagnosed anemia, and his likely chronic obstructive pulmonary disease from years of smoking, Roosevelt seems to have developed a case of secondary metabolic encephalopathy, characterized by intermittent periods of clouded consciousness, including periods of time when he would seem to fall asleep, gaze absently with his mouth open, and fail to remember certain activities and behaviors, including important events.

Because this condition manifested intermittently, it did not impact all his decisions and actions. Most notably, it appears not to have affected Roosevelt's performance at Yalta, the conference that many point to as a clear example of Roosevelt's failure to assert his will against Stalin. Instead, Roosevelt managed to secure the two things he cared about most: Soviet agreement to the United Nations and its future cooperation in the war against Japan. Other areas in which he failed to exert more influence over Stalin, including issues related to Germany and Poland, were precluded by a military situation that clearly favored Soviet forces in those regions.

However, there do appear to be several areas in which Roosevelt's medical condition did exert a negative impact on his decisions. His quick reversal and brief consideration of the campaign against Japan in Hawaii in July of 1944 provides one example where Roosevelt's fatigue, lack of engagement, and inability to focus and concentrate appears to have led him to support a campaign in the Philippines that later proved disastrously bloody. Perhaps a similar campaign against Japan through Formosa would have been equally bloody, but the decision deserved more consideration than two hours, especially when one of the principal players, General MacArthur, held a vested personal interest in the position he advocated, and Roosevelt had previously favored Nimitz's alternative approach.

Similarly, Roosevelt appears to have paid insufficient attention to the postwar plan for Germany at the Québec conference, where he endorsed the ill-fated Morgenthau plan to dismember and deindustrialize Germany after the war. Without consulting his advisers in the State Department or elsewhere, Roosevelt supported the plan offered by his friend Treasury Secretary Morgenthau to seek revenge against Germany, as well as to prevent a future German rise to power, threatening peace once again. When Churchill opposed the plan, Roosevelt bribed him into compliance. Once Roosevelt became aware of the opposition engendered by the plan within his own administration and the more general American public, he backed off, claiming that he did not even remember signing the memo at Québec. Had the plan been implemented, it would have been a disaster, wreaking havoc on European economic reconstruction in general and sowing the seeds of German discontent. Obviously, this error did not prove as consequential because Roosevelt was able to reverse it upon consultation with other government officials before it caused any real damage.

Finally, Roosevelt seems to have disengaged from the political decisions surrounding the nomination of his vice-presidential running mate in 1944. In addition, he never took the time or showed any interest in informing Truman about the workings of the American government or the foreign policy deals that he had conducted while president.

Two important points deserve reiteration at this point. First, Roosevelt suffered greatly at the hands of incompetent medical care under the treatment of Admiral Ross McIntire. An ambitious man who believed that the president's health should be kept secret even from the man himself, he neither recognized nor treated Roosevelt's high blood pressure as it emerged. Had Anna not insisted that a specialist be consulted after Roosevelt failed to recover following his trip to Tehran in late 1943, it is highly likely that Roosevelt would not have lived through the end of 1944. Once McIntire was forced to bring Bruenn in on the case, Roosevelt received what little expert care was available at the time. Digitalis, weight loss, smoking reduction, and rest clearly added to the length of his life. How much longer he might have lived had Bruenn been brought into the case sooner can never be known, but it might well have been months to even a year. Had modern medicines been available at the time to control Roosevelt's blood pressure, he might have lived even longer. Sadly, McIntire was never held accountable for his malpractice and incompetence. No evidence of his mistakes exists, because McIntire himself probably destroyed Roosevelt's medical records.

Second, the true impact of Roosevelt's illness on the conduct of American foreign policy lay in his premature death. Because Roosevelt was not around to follow through on the agreements made at Yalta and elsewhere, it can never be known how things might have turned out differently had he lived. He possessed much more experience in foreign policy and a much greater historical legacy with Stalin than his successor, Truman. Roosevelt's mantle of personal power, especially his personal relationship with Stalin, may have simply been too great a burden for Truman, or anyone else, to bear successfully, but he did not even try to pass along the legacy of his experience or understanding of the war or other leaders to his successor. Truman, for example, was not even made aware of the Manhattan Project's attempt to build an atomic bomb. Thus, in many ways, the deepest impact of Roosevelt's illness on his policy resulted from his inability to follow through on many of his plans and designs for the postwar world.

Had Roosevelt not been ill, the course of the military campaign in the Pacific might not have been as lengthy or as bloody. Others have argued that he might have even been able to prevent or lessen subsequent American involvement in Korea or Vietnam. The mistake Roosevelt almost made by originally endorsing the Morgenthau plan was overturned before it could do permanent damage. But Truman in many ways was not a worthy successor to Roosevelt in the realm of foreign policy, and Roosevelt's illness and his resultant lack of attention, interest, and awareness must be held at least partly responsible for the quick evolution into the Cold War which followed the end of the Second World War. But primarily, Roosevelt's illness caused his death, and his death left the biggest gap and the most harm in the immediate months and years after April 1945.

FIVE

ADDICTED TO POWER:
JOHN F. KENNEDY

Most people maintain two lingering images of President John F. Kennedy. One recalls a man who embodied tremendous youth, vigor, vibrance, intellectual acuity, and physical activity, always playing football or sailing; the second surrounds Jackie in her perfect pink suit crawling out of the back of the convertible in Dallas after Kennedy was shot in the head. These contrasting pictures reveal the dual reality of Kennedy's entire political life: that of a very sick man wrapped in images of youth, health, and vigor. In Kennedy's case, the robust image could hardly have been more divorced from reality. Ironically, although he was the youngest man ever to be elected president of the United States, he was in fact one of the sickest men to hold the office, thus exemplifying that youth often offers no protection from the ravages of illness. In reality, Kennedy's physical limitations, and his perseverance in the face of them, made him simultaneously the strongest and the most fragile of men.

The nature of Kennedy's health problems was even more complicated than Wilson's or Roosevelt's disabilities. Kennedy provides an instructive example of someone who was impaired by both illness and addiction. Three prominent issues deserve consideration in any investigation into Kennedy's life, health, and political behavior: his debilitating back problem; his Addison's disease; and, perhaps in response to the first two, his heavy reliance on medication, including steroids and amphetamines.

Above and beyond these concerns, Kennedy was a man who lived in extreme and often unrelieved physical pain, and he went to great lengths to hide this fact from the public. His brother Robert wrote in his memoir of Jack, *As We Remember Him*, that:

> At least one half of the days that he spent on this earth were days of intense physical pain. He had scarlet fever when he was very young and serious back pain when he was older. In between he had almost every conceivable ailment. When we were growing up together, we used to laugh about the great risk a mosquito took in biting Jack Kennedy – with some of his blood the mosquito was almost sure to die....I never heard him complain....Those who knew him well would know he was suffering only because his face was a little whiter, the lines around this eyes were a little deeper, his words a little sharper. Those who did not know him well detected nothing.[1]

As this comment from his brother suggests, Kennedy took literal pains to hide his disability from the public and those around him and had a great deal of experience with handling and hiding his physical illness and suffering. He had been plagued with a wide variety of illnesses and complaints in his younger years, as well as during his years in office. Aside from myriad childhood illnesses, he had suffered more enduring medical problems as well, including severe allergies, malaria, hypothyroidism, and Addison's disease.

Most of Kennedy's more serious health concerns derived from one of his two main chronic conditions, Addison's disease and his bad back. These problems were eventually managed, but, as is so often the case with serious chronic illness, the treatments themselves impaired Kennedy's subsequent health and behavior. The medications he took to stabilize his conditions caused their own independent side effects. The now-standard life-saving treatment for Addison's disease involved high maintenance doses of steroids. At least for some period of time while he was president, he also received procaine injections into his back. In addition, Kennedy often appeared to follow one legitimate medical regimen, while simultaneously availing himself of additional treatments at the hands of Dr. Max Jacobson, a German Jewish refugee known to the Manhattan elite circles as "Dr. Feelgood." Jacobson administered amphetamine and steroid injections; patients, typically unaware of the ingredients, felt happier and more energized, at least in the short term. However, in the long term, Jacobson created addicts, making people dependent on his services and his drugs.

Steroids and amphetamine use both have documented effects on an individual's ideation, motivation, and behavior. In Kennedy's case, the crucial question remains whether his medical conditions in general or his medications in particular affected his decision making in negative ways. Historians and others have examined this question with regard to Kennedy's decisions surrounding the Bay of Pigs debacle, his behavior at the 1961

Vienna Conference with Khrushchev, and his actions during the Cuban Missile Crisis.

This chapter concentrates on Kennedy's meeting with Khrushchev in Vienna subsequent to the Bay of Pigs incident and prior to the Cuban Missile Crisis. Most historians argue against a linkage of Kennedy's behavior during this crucial meeting to his illness and medication.[2] However, this analysis runs oddly contrary to Kennedy's own assessment of his performance at the time, not to mention that of his senior advisers, including former ambassador to the Soviet Union George Kennan. Medically, this time period is critical because the Vienna conference, unlike the Bay of Pigs, came after Kennedy had discovered Jacobson but before Jacobson was banished from the White House by Dr. Hans Kraus. Jacobson no longer visited the White House by the time of the Cuban Missile Crisis. Although Dr. Jacobson is listed in the White House record of injections kept by Dr. George Burkley in 1962–1963, no visits are recorded by him, although visits by Dr. Kraus and others are meticulously documented therein.[3] An additional interesting question revolves around not only what happened at the Vienna conference itself but also what might have happened had Kennedy not been so concerned with hiding his debilitating illness from public view. The true counterfactual question, though, is what Kennedy would have been like as a leader had he not been ill, and what might have happened in his presidency if he had not been so heavily medicated.

The discussion that follows is informed by careful consideration of the recently opened medical files at the John F. Kennedy Presidential Library.[4]

ILLNESS

From childhood, Kennedy frequently suffered from a wide range of often very serious illnesses. In the Kennedy family, Joseph Jr. was deemed the heir apparent. Joe, the golden boy, appeared strong and extroverted, ready and eager to claim his rightful political destiny. By contrast, John remained sickly, frail, and comparatively withdrawn. As a child, he seemed to catch every illness that circulated, contracting a near-fatal case of scarlet fever before the age of three, which required a two-month stay in the hospital.[5] He later caught measles and German measles, whooping cough, chicken pox, and diphtheria. At various points, he came down with bronchitis and pneumonia as well. He had his appendix removed in 1931 and later his tonsils and adenoids. In addition, he always suffered from bad allergies, asthma, and problems with his stomach. He was especially allergic to dogs and horses.[6] As his mother, Rose, later recalled,

> Even when he was laid out flat in bed from some new accident or disease, with his face thin and his freckles standing out against the pallor of his skin,

he could always smile or grin about his own bad luck, as if he had been victimized once again by some absurd joke that he should have been on guard against. He went along for many years thinking to himself – or at least trying to make others think – that he was a strong, robust, quite healthy person who just happened to be sick a good deal of the time.[7]

Only after Joe was shot down and killed over the English Channel during the Second World War did his father's political expectations and aspirations for John emerge. At this point, given his father Joe's high expectations, it became truly necessary for John to rise to the occasion and do his best to overcome his physical weaknesses in service of his own, and his father's, political ambitions.

Back Problems

At various stages of his political career, Kennedy blamed his back pain on either a football injury sustained while playing at Harvard or, later, as the result of a war injury that he endured when his PT-109 boat was chopped in half by a Japanese destroyer during World War II. At that time, Kennedy swam in the ocean for more than ten hours, while holding another man whom he rescued from the boat. He then had to survive without food or water for five or six days on an enemy island before finally being rescued. The myths about the origins of his back pain were perpetuated not only to hide his underlying medical infirmities but also to simultaneously project an image of health, vigor, courage, and sacrifice to the nation. Ironically, these myths served to hide the more remarkable accomplishment, for Kennedy's lifelong battles with chronic pain and illness were what adequately prepared him to survive his siege at sea. While most men in this situation would have easily given up, the pain Kennedy endured during those days may have felt like little more to him than what he dealt with every day; he was no more likely to give in to the pain in the Pacific than he was in Cambridge.

For their biography, *The Search for JFK*, Joan and Clay Blair interviewed Dr. Elmer Bartels, the physician who treated Kennedy for Addison's disease at the Lahey Clinic in Boston. Bartels came to care for Kennedy after his most severe Addisonian crisis and subsequent diagnosis in 1947. Dr. Bartels stated that Kennedy was born with a congenital deformity that caused the lifelong back pain. Kennedy's personal physician, Dr. Janet Travell, admitted in her oral history that Kennedy was born with the left side of his body significantly smaller than the right side. As a result of this structural abnormality, the discrepancy in the pressure on his spine when he walked led to his severe and sustained back pain. To help alleviate this problem, Travell offered several treatments. First, she had Kennedy wear a lift in his left shoe about three-eighths of an inch thick. She started with a quarter-inch lift and had to add more height later on. In addition, she encouraged him to wear a back brace. Another therapy began by chance. On the first day Kennedy visited her office, he sat in a rocking chair in her waiting room and discovered the furnishing that would become emblematic of his presidency. Rocking chairs offered a great deal more comfort for his back problem than ordinary ones. Finally, Travell offered a more unconventional and even dangerous treatment involving injection of procaine into Kennedy's back to alleviate his pain. Kennedy experienced immediate relief from these treatments, but they did nothing to address the underlying cause of his back problem. As soon as the drug wore off, he needed another injection. However, the real medical risk of this treatment lies in the injections themselves. Travell injected the procaine into Kennedy's spine.[8] But any injection in this area that accidentally hits the wrong place can cause either temporary or permanent paralysis. In this case, Kennedy was lucky not to have had this happen to him, given how many injections he received almost every day for several years.

Kennedy's back problems should have prevented him from military service altogether. He failed the physical for the army outright and would have been rejected from the navy as well if not for the machinations of his powerful father, who managed to prevent navy physicians from seeing Jack's entire medical record. The navy's high casualty rate in the war in the Pacific forced it to accept individuals they might have otherwise rejected on medical grounds.[9] When Kennedy volunteered for duty on the PT boats, the navy was so desperate for commanders of these craft that it did not even require a physical. Kennedy's medical surveys from the U.S. Naval Hospital in Chelsea reveal a long-standing and chronic problem with back pain. In addition, they also report persistent problems relating to gastrointestinal troubles, including an inability to gain weight. This second set of troubles comprises classic Addisonian symptoms and may have represented early stages in Kennedy's adrenal insufficiency. Kennedy's stomach troubles eventually led to his ultimate discharge from the navy on February 15, 1945, stating that he "is incapacitated for active service in the Naval Reserve by reason of colitis, chronic; that the incapacity for naval service is permanent."[10]

Kennedy's medical record during his relatively brief stint in the navy of two years and ten months is quite lengthy. Found physically fit for active duty on October 23, 1941, Kennedy was admitted to the hospital in South Carolina in April 1942 with "dislocation, chronic, recurrent (sacroiliac)." Kennedy indicated that his bad back had begun causing problems in earnest in 1940, following a tennis match at Harvard. Asked about his general history, Kennedy claimed that his "general health has always been good" and attributed his bad back to a football injury sustained while playing at Harvard. Only his appendectomy in 1932 is reported as abnormal. In May 1942 he was readmitted to the hospital with the same back complaint. At this time, Kennedy was upset that he had not received sea duty and wanted to do what he could to get cleared for such duty. Kennedy was given some exercises, and his back improved. His diagnosis was changed to "Strain, muscular, lower back" on June 15, 1942, and he was discharged for sea duty and given command of his own PT boat in the Pacific on June 23, 1942.[11]

Kennedy's stomach complaints started early and persisted as well. These are important because early Addison's disease often presents as a cluster of gastrointestinal problems. Yet these early warning signs seemed to have been missed by the medical personnel who examined him. In early 1943 he was admitted to the hospital with acute gastroenteritis. At that time, his blood pressure was a relatively low 90/60, which can again be seen as indicative of early adrenal failure.

In the medical report issued by the navy on October 16, 1944, the evaluating doctors indicated that Kennedy had been admitted to the hospital on June 11, 1944, following a fall on board his ship on August 1, 1943. This fall had produced back pain. No mention is made of the intervening ten months between the accident and the treatment, although it is possible that medical reports from this period are missing. In May 1944 the unusual step was taken of giving Kennedy leave to obtain service at the Lahey Clinic and not at a naval hospital. At the Lahey Clinic in Boston, his doctors found a herniation of his fifth lumbar intervertebral disc. Following this discovery, Dr. James Poppen performed surgery on June 23, 1944, in which some soft disc material in the interspace area was removed.[12] From Kennedy's perspective, this surgery did not seem to help his pain at all.

While at the Lahey Clinic, Kennedy was also examined by Dr. Sara Jordan for his gastrointestinal problems. After she took x-rays and conducted other tests, she found significant spasm in the duodenum and colon. She also found a "lipping of the base of the cap which was suggestive of a duodenal ulcer scar," though no evidence of an ulcer. She put Kennedy on antispasmodic medicine.

Kennedy returned to active duty on August 4, 1944, with continued pain in both his back and his abdomen. The navy report characterized Kennedy's condition at the time as follows: "The neurosurgeon at the hospital did not feel that the operation had corrected the condition and that some other cause might underlie the neuritis of the left sciatic nerve. . . . Review of the films from the Lahey clinic by the roentgenologist here failed to reveal any definite abnormality in the G. I. tract."[13]

Kennedy was again admitted to the hospital in Miami, Florida, on November 25, 1944, with chronic colitis. Following this admission, Kennedy was recommended for the Naval Retiring Board. Kennedy chose not to appear in person at that hearing.

By December 6, Kennedy's condition had not improved much, and he was readmitted to the hospital with chronic colitis. At that time, the military report of medical survey indicated that Kennedy had had an attack of malaria, benign, tertian, while at the Lahey Clinic during the earlier visit, something not indicated on the earlier report. This report states that Kennedy's back pain had improved, but that the pain on his lower left side had not remitted. Moreover, Kennedy dated the appearance of this stomach pain to his incident in the Pacific when the Japanese ship cut his PT-109 boat in half. According to this report, Kennedy spent more than 50 hours in the water at that time, although earlier reports indicate he spent 10 hours in the water. Further, this pain was sufficiently different from similar pain he had experienced in 1938, when he was diagnosed with "severe spastic colitis," meaning that his current chronic colitis would now be attributed to a service-related injury. This would ensure not only full retirement benefits for later treatment related to the condition but a more positive political attribution for subsequent limitations as well.

Kennedy's continuing back pain required two different surgeries. The first, already noted, took place in 1944, following his return from the war in the Pacific, before he was diagnosed with Addison's disease. By all accounts, that surgery was not successful: it did not alleviate his pain and left him very depressed. His condition continued to deteriorate. By 1954 Kennedy's fourth lumbar vertebra had narrowed, his fifth had collapsed, and he had compression fractures elsewhere in his lower spine.[14] He had difficulty walking and increasingly had to rely on crutches to get around. So in 1955 he underwent another, more successful, surgery to fuse his lumbosacral and sacroiliac vertebrae. His mother, Rose, later said that "Jack was determined to have the operation. He told his father that even if the risks were fifty-fifty, he would rather be dead than spend the rest of his life hobbling on crutches and paralyzed by pain."[15]

This surgery was much more serious because of the intervening onset of Addison's disease. Before Kennedy's time, few Addison's patients could be operated on for fear of subsequent infection; their bodies proved unable to resist infection because of their inability to marshal the necessarily output of stress hormones from the adrenal glands. As a result, most Addison's patients would die either during or just after surgery from shock or infection. Most doctors advised Kennedy against a second surgery, but Kennedy convinced Dr. Philip Wilson and Dr. Ephraim Shorr to undertake the challenge. By providing Kennedy with high doses of hydrocortisone immediately before and during surgery, they performed the operation without Kennedy dying on the table. However, Kennedy immediately contracted a major staph infection. Doctors administered high doses of steroids and antibiotics. He was administered the last rites of the Catholic Church and almost died. In an oral history, Arthur Krock of the *New York Times* noted that Kennedy's father, Joe, showed up at his office and wept openly, admitting that he was afraid Jack was going to die. At the last minute, one of the antibiotics began to work and Kennedy survived. But he survived with a gaping, open wound in his back that Dr. Travell said lasted from 1954 until 1957.

Kennedy spent two months in the hospital and was admitted twice more in the following months for another surgery to remove the metal plate that had been implanted during the original surgery and for other follow-up treatments. Doctors believed that staph had harbored in the metal plate that had been inserted into Kennedy's back and was likely the source of his infection. It was during the long recovery from this surgery that Kennedy wrote his Pulitzer Prize–winning book, *Profiles in Courage.*

Kennedy's ultimately successful surgery was so novel that Wilson wrote up the results in the *American Medical Association Archives of Surgery* in 1955. Though not identified by name, the patient referred to in the article about the management of adrenal insufficiency during surgery is clearly Kennedy. The article refers to a thirty-seven-year-old man who had the same surgery as Kennedy on the same date at the same hospital by the same doctor. Kennedy's surgery represented a genuine medical breakthrough in the surgical treatment of Addison patients:

> A man of 37 years of age had Addison's disease for seven years. He has been managed fairly successfully for several years on a program of desoxycortico-sterone acetate (DOCA) pellets of 150 mg. implanted every three months and cortisone in doses of 25 mg. daily orally. Owing to a back injury, he had a great deal of back pain which interfered with his daily routine. Orthopedic consultation suggested that he might be helped by a lumbosacral fusion together with a sacroiliac fusion. Because of the severe degree of trauma involved in these operations and because of the patient's adrenocortical insufficiency due to Addison's disease, it seemed dangerous to proceed with these operations. However, since this young man would become incapacitated without surgical intervention, it was decided, reluctantly, to perform the operations by doing the two different procedures at different times if necessary by having a team versed in endocrinology and surgical physiology help in the management of this patient before, during and after the operation.[16]

During this time, Kennedy had one of the highest rates of absenteeism in the Senate. His work there clearly suffered, and he sponsored no legislation. Most notably, Kennedy did not vote in the censure of Senator Joseph McCarthy. Many argue that Kennedy hid behind his illness in order not to take a stand on this important but controversial issue. Kennedy's failure to take a stand on this issue, despite what he later said about how he would have voted for the censure if he had been able, made many Democratic party stalwarts distrust Kennedy and his true motives through the time of the 1960 Democratic presidential nomination meetings.

Following the second surgery, which initially appeared unsuccessful because he remained in pain, Kennedy began to see his personal physician, Janet Travell. He first came to see her on May 26, 1955. He was brought by Dr. Shorr, who had been treating Kennedy for his Addison's disease. Kennedy came seeking help for pain in his back and his knee. She described his condition as follows: "He was thin, he was ill, his nutrition was poor, he was on crutches. There were two steps from the street into my office and he could hardly navigate these."[17] It was during this visit that he discovered the comfort of sitting in a rocking chair and later ordered one for the Oval Office. Through the use of vapocoolant therapy, she was able to achieve success in increasing Kennedy's range of motion in his knee within about fifteen or twenty minutes. From her office, he was admitted to New York Hospital for tests and treatments of his back pain. Travell began by giving Kennedy injections of procaine, a local anesthetic, into the trigger points along the spine, from which he achieved immediate, if temporary, relief. In addition to the danger of infection, such injections fail to provide any long-term solution, because they mask the pain only for short periods of time without really addressing the underlying causes, which should more appropriately be treated with an aggressive program of physical therapy. In addition, such injections raise the risk of reinjury, because it becomes possible to unduly strain muscles without being aware of it at the time due to the local analgesic effect of the drug. By the time Kennedy became president, he was receiving two to three shots a day from Travell.

Kennedy continued to have serious problems with infections at the site of his surgery for some time. The recently opened medical files show that Kennedy was admitted to the hospital between September 13 and October 1, 1957, for an incision and drainage of a lumbar abscess. The culture of this abscess showed a "very serious" hemolytic staphylococcus aureus, which was "resistant to penicillin, terramycin, and tetracycline." When he was discharged, Kennedy was released on a medication protocol of "erythromycin, 500 mg 3 × a day, microstatin 500,000 units 3 × a day, streptomycin, .5 IM 2 × week, meticorten 5 mg, 2 tablets a day, Florinef 1 mg two tablets in morning, methyl testosterone 25 mg a day." In addition, he was also treated with 5 milligrams of isoniazid for tuberculosis after two strong positive tuberculin tests.[18]

Robert Dallek suggests that Kennedy's back problem may have been precipitated by osteoporosis resulting from large doses of steroids, including DOCA, which Dallek indicates Kennedy may have taken as early as 1937 or 1938 as treatment for his colitis.[19] One possible problem with this speculation is that if Kennedy was taking steroids at this time, his stomach condition should have improved from the antiinflammatory effects provided by the steroids. But nothing in the record indicates that his condition improved; if anything, his colitis continued to trouble him until his proper

Addisonian diagnosis in 1947. While long-term or high levels of steroid use can cause bone degeneration, it would have been nearly impossible for Kennedy to get hold of sufficient steroids in the late 1930s and early 1940s to cause such a problem because they were simply not available, even to someone with a large amount of money. Steroid development remained in its infancy at this time, and the standard medical textbook, *Cecil's Handbook of Medicine* (1944), says that in early trials, DOCA, which was ingested orally at first, caused hypertension and cardiac failure and "was not generally available for general use."[20] DOCA came into common use only later, once its mode of ingestion had been adapted as pellets inserted into the thigh for slower, steadier rates of adsorption. More importantly, even if Kennedy were to have obtained some DOCA in the late 1930s, this compound represents a "mineral steroid" and not a "glucocortoid," such as cortisone or prednisone, and it is the latter, not the former, whose overuse causes osteoporosis. While Kennedy took such compounds later in life, they were not synthesized or widely used until the 1950s, so he would not have been able to take sufficient doses to cause osteoporosis before this time. Further, Robert Gilbert interviewed two of Kennedy's physicians at the Lahey Clinic, Charles Fager and Robert Wise, and both denied that Kennedy suffered from osteoporosis. Given that Travell and Burkley, Kennedy's doctors, provide consistent and reasonable explanations for Kennedy's back problem resulting from his congenital deformity, there is no reason to suppose that early steroid use caused a problem, especially given that such a large intake would have predated their general availability.

By the time that Kennedy entered the White House, the other White House physician, Admiral Burkley, a navy physician and head of the military support unit, observed Travell's treatment of Kennedy with disapproval and suspicion. He called in Dr. Hans Kraus, a physical therapy expert from New York, who subsequently came down from New York several times a week to treat Kennedy with an extensive program of exercises and physical therapy. Kennedy's father had had the White House pool area redecorated, and Kennedy took to swimming regularly as part of his new exercise regimen. Kennedy's back improved rapidly.

A great deal of byzantine internecine warfare developed between Dr. Travell and Drs. Burkley and Kraus in terms of the best treatment for Kennedy's back problem, among other things. Kennedy himself did not help matters, continuing to go behind Burkley's back to seek procaine injections from Travell, although much less frequently, until at least August 1963. However, Burkley and Kraus called a meeting in December 1961 with Travell and Kennedy and, in front of Kennedy, told Travell that her services were no longer needed, although she was kept on at the White House in service to Jacqueline Kennedy and their children. The cause of the dismissal surrounded Travell's extensive use of procaine injections to alleviate Kennedy's back pain. In Kraus's notes for January 1, 1962, he wrote: "I stated that I did not wish Inj. to be given without my approval as long as I was responsible for this phase of Rx. I wished to decide when or how many inj. to be given and give them myself. So stated in presence of K., Dr. T, Dr. B and Dr. W."[21] By February 3, 1962, Burkley's distrust of Travell became obvious in the following note, which he signed:

> [R]equested the medical records on X for the last 6 months. Dr. Travell said she would like to straighten them up before she gives them to me. I said that this was not necessary, but she said she would like to straighten them up.... Within the last few days, Dr. Travell has been inferring that all the recent improvements of X's condition is due to the fact that he is now getting gamma globulin and injections of vitamins.... Several days ago while discussing the chair for the helicopter a very obvious effort to cover information on the upper part of the sheet by covering it with an additional paper. Contents were not divulged to me.[22]

While Kennedy occasionally appeared to seek additional injections from Travell without Burkley's approval, he increasingly relied on Burkley as his back improved. But Burkley was continually required to mediate between Travell and Kraus. The degree of hostility between these doctors can be inferred from the note that Jacqueline Kennedy wrote to Burkley in August of 1963: "I have asked Dr. Travell to put suitable light bulbs and reading lights in all the places where the president and I read in the White House. So, please let's not get excited if you see her tip-toeing up to our floor in the elevator!"[23]

But the doctors' disagreements presented the potential for political fall-out as well, which is at least partly why Travell's White House employment was continued after her service to the president was terminated. In April 1962, for example, Travell gave Kennedy an injection that she believed Kraus approved because he did not "raise the roof" at the time. However, Kraus later told Burkley that he strongly disapproved of Travell's use of procaine because it slowed down the president's progress in physical therapy.[24] By the end of May 1963, the battle of the doctors had not abated despite the change in formal command. On May 29, 1963, following three injections over the previous three days, Burkley noted his concern about the political implications of Travell's actions and her disagreements with Dr. Kraus:

> [R]eceived a call from Dr. K[raus] at 5:30 p.m. And he stated that he had just received a call from Dr. Travell stating that X-1 [Jackie] was anxious to know if a nerve block would be beneficial in the treatment of X [Kennedy]. Dr. K stated that he would discuss the matter with X and not with X-1 or Dr. Travell. He also stated that he felt that it would not be beneficial. I spoke to him and then had him transferred to Mrs. L[incoln, Kennedy's personal secretary] who further transferred him to X and he informed X that he was

confident that this present distress would be relieved shortly and that a nerve block would not be beneficial and in fact might be detrimental. I talked further with Mrs. L and it is the impression that this is a planned procedure with ulterior motives behind it. I have arranged a talk with Mr. O'd[onnell] concerning the same angle. This could have drastic political implications if employed and made public. The possibility of a slip to the press suggesting that nerve blocks are to be done would have wide spread interest and would cause all kind of conjectures as to the fitness of X to have another term.[25]

Burkley's memo of January 10, 1963, concerning Travell's final dismissal from any control over Kennedy's medication is illuminating in this regard as well:

I went to Dr. Travell's office and gave her the report from yesterday. I then told her that the president had stated that I was to be in charge of his medication and that all consultants would clear through me. She made no statement and there was no change in her expression and no stop in her conversation. She simply stated that I had been giving penicillin on two occasions and that I had only given it for one day each and that was the best way for the organism to build up an immunity to the use of penicillin. I did not follow through to tell her that Dr. Taylor had used this technic [sic] on several occasions when there was only a question of whether a throat infection was present. . . . she then said she wanted to speak to Dr. Boles and talk with him so she would not get it third hand. . . . I again told her that the President's desire was that the treatment would be under my care and that consultants would consult through me. She again made no statement and had no change of expression. . . . Dr Boles requested specifically that Dr. Travell not be informed of his intended visit and that she was not to be informed of the enema being given. This will be complied with. Following the conversation, I spoke with Dr. Taylor regarding the use of penicillin that was given and he stated that in this particular case it had been felt advisable to give a preliminary injection as a prophylactic use rather than as treatment and that subsequent administration needed no further treatment. . . . Mr. O'Donnell asked me to contact Dr. Cohen with the view of checking on the possibility of placing Dr. Travell in another area.[26]

Kennedy received a truly phenomenal number of penicillin injections during his presidency. He received several injections a month, mostly at his request. Often the medical records state that there was no indication for treatment, but Kennedy would ask for it, and it would be administered. The physician who appeared most compliant with Kennedy's requests in this regard was Dr. Taylor, his ear, nose, and throat doctor. While Travell was correct that insufficient treatment with penicillin can produce organisms resistant to infection, Kennedy was often treated with one-time high-dose injections when it did not appear medically indicated for ear, nose, and throat complaints. Burkley's files contain a letter from Taylor on the date of his meeting with Travell justifying his use of penicillin in the president's case:

> First, single injections of penicillin. I want to emphasize that in my opinion the danger of developing resistant strains of organisms in this case is so slight that I feel it can be disregarded. Secondly, the possibility of the patient developing a sensitivity to penicillin must be considered.... While it is possible for anyone to develop a penicillin sensitivity, your patient has had large doses of penicillin in the past and has shown no signs of sensitivity. In addition, it is extremely important in that case that antibiotics be given early in order to prevent acute sinusitis or other complications from developing. If he feels that an infection is starting, I would never hesitate to use penicillin. If the infection does not develop, and symptoms subside, I would likewise not hesitate to discontinue this medication. We have done this on two well-documented occasions in the past and I see no reason to change this policy.[27]

Even in the late 1960s, few things besides strep and venereal disease were susceptible to penicillin. Given Kennedy's evident and persistent concern about urinary tract infections and other prostate problems, all without any evidence of venereal infection in the medical record, and given his documented sexual promiscuity, it seems possible that Kennedy requested penicillin prophylactically against his fear of infection with venereal disease. Dr. Travell, knowing this, offered a veiled threat to Burkley about what she knew about Kennedy's sexual activities once her own position was threatened, and this threat, once communicated to Kennedy's political adviser, Kenneth O'Donnell, assured her continued presence at the White House throughout the rest of Kennedy's presidency.

Thus, although Travell was cut off from direct care for Kennedy after this period, she continued to serve in the White House, helping Jackie Kennedy with the birth and care of her children. Though not a pediatrician or a gynecologist, Travell oversaw the tragic circumstances surrounding the premature birth and death of the Kennedys' youngest son, Patrick.

In retrospect, and in comparison to the previously closed files, Dr. Travell's oral history remains more revealing than Dr. Burkley's. She states that when she first admitted Kennedy to New York Hospital in 1955, she discovered that he suffered from hypothyroidism. She treated him with Cytomel, a thyroid medication, at a dose of twenty-five micrograms twice a day. She argued, correctly, that both thyroid and adrenal insufficiency can cause severe muscle spasms and that Kennedy's structural back pain could only have been greatly exacerbated by these conditions. She also found that Kennedy was extremely anemic, a characteristic of Addison's disease. This anemia did not result from iron deficiency, as it had in the case of Roosevelt, but rather from vitamin B deficiency. She treated this condition successfully with vitamin B injections. Finally, Dr. Travell called in

Dr. Paul de Gara to begin regular allergy injections for Kennedy, to reduce the impact of his allergies on his asthma and respiratory health. Kennedy's severe allergies, particularly to dog hair, required that special bedding and other materials be transported with him whenever he traveled.

Addison's Disease

Kennedy's second major health problem, Addison's disease, was the most serious of all his ailments. Although the records indicate that Kennedy probably did not have a proper diagnosis of the disease until he suffered a full-blown Addisonian crisis during his trip to England in 1947, at which time he almost died, the evidence suggests that he had ailments consistent with early signs of the illness since about the time he was thirteen.[28] While an Addisonian crisis is a genuinely life-threatening condition, it is not uncommon for the illness to have a long, insidious onset, and Kennedy may have experienced an earlier, undiagnosed Addisonian crisis. In 1946, he became very ill after participating in a "Bunker Hill" parade during the congressional races. Following that event, an aide recalled that he had looked yellow and blue and had collapsed. At that time, Kennedy almost died; he was given the last rites of the Catholic Church.[29]

Addison's disease was first documented in England by Dr. Thomas Addison in 1855, but it is believed to have existed before then. For example, Addison's appears to have been the illness that killed Jane Austen in the early 1800s. Addison originally described the progress of the disease as follows:

> The leading and characteristic features of the marked state to which I would direct attention are anemia, a general languor and disability, a remarkable feebleness of the heart's action, irritability of the stomach, and a peculiar change of color of the skin occurring in connection with the diseased condition....
>
> The patient ... has been observed gradually to fall off in general health; he becomes languid and weak, indisposed to either bodily or mental exertion; the appetite is impaired or entirely lost ... slight pain from time to time referred to in the region of the stomach....
>
> We discover a most remarkable, and ... characteristic discoloration taking place in the skin.... The body wastes ... the pulse becomes smaller and weaker, and ... the patient at length gradually sinks and expires.[30]

Before Kennedy, most people who suffered from this illness did not live very long. In the early days, Addison's most commonly resulted from tuberculosis which subsequently ravaged the adrenal gland. But the most common form now diagnosed appears to result from an autoimmune disorder which is possibly hereditary in nature. For example, Eunice Kennedy Shriver, Jack's sister, also suffers from the disorder.

The adrenal glands are two tiny glands that sit on top of each kidney and are crucial in the production of several hormones. They are composed of two separate parts. The inner portion, the medulla, produces epinephrine. The outer portion, or cortex, is the section affected by Addison's disease. This section produces three sets of hormones: testosterone, which in healthy males is mostly produced by the testes; aldosterone, the hormone that regulates blood pressure by signaling the kidneys to retain salt at appropriate levels; and cortisol, the main stress hormone.[31] When a patient dies of an Addisonian crisis, he most commonly dies because of the total collapse of the circulatory system due to low blood pressure. In the days before modern drugs, Addisonian patients were put on high-salt, low-potassium diets to help manage their condition, and Kennedy occasionally took salt tablets when under stress. In Addison's disease, the patient is eventually unable to produce any of these three hormones in the adrenals because of the destruction of the adrenal cortex.

The treatment of Addison's disease provides a remarkable study in the miracle of modern medical science. In 1944 the condition was considered invariably fatal in short course: "Addison's disease usually pursues a gradually downward course with striking remission and acute exacerbation that may attend the severity of a crisis. Crisis and death often follow stress and strain, overexertion, exposure, acute infection, surgical procedures or administration of purgatives...at most, a dozen patients have survived ten years." The prognosis "has always and should continue to be regarded as extremely grave...this holds true regardless of the excellent immediate reports from the use of salt or of cortical hormone. However, with better and more modern treatment the prognosis is improving and when adequate cortical extract is available, death from hormone insufficiency should be largely preventable." Interestingly, *Cecil's* considered "the psychic effects of treatment are often as profound as the physical."[32] By 1967 the picture had changed radically. Standard treatment with glucocortoid therapy had become essential for the restoration of a normal life-span in Addison's patients. The administration of this hormone improved appetite, body weight, vascular strength, and general feelings of well-being. *Cecil's Textbook of Medicine* recommended maintenance dosage of between twenty-five and fifty milligrams of cortisone a day with increased levels under conditions of great activity or stress. Mineral steroids such as DOCA or Florinef were also recommended. The use of supplemental androgens remained discretionary: "in the presence of normal testicular function, male patients with Addison's do not require androgen replacement therapy...patients vary in response to androgens. Some note an increased sense of well-being, increased libido or muscular strength; some notice no difference."[33]

While visiting Ireland in September 1947 with Pamela Churchill, Kennedy became violently ill, and weakness, nausea, and vomiting overcame

the young man. As Kennedy's condition worsened, he was flown to
London and admitted to the London Clinic, where he was diagnosed   h
as having an Addisonian crisis. One medical textbook describes it as
follows:

> In most cases, Addison's disease is insidious in its evolution, (and) adrenal
> destruction is a gradual process....
> When more than 90% of the adrenal cortex has been destroyed...the
> patient develops the clinical disease as it was seen by Addison. "Addisonian
> crisis" is the term applied to the patient whose hypotension progresses to
> shock, and, if untreated, death. Addisonian crisis is characterized by anorexia,
> vomiting, abdominal pain, apathy, confusion, and extreme weakness.[34]

In London, Kennedy was first diagnosed with Addison's by Dr. Daniel
Davis, Lord Beaverbrook's personal physician. Dr. Davis told Pamela
Churchill that Kennedy had less than a year to live.[35] At that time, Davis's
dire prediction rested on sound medical experience. As late as the 1920s,
more than 90 percent of Addison's patients died within five years of
diagnosis.[36] Once the idea of a high-salt diet was instituted, that number dropped slightly to 78 percent.

Fortunately for Kennedy, however, a brand new medical advance saved
his life and altered his still dim prospects for improvement. Once back in
Boston, Kennedy was treated by Lahey Clinic physician Dr. Elmer Bartels,
an endocrinologist. Dr. Bartels treated Kennedy with this new substance,
desoxycorticosterone (DOCA), a corticosteroid designed to help the body
maintain a proper salt balance. DOCA is an extract of adrenal cortex that
was synthesized by Dr. Swengle in the early 1940s. In other words, DOCA
replaced aldosterone in the body. This drug was administered as pellets
implanted into Kennedy's thigh and replaced every three months for life.
This treatment lengthened the lives of Addison's patients but still did not
replace the critical hormone cortisol. Later, Dr. Lewis Sarett, working for
Merck, developed a synthetic version of cortisone that was marketed by
1950; John Kennedy was one of the very first patients to receive this drug
as well. For the first time, patients could now expect to live a relatively
normal life-span.

There is no question that Kennedy knew that he had Addison's disease
by the time he returned to Boston and came under the care of Dr. Bartels.
Dr Bartels remembered:

> He was not in the crisis stage when he returned to Boston, as he'd been on
> active treatment....
> I'm sure that's the first time Jack knew he had Addison's disease. There are
> certain tests one does to confirm the diagnosis, although the clinical history
> is quite definite. So on the clinical grounds and laboratory studies, it was
> confirmed that that was the problem. Addison's disease.[37]

Despite maintenance doses of these essential synthetic drugs, however, additional stress can still place an Addison's patient in dire crisis if not enough additional cortisone is administered during times of physical or psychological stress or crisis. While on a trip to Okinawa with his brother Robert in 1952, Kennedy underwent a second Addisonian crisis and almost died, but in the end he was saved by extra doses of cortisone.

After the administration of these new steroid drugs, Kennedy's health started to improve rapidly, and for the first time pictures reveal that he was able to put on weight. Keeping weight on continued to prove a real problem for Kennedy for most of his life. He was often weighed twice a day, and his doctors usually temporarily increased his dosage of testosterone when his weight fell below 170. Typically, Addison's patients suffer depression, apathy, and fatigue, which remit with cortisone treatment. Someone on these drugs, at least at the early stages, would be expected to have mood effects including euphoria, exuberance, and newfound ambition. These effects can last months to years. It was around this time, for example, that Jack married Jacqueline Bouvier. Other considerations may have entered Kennedy's decision to marry, including political ambition and desire for children, but the timing of this event seems at least partly influenced by the addition of cortisone to his treatment. After all, although Jack had met Jackie a few times before 1950, he did not pursue her avidly until shortly after he started taking cortisone. In addition, his political ambition grew as well, and he decided to run for the Senate, after refusing to run for governor of Massachusetts the previous term.

Kennedy's Addison's disease was never made fully public during his lifetime. The only time it really broke into the open was during the Democratic National Convention in 1960. Kennedy, ironically, made some comments about the importance of having a young and vigorous leader as president. These statements came after eight years of Eisenhower's presidency, during which he had a heart attack, a stroke, and surgery for ileitis while in office. Interestingly, according to Nixon's doctor, John Lungren, Nixon asked about rumors he had heard that Kennedy suffered from Addison's disease. Lungren confirmed these rumors, citing "reliable sources" and explained the disease, its severity, and its treatment to Nixon, concluding with the statement that as long as Addison's was properly managed, all bodily and mental functions could operate adequately. According to Lungren, Nixon listened carefully to his discussion and then declared, "This is a personal subject and we will not use it in this campaign."[38] Given the close nature of this race, Nixon's refusal to turn Kennedy's illness to his own advantage seems remarkable, although he may have feared that such an attack might precipitate a public backlash against him. Dewey had also considered making an issue of Franklin Roosevelt's more widely recognized health problems in 1944 and decided not to do so.

Although Kennedy's comment was directed at the Republicans because of Eisenhower's age and previous health problems, Lyndon Johnson also took offense because of his previous heart attack. One of Johnson's advisers, India Edwards, along with John Connelly, revealed to the press that Kennedy had Addison's disease. The Kennedy camp, anticipating potential problems along this line, responded with a carefully worded statement by Dr. Travell and Dr. Cohen, another physician who had treated Kennedy, essentially denying that Kennedy suffered from "classical" Addison's disease. In her oral history, taken by Kennedy speechwriter Ted Sorensen, Travell mentions that originally Dr. Cohen did not want any part of writing this statement. After she persuaded him that it was part of his medical duty to his patient, Cohen agreed under the condition that he not be required to sign his name. With this agreement, the two doctors spent five or six hours carefully crafting this statement. When the campaign people demanded signatures to ensure credibility, Cohen signed the document under duress. Later, both Cohen's and Travell's offices were broken into, and medical records were disturbed. Kennedy's medical records were not kept in these offices and so nothing of his was taken, but the presumption remained that the break-ins were motivated by those who wanted medical information that could be used to damage Kennedy politically. Others have provided an alternative explanation for the break-ins. Dallek speculates that Nixon's people broke into Dr. Cohen's offices to find Kennedy's records because of the similarity between this event and the Watergate tactics, as well as the break-in at Daniel Ellsberg's psychiatrist's office in Los Angeles.[39] Obviously, Lungren contradicts this claim. If Lungren is telling the truth, there appears to be no reason for the break-in because Nixon already knew of Kennedy's condition and had decided not to use it.

The declaration concerning Kennedy's Addison's disease remained a masterful statement, brilliant in its double talk:

> In 1943, when the PT boat which he [JFK] commanded was blown up, he was subjected to extraordinarily severe stress in a terrific ordeal of swimming to rescue his men. This, together perhaps with his subsequent malaria, resulted in a depletion of adrenal function from which he is now rehabilitated.
>
> Concerning the question of Addison's disease, which has been raised. This disease was described by Thomas Addison in 1855 and is characterized by bluish discoloration of the mucous membranes of the mouth and permanent deep pigmentation or tanning of the skin. Pigmentation appears early and it is the most striking physical sign of the disease. Senator Kennedy has never had any abnormal pigmentation of the skin or mucous membranes; it would be readily visible.
>
> Senator Kennedy has tremendous physical stamina. He has above-average resistance to infections, such as influenza.[40]

Kennedy's tanned skin was readily visible. He often attributed it to summers on Cape Cod or winters in Florida, and his ironically healthy appearance helped him in the first televised debates against the pasty-looking Nixon. Robert Kennedy participated in crafting the final version of the doctor's statement that was released to the press:

> John F. Kennedy does not now nor has he ever had an ailment described classically as Addison's disease, which is a tuberculose destruction of the adrenal gland. Any statement to the contrary is malicious and false . . . in the postwar period, (he had) some mild adrenal insufficiency. This is not in any way a dangerous condition and it is possible that even this might have been corrected over the years since an ACTH (adrenocorticotropic) stimulation test for adrenal function was considered normal in December 1958. Doctors have stated that this condition he has had might well have arisen out of his wartime experiences of shock and continued malaria.[41]

Even in the 1966 oral history Travell gave after Kennedy's assassination, she argued that Kennedy never suffered from the "classical" form of Addison's disease and insisted on calling his condition one of "adrenal insufficiency" throughout. While it may have been technically true that Kennedy did not suffer from Addison's disease in a classical sense, he did have it nonetheless. "Classical," in the medical sense, at least, refers to the form of adrenal insufficiency that resulted from tuberculosis, the most common form seen by Thomas Addison in the 1850s. In 1944, *Cecil's Textbook of Medicine* indicated that about 10–20 percent of Addison's cases did not derive from tuberculosis and that four-fifths of the gland would need to be destroyed before the syndrome appears in a clinical sense.[42] Because Kennedy had never had tuberculosis, he thus did not have a "classical case." This hair-splitting, however, does not diminish the fact that Kennedy's life was dependent, day to day, on cortisone pills and DOCA pellets due to an autoimmune manifestation of Addison's.

Other aspects of the public statement were misleading as well. Kennedy's "rehabilitation" depended on the DOCA and cortisone that he took regularly. Further, such treatments would be expected to clear up the pigmentation characteristic of the disease, as well as induce greater than normal resistance to typical infectious agents. For her help in formulating this statement for the press, Travell was rewarded with the position of personal physician to the president when Kennedy was elected. This factor may also have contributed to her retention by the White House as Jackie's doctor after she was relieved of her duties as Kennedy's primary physician.

The statement to the press worked well on a number of levels. It reinforced the belief that whatever difficulties Kennedy might have, or continue to manifest, including his bad back, were attributable to his war injury, thus making the public feel compassion for him rather than scorn or fear. In addition, his injuries encouraged respect and admiration for his courage in the war. These attributions prompted the public to frame Kennedy's infirmities from the perspective of his heroism and sacrifice during the war. The statement also succeeded in reassuring the public that Kennedy was not really sick. Twice more, reporters accurately noted the connection between Kennedy and the Addison's patient mentioned in the 1955 medical journal. Once in 1961, the allegation went unnoticed. And once in 1967, Dr. John Nichols raised the issue in the *AMA Journal*, but again the topic failed to attract any additional interest, probably because Kennedy was already dead. Some did try to get more precise information on his adrenal glands from the autopsy report. Unusually, this information, standard in an autopsy, was omitted from Kennedy's. About a year after the autopsy report was released, the editor of the *New England Journal of Medicine* requested information about Kennedy's adrenals from Admiral Burkley. Burkley never responded to the inquiry.

Drugs

Because of his many and serious health problems, Kennedy required a certain amount of medication every day just to survive. In addition, Kennedy also availed himself of the unethical and unorthodox treatments of Dr. Max Jacobson, who gave Kennedy injections of steroids and amphetamines on a regular basis throughout his presidency.

Steroid Medication

Kennedy took a diverse array of medications. According to Travell's oral history, he took the following medication and vitamins every day: "vitamin C, some Cytomel, a little meticorten, hydrocortisone, a small dose of Florinef (nine-alpha-fluorohydrocotisone) and a tablet of calcium." In addition, Kennedy sometimes took some antispasmodics for his back pain. This regimen supplemented the DOCA pellets that were implanted in his thigh every three months. According to Sorensen, Kennedy "used more pills, potions, poultices, and other paraphernalia than would be found in a small dispensary."[43] When asked if Kennedy was concerned that he was too dependent on these drugs, Travell replied that "[t]hese are not drugs":

> If you add vitamins and some calcium – nutritional supplements – and hormone replacement – a little thyroid and the things his adrenals didn't make, to bring the level up to a physiological level, that is quite different from the use of, let us say, the adrenal corticosteroids for the anti-inflammatory treatment of rheumatoid arthritis in which massive, or suppressive doses are given way beyond the physiological level. Under the latter circumstances you're very likely to encounter unfortunate side effects. He really didn't take any drugs. He didn't tolerate aspirin well. He didn't like to take it. It was as much as

your life was worth to get him to take an aspirin. He didn't take sleeping pills. He wouldn't take medication for pain. He didn't want it. I think the record should be perfectly clear that the things that he did take were normal physiological constituents of the body, nothing more.[44]

Even at this, Travell underreported and simply lied about the medications Kennedy took daily. His medication regime was complicated enough that once Burkley took over, he improved on Travell's messy written notes, often jotted on the back of envelopes or napkins, by methodically instituting a typed sheet to record the president's morning and evening doses, with written additions and deletions on a daily basis. By October 1963 Kennedy's daily sheet included two types of cortisone, two types of testosterone, antihistamines, muscle relaxants, barbiturates (phenobarbital), and several treatments for his chronic diarrhea. In addition, he regularly received penicillin and allergy injections, drugs for prostate and urinary tract problems, and sleeping medications.[45] The "routine medications" kept in Kennedy's traveling medical bag, as documented by Dr. Burkley in 1961, included twenty-six different kinds of drugs.[46]

Many of these medications can cause side effects. Contrary to Travell's claim, cortisone is known to produce noticeable side effects, even when taken for legitimate medical reasons. In addition, because cortisone represents a treatment and not a cure for Addison's disease, more steroids are required over time, as the glands continue to progressively deteriorate. Further, additional medication is needed anytime that a patient undergoes a great deal of stress, including times of surgery or emotional upheaval. Often Addisonian patients are told to double or triple their normal steroid use during times of stress. Because Kennedy's job created a great deal of stress, he required increased dosage at particularly difficult times and higher levels in general over time. As dosage increases, the risk of excess use also increases in a commensurate fashion. Long-term use of glucocortoids can cause cataracts, bone degeneration, and eventually kidney problems. Overdose can cause high blood pressure, weight gain, heart failure, and death.

Other less ominous side effects can result from long-term use of steroids at therapeutic levels. For one thing, cortisone causes fluid retention and a visible look of "puffiness." In addition, it causes a particularly flushed look, especially immediately after injection. Early pictures of Kennedy show him to be quite thin around the head and neck, but by the time of his presidency he had acquired the moon-faced look typical of those who are on long-term cortisone maintenance. Janet Travell talks in her oral history about putting wood blocks under the head of Kennedy's bed to alleviate the puffiness around his eyes in the morning, although she attributes this puffiness not to the intake of cortisone but to severe allergies, from which he also suffered.

Steroid use can also precipitate a real change in an Addisonian's personality, and the shift from lethargy and depression to energy, optimism, and euphoria can last for months to years after the instigation of therapy. Both sides of this equation present problems. An untreated Addisonian patient manifests neuropsychological dysfunction, including abnormal brain waves on electroencephalograms, and adrenal insufficiency can cause depression, lethargy, and psychosis. Yet the side effects of steroid treatment can include an increased sense of well-being, cheerfulness, an increased ability to concentrate, and an increased libido. Some of these side effects may prove desirable, others less so.

Kennedy's sexual profligacy has become legendary since the time of his death. However, it appears that his heightened sexual interest, no doubt precipitated, at least in part, by his steroid use, caused other medical concerns as well. For these concerns, Kennedy had been introduced to Dr. Herbst in a letter from Dr. Vernon Dick, a urologist at the Lahey Clinic, who wrote, "Senator Kennedy has been a patient at the Lahey clinic at intervals since 1936, and has had quite a variety of conditions. The most serious of these has been Addison's disease which was first discovered and treatment instituted in October of 1947."[47] Medical records in the Kennedy library indicate that Dr. Herbst treated Kennedy on and off for a variety of bladder and prostate problems, and Kennedy appeared to be concerned about these problems. In his medical notes, Herbst records that on June 11, 1953, Kennedy asked the doctor about the impact of his condition on his fertility. Dr. Bert Park indicates that Herbst's notes report treatment for postgonococcal urethritis. While this is possible, I found no written indication of such in Herbst's medical file. Moreover, there is nothing in any of the other medical files that indicate any venereal disease infection. Dr. Robert Hopkins carefully reviewed laboratory data in the medical files at the Kennedy library and found no evidence of venereal disease; this does not mean, of course, that Kennedy never contracted such an illness in his lifetime, but it does mean that no evidentiary record of such infection exists in any of these medical files. However, there is no doubt that Herbst gave Kennedy repeated antibiotic and sulfonamide treatment for various urinary and prostate complaints over a period of about a decade, often at his insistence or instigation. Yet this pain may have actually originated elsewhere. Note that "pain in the loins is more frequent than is usually realized" in Addison's disease.[48]

Further, Dr. Burkley, for one, felt that at least some of Kennedy's prostate pain resulted from the cut of the back brace that he wore, which placed undue pressure on this region of his body. Herbst did mention Kennedy's assassination in his notes on November 22, 1963. A week later, Herbst wrote a final, odd comment in Kennedy's medical record: "Talked to Dr. Travell re sending report to Dr. Dick and was told that this record does not belong to me but to the country. This I did not agree with but am sending it to her for what is considered appropriate disposition. It is my considered opinion that John F. Kennedy experienced a profound psychochemical influence for the better in a spectacular way."[49]

Although there is no way to know for sure what this comment refers to, it may reflect Dr. Herbst's opinion concerning the impact of steroids on Kennedy's mood state. As noted in the earlier chapter on addiction, long-term steroid use can also produce a wide variety of more negative subtle behavioral effects over time, including agitation, restlessness, and insomnia. Importantly, excess use of steroids can lead to inappropriately impulsive behavior as well. In many ways, the effects of an overdose of steroids can appear remarkably similar to an overuse of amphetamines. Such symptoms can include anxiety, irritability, and even paranoia. As with amphetamine psychosis, steroid psychosis can develop from an overuse of steroids. Such overdose problems can produce disorientation, memory problems, agitation, hostility, and mania. L'Etang writes that Kennedy suffered from an episode of steroid psychosis prior to becoming president, but as there appears to be no corroborating evidence on this point, it must be taken as speculative.[50] If Kennedy were prone to steroid-induced mania, however, the prescribed antipsychotic medication, Stelazine, makes much more sense in this light.

Amphetamines

All of Kennedy's medical problems and treatments were further affected by his illicit use of amphetamines at the hands of Dr. Jacobson. To any objective observer, Dr. Jacobson's professional behavior seemed unconventional. He did not belong to any medical organizations, and none of the New York City hospitals would grant him privileges. Yet such censure did not prevent Jacobson from pursuing his own form of medicine. Often Jacobson did not tell his patients what was in the injections he administered, indicating that they included a combination of vitamins and hormones. While it is not clear whether Kennedy knew the composition of the injections he received, at least at the beginning, neither did he appear to want to find out. The regimen worked for him, thus explaining Kennedy's acceptance of it despite his willful ignorance of its constituents. As long as it made him feel better, that was all he cared about or needed to know. Robert Ferrell outlines Jacobson's descriptions of his treatments to his patients in a compelling and fascinating footnote:

Sometimes Jacobson took patients to his laboratory in the back of the office. "There were cauldrons and masses of rocks and things boiling around. It was like science fiction, the colored lights. Then he would show me what he described as uranium, which he put in the vials. Very often the vials had little rocks at the bottom to give energy, he said." Jacobson told patients he was involved in high level medical research. He told a House committee that he used "ultrasonic bombardment" to make medications, together with a strong magnetic field and the ability of certain minerals and precious stones to regain fluorescence. He said that in 1953 he was a coinventor of the laser microscope – that is, seven years before the first laser was developed. The device, he said, was more powerful than the best microscopes in use in the 1970s. Asked why no scientist used the invention, he said that unfortunately his partner was "completely insane" and ran off with the device and had not been heard from since.[51]

Dr. Jacobson ministered to a whole host of socially and politically elite patients in Manhattan in the late 1950s and early 1960s, including Tennessee Williams, Eddie Fisher, and Truman Capote. While amphetamines were not illegal at this time, Jacobson mixed these substances with other things that patients may not have been aware of, including vitamins, ground-up bone marrow, placenta, and electric eel parts.[52] Truman Capote, for one, stopped seeing Jacobson after experiencing a serious infection at an injection site. After Dr. Jacobson gave self-administration vials of his potion to Tennessee Williams for an extended period of time, Williams had to be hospitalized for a paranoid psychosis.[53] In addition, Mark Shaw, a Kennedy photographer and family friend, died of an apparent methamphetamine overdose while under Jacobson's care. The initial cause of death was labeled heart disease. However, while no evidence for such a cause was found in his autopsy, his organs contained major quantities of methamphetamines at the time of his death.[54]

In 1969 the Bureau of Narcotics and Dangerous Drugs seized all the substances under Jacobson's control. In one two-year period, Jacobson was unable to account for almost 1,500 grams of methamphetamine he was recorded as having purchased.[55] As a result of these findings, the New York State Board of Regents revoked Jacobson's medical license in 1975, citing numerous abuses, including "adulterated drugs consisting of filthy, putrid, and/or decomposed substances."[56] Not only did they find Jacobson guilty of forty-eight counts of unprofessional conduct,[57] but they also ascertained that Jacobson's methods were typically invariant with respect to symptoms. In other words, regardless of complaint, Jacobson treated all presenting medical problems with injections of the same ingredients, which invariably included both amphetamines and, ominously, steroids. In Kennedy's case, additional steroids presented particular problems, because they would have served only to accelerate and exacerbate the already disease-induced atrophy and destruction of his adrenal glands.

Although Jacobson claimed that the dosages he used were low, this was clearly not the case, at least in the samples of his substances seized and analyzed by New York State. He stated that he used about twenty-five-milligram doses of amphetamine, but patients often received more than one dose a day. As a comparison, when legitimate doctors prescribe such medications, typically for hyperactivity or narcolepsy, recommended dosages almost never exceed forty milligrams per day.[58] But the New York Board of Regents revealed that the vials in his office contained between thirty-five and fifty milligrams of amphetamine. The state of New York found that more than 90 percent of Jacobson's patients were mailed these vials for purposes of self-medication.[59]

The FBI found at least five of these vials in the White House in 1961. These vials contained high concentrations of both amphetamines and steroids. Robert Kennedy was so concerned with his brother's use of Jacobson's potions that he had fifteen additional vials analyzed, with results consistent with those obtained by the FBI. Apparently when Bobby confronted his brother with his findings, Jack replied, "I don't care if it's horse piss. It works."[60] One of the really serious problems with Kennedy availing himself of Jacobson's treatment, when it was added to the steroids he already took, is that he risked catapulting himself into unknowing periods of drug withdrawal. A person on steroids needs to come down very slowly, or their absence precipitates various problems, including vastly increased inability to fight common infections, already an Achilles' heel for an Addisonian patient. In addition, the person can feel swollen, lethargic, and agitated. In the original article that broke this story in the *New York Times* in 1972, Dr. Kraus indicated that he warned Kennedy about receiving any more treatments from Jacobson. He said he told the White House that, "if I ever heard he took another shot, I'd make sure it was known. No President with his finger on the red button has any business taking stuff like that." Dr. Burkley remained concerned about Kennedy's involvement with Jacobson as well:

> [C]all from Dr. C in New York. States that Dr. Bill Geller from memorial hospital came to his office and made the following statement: "He himself is quite perturbed and disturbed because he said a patient of his told him that a friend from the theatre advised the patient to see Max Jacobson, who is treating the president and that he could treat her with cortisone in such a way that she would look well and healthy as the president looks and that the president is now under treatment of Dr. Max Jacobson and that is the reason he is so healthy and well." The question of security of the medications which Dr. Jacobson uses as far as possible introduction of a substance deleterious to X should be considered as suggested by Dr. C.[61]

White House gate logs show that Jacobson visited the president in the White House thirty-four times before May 1962. Practicing neurosurgeon and medical historian Bert Park obtained a copy of Jacobson's memoir. Jacobson appears to have begun treating Kennedy and his wife prior to and after Kennedy's first state visit to Canada in May 1961, where he injured his back helping to plant a tree. In his autobiography, Jacobson claimed that "I worked with the Kennedys, I traveled with the Kennedys; I treated the Kennedys; they never would have made it without me." Jacobson goes on to state that his help was particularly essential to the president during the Vienna conference and the standoff between state and federal authorities concerning the integration of the University of Mississippi.[62] Various reports indicate several occasions in which Jacobson treated Kennedy with his infamous injections. For example, just prior to a speech Kennedy was to give before the United Nations on disarmament, he had laryngitis. Jacobson apparently injected Kennedy just above his voice box, and Kennedy's voice returned in a matter of minutes. It is possible that steroids, injected directly into this area, may have reduced inflammation sufficiently to allow the return of Kennedy's voice. On another occasion, several observers reported that Jacobson treated Kennedy for an infected hand and back pain in Vienna during Kennedy's conference with Khrushchev in 1961.

Side effects from amphetamine use present real dangers for decision making. Amphetamine use can cause people to suffer from nervousness, belligerence, irritability, impaired judgment, and overconfidence. Amphetamine overdose can cause psychosis. As early as 1938, three years after amphetamines were introduced in the treatment of narcolepsy, doctors were well aware that they could cause a psychotic reaction in someone taking large doses. As one textbook states, "experimental studies confirm the clinical observation that sufficiently large doses of amphetamine will induce paranoid psychosis in all individuals."[63] It was well established, even in Kennedy's time, that psychotic reactions could occur following as little as 100 milligrams in a day or 500 milligrams or more over the course of several days.[64] Amphetamine psychosis is essentially indistinguishable from any other form of psychosis, although shorter in duration, and related to dosage, being characterized by a person's inability to maintain connection with reality. An additional serious problem with the use of amphetamines, of course, exists not only while the person is high on the drug but also during the withdrawal period, when the user becomes subject to potentially severe and incapacitating periods of depression, depending on how much was ingested and for how long a period of time. This period of depression can drive an addict to seek more amphetamines before the crash becomes too bad.

Kennedy's use of these drugs remains troublesome from at least two perspectives. First, Kennedy was already taking legitimately moderately high doses of steroids for treatment of his Addison's disease. Overdoses of steroids can result in mania, paranoia, restlessness, agitation, anxiety, irritability, insomnia, and even delirium, any aspect of which can cause serious restrictions in the ability to render rational decisions in a timely manner. Second, amphetamines alone can carry their own set of side effects. Most typically, these include a sense of omnipotence and euphoria.

The person can go long periods of time without needing food or sleep. Sex drive is heightened. Concomitant use of steroids only exacerbates these effects. Both drugs, alone or in combination, are well known to suspend rational judgment and decision making.

Other Medications

Dallek writes that on at least one occasion Kennedy took Stelazine. Apparently, Kennedy was prescribed this drug by his gastroenterologist, Dr. Russell Boles, when Jackie told him that she was concerned that the antihistamines that Kennedy had been taking for his various allergies was making him depressed. She asked Boles to prescribe something that would lift Kennedy's mood without upsetting his stomach. At this point, Boles prescribed Stelazine for a short time.[65] Although on this occasion Kennedy stopped taking the drug after a few days, the medical record documents that he continued to take Stelazine on occasion throughout the rest of his life.

Stelazine is one of the class of conventional antipsychotics of the chemical class called piperazine phenothiazine. Stelazine is the trade name for the generic form of the drug, trifluoperazine. Kennedy was apparently taking the smallest amount possible, one milligram. Stelazine is often used as an antiemetic, to help prevent nausea, for example, after surgery. It is not an antihistamine, but it might easily be prescribed to lower anxiety. In such a case, doctors prescribe the drug on the basis of its side-effect profile, which emphasizes sedation. Stelazine remains an odd drug to have been given to Kennedy because one of the main side effects of this drug is that it induces hypotension, or low blood pressure, something any Addisonian patient and his doctor would drastically shy away from given its incipient danger in precipitating an Addisonian crisis.

VIENNA

One of the most important concerns raised about Kennedy's use of amphetamines at the hands of Dr. Jacobson comes in connection with his meeting Nikita Khrushchev in Vienna in June 1961. Kennedy chartered a separate transatlantic flight just for Jacobson and his wife, at taxpayers' expense. Jacobson did not travel on Air Force One with Drs. Travell and Burkley, nor did he attend official dinners and processionals in which the other two physicians participated.[66] Travell claimed not to have seen Jacobson in Vienna, and he was put in a different hotel from the others.[67] Reportedly, Jacobson injected Kennedy prior to meeting with French president DeGaulle in France as well as before his meetings in Vienna with Soviet premier Khrushchev.

The conference that Kennedy had with Khrushchev in Vienna on June 3 and 4, 1961, concerned a number of important international issues. These included Laos, China, Cuba, the nuclear test ban treaty, the German peace treaty and its implications for the settlement and control of Berlin, and ideological issues about the differences between communism and capitalism. By all accounts, the meeting was a chilly one, and the two men did not appear to get along very well. Kennedy emerged from the conference seemingly shell-shocked.

The most contentious issue that emerged in the talks surrounded Germany and Berlin. Kennedy believed that this was the real reason that Khrushchev had come to the meeting. Khrushchev presented Kennedy with an ultimatum. The Soviets wanted a peace treaty with Germany, after which "The U.S.S.R. would never under any conditions accept U.S. rights in Berlin after a peace treaty had been signed."[68] The Soviets argued that a peace treaty would end all formal occupation rights, thus leaving the question of control over West Berlin uncertain. The Soviets gave Kennedy until December to respond. Kennedy believed that DeGaulle seemed ready for war over the issue if necessary. Kennedy said that the Soviets should understand that hostile action over Berlin had a serious chance of leading to war.

Beschloss provides the most compelling account of this part of the meeting, and it is worth quoting at length for the flavor of the mood that it imparts:

> The President said that if Khrushchev was going to take this "drastic action" he must not believe the American commitment to Berlin was "serious." He was about to see Prime Minister Macmillan in London. He would have to tell him that the U.S.S.R. had presented him with a choice of "accepting the Soviet action on Berlin or having a face-to-face confrontation...."
>
> Khrushchev replied that in order to save Western prestige "we could agree that token contingents of troops, including Soviet troops, could be maintained in West Berlin. However, this would be not on the basis of some occupation rights, but on the basis of an agreement registered with the UN. Of course, access would be subject to the GDR's control because this is its prerogative." With steel in his eyes, he slammed his open hand on the table. "*I want peace. But if you want war, that is your problem.*"
>
> The chamber was deathly silent but for the loud ticking mantel clock. As DeGaulle had recommended, Kennedy replied, "*It is you, and not I, who wants to force a change.*"
>
> Khrushchev said that the Soviet Union had "no choice other than to accept the challenge. It must respond and it will respond. The calamities of war will be shared equally. War will take place only if the U.S. imposes it on the U.S.S.R. It is up to the U.S. to decide whether there will be peace or war." His decision to sign a peace treaty was "firm and irrevocable.... The Soviet Union will sign it in December if the U.S. refuses an interim agreement."
>
> Tight-lipped, Kennedy said, "If that is true, it's going to be a cold winter."

Years later, Khrushchev recalled that the President "looked not only anxious, but extremely upset. . . . I would have liked very much for us to part in a different mood. But there was nothing I could do to help him." Politics was "a merciless business."[69]

Declassified draft memos of the conversations between Kennedy and Khrushchev, released between February 1988 and May 1990, reveal a great deal of contentious ideological conversation. Kennedy appeared surprised by the ideological tone of the discussions and shocked and taken aback by Khrushchev's hard-line position on the German peace treaty and the question of Berlin. Rather than being unduly belligerent, as one might expect of someone hyped up on steroids and amphetamines, however, Kennedy's behavior seems almost the opposite. He did not appear eager to take the bait on war when Khrushchev presented Kennedy with his December ultimatum on Berlin.

Immediately after the meeting with Khrushchev, Kennedy reported feeling awful about how the meeting went. Prior to the conference, Kennedy had agreed to an interview right after the Khrushchev meeting with James Reston of the *New York Times*. The interview revealed Kennedy's distressed emotional state. Reston notes that Kennedy claimed that the meeting had been the "roughest of his life" and that Khrushchev had been "rude" and "savage." Referring to the ultimatum regarding Berlin, Kennedy said:

> I've got two problems. First, to figure out why he did it, and in such a hostile way. And second, to figure out what we can do about it.
>
> I think the first part is pretty easy to explain. I think he did it because of the Bay of Pigs. I think he thought that anyone who was so young and inexperienced as to get into that mess could be taken. And anyone who got into it and didn't see it through had no guts. So he just beat the hell out of me. . . . I've got a terrible problem. If he thinks I'm inexperienced and have no guts, until we remove those ideas we won't get anywhere with him. So we have to act.[70]

In his memoir, Reston claims that he was dumbfounded when here, for the first time, he heard Kennedy claim that the United States had to push back against the Soviets and that the place to do this was Vietnam. Although Eisenhower initially sent in troops, and Johnson increased their number in Vietnam much more than Kennedy, Reston traces the origins of American military intervention in Vietnam to this moment with Kennedy following his meeting with Khrushchev in Vienna and to Kennedy's need to prove himself to the Soviet leader.[71]

Many other senior advisers were upset and disappointed with the exchange between Kennedy and Khrushchev as well. Secretary of State Dean Rusk said he was "shocked" by Kennedy's discussion with Khrushchev over Berlin. "In diplomacy, you almost never use the word war. Kennedy was very upset.... He wasn't prepared for the brutality of Khrushchev's presentation.... Khrushchev was trying to act like a bully to this young President of the United States."[72] George Kennan, at the time Kennedy's ambassador to Yugoslavia and formerly the ambassador to the Soviet Union, argued in his oral history that Kennedy had not done a good job at the meeting:

> I was very disappointed when I read the account, which I was permitted to do, of his Vienna meeting and discussion with Khrushchev. I was shown the verbatim account of that.... I felt that he had not acquitted himself well on this occasion and that he had permitted Khrushchev to say many things which should have been challenged right there on the spot. But he, feeling his way, preferred to let Khrushchev talk and not to rebut any of this. I think this was a mistake. I think it definitely misled Khrushchev; I think Khrushchev failed to realize on that occasion what a man he was up against and, also, thought that he'd gotten away with many of his talking points; that he had placed Kennedy in a state of confusion where he had nothing to say in return.
>
> Q: That was June, 1961. Do you think this might have had some influence on Khrushchev's attitude toward Cuba and the placement of the missiles there?
>
> A; Yes, I do....
>
> Q:...Khrushchev's impression of Kennedy from that first interview in Vienna...would have encouraged an aggressive spirit on the part of the Soviets....
>
> A: I think so. I think they thought that this is a tongue-tied young man who's not forceful and who doesn't have any ideas of his own; they felt that they could get away with something.... He was, I felt, strangely tongue-tied in this interview with Khrushchev, and numbers of these typical, characteristic Communist exaggerations and false accusations were simply let pass, you see, instead of being replied to – being rebutted.
>
> Q: It was because he was young in office.
>
> A: Yes. He was feeling his way. I didn't feel, you know, that he was initially firm in his ideas of what he wanted to do with the communist problem.[73]

Other advisers also felt the meeting had not gone well. One of the men who urged the meeting, American ambassador to the Soviet Union Llewellyn Thompson, indicated in his oral history that Kennedy later gave him a hard time about this suggestion:

> Afterwards, the President used to tease me about this quite often saying "well, you were the fellow that urged this meeting. And that didn't come off very well." But then he also admitted that it had been valuable to him just to get to know Khrushchev, to know what he was like. I think, in retrospect, I'm sorry in a way that the discussion got off on ideological grounds – which is something I don't think that the President quite appreciated that fact that a Communist like Mr. Khrushchev could not yield on even if he wanted to. I mean he couldn't formally deny his own ideology. I think it is unfortunate that the dialogue started on that basis. There hadn't been worked out any very

clear scenario in advance. Had I realized it, it wouldn't have gotten so much on that basis. What, in effect, the President proposed was that neither side try to upset the balance of power. Khrushchev pointed out this is scarcely consistent with Communist hopes and ambitions and their beliefs that it was inevitable that this would be upset simply by the fact that in their view Communism was inevitable throughout the world.[74]

Some advisers also noted how upset Kennedy had seemed in the wake of his meeting with Khrushchev. Lem Billings claimed that Kennedy was "absolutely shook" by the meeting and that he had "never come face to face with such evil before." Robert Kennedy also agreed, noting that this was the first time Jack "had ever really come across somebody with whom he couldn't exchange ideas in a meaningful way." Apparently he told his brother that interacting with Khrushchev was "like dealing with Dad. All give and no take."[75] This event may have cemented Kennedy's desire for revenge against Khrushchev. In typically visceral style, Kennedy remarked of Khrushchev after the Cuban Missile Crisis that he had "cut his balls off."[76]

Leaders in the international world noticed Kennedy's concern about the way the conference had gone as well. Immediately after the meeting in Vienna, Kennedy met with British prime minister Harold Macmillan. Macmillan wrote in his diary that Kennedy "talked all the way up on his experiences. He had 'laid great hopes' on the summit but for the first time in his life 'met a man wholly impervious to his charm.'" Kennedy told Macmillan that Khrushchev was "much more of a barbarian" than he thought. Macmillan recorded in his diary that Kennedy "seemed rather stunned. . . . like somebody meeting Napoleon (at the height of his power) for the first time."[77] This claim seems at odds with Kennedy's typical style. Kennedy had no prior reason to expect Khrushchev to be accommodationist. Kennedy's charm may have been legend, but Kennedy was not so foolish as to believe that personality alone could solve deep structural problems.

At the time, Khrushchev did appear to be signaling to the world with his ultimatum that he believed the young and inexperienced Kennedy could be blackmailed, intimidated, and humiliated. Following the meeting with Khrushchev, Kennedy sent Jacobson packing, saying that his services were no longer desired. Yet, the next day in London, obviously depressed, Kennedy sent for Jacobson once again. Following his return to Washington, Kennedy held no press conferences for over a month. Blaming his back, Kennedy remained out of view from the public during what some speculate was an amphetamine withdrawal.[78] Such withdrawals are typically characterized by profound and lengthy depressions. During this period, there is no record of Jacobson visiting the White House. After Jackie returned to Washington, however, he returned to the White House;

at that point, Jacobson started coming back to the White House one to four times a week to treat her, although no record exists that he also treated Jack at this time. Given the meticulous care Burkley paid to Kennedy's medical care at this point, such attention would have been unlikely to escape Burkley's observations or logs.

In his report to the Congress concerning the conference on June 7, 1961, Kennedy told the leadership about the meeting, but he did not go into detail about the level of hostility that had existed between the two leaders during the discussion over Berlin. Kennedy said that Khrushchev believed that the two powers now had a nuclear balance, but that the Soviet Union held superiority in conventional forces, which would place the Soviets at an advantage in local conflicts. What Kennedy did not report to the congressional leadership was his awareness of a large nuclear missile gap in America's favor.[79] In addition, Khrushchev argued that another type of war, the war of liberation, was a sacred type of conflict that the Soviets would continue to support. In his view, Iran and South Korea verged on collapse. The Soviets did agree that Laos should remain neutral, although Kennedy did not think that Khrushchev appeared all that interested in the issue. According to Kennedy's report, Khrushchev went on to say that Castro was not a communist but that the United States was turning him into one. On the issue of disarmament, Khrushchev advocated for combining the limited test ban talks with wider disarmament talks. Kennedy claimed that the Soviets had lost interest in the test ban treaty. Khrushchev threatened to begin testing when the United States did so.

When asked by Congressman John McCormack at the end of the meeting what Khrushchev had been like,

> The President replied that he was very tough.... He had not been disagreeable. He came to talk on Germany. He wanted "to know whether we would fight" and that was why the President went back after lunch to make our position very plain. Then Khrushchev had said that if there has to be war, then let it come now, and the President "gave him a box of sandwich glass and left." The President felt it was going to be very close, and awfully tough. The Soviets feel that our edge is gone on the nuclear side.[80]

Kennedy's address to the nation was less specific but not much more optimistic:

> Mr. Khrushchev and I had a very full and frank exchange of views on all the major issues now dividing our two nations. I will tell you that it was a very grim two days. There was no discourtesy, no loss of temper, no threats or ultimatums by either side. No advantage or concession was either gained or given – no major decision was either planned or taken – no dramatic progress was achieved or pretended....
>
> For it was obvious in these talks that neither of us had ever received so clear a view of what the other considered to be vital....

For the facts of the matter are that the Soviets and ourselves give wholly different meanings to the same words: war, peace, neutralism and popular will. We have wholly different views of right and wrong, of what is an internal affair and what is aggression – and, above all, we have wholly different concepts of the world and where it is going. Only by searching discussion did Mr. Khrushchev and I begin to see how each of us viewed the future. Our views clashed – the outlook was dark – but at least we knew where we stood....

But our most somber talks were on the subject of Germany and Berlin. I made unmistakably clear to Mr. Khrushchev that the security of all Western Europe depended on our presence and our access rights to West Berlin – that, regardless of what he unilaterally said or signed, those rights would be unaffected since they were based on victory and law, not on sufferance ... and that we were determined to maintain those rights at any risk, and thus maintain our obligation to the people of West Berlin and their right to choose their own government. Mr. Khrushchev in turn presented his views in detail, demanding an end to our rights.... He was equally determined. It was a chilling exchange....

But let me give you my impression of Mr. Khrushchev. Outside the meeting room, he was capable of good humor, and showed real affection toward his family, first hand knowledge of agriculture, and at all times tremendous energy and drive. But he is also able, tough and vigorous – a very skillful and clever leader who is not afraid to use power or take chances. He is too dedicated to his party and his country, too well-versed in the history and doctrines of both, to change his view of the world. He is well-read and well-informed.... In talking with me he was shrewd and resourceful, never rude, rarely heated, and not at all impulsive.[81]

Khrushchev's report on his talks with Kennedy, issued June 16, 1961, carried a more ideological and less personal tone.[82]

Was Kennedy's behavior, as some have claimed, reckless at Vienna? The records and transcripts seem to indicate that Kennedy appears frightened, shocked, and disoriented by his meeting with Khrushchev. This seems odd, given his previously strongly proactive behavior in the earlier Bay of Pigs incident. In that case, he overrode many of Eisenhower's military plans, changes that included the cancellation of air cover for purposes of secrecy, which helped to doom the mission to failure. Such unrealistically optimistic and overconfident belief in the success of his plan would have been consistent with high doses of cortisone. Yet, in Vienna, Kennedy appeared stunned by the Soviet ultimatum on Berlin and shocked at what he perceived to be Khrushchev's brutal behavior toward him.

Kennedy's bad back may have contributed to his compromised performance, a possibility suggested by Charles Bartlett: "I think his problem with Vienna was his damned back ... when that back went off, Jack was off.... My impression was that he was not in top shape in Vienna."[83]

Kennedy certainly endured back pain in Vienna; many anecdotes mention how much time he spent in the bathtub trying to alleviate it. Kennedy's medical record shows that he often took narcotics for back pain and other ailments. Because Kennedy was traveling abroad, his medical record does not contain his medication dosage for this exact time, but the record does indicate that upon his return, on June 20, 1961, he took 30 milligrams of Darvon at noon and 2 capsules of 65 milligrams each of Darvon at 6 p.m., with an additional dosage in between at 2:30. This dosage is sufficiently high (double the current recommended dosage for moderate pain) that it is highly unlikely that he began taking this amount at this time because it would have been too sedating unless he was already adjusted to the medication; it is more likely that he had built up to the dosage over the previous few weeks at least.[84] Such drugs not only would have counteracted the effects of the steroids and amphetamines he took but also may have exerted a stronger effect on his immediate mood, because he did not take these kinds of drugs as often or in as high a dosage. Such narcotic usage would explain behavior that was more passive and less forceful than might have been expected by either a leader in top form or one under the influence of steroids and amphetamines.

Regardless of the reason for his poor performance, Kennedy did not feel that he had handled things well at Vienna with Khrushchev. Kennedy's banishment of Jacobson subsequent to his return from Vienna may indicate his awareness that these treatments might backfire. Khrushchev left with the impression that Kennedy was young and inexperienced and could be pushed around. Many, including Kennan, believe that this impression set up and encouraged the Soviet's risky action of placing the missiles in Cuba in October of the following year. Indeed, one of Khrushchev's aides, Fyodor Burlatsky, reported that Khrushchev felt Kennedy had "more the look of an advisor, not a political decision maker or President. Maybe in a crisis he would be an advisor, but not even the most influential."[85]

Yet there remain a couple of additional reasons why Kennedy's behavior appears paradoxical, given the nature and large doses of medications and treatments he received at the time, but may not actually be so under more careful scrutiny. First, amphetamines have a relatively short half-life. A single injection on one day, which is all that Jacobson claimed he administered to Kennedy in Berlin (he admits additional treatments in France prior to and in London subsequent to Vienna), would not be expected to affect a person for two days. Second, by this time, Kennedy had been taking reasonably high doses of steroids for almost fifteen years. His tolerance at this point would have been extremely high. He would have needed a huge increase in dosage to precipitate any additional mental effects at this point. In addition, recall that individuals under stress require more cortisone. When a person's body really needs the drug to combat stress, the immediate mental side effects simply do not manifest in the same sort of way as when the person does not really need the medication; this is similarly true for narcotics that are needed for control of genuine physical pain. Kennedy would have been used to boosting his dosage during stressful times, such as the conference in Vienna. At the meeting, General Snyder noted Kennedy's sweating brow in the cold and said to Admiral Radford, the chairman of the Joint Chiefs of Staff, that Kennedy usually received only one shot of cortisone for his back but must have received two that day, due to the added stress, and that this extra dose had been responsible for the excess sweating. Snyder commented that people hooked on cortisone went from a high to a low as the medicine wore off. He expressed his concern to Radford: "I hate to think of what might happen to this country if Kennedy is required at three a.m. to make a decision affecting the national security."[86]

Much more likely is the consideration that Kennedy was suffering from an amphetamine withdrawal at Vienna. He apparently received fewer amphetamine shots than usual, maybe because of his concern about their effect on his judgment. The sweating that Snyder noted also constitutes a classic symptom of amphetamine intoxication, which is characterized by at least two of the following symptoms, within one hour of use: heart skips, dilated pupils, high blood pressure, sweating, nausea or vomiting (a symptom Kennedy frequently experienced as a consequence of Addison's disease anyway), and hallucinations.[87] Amphetamine withdrawal can similarly cause a wide variety of side effects, the most characteristic of which is depression, but which also include fatigue, sleep disturbances, anxiety, and physical agitation.[88] As a basic textbook on the subject relates, "[w]hen high levels of amphetamine have been continuously used for an extended time, the depression that results may be quite severe and may be accompanied by suicidal thoughts and suicide attempts."[89] Amphetamines' short half-life lasts for about three to five hours in the body, after which withdrawal can set in.[90]

An examination of the facts of the Vienna conference indicates that a diagnosis of amphetamine withdrawal presents a much more logical, comprehensive explanation for Kennedy's behavior than any other. First, Kennedy's behavior did not serve his interests or that of his country; he had no reason to act as he did. Second, attributing his passivity with Khrushchev to youthful indiscretion seems implausible. By this time, Kennedy was an extremely sophisticated political actor who had been an active politician for many years, and he was part of a highly political family. His father, Joe, was a strong anticommunist, even being accused of harboring Nazi sympathies prior to the war. His brother Bobby worked for Joseph McCarthy in the 1950s. Kennedy himself took a very bellicose stand against communism in the 1960 election, even placing himself to the right of Republican president Eisenhower on the issue. In addition,

Kennedy should have known that Khrushchev would be tough with him; at the very least, DeGaulle must have prepared him for this eventuality before the meeting. Finally, for anyone who has ever watched Kennedy's press conferences, especially in light of the performance of later, healthier presidents, there is simply no question that Kennedy was impressively quick on his feet, smart, witty, clever, charming, resilient, and resourceful. He clearly had the ideology to stand up to Khrushchev and the skills to do so.

So, why did he simply sit back and take a paddling from Khrushchev without response? The most reasonable and comprehensive explanation lies in his concurrent amphetamine withdrawal, a drug-induced depression and passivity that Kennedy was unable to physiologically overcome at the time. And his reported depression, his self-critical evaluation of his performance to intimates and advisers afterward, and his absence from public view for more than a month seem to confirm a diagnosis of serious depression. Most tellingly, upon his return, Kennedy suffered from a series of very high fevers, ranging from 103 to 105 degrees, a common side effect of amphetamine withdrawal. One set lasted between June 22 and 26, 1961, and the second set occurred in early July. Travell, Kennedy's primary doctor at the time, administered penicillin, codeine, and a sleeping pill. During the July episode, she increased his testosterone dosage from 10 to 25 milligrams a day and added an additional steroid, aristocort. Each set of fevers went very high very fast and came down to normal almost as quickly, within 48 hours, a pattern typical of amphetamine withdrawal.[91] While it is possible that the fevers resulted from an episode of malaria, none of the doctors mention that as a possibility at the time. Further, Kennedy had been successfully treated with an antimalarial drug, Aralen, in July 1953 at George Washington Hospital, after being diagnosed with *Plasmodium vivox* malaria, and had not had a diagnosed recurrence since.[92] Interestingly, at the time, one of his doctors, Dr. Pitts, wrote a note in the file questioning the diagnosis of Addison's, seeing the drop in adrenal function as secondary to malaria.[93] Kennedy's later course of illness disproves this hypothesis however.

In Vienna, Kennedy's behavior seems remarkably similar to that which Anthony Eden displayed in the Suez crisis in 1956.[94] Eden had become addicted to amphetamines during the course of his biliary tract disease and consequent difficult surgical operations. This included treatment at the Lahey Clinic in Boston for repair of the major bile duct, injured at the time of the earlier surgery. Eden's doctor, under duress, administered massive doses of amphetamines to Eden during the early phases of the crisis when Eden wanted to stay awake and alert. When Eden had not slept in days, and his advisers began to worry that he was becoming clinically paranoid, his doctor cut him off, precipitating severe withdrawal, depression, and high fever. Eden's bad judgment in this period cost Britain terribly, because, despite repeated statements to the contrary, Eden never believed that Eisenhower would fail to support British military interests in the Gulf in the end. The British government was forced to ship him off to the Bahamas under the unconvincing excuse of a high fever from malaria and replace him with Harold Macmillan in the midst of the crisis. As is commonly known, this crisis caused disastrous effects, precipitating not only the collapse of Eden's government but also a run on the pound sterling and a costly war.

CONCLUSIONS

Robert Gilbert argues that there were several ways in which Kennedy's illness may have affected his presidency, and most of these influences were positive in nature. Because Kennedy was ill so much of the time, he picked up a useful lifelong habit and fondness for reading and learning. Kennedy's various illnesses also contributed toward establishing a bad reputation for him in Congress, especially during his first term in the Senate, where he racked up one of the most impressive absenteeism records in history. His failure to vote in the case of McCarthy's censure proved politically problematic for him at critical junctures during his future political career. But many Democrats believed that Kennedy used his illness to escape a politically difficult decision, and his failure to vote against McCarthy hurt his reputation in Congress from that time forward among many Democrats.

Gilbert also argues that Kennedy's illnesses gave him a sense of urgency about his life. Both Wilson and Roosevelt also seemed to share this strong sense of terminal urgency.[95] They may have all felt, in one way or another, for various reasons, that time was short, and they needed to do their utmost to accomplish as much as they could in the time remaining. Kennedy's youth at various points in his career supports Gilbert's claim that Kennedy feared a premature death. He was twenty-nine when he ran for the House of Representatives, thirty-five when he ran for the Senate, and forty-three when he became the youngest elected American president in history. This aspect of Kennedy's character may also have contributed to his enormous drive to excel, even in the face of great pain and illness. However, these facts can just as readily be accounted for by the pressure that Jack's father, Joe, placed on his son to achieve great things in the wake of his older brother Joe's death.

According to Gilbert, Kennedy's illnesses made him particularly concerned with issues of health and health care and motivated his Medicare legislation. For instance, Kennedy established a child health division in the Public Health Service nineteen days after his inauguration; at that time, he noted that this plan held particular interest for him. In this feature,

Kennedy again resembles Roosevelt, who implemented aspects of his New Deal legislation in part to help others who were suffering in various ways as a result of the Great Depression. Finally, both Gilbert and Dallek suggest that Kennedy's suffering helped him to develop a kind of strength of character and sense of detachment that aided him in his job as president, especially in crisis situations like the Cuban Missile Crisis.

Dallek argues that one of Kennedy's most impressive accomplishments while president was to hold the military-industrial complex at bay and refuse to place more troops in Vietnam. If this was in fact the case, and some argue that Kennedy would have become just as involved in Vietnam as Johnson had he lived, Kennedy's detachment may have aided him in standing up to those who tried to persuade him of positions that opposed his own. Again, this characteristic of cool detachment appears to be something that Kennedy shared with Roosevelt.

At least one other medical biographer does not believe that Kennedy's performance, even in acknowledged successes like the Cuban Missile Crisis, is cause for celebration. As Hugh L'Etang writes,

> Defective judgment and poor leadership during the fiasco at the Bay of Pigs in 1961 is not necessarily attributable to his own inexperience and to the failures of his advisors. Nor is his brilliant statesmanship during the Cuban Missile Crisis one year later entirely explained by added experience and better advisers. The tragic pilgrimage to Texas in November 1963, taken against sober advice and in defiance of the openly expressed hatred in Dallas, should not be dismissed as the casual fatalism of a man who once admitted that an American President could be killed at any time; there could be elements of imprudent overconfidence and unfounded optimism that influenced the fatal decision. [96]

The final characteristics that L'Etang notes are classic side effects from the use of steroids. Yet despite all of Kennedy's medical difficulties and problems with treatment, the Kennedy myth continues. For example, several analysts claim that Kennedy's ability to overcome his health problems demonstrates his courage and determination.[97] This is certainly true. Others argue that his illness is, in part, what prompted him to seek political office and strive to live each day as his last.[98] This may also be true. But what also remains true, over and above all the personal troubles he may have courageously overcome, is that his illness and its treatment endangered not only his own life but also the lives of the people under his leadership. Kennedy never seemed to take account of that consideration. As Crispell and Gomez write, the issue is not what did happen but what could have happened.[99] Even Kennedy himself told his aide Arthur Schlesinger that someone with real Addison's disease should not run for president but then concluded the thought by saying he did not have it. The fact remains that a leader who is seriously impaired by pain, is required to take heavy doses of medications with known psychotropic side effects in order to stay alive, and also abuses drugs is not a reliable and responsible man, even if he is exceptionally courageous. While the negative side effects of some of this medication, such as amphetamines, may not have been fully understood and appreciated at the time, the effects of other medication, such as phenobarbital, Darvon, and others were well established.

Ironically, chances are that Kennedy would not have lived much beyond the time of his assassination at any rate because he took such high doses of steroids for so long. Chronic use of steroids can lead to serious medical problems, most notably bone degeneration. Kennedy was one of the first patients to be put on synthetic steroids for the medical management of Addison's, and doctors were just beginning to understand how much patients needed to get by, without taking so much as to harm them. As a result, at that time many patients, including Kennedy, took more steroids than they needed and thus were likely to suffer from the iatrogenic sequelae of their usage.

Yet Kennedy radiated youth and vigor. The myth became the man, and Kennedy strove, until the assassin's bullet ended his life, to keep up the fiction that he was healthy and vigorous, when in fact he suffered from multiple serious and debilitating illnesses. And despite the cortisone and DOCA, a simple tooth extraction, urinary tract infection, or other simple virus, particularly under conditions of stress, could have felled him as quickly as the gunshot.

SIX

BORDERING ON SANITY: RICHARD NIXON

About Richard Nixon, Henry Kissinger once said, "Can you imagine what this man would have been like if somebody loved him? I don't think anybody ever did, not his parents, not his peers.... He would have been a great, great man had somebody loved him."[1] Would love have been sufficient to save Nixon from the excesses that defined his presidency? Or was its lack the motive for his many numerous accomplishments in spite of his limitations?

This chapter differs from those that come before because its subject revolves around a president whose infirmities were psychological and not physical in origin. Without the kind of consensual diagnosis of physical illness found in the earlier chapters, and the necessarily less precise nature of psychological impairments, this examination of Nixon may seem out of place. To examine psychological factors, analysts must examine psychological theories and motives. Despite the lack of agreement surrounding the source and manifestation of Nixon's psychological limitations, his mental health in office often seemed precarious and fragile. As Lasswell argued, leaders often project their personal needs and desires onto the public sphere, making an examination of leaders' motives both important and necessary. Nixon's presidency thus offers an opportunity to explore the ways in which psychological limitations can exert an impact on foreign policy.

Various presidents in American political history have undergone forms of historical renaissance despite fairly undistinguished terms in office. For example, Herbert Hoover, as director of the American Relief Administration before he assumed the presidency, sent food aid to Bolshevik Russia during the severe famines of the 1920s, an act that saved millions from death by starvation.[2] Jimmy Carter went from what many considered a failed presidency to a distinguished "postpresidency," establishing Habitat for Humanity to build houses for poor people, becoming a very respected election observer throughout the Third World, and serving as peacemaker in Haiti for President Bill Clinton in 1994. His impressive service for causes of peace and justice throughout the world culminated in his Nobel Peace Prize in 2003. But no president in American history has endured the political ups and downs experienced by Richard Nixon over the course of his life.

The number and extremity of Nixon's political renaissances are amazing and unusual. Not only did he recover from defeat in the 1960 presidential race and the 1962 California gubernatorial campaign to become elected president in 1968, but he almost single-handedly resurrected his position on the American political landscape following the most ignominious political defeat in U.S. history when he was forced to resign the presidency in 1974. Unlike Carter, who won his way back into his country's affection through consistent hard work and good deeds, Nixon rehabilitated himself by writing books, giving speeches, and slowly reconnecting with former political allies such as President Ronald Reagan, all essentially without openly acknowledging or admitting the personal and political mistakes that brought about his downfall.

In this regard, Nixon quintessentially understood the important role of myth and history in political culture. When Henry Kissinger tried to comfort Nixon after he left the presidency, he told him that history would judge him to have been a great president. Nixon replied, "that depends, Henry, on who writes that history."[3] By 1985, when Nixon gave an interview to Barbara Walters, he had determined who would accomplish that task. Quoting Winston Churchill, Nixon told Walters that "history will be very kind to me, because I intend to write it."[4] And so he did, authoring more than eight books and numerous articles between the time of his resignation and his death. Indeed, the final chapter of his life resembles the myth of the Phoenix rising from the ashes much more than that of Icarus, who flew too close to the sun with wings of wax that melted, leading to his downfall and death. This does not imply, however, that the evaluation of his presidency was not plagued by his personal limitations: of forty-three presidents, the Ridings-McIver list ranks him thirtieth, and the Schlesinger Poll considers him a "failure" as president.[5]

Richard Nixon was a source of fascination, reprobation, and even acclaim before his presidency, which was marred by massive controversies and allegations concerning his lies and corruption involving both Watergate and Vietnam and which culminated in the only presidential resignation in U.S. history on August 8, 1974. A great deal has been written about his leadership since. What is notable is the extreme position that most analysts take: Nixon as evil incarnate; Nixon as great statesman; Nixon as madman.[6] Few treatments attempt to explain how a supposedly evil or insane man was able to accomplish such political feats as opening the United States to China, achieving major arms control agreements with the Soviet Union during the height of the Cold War, or helping to bring about some peace and stability, if only for a time, in the Middle East. Similarly, those defenders and loyalists who view Nixon as a victim of his time or the so-called liberal media seem perfectly capable of justifying the lies and destruction that surrounded the secret bombing and invasion of Cambodia or the riskiness of the Watergate break-in and cover-up. In short, how can a man who angrily tells the press following his defeat by Pat Brown in the 1962 California gubernatorial race that "you won't have Nixon to kick around any more"[7] later become a two-term president?

Nixon's family history was rife with reasons and causes for his personality development. Analysts attempting to develop psychological arguments for Nixon's traits and behaviors suggest he was a narcissist who also displayed paranoid features on occasion. In these characterizations, Nixon appears to suffer from a variety of problems, including survivor guilt with its consequent drive to succeed, a simultaneous and oppositional fear of success, and a tendency to respond with rage in the face of humiliation, shame, or negative evaluation. And Nixon manifested many if not all of these characteristics in both his personal and political life. Yet he managed to achieve remarkable and impressive accomplishments with China and the Soviets, while still undercutting himself in the areas of Vietnam and Watergate. How is this possible?

Evidence suggests that Nixon's psychological problems may have been more subtle and more profound than straight narcissism or paranoia might indicate. It seems possible that Nixon suffered from a borderline personality disorder. This chapter attempts to delineate Nixon's childhood and adolescent background, which served to shape his personality. A brief description of some of the main psychological analyses of Nixon follows. This section is, by necessity, largely theoretical, drawing on earlier psychoanalytic work.[8] This is largely because Nixon's life story seems to easily engage and adapt to analytic concepts and interpretations. The next section provides a more detailed explanation of the various psychiatric symptoms Nixon displayed. The final section examines the way in which a borderline tendency may inform the specific foreign policy decisions he made. Although the bulk of the discussion here centers on his decisions to secretly bomb and invade Cambodia in 1969–1970 and to engage in the so-called Christmas bombing over North Vietnam in December 1972, other, more positive, aspects of foreign policy are also considered.

NIXON'S FAMILY HISTORY

More than most, it is impossible to understand Richard Nixon and the decision maker he became without knowing about his family of origin and his childhood. The Nixon family name, Celtic in origin, means "he wins" or "he faileth not."[9] The family had a long and distinguished political and military history in America that could be traced back to James Nixon, who arrived from Ireland in the 1730s. James's two sons fought in the Revolutionary War, and one of them, George, crossed the Delaware with George Washington. Another family member, Sheriff John Nixon of Philadelphia, read the Declaration of Independence for the first time in public.[10] George's grandson, George III, died in the battle of Gettysburg. George III was Frank Nixon's grandfather.[11] Frank was Richard's father. But George III's virtue and valor appear to have skipped a generation. By all accounts, his grandson was angry, mean, and desperately unhappy – succinctly put, Frank was a loser. Even Richard Nixon's younger brother Edward took to calling their father "the executioner."[12]

Good reasons existed to explain Frank's bad temper. His mother died of tuberculosis when he was eight years old. His father proceeded to marry a woman who acted as the veritable wicked stepmother of fairy tale proportions. He dropped out of school in the fourth grade. He ran away from home when he was fourteen. He drifted for a while from place to place and job to job. The only meaningful event that took place in his youth occurred when he was in Ohio at a town where William McKinley made a presidential campaign stop in 1896. Frank, who had a horse, was put at the head of the welcoming party and introduced to McKinley in person. When McKinley inquired as to how the young Frank was going to vote, Nixon replied, "Republican, of course!" thus changing his family's historical political party affiliation from Democrat to Republican.

Frank Nixon eventually took a job with the Columbus Railway and Light Company in Ohio in 1906. There he organized the workers in support of a lawyer who sought a seat in the state senate. When the man was elected, he passed legislation to make the workers' conditions more palatable.[13] Typically, Frank was not able to make anything lasting of his fleeting political victory. When he was twenty-eight, he moved to southern California, where he got a job as a motorman for Pacific Electric Railway Company, driving between Los Angeles and Whittier. One day, his motorcar hit an automobile, and he was fired from his job. When this happened, Frank decided to become a farmer in the small Quaker town of Whittier. There he met Hannah Milhous, the daughter of a prominent Quaker. Although they did not share a religion, Hannah having been raised a Quaker and Frank a Methodist, they married four months after they first met, in February 1908. They went on to have five sons, of which

Richard was the second. They named all of their children after prominent English kings.

Hannah Milhous's family background was ethnically German, but her ancestors had moved to England and been given an estate in Ireland in return for their service to Oliver Cromwell. There they became followers of William Penn and devout Quakers. Her first ancestor to come to America was Thomas Milhous, who settled in Pennsylvania in 1729. By all accounts, Hannah lived the life of a devout Quaker. Many described her as a "saint," including her son Richard. In his final speech to his staffers on August 9, the day after his resignation, Nixon said about his mother, "yes, she will have no books written about her. But she was a saint."[14] Nixon's youthful hero, Woodrow Wilson, had also referred to his mother as a saint; yet an objective observer might view the two women differently, particularly in their inability to shield their young sons from their fathers' wrath. Hannah was quiet, hardworking, strong, religious, and devoted to values of honesty, integrity, and forbearance. Above all things, she believed in self-control. Overt emotional expression remained outside her vocabulary. Her restraint might easily have been felt as cold, withholding distance. She punished her children with "quietly eviscerating little talks."[15] Everyone in her family seemed to believe that she had married beneath her, and Frank was never totally accepted by her family. Indeed, it is hard to imagine a more opposite pair of psychological temperaments in a set of parents than those which Hannah Milhous and Frank Nixon embodied.

Despite his marriage, Frank continued to display continual wanderlust. He moved the family to Bakersfield and then Yorba Linda, where he built a Sears kit house without electricity or running water. He also started a short-lived and ultimately failed lemon farm with his father-in-law's money. Richard Nixon was born here on January 9, 1913. By all reports, Nixon was a crybaby from birth and kept the habit up much longer than most children. His family took to calling him "the screamer,"[16] and even Nixon himself recalled that he was "the biggest cry-baby in Yorba Linda."[17] Analysts make much of the fact that when Richard was six months old he was forced to share his mother's breast milk with his cousin, Russell Harrison, because Hannah's sister Elizabeth was too ill to care for him. When he was nine months old, Hannah had to be hospitalized for a mastoid infection and was separated from Richard in an even more pronounced physical way. By the time Richard was two, his brother Donald was born, and Hannah appeared to be overwhelmed by all the demands made on her by her husband, their children, and their precarious financial situation. When Richard was six, Hannah was forced to go to work for the Sunkist lemon packing company to keep the family afloat financially. Richard went along and helped sweep and perform other menial tasks, as did his brother Donald. In 1922 Frank gave up on the farm and bought a small gas station in Whittier, to which he later added a general store.

Angry and frustrated, Frank often lashed out at his children, brutally punishing them physically. For example, once when Frank caught Richard and his older brother Harold swimming in the irrigation canal that ran behind the house against his expressed wishes, he pulled them out and then threw them back in again. One of the boys' aunts witnessed Frank's actions and intervened, yelling, "You'll kill them, Frank! You'll kill them."[18] Nixon himself reported that his father had a bad temper and was "sometimes impatient and – well – rather grouchy with most people" and that he had "tempestuous arguments with my brothers Harold and Don and their shouting could be heard all through the neighborhood."[19] But Richard learned how to circumvent these fights early on. He recalled, "I used to tell my brothers not to argue with him. . . . Dad was very strict and expected to be obeyed under all circumstances. He had a hot temper, and I learned very early that the only way to deal with him was to abide by the rules he laid down. Otherwise I would probably have felt the touch of the ruler or the strap as my brothers did."[20] Hannah later confirmed that although Frank "would not hesitate using the strap or rod on the boys when they did wrong," she did not remember "that he ever spanked Richard."[21]

Psychobiographers argue that Frank produced in young Richard an identification with the aggressor. Steinberg perhaps expressed it best when she wrote that the spankings

> fostered an identification with his aggressive father as a way of coping with this feared authority figure. It also led to a deep-seated wish to avenge himself on his authoritarian father by administering equal humiliations to a succession of perceived tormentors and surrogate fathers – opposition politicians, the press, college students and so on. In later life, the control over his emotions which Nixon tried so hard to maintain would shatter when his self-esteem was attacked, and he would lash out in a manner similar to that which he had experienced at the hands of his father.[22]

Nixon's and Wilson's responses to powerful male authority figures who might seek to challenge their will suggest a similar source and dynamic. In addition to Frank's ill treatment of his sons, physical and emotional separation from his mother defined Richard's adolescence. Aside from his early physical separations from her, he felt her to be emotionally distant as well. Even Hannah seemed to notice, and seemingly resent, Richard's neediness toward her; "as a youngster, Richard seemed to need me more than my four other sons did. As a schoolboy, he used to like to have me sit with him. . . . But it wasn't that Richard needed my help with his work. Rather, it was just that he liked to have me around."[23] Most psychological analyses of Richard's relationship with his mother point to her lack of emotional nurturance of him as the signal event that shaped his later personality structure. This perspective reflects the psychoanalytic bias that assumes that the mother is the source of all problems that emerge in the child. But in Richard Nixon's case, it does appear that his mother was not quite "good enough" in the parenting role.[24]

Psychodynamic interpretations of Nixon's personality often cite a letter he wrote as part of a school assignment when he was about ten years old to illustrate this point. Whether or not a reader buys into the more heavily Freudian interpretations of this letter, the imagery speaks to loneliness, helplessness, and desolation:

November 12, 1923

My Dear Master:

The two dogs that you left with me are very bad to me. Their dog, Jim, is very old and he will never talk or play with me. One Saturday the boys went hunting. Jim and myself went with them. While going through the woods one of the boys triped [sic] and fell on me. I lost my temper and bit him. He kiked [sic] me in the side and we started on. While we were walking I saw a black round thing in a tree. I hit it with my paw. A swarm of black thing came out of it. I felt pain all over. I started to run and as both of my eyes were swelled shut I fell into a pond. When I got hom [sic] I was very sore. I wish you would come home right now.

Your good dog,
Richard[25]

Most observers assume this was a letter intended for his mother; they interpret Jim as representing his father and the other dogs as representing his brothers. Some interpretations of this letter are so extreme as to provide caricatures of psychoanalysis.[26] Others appear to present more reasonable interpretations. One biographer points to the way in which Nixon's imagery demonstrates his self-pity, his perceived sense of vulnerability, his desire for his mother's love, and his early tendency to react violently – and orally, by biting – to threats.[27] Another notes the way in which Nixon's early sense of persecution and paranoia manifests in the letter.[28] Regardless of how one reads the letter, Nixon spent a great deal of his formative years in physical or emotional distance from his mother. These separations continued into Richard's adolescence. At twelve, he was shipped off for the summer to his aunt, Jane Beeson, a piano teacher who lived a couple of hundred miles away from his family, from whom he learned to play the instrument. Later, he was sent to live with a paternal uncle in Fullerton, California, where he attended his first two years of high school.[29]

163

Of all of Nixon's early experiences, none had the impact of the deaths of his two brothers. Their loss formed the definitive shaping experiences in his life. Shortly after his return from his Aunt Jane's, Richard was again sent away with his brother Donald to another aunt when his brother Arthur fell ill. On August 11, 1925, at age seven, Arthur died of bacterial meningitis. Two years later, when Richard was fourteen, Harold, the parents' first and favorite son, was stricken with tuberculosis. Thus began a six-year odyssey where Hannah almost exclusively nursed Harold, taking him to Arizona for a better climate and leaving Frank and the boys alone for long periods of time. Frank sold part of his land to help pay for Harold's care at the sanitarium in Arizona, and Hannah took in other patients to help pay the bills as well. As Nixon later recalled, "if it hadn't been for the expense of my brother's sickness we would have been fairly well off, with the store. I remember my dad sold half of the acre on which our house was located in order to pay medical bills."[30]

Richard visited Hannah during the summer, working as a carnival barker among other things to help support the family. Richard recalled his mother's sacrifices at this time during his emotionally laden final speech to his remaining loyal staff at the White House on the day after his resignation: "My mother was a saint. And I think of her – two boys dying of tuberculosis – nursing four others in order that she could take care of my older brother for three years in Arizona and seeing each of them die and when they died, it was like one of her own."[31] While she was taking care of Harold in Arizona, Frank visited occasionally and Hannah found herself pregnant once again; she gave birth to Edward in 1930. Harold eventually died in 1932. The cost of his care prevented Richard from attending either Harvard or Yale for college, places where he had been invited to apply for scholarships. Instead, he stayed in town to help his parents run the family gas station and general store and attended Whittier College.

In his studies of survivors of Hiroshima and Nazi concentration camps, Robert Lifton discussed the notion of "survivor guilt," referring to those who survived the horrors that killed so many others around them. He argued that such survivors can come to identify with the dead, because often only simple accidents of fate separate them from those they have lost, and as a result of their experiences, survivors develop a kind of "psychic numbing."[32] Lifton was not the first to discuss such dynamics. His ideas draw on Freud's notion of "wrecked by success." In his own self-analysis, Freud explained his fainting attacks by remembering how he wanted his baby brother Julius to die. When Julius actually did die, Freud was overcome with guilt and connected that past experience with his later symptomatology to interpret the origins of his fainting as his own form of survivor guilt.[33] As a result of his own analysis, Freud concluded that a "wrecked by success" syndrome can occur whenever a person either survives a sibling's death or accomplishes more than a parent.

When a sibling dies, survivor guilt is not uncommon. The child asks why he lived while another died. This can be especially problematic if the child never liked the sibling or saw him as a competitor for the parents' affection. By all accounts, Arthur was a difficult child, but one whom Richard liked and got along with well. Harold was another story; he was the first and favorite son, the easygoing boy who absorbed Hannah's already scarce attentions and affections for more than six years. Any normal child might feel some small glee at a competitor's demise, especially if it means more love and attention for oneself. Such feelings are quickly followed by intense guilt about having such animosity toward one's sibling, especially in the face of the parents' obvious and authentic grief. The child witnesses his parents' grief and with normal childhood grandiosity believes that he possesses the power to overcome it. His inevitable failure to do so sets the child up for a permanent, uneasy sense of failure, anxiety, and guilt, as he recognizes the implicit, unacknowledged, and unachievable expectation on the part of the parents toward the remaining child to somehow make up for the death of the sibling. Such a child does not possess the ability to confront the parents directly. But both parents and child, often unconsciously, expect the child to alleviate the parents' grief. Achieving this task inevitably proves impossible to accomplish. As a result, the parents remain vaguely disappointed with the child, and the child is left feeling curiously impotent and unloved, often blaming himself and remaining unaware of the way in which his parents' suffering was unconsciously projected onto him.

Hannah recalled that, following Arthur's death, "I can still see Richard when he came back. He slipped into a big chair and sat staring into space, silent and dry-eyed in the undemonstrative way in which because of choked, deep feeling, he was always to face tragedy. I think it was Arthur's passing that first stirred within Richard a determination to help make up for our loss by making us very proud of him. Now his need to succeed became even stronger."[34] This sentiment only strengthened upon the death of his brother Harold, again according to his mother, Hannah:

> Hearing the shocking news, Richard who was twenty, behaved very much the same way he had behaved when Arthur had died eight years before. He sank into deep, impenetrable silence. From that time on, it seemed that Richard was trying to be three sons in one, striving even harder than before to make up to his father and me for our loss. With the death of Harold his determination to make us proud of him seemed greatly intensified. Unconsciously, too, I think that Richard may have felt a kind of guilt that Harold and Arthur were dead and that he was alive.[35]

Richard's ability to attend law school on the money set aside for Harold's medical care could have served to exacerbate the young Nixon's sense of survivor guilt as well.[36] In a story written in May 1930 about his brother Arthur, Nixon was able to express his own inability to get over Arthur's death and the drive his loss instilled: "there is a growing tendency among college students to let their childhood beliefs be forgotten. Especially we find this true when we speak of the divine creator and his plans for us. I thought I would also become that way, but I find that it is almost impossible for me to do so.... And so when I am tired and worried, and am almost ready to quit trying to live as I should, I look up and see the picture of [Arthur]."[37] Indeed, Nixon claimed to have cried every day of his life over his brother's death.

Explanations for Nixon's Personality

Most of the literature on Nixon's personality or psychological status derives from a deeply psychodynamic perspective. Unfortunately, like a great deal of such psychoanalytically informed biography, much of this work goes beyond existing evidence both to infer, especially from childhood, evidence based on outcome and to explain outcomes in terms of theoretical expectations more than on actual childhood experiences.[38] This review examines only those explorations of Nixon's personality that appear to rest on credible evidence and psychodynamic argument. Discussions of these arguments are intended to establish background on the existing descriptions of Nixon's character and to provide contrast for the more medically formulated psychiatric assessments that follow.

Much of the early work of Nixon's psychobiographers starts with the assumption that because he did things they consider to be bad, Nixon himself must have possessed some kind of pathology. They seek to explain and interpret his personality using a wide variety of psychodynamic or psychiatric terms or labels. As Greenberg notes, "[w]ith his alternating bouts of caged-in restraint and explosive anger, Nixon was a textbook case of the psychoanalytic precept that repressed feelings affect people's behavior in unplanned ways."[39] Most of these interpretations locate the source and outcomes of Nixon's political troubles in his psychological limitations. In general, these psychodynamic studies find the origins of Nixon's psychological problems in some combination of his angry and abusive father, his cold, withholding, and unloving mother, and the deaths of his two brothers when he was young. These loose foundations then create a weakened edifice in Nixon that later becomes wracked with variations of rage, paranoia, shame, guilt, and narcissism.[40]

Because the details of Richard Nixon's early life encourage and support a psychodynamic interpretation, such analysis often appears to make sense. Nixon's rage can alternatively be understood as identification with his father, the aggressor, someone who modeled the behavior of reacting violently to insult or injury, or instead as an attempt to react against authority in the way he must have wanted but was never allowed, to respond directly to his father. Nixon's aloofness, isolation, repression of emotion, social awkwardness, and seeming coldness appear to derive from his mother's religion, personality, and socialization. Nixon's alternating attempts to achieve peace in places like the Middle East and to pursue war through his ferocious bombing of North Vietnam reflect the extreme divergences in his parental modeling. In turn, an analyst can see Nixon's guilt resulting from surviving his two brother's deaths and his narcissism growing out of his parents' inability to provide adequate love and nurturance to Richard while he was growing up.

Although most of Nixon's psychobiographers achieve consensus around these issues, specific analysts emphasize different points. Bruce Mazlish, for example, focuses on what he sees as Nixon's profound fear of death. As evidence for the origins of this fear, Mazlish points not only to the deaths of Nixon's two brothers, but also to the very serious injuries that Nixon sustained when he was quite young. For example, when Richard was two or three a team of horses almost killed him; he sustained a serious head injury that required surgery. At four, he nearly died of pneumonia. Such early brushes with death might have engendered a sustained lifetime fear of illness and death. Nixon appeared prone to psychosomatic illness; he demonstrated a lifelong proclivity toward sinus problems that always appeared to manifest around the anniversaries of his parents' deaths, for instance.[41]

A milder form of this argument can be found in James Johnson's psychoanalytic interpretation of the Nixon tapes when he writes, "I believe that the wounds Nixon felt when his brothers died contributed to his generally fearful approach to life, as if he were somehow going to be punished for their deaths. This vague fear of retaliation ... [left] Nixon with an unusually strong sensitivity about this potency."[42] Support for this last argument can only be found early in Nixon's life, when he apparently closed the drapes while he was doing dishes to prevent anyone from watching him doing what he perceived to be "women's work." While many men in the 1920s may have worried about being considered effeminate or weak for engaging in women's work, the lengths to which Nixon went to avoid being observed suggest a concern about perceptions of his manliness. The psychoanalytic understanding then assumes that Nixon's earlier losses made him unusually fearful of the world, because he anticipated, based on experience, a life characterized by pain and loss. Because of his survivor's guilt, he also remained particularly susceptible to vague superstitions about retaliation for his sin of living, thus making him acutely sensitive to challenges to his strength and potency, because he would have felt basically unable to defend himself against a cold, hostile, and unpredictable world. Thus, challenges to his strength elicited his guilt, making him strike out against those who reminded him of his inability to save his brother from death.

And yet the most serious illness Nixon contracted as an adult was phlebitis in his left leg, which emerged just before his presidential resignation and did not resolve for some time. This experience presents the major contradiction to Mazlish's theory concerning Nixon's fear of death. In particular, not only did Nixon fail to seek treatment for his condition until it was quite severe, letting the blood clot threaten his life for months, but he also refused to listen to his doctor, Walter Tkach, before and during his extensive foreign travel in June 1974, which exacerbated his condition.

Following his resignation, Nixon returned to his long-term doctor, John Lungren, in California. Despite aggressive noninvasive treatment, Nixon's condition worsened. His psychological condition at the time no doubt exacerbated the already precarious state of his physical health. Depression, for example, inhibits the body's ability to manufacture various hormones, including those essential for blood coagulation. Eventually, despite drugs that would usually break up a clot, but did not appear to work in Nixon's case, he required surgery to remove the blood clot from his left leg. Nixon all but died immediately after the surgery. At the time, many observers were skeptical about the true nature and severity of Nixon's illness, because it coincided with the time during which he was supposed to fly to Washington to testify in the Watergate trial. At the time, the presiding judge, John Sirica, ordered a panel of three prominent physicians to examine Nixon and confirm Lungren's diagnosis and treatment. He then ruled that Nixon did not have to testify at that time, as originally scheduled.[43] The timing of this illness would suggest that the stress of Nixon's situation made him more vulnerable to disease. Nevertheless, it still seems unlikely that a man primarily driven by a fear of death, as Mazlish claims, would defy and disregard serious medical advice concerning a life-threatening illness as Nixon did from June until late August 1974.

Psychobiographers find evidence of Nixon's sense of survivor guilt in his decision to tape conversations at the White House. On the one hand, he may have felt an obligation to history to record his actions and decisions. He may also have wanted insurance against future betrayal by subordinates, as well as contemporaneous material for blackmail. In his memoirs, Nixon claims that he installed the taping system to help him write his memoirs and to protect himself from "revisionist histories." On the other hand, Nixon's self-taping can be viewed as a demonstration of his grandiosity as well as his sense of paranoia. Obviously he realized that what he did and said was important enough to preserve for posterity, even if some of these tapes might prove self-incriminating in the meantime. Although such activity is not odd for a president, Nixon also taped himself to record not only his own thoughts, actions, and decisions but those of others as well. He wanted to make sure that he could catch or threaten anyone who might be out to get him, or might try to accuse him of lies, secrets, and deception. As Nixon wrote, "These tapes were my best insurance against the unforeseeable future. I was prepared to believe that others, even people close to me, would turn against me . . . and in that case the tapes would give me at least some protection."[44] Later, Nixon acknowledged a self-destructive element in the taping in his famous David Frost interviews in 1977 when he said, "I gave them the sword, and they stuck it [in], and they twisted it with relish!"[45]

Finally, Nixon's puzzling retention of the tapes requires explanation. He refused to destroy them even when it became clear that they had become an instrument of his own impending presidential conflagration. True, Nixon's secretary, Rosemary Woods, either on her own or under Nixon's direction, did erase a crucial eighteen-minute section of one of the tapes. But the tapes were not destroyed in their entirety, as might be expected if only paranoia and grandiosity were at play. Instead, psychobiographers such as Fawn Brodie see Nixon's guilt being manifest in his conscious self-exposure, both in keeping the tapes and later in releasing parts of them. She argued that Nixon desired to "exhibit his own nakedness, his ineffable dirtiness."[46] So, as psychobiographer Peter Loewenberg writes about Nixon's survivor guilt, Nixon "unconsciously needed to fail, in order to appease his guilt."[47] Johnson renders a similar interpretation, as does Abrahamsen, although Abrahamsen locates the source of Nixon's survivor guilt in a slightly different place. Abrahamsen argues that Nixon's guilt derived from his tremendous unmet desire for his mother's love; when his brothers' deaths allowed his mother to give him more time, attention, and devotion, he experienced "survivor guilt."[48]

Psychobiographers have seen evidence of Nixon's paranoia in his Watergate activities and cover-up. The difficulty with this interpretation lies in the fact that, in retrospect, it seems obvious that Nixon did not need inside information in order to win the 1972 presidential election. In the spring of that year it is possible that he felt more of a threat to his political career at the time than seems justifiable in retrospect. Regardless, Nixon's Watergate cover-up activities can be viewed as a psychologically motivated extension of his own self-taping and an expression of his fear that others were out to get him. In his case, this perception was not always paranoid, but often real, complicating any attempt to disentangle strategic from pathological motives. As the old adage proclaims, "just because you are paranoid does not mean they are not out to get you." These self-taping activities demonstrate Nixon's inability to control rage toward those he believed were judging or thwarting him politically or personally. Recall Freud's notion of being "wrecked by success." Freud argued that individuals who suffer from this syndrome often sabotage themselves just as they have achieved their goals, in an attempt to assuage their guilt for surviving a sibling or outperforming a parent. Nixon had achieved the former and more than accomplished the latter. Even Kissinger poignantly pointed to Nixon's sense of emptiness at a moment of great triumph during his second presidential inauguration:

> He too seemed as if he could not really believe it had all happened; a term in office had not abated his sense of wonder at being there. And he seemed, if not really happy, indeed quite detached.
>
> Triumph seemed to fill Nixon with a sense of ephemerality. He was, as he never tired of repeating, at his best under pressure. Indeed, it was sometimes difficult to avoid the impression that he needed crises as a motivating force – and that success became not a goal but an obsession so that once achieved he would not know what to do with it.... Through it all Richard Nixon moved as if he were himself a spectator, not a principal.... And yet there was about him this day a quality of remoteness, as if he could never quite bring himself to leave the inhospitable and hostile world that he inhabited, that he may have hated but at least had come to terms with.[49]

Nixon's sense of emptiness in the face of victory and success mimic Wilson's earlier responses. All of the psychoanalytically informed analyses of Nixon tend to focus on the preceding issues. Remarkable consistency exists among them in many areas. David Greenberg sums them up most eloquently when he writes that each psychobiographer "painted Nixon as an insecure, narcissistic personality whose childhood injuries instilled a drive to achieve, a sense of guilt over his success, and a frail ego to which small injuries triggered angry outbursts."[50] And yet the real conundrum of Nixon's life lies not in the insight that his troubled childhood led to personal and political difficulties later in life. Rather, the true puzzle rests in how Nixon could have achieved so much, been so successful, and reached the pinnacle of American political power despite this background, only to bring himself down by his own psychologically driven actions and decisions in the end. Loewenberg in particular notes Nixon's many "ego strengths and adaptations in his long political career."[51] Greenberg concludes that the psychobiographers "focused so unremittingly on his lying, his narcissism, his rage and other shortcomings that they didn't adequately explain how he had risen as high as he did."[52]

In their psychobiography of Nixon, Vamik Volkan, Norman Itzkowitz, and Andrew Dod attempt to take on the question of how Nixon could be so successful in some areas of policy making and such a failure in others.[53] They make their argument based on the implicit assumption that narcissistic personality disorders can include aspects that are "split off" from the dominant personality of grandiosity, which constitutes a compulsive form of self-devaluation. They pose three faces of Richard Nixon.

In one, the grandiose Nixon is seen to strive for superiority and major accomplishments, using his achievements to further bolster his sense of uniqueness and assure his positive place in history. This Nixon is found in the president who worked closely with Kissinger to try to solve the problem in Vietnam through the ultimately failed policy of Vietnamization, trying to turn control of South Vietnam over to the Vietnamese themselves.

The second face of Nixon they call the peacemaker. The peacemaker reflects the psychoanalytic perspective that narcissists combine unhealthy grandiosity with unrealistic self-devaluation, which is normally split off from the dominant grandiose personality. However, because all people are understood to strive for personal growth and development, even narcissists attempt to integrate the black and the white in themselves, attempting to combine their grandiose and hungry selves into one person. When a narcissist achieves such integration, however briefly, he can not only achieve peace inside himself by combining his normally split halves but can also serve as a peacemaker for the world.[54] From this perspective, Volkan et al. argue that Nixon had moments of achieving such peaceful integration. Perhaps the most notable of these accomplishments from a psychoanalytic perspective was Nixon's notion of linkage, his attempt to advance U.S.-Soviet relations by linking progress in areas of importance to the Soviets, such as strategic arms talks, U.S. trade, and the Middle East peace process, with progress in areas of importance to the U.S., especially Vietnam. Evidence for this peacemaking impulse can also be seen in Nixon's policies of détente with the Soviet Union, his attempt to unite a divided Berlin, and his rapprochement with China.

The third face of Nixon represents his paranoid self, the one that emerges when the split-off hungry self, filled with extreme feelings of debasement, takes precedence. This is the face of the destructive Nixon. If a person feels badly about himself as a result of how he feels about the way other people treat him or think about him, one of the simplest ways to feel better is then to project that anger outward, away from the self toward those who appear to cause the pain. In short, when someone gets hurt, they want to lash out at the person who harmed them and exert revenge upon them. When Nixon felt humiliated, threatened, or otherwise judged, he was unable to accept the resulting feelings of shame and rejection, and which he was normally able to successfully repress or control. So, he projected these feelings onto others and sought to destroy those others, incorrectly feeling that if he could accomplish this, he could simultaneously destroy his bad feelings toward himself. This Nixon emerges in his decisions to bomb, in secret, and then invade Cambodia, and also in his decisions surrounding the Christmas bombing of North Vietnam. In this way, Nixon reacted with rage, anger, violence, and aggression against those he felt had shamed or humiliated him.

The best psychological analysis of Richard Nixon focuses on just these issues of shame, humiliation, and subsequent aggressive action in Vietnam. Blema Steinberg wrote a masterful treatment of Nixon as an angry narcissist from this perspective.[55] She notes the way in which narcissists are not simply overly self-involved but also use success and recognition as a substitute for the parental love they so desperately desire but were never able to achieve. Somehow narcissists learn, or come to believe, that if they are just smart enough or successful enough, their parents or others will offer them the love they crave but never receive. And, of course, this strategy never works, because conditional love always feels tenuous, ephemeral, and inadequate. What narcissists want, like anyone else, is to be loved for who they are, not what they do. The irony, of course, lies in the fact that not only do narcissists pretend not to care what others think or feel about them but also they remain particularly sensitive to any kind of slight or rejection because such feelings of deprivation rest barely below the surface at all times. In addition, they often remain oblivious to the hurt and pain they inflict on others. Obviously, narcissism can manifest itself in several different ways. Steinberg focuses on the way in which Nixon tended to use force when he felt humiliation in an attempt to bolster his low sense of self-worth.

Steinberg carefully traces the origins of Nixon's narcissism in his childhood and then documents the way in which this dynamic played out on the international scene, as evidenced by his decisions and actions in first bombing and later invading Cambodia in 1969–1970. Steinberg's take on Nixon draws on a psychoanalytic framework, as do many of the other analyses of his life. She notes, as does Fawn Brodie, that Nixon came to believe that he could garner his parents' love only through his intellectual success. His mother recognized early that Richard was gifted and worked hard to teach him to read before he entered school; she insisted that he have his own room in which to study, while the other three boys shared the second bedroom. Not able to secure his mother's love in other ways, Nixon learned that his intellectual skills were a source of pride and accomplishment for his mother, and he believed it could earn him some affection from her. As Steinberg writes, young Richard saw his successes as both the price of his mother's love and the expiation of the survivor guilt he felt concerning the loss of his brothers. This structure, whereby a child feels that his parent's love remains contingent on his success and achievements, serves as a common precursor to the development of a narcissistic personality. According to Steinberg, a child who learns the lesson that love depends on achievement can establish only a very weak and fragile sense of self, because that edifice forever rests on the feeling of emptiness derived from profound deprivations in early parenting. The belief that love comes only with success induces shame, thereby driving the person to strive for ever greater accomplishments in order to shore up his fragile sense of self-worth. When success is not forthcoming, the individual experiences his underlying fear, shame, humiliation, and deprivation of love, leading him to lash out in rage and violence toward those who make him feel that way. Nixon's infamous "you won't have Nixon to kick around anymore" speech can be understood in this light.

Steinberg argues that Richard learned to control and repress his emotions from his psychologically distant Quaker mother. She believed in "silent punishment – in making a child sit quietly while he thinks through what he has done. That makes it punishment. It gets better results."[56] Nixon remembered his mother's punishments as much worse than his father's beatings: "But I do know that we dreaded far more than my father's hand, her tongue. It was never sharp, but she would just sit you down and she would talk very quietly and then when you got through you had been through an emotional experience."[57] These powerfully quiet punishments poured the foundation of Nixon's sensitivity to shame early in life.

According to Steinberg, Nixon also identified with his father, the aggressor. In attempting to balance these parental influences, Nixon learned a reasonable degree of control over his emotions until he felt ashamed or humiliated, in which case he lashed out at those who he felt had disrespected him. Steinberg argued that Nixon often projected this displaced anger outward, at enemies real and imagined, from his domestic Democratic opposition in Watergate to his Cambodian and Vietnamese enemies in war.

Yet this explanation, while obvious on its face, is not satisfying. While it is normal to assume prototypical gender roles, such that men are seen as aggressors and women as more nurturing, such a notion need not preclude the possibility that the true aggressor in a family might be the mother. This seems to be the case in Nixon's experience. While Frank's rage was more obvious, it was also more transient. Perhaps the real aggressor that Nixon identified with was not this father but his mother, who remained quietly humiliating. Donald Nixon, Richard's younger brother, believed that Richard was more like their mother than any of the other sons: "Dick always planned things out. He didn't do things accidentally. He had more of Mother's traits than any of us. He wouldn't argue much with me, but once, when he had just about as much as he could take, he cut loose and kept at it for a half hour. He didn't leave out anything. I've had a lot of respect for him ever since for the way he can keep things on his mind."[58]

All agree that the note he wrote as a young boy, addressed to "my dear master" was meant for his mother. Nixon himself stated that her quiet forms of retribution were more psychologically devastating than his father's beatings. Although Richard may not have held her responsible for the deaths of his two brothers, he held her accountable for his own emotional crucifixion. After all, the most aggressive action that a mother can take toward her child is to deny him her love. This framework hands Hannah incredible power in Richard's life. If his mother was the aggressor that Nixon identified with, and not his more rageful father, his ambivalence about the use of violence becomes more understandable. Her rage manifested in quiet, determined, calculated ways, not in explosive impulsivity. And, so, it appeared, did Nixon's anger display in the ways he tried to keep his unacceptable actions, both domestic and international, secret.

Medical Analyses

Nixon had at least two doctors, Dr. Arnold Hutschnecker and Dr. John Lungren, who felt it to be their duty to come to his defense in writing, despite issues of doctor-patient confidentiality. Dr. Hutschnecker's treatment of Nixon caused some interest in the 1960 election because Hutschnecker had treated Nixon as an internist. Hutschnecker later became a psychiatrist, raising some question about whether Nixon had seen Hutschnecker in a psychotherapeutic context. As an internist, Hutschnecker was known for being an expert on psychosomatic illness.

Nixon's relationship with Hutschnecker was complex. Nixon met the doctor in 1951 after a colleague gave Nixon a copy of Hutschnecker's popular psychology book on psychosomatic illness, *Will to Live*. Nixon liked the book and continued to recommend it for years, even as president. He sought out the doctor for treatment of insomnia and continued to see him for four years. In 1955 gossip columnist Walter Winchell broke the story that Nixon was seeing a psychiatrist, after which Nixon stopped the visits. However, he continued to see the doctor, now as a friend, in a social capacity, for a long time. One of the last remaining items in Nixon's desk upon his resignation was a letter from Hutschnecker. And Hutschnecker was the one who held Nixon's hand as he cried at his wife Pat's funeral.[59]

Following a media feeding frenzy surrounding the Winchell allegation, Dr. Arnold Hutschnecker acknowledged that he had been Nixon's doctor but refused to disclose any details of their relationship: "What I as a physician am allowed to say is that Mr. Nixon came for physical checkups, none of which showed any evidence of any illness."[60] Later in the same article, he reiterates, "During the entire period that I treated Mr. Nixon, I detected no sign of mental illness in him."[61]

However, in the context of his article entitled "President Nixon's Former Doctor Writes about the Mental Health of Our Leaders," Hutschnecker discussed how the public should evaluate the leadership qualities of an individual in the nuclear age. He posited that the answer lay in considering "a man's drive for power, his personality, emotional makeup, motivation and goals."[62] He then presented a leadership typology that he claimed was based on Pavlovian techniques.[63] He discussed four leadership types: strong-excitatory; lively; calm-imperturbable; and weak-inhibitory. Hutschnecker's typology is matched almost exactly by the active-passive and positive-negative dimensions upon which James David Barber later based his fourfold model of presidential leadership.[64] Hutschnecker wrote that the first type of leaders, strong-excitatory, driven by hostile and aggressive urges, represented the majority of all leaders. He went on to say that because the first and last, weak-inhibitory, type were the most likely to crack under pressure, the second type, lively, would make the best leaders.

In the context of this discussion, however, Hutschnecker makes an interesting point about the will to power but without mentioning Nixon. "When a man seeks excessive power, what moves him is an urge to fulfill neurotic needs. Most of these go back to a child's feelings of smallness and a compulsion to compensate for his helplessness by attaining omnipotence."[65] He ended with two somewhat unique suggestions for improving the quality of leadership in America. First, he suggested that all high school or college students undergo psychiatric testing. The purpose of this would be twofold: first, to find and treat existing mental illness early; and second, to detect and prohibit psychopathic personalities from reaching high positions of power. He believed that children on a criminal path should be exiled from society. He argued that such a test should be a requirement for highly responsible jobs. However, he did not comment on issues of misdiagnosis, privacy, civil rights, the misuse of such information, or the possible stigmatization of the mentally ill as a result of this process. Second, he advocated for a department of peace, which would require a cabinet-level position designed to "explore the psychodynamics of peace, the study of the techniques and sublimation of human aggression."[66] In a later article, he wrote, "I cannot help think[ing] that if an American President had a staff psychiatrist, perhaps a case such as Watergate might not have had a chance to develop."[67]

His retrospective contention would appear to undercut his earlier claims that he had seen no mental illness in Nixon in the 1950s and felt no compulsion to "weed" Nixon out of politics. Similarly, his arguments seem to contradict each other; if you can discover and prevent those with mental illness from reaching high office, why then would prominent officials need a staff psychiatrist? And if such identification were straightforward, why couldn't he see signs of problems in Nixon? The frequency with which mental illness can arise in later life among those not previously vulnerable raises a problem for his argument. However, early warning might provide the type of supportive intervention that could prove critical in stressful times.

The second physician to comment on Nixon was John Lungren, who served as Nixon's personal physician and friend from 1952 until just shortly before Nixon's death. Lungren decided early on in their relation-ship that he wanted to write a book about Nixon and obtained a full release from medical confidentiality on December 21, 1975. Nixon put no restraints in his release letter. This fact is interesting in itself. Imposing no restraints whatsoever on a biography of himself written by his medical doctor does not seem to be the act of a paranoid personality. It does, how-ever, speak to a kind of narcissism. Lungren did not write his biography until after Nixon's death, spending the last five years of his life, while he himself was dying, writing the book with his son, a prominent California politician in his own right. Lungren's perspective is sympathetic toward Nixon and defensive against those who would attack him, but not blind to Nixon's failings.

In the foreword to Lungren's book, Rick Perlstein writes, "The issue of vulnerability – repressing it, belatedly acknowledging it, fighting it, hid-ing it, probing it, exploiting it in others, and even, in strategic moments, exploiting it in himself – was central to Richard Nixon's life."[68] What emerges from Lungren's portrait of Nixon, which largely focuses on Nixon's battle for life following his phlebitis crisis, is a man totally destroyed by what he had undergone during his presidency. Lungren quotes Nixon as having asked him "with impassioned consternation: 'Pat and I would both like to know – *what did we do wrong?*'"[69] Unlike most, Lungren argues that Nixon did reflect on his presidential mistakes after his resignation and felt remorse for them:

Nixon's growing self-awareness would later deepen into dreadful self-recognition that would reach a catharsis of conscience during the seminal David Frost interviews of March 1977. As he confronted his own actions, the consequences flowing from his own fallibility would fill Nixon with great sorrow and deep contrition. Nixon lamented that he had gravely harmed democracy in America by estranging a generation of young people from pol-itics and by losing the chance for a generation of peace.[70]

While acknowledging that Nixon agreed to the Frost interviews because he needed the money to pay off legal and medical debts, Lungren does not mention that these interviews represented a brilliant political move on Nixon's part as well; he understood that his reentry into the world he had left in disgrace must be presaged by a meaningful mea culpa.

In no way self-serving in his tone, Lungren still emerges as a skilled, car-ing, and compassionate physician who helped bring Nixon back to life, by saving not only his physical life through surgery but also his psychological life by encouraging Nixon to write, speak, see friends, and reengage in life after his illness and disgrace. Unlike most of Nixon's psychobiogra-phers, Lungren focuses on Nixon's many accomplishments, particularly his opening of China.

But Lungren also notes two important characteristics in Nixon that repeatedly disturbed him. He observes that Nixon seemed to have an ambivalent relationship to loyalty. On the one hand, he would reward a particular type of sycophantic loyalty, while simultaneously punishing more authentically loyal advisers who offered constructive forms of criticism. First, he found Nixon's penchant for surrounding himself with those who agreed with him to be troublesome:

> I found [William P.] Rogers personable and likeable; however, he frequently offered gratuitous praise instead of candor and constructive criticism. Unfortunately, Rogers was a yes-man and would tell Nixon that he was great and that everything was fine when it was not. Rogers personified a disturbing pattern in Nixon that I perceived as he rose to great positions of power: a predilection to surround himself with advisers who were completely subservient.
>
> At times, loyal and trusted advisers who were not afraid to tell Nixon when he was wrong were shunted aside. There usually were advisers who were personally and intellectually secure, who wanted and needed nothing from Nixon. Their forthright counsel was allowed to wane in favor of influence from those who feared jeopardizing their own acquired power and position.[71]

The discussion of Rogers appears particularly compelling in light of the fact that Nixon was known for frequently humiliating him. Some people found this behavior odd, but this pattern in Nixon may have gratified his important psychological need for repeating the rejection he himself experienced from the other perspective.

Lungren's other concern related to a lack of loyalty that Nixon displayed toward his dutiful subordinates. In 1969 the Nixon administration tried for five months to elevate John Knowles as assistant secretary of health, education, and welfare for health and scientific activities. This nomination was supported by previous Nixon favorite Robert Finch, secretary of health, education, and welfare. But this nomination got Nixon into trouble when it was strongly opposed by the American Medical Association and Senate Minority Leader Everett McKinley Dirksen.[72] This debacle led Nixon to brush Finch aside:

> [Robert] Finch's travails revealed a troubling characteristic of Nixon and the political world in general that I could neither fathom nor condone – the tendency to discard loyal aides when they became disposable. The pattern was familiar – the aide would never be informed directly, overtly ostracized, or summarily dismissed. He was merely ignored, cut out of key meetings, gradually stripped of responsibility; given a position with no authority, and, in effect, shoved into a corner. . . . Nixon suffered unnecessary political defeats without their constructive counsel and mature and balanced perspective.[73]

Nixon followed such patterns in a repeated sequencing of firing top administration officials. Notable dismissals included Assistant to the

President for Domestic Affairs John Ehrlichman and White House Chief of Staff Bob Haldeman on April 30, 1973. He also fired White House Counsel to the President John Dean at this time. Alexander Haig then replaced Bob Haldeman as White House chief of staff. Later, in the so-called "Saturday Night Massacre" of October 20, 1973, Nixon forced resignations from Attorney General Elliot L. Richardson and his deputy, William D. Ruckelshaus, who refused to fire Special Prosecutor Archibald Cox. Nixon then appointed U.S. Solicitor General Robert Bork as acting Attorney General; Bork then fired Cox. These last terminations were undertaken in a last-ditch attempt to save his presidency in the wake of the Watergate investigations.

In many respects, Nixon's style mimics his own earlier rejection at the hands of President Eisenhower. Eisenhower did not like or trust Nixon, had not wanted Nixon as a running mate on the 1952 ticket, and certainly did not want him on the second ticket in 1956, from where he would, as a consequence, become the presumptive nominee for the Republican nomination in 1960. As a result, Eisenhower engaged in many slights toward Nixon. In 1952, however, many Republicans found Nixon a good balance on the ticket for Eisenhower because of his youth and California geographical credentials; he was also one of the few candidates acceptable to both the Eisenhower people and the old guard in the Republican Party, and they felt this would help prevent a repeat of the electoral defeat the party suffered in 1948. But many others, including Eisenhower, did not consider Nixon trustworthy.

Barely two months after the convention, the New York Post ran a story accusing Nixon of misappropriating $16,000 for personal use. This secret fund, ostensibly for office expenses and travel, came from about seventy of his California millionaire backers. The scandal surrounding Nixon's fund all but drove him off the ticket, as the Washington Post and the New York Herald Tribune called for his resignation.[74] Eisenhower himself refused to commit himself either for or against Nixon: "I have come to the conclusion that you are the one who has to decide what to do.... If the impression got around that you got off the ticket because I forced you to get off, it is going to be very bad. On the other hand, if I issue a statement now backing you up, in effect people will accuse me of condoning wrongdoing."[75] Nixon wrote out a letter of withdrawal, but his campaign manager Murray Chotiner tore it up. Never overtly hostile, Ike essentially expected Nixon to take it upon himself to resign as the vice-presidential candidate. On the night of his speech to the nation to address this crisis, one of Eisenhower's men, Tom Dewey, told Nixon that everyone thought it would be best if he resigned. When Dewey asked Nixon what he was going to do, Nixon replied: "Just tell them I haven't the slightest idea as to what I am going to do and if they want to find out they'd better listen to the broadcast. And tell them I know something about politics too!" Nixon then proceeded to give his famous Checkers speech, one of the most successful resurrection speeches in American history, so-called after the name of the dog given to his daughter that he mentioned in the speech. Eisenhower was forced by public opinion to keep Nixon on the ticket.

In 1956 Eisenhower wanted to run Treasury Secretary Robert Anderson as his vice-presidential running mate, a candidate who would never have flown with the party regulars because he was a Democrat. Nonetheless, Eisenhower tried hard to get Nixon to drop out of the race voluntarily. He offered him a position as secretary of defense; he encouraged him to run for the Senate. But Nixon insisted on continuing on as vice president and Eisenhower, not willing to cause a party rift just prior to his reelection, accepted Nixon once again. In 1960, Eisenhower refused to formally endorse Nixon for president. In the case of Nixon and Eisenhower, whatever paranoia Nixon experienced had a basis in reality.

Additional Commentary

At least one psychobiographical treatment of Nixon does not rest on psychodynamic assumptions. David Winter and Leslie Carlson undertook an analysis of Nixon using his 1969 first inaugural address to determine Nixon's drives from his rhetoric, applying David McClelland's theoretical conceptions of motive. They validated their findings using the memoirs of six Nixon presidential aides.

An achievement motive refers to a person's drive for excellence and accomplishment. Nixon's preoccupation with being the first one to accomplish something, such as opening China to the West, would represent an example of this motive. Need for affiliation refers to the desire to be loved, acknowledged, and appreciated. Under conditions of stress, those with a high affiliation motive can often exhibit defensive behavior, fearing rejection if they make a wrong move. In other words, people with a high affiliation motive can appear paradoxical in action; if they feel threatened, they tend to react with aggression rather than in a prosocial way. The power motive describes the wish for status and prestige. This motive is seen to accentuate impulsive behaviors, including high-risk activities such as binge drinking, aggressive action, or sexual promiscuity. What is striking about this analysis is that it supposes contingent behavior. A high-affiliation leader does well in good times but can become erratic under stress, proving less likely to take advice from experts than friends and reciprocating dislike where it is assumed to exist.[76] These authors concluded that Nixon possessed a high motive for achievement and for intimacy and affiliation and only an average motive for power.

PSYCHIATRIC DIAGNOSES

Most the authors who have assessed Nixon's behavior have assumed that he suffered from some form of narcissism. From a medical and psychiatric perspective, narcissism constitutes one of ten different so-called personality disorders. Unlike more acute or transitory psychiatric disorders such as substance abuse or depression, personality disorders are distinguished by their pervasive and enduring nature. According to the *Diagnostic and Statistical Manual of Mental Disorders*, a personality disorder is defined as "an enduring pattern of inner experience and behavior that deviates markedly from the expectations of an individual's culture, is pervasive and inflexible, has an onset in adolescence or early adulthood, is stable over time, and leads to distress or impairment."[77] Some disorders, such as schizotypal, tend to cause more severe impairment than others, such as a dependent personality disorder, and many, like narcissism, can cause more difficulty for those around the affected individual than for the person himself. It is possible for one person to suffer from more than one personality disorder at a time.

The ten personality disorders are broken into three groups. Narcissism belongs in the second cluster of disorders, typically defined by their dramatic nature. About three-quarters of narcissists are male. While it seems to affect less than 1 percent of people in the general population, it seems likely that certain professions, such as politics, include a higher percentage of narcissists because affected individuals tend to self-select into political positions that offer the kind of fame or power they feel they need or deserve. The characteristics defining narcissism include grandiosity; extreme need for admiration, attention, and special treatment; and a profound lack of empathy. Typical elements of the disorder include a grandiose sense of self-importance; preoccupation with fantasies of unlimited success, power, beauty, or love: a belief that one is special and unique and can be understood only by similarly gifted or high-status people; demands for excessive admiration; a vast sense of entitlement; a tendency for greatly exploiting others; lack of empathy; enormous envy; and tremendous arrogance.

Nixon demonstrated many of these characteristics in his personal and political life. Without at least a somewhat grandiose sense of his own self-importance, he might never have run for president again after his close defeat by Kennedy in 1960 and his subsequent loss to Pat Brown in the 1962 California gubernatorial race. But Nixon was not only a man compelled to be the first and the best; also he continually participated in his own political resurrection, rising from the ashes of defeat time and again, at least partly because of his belief in his own importance. In this way, Nixon closely modeled his mother's strong-willed persistence in the face of adversity, although his domain of action was political while hers was personal. Nixon's obsession with his own personal political power, from Watergate to Vietnam, betrays his preoccupation with unlimited power and smacks of arrogance. And his ability to dismiss long-standing and loyal aides when his political future was on the line, including intimate advisers such as John Ehrlichman and Bob Haldeman, reflects both his interpersonal exploitativeness and his lack of empathy. Most remarkably, after firing Haldeman, Nixon tried to prevail on him to find out how well the speech announcing the forced resignations had been received. Even Haldeman was stunned by Nixon's lack of understanding and empathy in this regard:

> P[resident] called in the afternoon from Camp David, where he was working on his speech for tonight. Sounded terrible, said, well, I just wanted you to know that I still love you.... Said basically, I have all resignations in hand, don't I? And I said that he did.... It was interesting that I called him, and they said he wasn't taking calls, but he called back a little after ten. I said well, You've got it behind you now, and you should approach it that way. He said it was a very tough thing, and I'll never mention it again. Then he got to feeling sorry for himself. He said Cap is the only Cabinet officer who's called. I told him that the operators were telling people that you weren't taking calls. Said to me you're a strong man, you've got to keep the faith, you're going to win this, God Bless You.
>
> Then he asked me if I thought I could do some checking around on reaction to the speech as I had done in the past, and I said no, I didn't think I could. He realized that was the case. He called again about midnight, rather bitter. Said Kissinger's reaction was typical, he's waiting to see how it comes out. Said again, keep the faith, and that was that.[78]

In a demonstration of his overall sense of grandiosity and narcissism, Nixon explained his desire to run for the presidency in 1960, over his wife's objections, because he had "never been in center stage, in the leading role.... And I'll never be satisfied until I'm in that role."[79] Of course, the confidence inherent in narcissism can lead its victim to accomplish great things because the individual never has any conscious doubt that he can achieve what others cannot by outsmarting and outmaneuvering the less talented opposition.

In addition, Nixon was thought to envy some of his competitors, such as Jack Kennedy. Nixon's envy of Kennedy could have had its roots in his counterpart's obvious success, wealth, good looks, and easy personal skills. It may have also reflected his envy over the obvious love that Jack's mother lavished on him, while Nixon's own mother remained frustratingly aloof. In a telling set of interviews conducted by Bela Kortnizer during the 1960 presidential election campaign, he asked each mother if she thought her son would make a good president. Rose Kennedy bubbled, "He would make a wonderful President." Hannah Nixon dourly replied that Nixon would be a good president "if God is on his side."[80]

Nixon cannot have felt that this contrast reflected well on him. While he may not have seen his mother's response as an explicit betrayal, it did not help his candidacy and thus may have easily sparked his anger and envy toward Kennedy for having all that Nixon had felt deprived of, including maternal love. Arnold Hutschnecker, Nixon's physician, felt that Nixon's awkwardness in his televised debates with Kennedy derived from his fear of his mother's observation: "I was convinced of the connection between being in front of the camera and being in front of his mother.... Multiply the singular face of a critical mother watching the flaws, to the flaws seen by millions, then one can better comprehend the telegenic awkwardness of Nixon.... I believe that the image of the saintly but stern face of his mother defeated him more than any other factor... he wanted his mother to believe him perfect. That was his problem."[81]

When Andre Watts played piano at the Eisenhower presidential inaugural, Hannah turned to Richard during the intermission and said, "Now Richard, if thee had practiced more on the piano, thee could been down there instead of up here."[82] Even during one of Nixon's greatest moments of political triumph, his inauguration as vice president, his mother choose to remind him that his musical discipline and talents failed to impress her. Hannah Nixon died in 1967, the year before Richard was elected president.

Another personality disorder that Nixon may fit into is the paranoid, which falls into the first group, the one usually referred to as odd or eccentric. In this disorder, the person suffers from a severe sense of distrust and suspiciousness of others. The person often assigns malignant intent to the motives and actions of others where another might see no evidence of such malevolence. This disorder is characterized by features that include suspicion, without cause, that others are hurting, exploiting, or deceiving the person; preoccupation with unjustified doubts about the loyalty and trustworthiness of others; reluctance to share confidences for fear of them being used against the person; reading hidden threats into everyday words or events; bearing grudges; perceiving attack on the person's character where none exists and reacting quickly in an angry or threatening manner; and recurrent suspicions of infidelity on the part of one's partner.

Nixon seems to manifest many of these symptoms over the course of his life. In particular, he never seemed able to truly trust or confide in another person fully. While vice president, Nixon himself said, "in my job you can't enjoy the luxury of intimate personal friendships. You can't confide absolutely in *anyone*."[83] Nixon's views notwithstanding, many men as vice president have kept up close friendships while on the job. Bryce Harlow, one of Nixon's presidential aides, believed that Nixon "was hurt very deeply by somebody... someone he deeply trusted. Hurt so badly he never got over it and never trusted anybody again."[84] This may be the case, or it may be that his parents were the ones who hurt him deeply and failed to either teach or model trust for their son. Or, as one biographer succinctly stated, "beginning with his parents, other people have always brought Nixon grief."[85] Nixon's long-standing obsession with the Kennedys and their desire to do him harm may have stemmed from the reality of his 1960 loss to Jack in the presidential race but endured and grew well beyond what a reasonable person might expect.

Finally, a common question raised about Nixon is, Who is the real Richard Nixon? Greenberg's book revolves around the many and varied images that Nixon holds in American culture and society. Even sophisticated psychobiographers like Volkan and his colleagues are left presenting notions of "the three faces" of Nixon. Many images of Nixon appear contradictory in retrospect: how is it that a man who opened China and achieved détente with the Soviets could bring himself down with, in essence, the cover-up of a petty theft? The most revealing reflection on this question of who the real Richard Nixon was is offered by John Ehrlichman:

> I imagine you will get as many answers as you ask questions. Everybody sees him differently, and that was one of the problems working (with) him. He was a man who presented an aspect to each individual that he came into contact with, and it was different to some degree to the aspect that he presented to everyone else. I account for this by the fact that he was a person who genuinely disliked face-to-face controversy. He would find out what the visitors' interests were and get them talking about themselves and size up how to best get along without a clash. He was pretty much all things to all people, to the extent that he could be. If he had someone in there who was profane, then he was profane. If he had someone in there who was not profane, he was not profane.[86]

This description reflects an almost textbook understanding of someone who suffers from a borderline personality disorder, replaces identity with role, and attempts to be all things to all people because there is no deeply held sense of self.

Nixon's discomfort around people, especially in social situations, has been frequently noted by his advisers and associates in their memoirs. Writing in 1979 of his first meeting with Nixon, Kissinger noted that "Richard Nixon has to this day not overcome his own social inhibitions."[87] When Kissinger first met Nixon to discuss the possibility of joining his administration, he wrote that "Nixon was painfully shy. Meeting new people filled him with vague dread, especially if they were in a position to rebuff or contradict him. As was his habit before such appointments, Nixon was probably in an adjoining room settling his nerves and reviewing his remarks, no doubt jotted down on a yellow tablet that he never displayed to his visitors."[88] Kissinger agreed with Ehrlichman that Nixon could not bear face-to-face confrontation with others:

"Almost invariably during his Presidency his decisions were courageous and strong and often taken in loneliness against all expert advice. But wherever possible Nixon made his decisions in solitude on the basis of memoranda or with a few very intimate aides. He abhorred confronting colleagues with whom he disagreed and he could not bring himself to face a disapproving friend."[89] Kissinger further notes that Nixon employed a particular mechanism to avoid such unpleasant interactions:

> During periods when he withdrew he counted on his assistants to carry on the day-to-day decisions; during spasms of extreme activity he relied on his assistants to screen his more impetuous commands. They were needed to prevent the face-to-face confrontations he so disliked and dreaded. And they were to protect Nixon against impulsive visitors or the tendency to agree with the visitors he did receive. Haldeman's staff system did not "isolate" the President as was often alleged; Nixon insisted on isolating himself; it was the only way in which he could marshal his psychological resources.[90]

Haldeman reports an incident with Nixon that confirms Kissinger's claims. On Wednesday, May 17, 1971, Nixon had a hard time mediating a conflict between Rogers and Kissinger over the SALT treaty. After talking to Rogers, "right after he hung up the P heaved a deep sigh, looked out the window, and said it would be goddamn easy to run this office if you didn't have to deal with people."[91] This comment proves especially revealing about Nixon for a number of reasons. First, as Kissinger's and Haldeman's memoirs attest, Nixon was the one who encouraged Kissinger to engage in the behaviors that so angered Rogers, yet he fails to take responsibility for his part in creating the personnel troubles such antagonisms created. Second, as Kissinger's comments above attest, Nixon was very uncomfortable around people in general, but simultaneously, and ironically, he often hated to be alone, so he would often call Haldeman, Ehrlichman, or Kissinger to be with him when nothing else was scheduled. Having just anyone around was not sufficient, because anyone other than intimates created anxiety. But for someone who experienced so much social awkwardness, Nixon kept Haldeman in particular on a very close leash.

A borderline disorder is part of the dramatic cluster, along with narcissism. Borderline gets its name from the early psychoanalytic assumption that those who exhibited this disorder sat on the "borderline" between neurotic and psychotic disorders. Many borderline features combine and reflect some of the criteria outlined in the narcissistic and paranoid disorders. The disorder is defined as one where the person manifests "instability of interpersonal relationships, self-image, and affects, and marked impulsivity."[92] This personality pattern is reflected in the tendency to avoid real or imagined abandonment; unstable and intense interpersonal relationships; unstable sense of self; impulsivity, including substance abuse; suicidal behavior; unstable mood; chronic feelings of emptiness; inappropriate anger, or inability to control anger; and transient, stress-related paranoid ideation.

One feature of Nixon's life may be relevant in this context. Nixon married his second real girlfriend, Catherine "Pat" Ryan, after his first girlfriend, Ola Florence Welch, married Nixon's former football team-mate Gail Jobe. Richard met Pat at Whittier College in 1939. Pat had her own troubled childhood, which may have provided some of the basis for common experience between the two. As David Halberstam described it,

> Pat Nixon. I think she's heartbreaking. She has a childhood so harsh it is Dickensian. It is hard as if she lived in the time of Charles Dickens. It's hard to imagine anyone with so difficult a life. Her mother, who's the one person she really loves, dies when she's young. Her father dies. She raises her brothers, cooks for them, keeps house, cleans, and then goes off and studies herself, puts herself through school. Utterly admirable, really beautiful when she was young, eventually marries Richard Nixon.[93]

At first, Pat did not like Richard or respond to him. But Nixon was intensely persistent, often driving her back and forth to her dates with other men, for two years. When she finally relented and married him, many observers commented on the seemingly cold and distant nature of their relationship. Arnold Hutschnecker, Nixon's physician, said he heard from Pat "how much she detested politics. She wanted a simple life...wanted to be a housewife. But he couldn't. He liked to be in the thick of things." Hutschnecker argued that, while Pat was loyal to her husband, giving him support and encouragement, Nixon saw Pat as "his sun – to a degree that was not entirely healthy. He was devoted but that was like the relationship with his mother... one-sided. He was very dependent on her." And, indeed, when Pat died, Nixon gave a moving eulogy and openly cried over his loss of her.

Some, including Nixon's press aide, James Bassett, claimed that Nixon had first consulted Hutschnecker for treatment of impotence. Although Hutschnecker had received written permission from Nixon to speak after his death, he remained circumspect about this particular issue. While he would not answer a specific question about whether Nixon suffered from impotence, he discussed the problem in more general terms with his interviewer: "Every boy has an imprint of his mother as an ideal. And unless he drowns out that ideal woman, he cannot do sex....If someone was like a mother and a saint, you don't have sex. That far I can go."[94] This pattern of alternating intense and cold personal relationships remains characteristic of borderline personality disorders.

Nixon's unstable sense of self may also meet the criteria for a borderline disorder. While it might be easy to disregard Ehrlichman's earlier quote as simply reflecting an astute politician's desire to please, Ehrlichman was a sophisticated political actor who was used to watching politicians manipulate individuals in order to achieve their goals. And yet it is within this context that Ehrlichman makes his claim about the extreme nature of Nixon's personal instability. Evidence of Nixon's impulsivity in the form of substance abuse exists as well.[95] In May, Nixon himself became worried that word would leak that he had been drunk during the early phases of a crisis involving the North Koreans' attacking an American reconnaissance plane. At that time, Kissinger aide Lawrence Eagleburger commented, "[h]ere's the President of the United States, ranting and raving – drunk in the middle of a crisis."[96] Many authors speak to Nixon's increasing problems with alcohol abuse as the problems in his presidency worsened. Nixon's drinking became of particular concern to Kissinger, who apparently would "poke fun at 'my drunken friend' the way most people who joke about things that really scared them."[97] Kissinger's staff also became alarmed by Nixon's drinking and took to listening in on their late night conversations.

Further, depending on how liberally the notion of suicide is taken, Nixon surely demonstrated a willingness to take severe, life-threatening risks with his health, especially when he refused treatment for the phlebitis in his left leg just prior to his resignation. He also participated in his own political suicide, bringing about the condition and situation that precipitated his own downfall. In addition, he often demonstrated an inability to control his anger, even in press conferences, but especially toward his political enemies, both abroad and at home. Finally, as noted earlier, Nixon's tapes, and his justification for them, display his paranoid ideation.

What is the purpose and meaning of this litany of diagnostic categories? Does it help observers understand Nixon any better? Nixon was a unique and tortured man who experienced extremely unusual and intense highs and lows throughout his life. What these diagnoses illustrate is particular patterns of behavior that cluster together and reflect an ongoing and pervasive set of attitudes and behaviors toward the world around oneself. Such people are less responsive to their environment and more likely to impose their view of events upon it. If these categories help observers illuminate a person's understanding of his world, his place in it, and his interactions with others, they can provide starting points for analysis and understanding.

Richard Nixon appears to have been especially unlucky. His father's bad temper and shiftlessness may have reflected some kind of psychological vulnerability. In addition, Nixon grew up under painful circumstances where he needed more love than either his emotionally remote mother or his violent father could provide. Two of his brothers died when he was young. In the face of such stress and rejection, he had to learn to love himself if he was to survive. No one else helped him flourish. He learned that only success could bring the approval he craved; failure only endorsed his deep-seated sense of his own basic lack of self-worth, creating rage and vindictiveness, especially when shame or humiliation reminded him of this fact. Nixon's narcissism and paranoia can be seen as survival strategies, which, while essential in his youth, proved maladaptive in his future political life.[98]

CAMBODIA AND VIETNAM

When Nixon was elected president in 1968, he understood that the Vietnam War was both emblematic and symptomatic of the decline in postwar U.S. hegemony. Nixon had a plan to turn this tide around, and the head of his National Security Council, Henry Kissinger, became his partner in undertaking the laudable goal of peace with honor. Kissinger may have been picked as Nixon's alter ego for many reasons, but perhaps one journalist's observation provides the most revealing explanation: "Nixon had a consuming need for flattery and Kissinger a consuming need to provide it."[99]

Beginning in 1969, Nixon embarked on a plan to end American involvement in Vietnam through a strategy that involved the gradual withdrawal of American troops from the region, the strengthening of South Vietnamese troops and government in a policy that came to be known as Vietnamization, American military action against guerrilla forces, détente with the Soviets that included linkage of things they wanted for help with Vietnam, and negotiations with the North Vietnamese. Part of the explanation lies in Nixon's insight into how others perceived him and his strategic use of this understanding. Similar to Thomas Schelling's notion of the "rationality of irrationality," Nixon believed that his Madman theory, as well as his use of linkage politics with the Soviets, may have served to integrate and synthesize the two faces of Nixon that others saw as distinct. Specifically, as recalled by Haldeman,

> The threat was the key, and Nixon coined a phrase for his theory which I'm sure will bring smiles of delight to Nixon-haters everywhere. We were walking along a foggy beach after a long day of speech writing. He said, "I call it the Madman theory, Bob. I want the North Vietnamese to believe I've reached the point where I might do anything to stop the war. We'll just slip the word to them that, "for God's sake, you know Nixon is obsessed about Communism. We can't restrain him when he's angry–and he has his hand on the nuclear button" – and Ho Chi Minh himself will be in Paris in two days begging for peace.[100]

Nixon believed that he could garner a strategic advantage in his negotiations with the North Vietnamese by appearing to be more irrational than he was. The problem arose, however, because the North Vietnamese seemed to believe that Nixon was crazy like a fox and not simply crazy. As the vice minister of foreign affairs and a top aide to Le Duc Tho in his negotiations with Kissinger in Paris later reported, "he would like to show to the Vietnamese that he was a changeable [unpredictable] person, that he can surprise – how to say, a big stick surprise. But this backfired on Nixon, because we saw that Nixon could not have a big stick, because of the step-by-step withdrawal of American forces. That means the stick becomes smaller and smaller."[101] This so-called Madman theory remained central to Nixon's comprehensive strategy from the start, as early as 1968, whereby he hoped to scare the North Vietnamese, and the Soviets, into complying with American demands through the threat of excessive force. As Kimball writes,

> [T]he madman theory lay at the heart of the president's strategy for dealing with foreign adversaries, such as North Vietnam and the Soviet Union. This striking phrase, Haldeman reported, was Nixon's alternative name for the "principle of a threat of excessive force." Nixon thought that military force was an essential component of diplomacy because of its coercive power, but its coercive power, he believed, could be enhanced if his opponents could be convinced that he was capable of or intent upon using extreme force, since this would suggest that he possessed one or more of the interrelated qualities of madness.... he meant to convey his supposed madness as irrationality, unpredictability, unorthodoxy, reckless risk-taking, obsession, and fury.[102]

Perhaps his deeply conflicted childhood made the notion of putting irrationality to constructive use particularly attractive. It allowed him to act out his impulses in a way that could accomplish the important, and justifiable, goal of peace.

Common understanding assumes that Vietnamization, which sought to help the South Vietnamese allies without America doing everything, in an attempt to gradually turn control of South Vietnam over to the South Vietnamese, was Nixon's main strategy to end the war. Instead, Vietnamization was only part of Nixon's larger goal of undertaking a slower withdrawal of American forces in order to ensure a "decent interval" between the end of American occupation and the fall of the South Vietnamese government.

Vietnamization was in reality the fall-back strategy for Nixon and Kissinger, who originally advocated a much more aggressive approach to the war in Vietnam.[103] In September 1969 Nixon even contemplated a major escalation in the war – code-named Duck Hook – which encompassed a plan to bomb military and economic sites around Hanoi, mine the harbor at Haiphong, increase ground operations in the demilitarized zone between North and South, interdict supply lines in and out of Cambodia, and bomb North Vietnam's rail and communications systems, bridges to China, and the dikes on the northern rivers. The administration expected that bombing the dikes in particular could lead to more than a million deaths by drowning. Eventually Nixon abandoned this plan in favor of a worldwide nuclear alert designed to signal to the Soviets the seriousness of his intent. Part of the reason he moved away from Duck Hook revolved around the timing and how close the announcement of this policy would be to major scheduled antiwar demonstrations; Nixon believed that such timing would undermine its credibility. Clearly part of his Madman approach, Nixon's attempt to scare the Soviets failed because they failed to respond to the alert. Later still, in the fall of 1970, Nixon once again contemplated a more aggressive alternative dubbed the Bug-out option, which would have combined rapid troop withdrawal with massive air and naval operations, but without negotiations.

Nixon's strategy ultimately failed. The North Vietnamese continued to use the Ho Chi Minh trail, which led through parts of Laos and Cambodia, to resupply their forces in the South. Without informing the American people, or explaining anything to Congress, Nixon began secretly bombing North Vietnamese sanctuaries in Cambodia on March 18, 1969. The following year, Prince Sihanouk of Cambodia, who had broken relations with the United States in 1965, but did not object when Nixon began his secret bombing, was overthrown by his prime minister General Lon Nol on March 18, 1970. Nol was more sympathetic to the American cause, giving Nixon an excuse to launch a land invasion of Cambodia on April 30, 1970. Even Dean Acheson had his doubts about the invasion. He told a friend that Nixon was the only horse he knew who would run back into a burning barn.[104] The main thing Nixon accomplished with his land invasion was the outcome he was trying to prevent from the outset: the wider and deeper incursion of the communist forces, the Khmer Rouge, throughout Cambodia, and worse still, their ultimate victory, sealed by their leader Pol Pot's brutal murder of more than 1 million of his own people.

In addition, the Cambodian invasion signaled the real start of violent antiwar protests at home. American college campuses blew up; 450 went on strike to protest the invasion. People marched on Washington. In early May, antiwar protestors at Kent State University were shot by the Ohio National Guard; four students died as a result. Neil Young's protest song, "Ohio," which memorialized the incident, quickly became an antiwar anthem, with lyrics that included the line, "Tin soldiers and Nixon's coming; We're finally on our own; This summer I hear the drumming; Four dead in Ohio." The picture of the screaming woman kneeling over one of the dead students provided an American bookend to the searing image of the Buddhist monk who set himself on fire in Vietnam to protest the war. Ten days later, two black students were killed in antiwar demonstrations at Jackson State in Mississippi, an event that received much less attention than the earlier killing of white students in Ohio.

On the night of the Kent State shootings, Nixon, who had previously called the student protestors "bums," stayed up all night. He made fifty-one phone calls. Kissinger believed he was "on the verge of a nervous breakdown."[105] Then, most bizarrely of all, he went to the Lincoln memorial to meet with young antiwar protestors who were camped out there. He rambled at length with some of the students, telling them at one point, "I am a devout Quaker, I'm against killing as much as you are, and I want to bring the boys home." He then asked to be driven to the Capitol, where he spoke at great length to a cleaning woman about his dead mother, whom he called a "saint."[106] The morning papers were filled with Nixon's erratic stunt, and the students complained that he had seemed indifferent to their concerns.

The Cambodian invasion provided a turning point for the domestic American response to the war in Vietnam. For the first time since the initial American troops had been sent in, Congress acted to prohibit U.S. troops from reentering Cambodia after the June 30 pullout date that Nixon had set in the wake of the campus shootings.

Congress's action, however, did not stop Nixon's rage from continuing to be vented on Vietnam. Between 1969 and early 1973, Nixon dropped an average of one ton of bombs each minute. Senator Fulbright agreed when the *Washington Post* labeled Nixon "the greatest bomber of all time."[107] This is not slim praise in light of the fact that between July 1965 and December 1967, the Johnson administration dropped more tons of bombs on Vietnam than all the allies had dropped on Europe during the Second World War.[108]

Throughout this period, Nixon remained committed to demonstrating his Madman theory of using the threat of excessive force to try to psychologically pressure the North Vietnamese into concessions at the negotiation table. But some documents reveal that his threat may not have been entirely strategic in nature. In a conversation between Nixon and Kissinger on April 25, 1972, Nixon contemplated the use of nuclear weapons:

NIXON: – docks, and, I still think we ought to take the dikes out now.
KISSINGER: I think –
NIXON: Will that drown people?
KISSINGER: That will drown about 200,000 people –
NIXON: Well, no, no, no, no, no, no. I'd rather use a nuclear bomb. Have you got that ready?
KISSINGER: Now that, I think, would just be, uh, too much, uh –
NIXON: A nuclear bomb, does that bother you?
KISSINGER: (unclear) he wouldn't do that anyway.
NIXON: I just want you to think big, Henry, for Christ's sake.[109]

Kissinger and Nixon's other advisers understood an important point: Nixon's bark was often worse than his bite. Kissinger himself noted that he often ignored Nixon's more extreme and excessively aggressive directives, understanding that "Nixon was entitled to some release for his nervous tension."[110] While Nixon often swore up and down that he would engage in a major escalation in Vietnam, including the consideration of nuclear options, he just as often would back away, as he did in this encounter. Kissinger and others quickly learned that they could safely ignore many of Nixon's spontaneous orders because he often changed his mind and would eventually offer another plan. While this dynamic may prove highly functional in a political sense by giving Nixon a way to feel strong and decisive without actually implementing foolish strategies, it also fits with the personality characteristics one would expect of a borderline.

By October 1972 Kissinger announced that "Peace is at hand," but the proposed treaty was rejected because South Vietnam's President Thieu realized that without American support it was highly likely that his government would fall to the North Vietnamese. Nixon then decided to use force against the North to demonstrate his commitment to the South should North Vietnam violate the treaty. At the time, Nixon once again invoked his Madman theory, saying that he "did not care if the whole world thought he was crazy" because "the Russians and the Chinese might think they were dealing with a madman and so had better force North Vietnam into a settlement before the whole world was consumed in a larger war."[111] At that time, Nixon unveiled his infamous "linebacker II" operation, which involved bombing around Hanoi and was designed to demonstrate his "brutal unpredictability."[112]

A peace settlement was eventually reached in January 1973, when the United States dropped the demand that North Vietnamese troop pullbacks accompany American withdrawal in combination with the North dropping its requirement that the government in the South be replaced. These concessions cleared the final roadblocks to the achievement of a peace accord. Congress voted to prevent Nixon from dropping any more bombs in the entire region after July 1, 1973. Later that year, Congress passed the War Powers Act, designed to force the president to consult with Congress before sending troops into combat, and demanding troop withdrawals after ninety days unless approved by Congress in the interim. Nixon flew into a rage and vetoed the legislation, which passed with a congressional override. Following Nixon's resignation in the wake of the Watergate allegations, South Vietnam fell on April 30, 1975, shortly after the last American troops left in March 1974.

Nixon's farewell speech can be read to reflect his own experience in office, as much as it offered advice to others. Inveighing others to realize that when "someone dear to us dies...we lose an election...suffer a defeat," it represents only a beginning and not an end, Nixon went on to admonish his listeners to "always give your best. Never get discouraged. Never be petty. Always remember others may hate you but those who hate you don't win unless you hate them. And then you destroy yourself."[113]

Psychodynamic Explanations

So why did Nixon proceed with his violent Vietnam tactics as he did, destructive as it was to his objectives, the country, his allies, and his own domestic political interests? He bombed and invaded Cambodia without informing the American public or Congress; he presided over the largest and most violent antiwar demonstrations in American history; and he dropped more bombs on the North Vietnamese than any president had dropped on any country in U.S. history. All this, and he never achieved the full military or political objectives he sought. While strategic and political reasons existed to justify the bombing of North Vietnam, Blema Steinberg offers a compelling explanation of how Nixon's personal motives helped drive his political behavior when she writes:

> The fact is that Nixon's strategic and domestic perceptions were animated by an underlying psychological dimension. His need to be perceived as invincible, in conjunction with his vulnerable self-esteem, led him to perceive any challenge to his policies, domestic or foreign, as a function of his opponents' desire to humiliate him personally. Both his decision to bomb Cambodia in March 1969 and his subsequent decision to invade it in April 1970 followed on the heels of foreign and domestic attacks that he deemed insulting and hurtful. Nixon chose Cambodia as the place where he could displace his rage.[114]

In mentioning domestic attacks, Steinberg refers to the serial rejection of two of Nixon's Supreme Court nominations, Carswell and Haynesworth. These domestic fights preceded more powerful military actions. Steinberg's claim is consistent with the way Lasswell described political man in his early work as someone who displaces his private needs onto public objects and then rationalizes his actions as being in the public interest, implying that behavior is often greatly influenced by unconscious motives.[115]

The conundrum of Nixon's ability to accomplish great things while simultaneously undermining his own success may have different explanations. From the more psychodynamic perspective that Nixon's early life seems to call for, Nixon was torn between two quite different parents. His parents not only possessed different personal styles but also expressed themselves differently. Young Richard was desperate to obtain their love, which was never adequately forthcoming. For children exposed to or influenced by one parent more than the other, it may only prove necessary to examine one relationship carefully. But in Nixon's case, he was exposed to both parents, and both parents influenced his later development. In this way, Nixon can be said to have introjected both parents, his withdrawn, rigid, emotionally controlled mother and his enraged, vengeful father. In an interview conducted after Nixon's death, his former doctor, Arnold Hutschnecker, argued that while Nixon's father was vicious, the real problem lay with his mother: "Clinically, it started with his mother. Nixon's mother was *so* religious that he was trapped in many ways. I wouldn't say that he was really religious but he was totally devoted to his mother – like a robot if you want. Even to the last, you know, he was kneeling down to pray every day. He was completely smothered. His mother was really his downfall."[116]

It does not require much of a stretch to suppose that Nixon entered into a kind of constant war within himself over his own identity. Even Hutschnecker described Nixon in these terms: "Nixon was an enigma, not just to me but to himself."[117] The juxtaposition of ordering bombing while simultaneously telling students that he hated killing as much as they did speaks to these warring elements in his character. Feeling chronically deprived of, and desperate for, love, Nixon's inner conflict may have made him both malleable to others' demands and expectations, in his insatiable need for love and approval, and paranoid that others might find out how inadequate he felt himself to be. As one biographer argued, Nixon was likely to do well in an international crisis so long as it was not personal: "the threat of world war poses less of a vexation for Nixon than the outcome of Watergate . . . and other personal scandals."[118] But when challenges became personal, Nixon's reaction took on an entirely different tenor. In particular, his anger was especially triggered when others touched on those issues which were most salient to his own self-criticism, relating to his personal inadequacies regarding either the strength of his character, which reminded him of his mother's criticisms, or his strength of conviction, which brought to mind the weakness demonstrated by his father. In his interview, Hutschnecker argued that Nixon felt guilt for "having pursued politics in the vindictive style of his father rather than the 'saintly' path of his mother. Nixon's fervent wish, the doctor felt, was that someday he would be able to say to Hannah, 'Mother, I have made peace. Now I am worthy of you.'"[119]

In this case, Nixon would have been caught between his parents' mutually exclusive expectations; he could elicit attention from his mother only when he succeeded; but he could not allow himself to surpass his father's success without punishing himself for it. Add survivor guilt over the death of two brothers, the incredible pressure to live and succeed for three in an attempt to abnegate his parents' sense of loss, and it becomes possible to even empathize a little with the psychological pressures that Nixon endured. Not only was he caught between control and rage but also between success and failure. In such circumstances, it seems likely that Nixon would seek out external conflict as a means by which to overcome the warring pressures within himself. In times of internal crisis, for someone whose life is fraught with fighting such psychological demons, it may seem much easier to seek out and resolve external conflicts as a way to help pacify and quell the warring elements in oneself.

Cognitive Explanation

The problem with psychodynamic explanations is that there exist no categories to account for risk taking, creativity, or the external pressure of political exigencies on behavior. Nixon's life leads to speculation about depth psychology, but that approach leaves out important features in Nixon's political experience. Nixon was a man at war at home and abroad. He appears to have believed that what he did in Southeast Asia was required to achieve a laudable goal, peace with honor. Yet how can analysts explain the irony of employing violent, aggressive means to accomplish peaceful ends? Did Nixon simply worship aggression, as he seemed to worship his mother, from afar and with full awareness of its ultimate futility? Or was there something else going on? Did Nixon simply adhere to a particular risk-taking propensity that is common among many?

Prospect theory presents just such a nonpsychodynamic, but no less psychological, interpretation of Nixon's successes and failures. Psychologists Amos Tversky and Daniel Kahneman developed a theory to explain risk taking in decision making called prospect theory.[120] To vastly simplify, they argue that when things are going well, people tend to be cautious and conservative in their decision-making strategies, but if things are going badly, or if they look as though they are going to get worse quickly, people appear more willing to take risks, especially for a chance to recoup a former loss. Like many others, Nixon may have preferred, in general, to act in domains where he felt more comfortable or competent. Indeed, Nixon was always someone who found domestic policy to be a waste of time and talent. He referred to it as "building outhouses in Peoria."[121]

But foreign affairs represented something else altogether. It offered a venue that encourages both the best and worst of a leader's character to emerge. Foreign affairs typically allows the president more freedom, and perhaps more impact. In this arena, Nixon was most interested, most comfortable, and most skilled. Here Nixon accomplished the most good – in opening the United States to China, engaging the Soviets in détente, and helping move the Middle East peace process along. It was also the area where he appeared to take the greatest risks, including clandestine incursions into Cambodia and Laos and expanding the bombing raids on North Vietnam during the Vietnam War.

When acting in the arena of foreign affairs where he was most comfortable and when things were going well, Nixon proved able to provide cautious and distinguished decision making and leadership, as he did toward China, the Soviet Union, and in the Middle East. However, when things were going badly, as in Vietnam, he appeared willing to take greater risks, such as authorizing the secret bombing of Cambodia, invading Cambodia and later Laos, and continuing the bombing of the North Vietnamese long after such attacks could realistically have been expected to generate a more favorable peace accord.

Similarly, in domestic policy, in which Nixon showed less interest, he tried to accomplish some positive things, such as the Family Assistance Plan. Creating it with the assistance of Urban Affairs Council Secretary Daniel Patrick Moynihan, Nixon sought to replace bureaucratic programs like Aid to Families with Dependent Children and Medicaid with direct cash payments. The program received criticism from both sides of the aisle, with Democrats feeling that the amount Nixon offered, about $1600 to a family of four, was insufficient, and Republicans opposing direct cash payments to people who did not work. Nixon tried for several years to advance the program and finally abandoned it just prior to the 1972 election cycle. However, when things were not going well as a result of the war in Vietnam, Nixon proved more willing to take risks to recover his popularity and power by authorizing his "plumber's unit" to break into Democratic headquarters and then lying to cover it up. Such an analysis, which rests on Nixon's understanding of his situation, requires no assumption of mental illness in order to explain his seeming shifts between comfortable competence and risk taking.

What is especially compelling about a prospect theory interpretation of Nixon's behavior is that his experience can be used to stretch the potential implications of the theory itself. In Nixon's case, his emotions, in the forms of shame and humiliation, in large part determined his characterization of domain. Critics argue that prospect theory cannot be generalized because it fails to account for individual differences in the framing of domain, as positive or negative. But perhaps these differences derive from emotive sources that the original laboratory demonstrations of prospect theory did not explore. If this happens to be the case, as appears to be true at least in Nixon's case, then emotion does help determine behavior, not in the direct way it has traditionally been understood, but rather through its influence on a person's cognitive construction of the appropriate reference point that determines risk-taking propensity. In this way, shame may have served as a kind of trigger for plunging Nixon into a domain of loss. There may be times when it is crucial for a president to take military risks, but determining when to do so remains a key aspect of skilled decision making.

And it may be that a healthy emotional life can effectively shift a leader's reference point back, in a way that makes risk taking less likely.

CONCLUSIONS

Richard Nixon was a complicated, intermittently successful, tortured, and tragic figure. He accomplished some important achievements in American foreign policy. He also presided over a covert war in Southeast Asia and authorized improper surveillance of his domestic opposition, and then attempted to deceive the American public concerning such policies.

Some, like Elliot Richardson, Nixon's attorney general, argued that Nixon's success was a reflection of his insecurity: "My own feeling has always been that if you had adjusted or if you had somehow been able to eliminate the sense of insecurity felt by Nixon toward his place in the world, you would have at the same time removed the very source of his drive. I don't think that he would even have been President at all."[122]

Other observers agree that Nixon was driven by his sense of psychological deprivation. Roger Ailes claimed that Nixon's "overriding motives were to do great things for the world, coupled with his own personal need for attention, acceptance, and praise, something that I think he was starved of during youth because I don't think that he came from a demonstrative family. His family never said, 'Hey, Dick, I think you're doing a great job, and we are proud of you.' And like all of us, he needed those things, and so he sought them in the outside world."[123]

But was Richard Nixon's downfall the predictable and inevitable outcome of a tragic and doomed personality playing out its inevitable fate? Or was it simply the accidental by-product of a man responding to the challenges presented by his office in a rational, if immoral, way? Would Nixon have possessed the drive to become president if he had not suffered from early psychological deprivations?

SEVEN

THE TWENTY-FIFTH AMENDMENT

Rules surrounding presidential succession have never been entirely clear or straightforward. The original framers of the Constitution spent relatively little time on this issue and were heavily influenced by the existing state constitutions on gubernatorial provisions in designing their language on executive succession.[1] The original Constitution signed in 1787 did not contain a succession clause. It took until 1790 to obtain the necessary thirteen state approvals for Article II, Section 1, Clause 6, to be ratified:

> In Case of Removal of the President from Office, or of his Death, Resignation, or Inability to discharge the Powers and Duties of the said Office, the Same shall devolve on the Vice President, and the Congress may by Law Provide for the Case of Removal, Death, Resignation or Inability, both of the President and Vice-President, declaring what Officer shall then act as President, and such Officer shall act accordingly, until the Disability be removed, or a President shall be elected.

This section of the Constitution does not discuss the vice president taking over the president's job in full, but rather as serving temporarily until the president recovers or a presidential election is held. Note also that disability, or what should be considered to constitute disability, is not defined. Further, this paragraph conflates permanent kinds of disability, such as death and resignation, with potentially temporary forms of "inability."[2]

One of the delegates from Delaware, John Dickinson, asked at the time: "What is meant by the term disability and who shall be the judge of it?"[3] In the next two hundred years, government officials were not really able to provide an adequate consensual answer to that question.

Since Dickinson's time, scholars have discussed the issue of presidential disability and succession as the "Achilles' heel"[4] or the "blind spot"[5] in the Constitution. Concerns surrounding the succession issue arose early when James Madison grew gravely ill in 1813 with what was billed at the time as "bilious fever," from which he managed to recover after about four weeks.

A Presidential Succession Law was put into place in 1886 to address the issue. Several events had brought this law into being. In 1841 Vice President John Tyler took the oath of office after William Harrison died exactly one month after he caught pneumonia at his inauguration, thus overriding the earlier understanding of temporary service and setting a precedent for full succession. Then, President James Garfield was shot in the back on July 2, 1881. For eighty days, Garfield floated between life and death, while a succession of physicians stuck dirty fingers into the wound trying to remove the bullet, before dying of infection on September 19, 1881. Vice President Chester Arthur then took over as president, after hesitating to act in Garfield's stead during his illness. After Arthur's assumption to the presidency, there was no vice president, or president pro tempore or Speaker of the House. Fearing a potential succession crisis, President Arthur immediately convened a special session of Congress to elect a new president pro tempore. Four years later, under President Cleveland, Vice President Thomas Hendricks died in office, and there was again no president pro tempore or Speaker of the House. Cleveland stayed away from the funeral to reduce the likelihood of a succession crisis at that time. As a result of these events, Congress moved in 1886 to place cabinet members ahead of congressional leaders in the presidential line of succession.[6]

In this new instantiation, now following earlier practice, the second succession law officially declared that the president was to be succeeded in office by the vice president, followed by members of the cabinet in the order of their department's seniority. Seniority depended on the order in which departments were first created, with State coming first, followed by Treasury, then Defense, and so on. Many years later, President Truman and others argued against this succession law, claiming that it was undemocratic in nature because it devolved to nonelected officials immediately after the vice president.[7] This awareness led Congress to pass a new succession law in 1947, which placed two elected officials, the Speaker of the House of Representatives and the president pro tempore of the Senate, next in line for the presidency. They were, however, followed in line by the cabinet officers in the same order as under the 1886 law.

Interest in presidential succession grew again during Eisenhower's term after he had a massive heart attack in 1955, surgery for ileitis in 1956, and a stroke in 1957 that left him with some speech difficulties for a time afterward. Once again, in 1957, now former president Truman offered a suggestion for how to tackle the question of presidential disability and succession. When a president becomes ill, Truman suggested, a committee of seven members from the three branches of government should be created. This committee would then select a board of prominent physicians drawn from the best medical schools. These doctors would examine the president and report their findings to the committee. If the board found the president to be too permanently impaired to act as leader, the committee would tell Congress, which could then choose to appoint the vice president to the presidency by a two-thirds vote.[8]

While President Truman's suggestion was being discussed, Emmanuel Celler was conducting his own investigations into this succession issue as chairman of the House Judiciary Committee. He created a questionnaire for lawyers, politicians, and scholars that asked their opinions concerning the meaning of inability, how it should be determined, who should initiate proceedings in the case of presidential impairment, and how these processes should be formalized. Twenty-six experts responded. They suggested several methods for determining disability and several more for determining when it ceased. All the experts agreed that the process needed to work quickly and expertly. They wanted to preserve separation of powers, the role of the presidency, and a nonpartisan atmosphere.[9] The most influential proposal in these discussions was that offered by President Eisenhower's attorney general, Herbert Brownell, who suggested that the president himself might be able to certify the beginning and end of his inability, and that Congress and the vice president might find a way to depose him if he were unable or unwilling to act on his own. Several such suggestions were put forward, but the discrepancy in recommendations led to Congress's failure to act on the issue at the time. One of the reasons for this delay resulted from widespread personal loyalty to then long-standing Speaker of the House John McCormack, who was next in line for succession under the old rules.[10]

Nonetheless, the earlier discussions planted the seeds for what would blossom into the Twenty-fifth Amendment. The new Kennedy administration offered a variant on an old theme when it proposed a new Senate Joint Resolution on the matter, putting forward a version of the bill that was similar to the position advocated by Brownell but modified by his successor during the Eisenhower administration, Attorney General William Rogers. This proposal did not require constitutional action. Ironically, further progress on the issue was buried with the death of Senate Subcommittee Chairman Estes Kefauver. In another cruel and ironic twist of fate, water for the seeds of legislation on presidential impairment resulted from the assassination of President Kennedy. Following his death, the American Bar Association undertook a study of the succession issue in early 1964. Senator Birch Bayh came in as the new chairman of the Senate Subcommittee and managed to push through Senate Joint

Resolution 139. This bill, quite similar to the original Brownell proposal, passed the Senate unanimously on September 29, 1964. The following year, both houses passed the amendment in July 1965. It was ratified by the required thirty-eight states on February 10, 1967, and formally added as the Twenty-fifth Amendment to the Constitution on February 23, 1967.

SECTIONS OF THE AMENDMENT

The Twenty-fifth Amendment contains four sections:

1. In case of the removal of the President from office or of his death or resignation, the Vice President shall become President.
2. Whenever there is a vacancy in the office of the Vice-President, the President shall nominate a Vice President who shall take office upon confirmation by a majority vote of both Houses of Congress.
3. Whenever the President transfers to the President pro tempore of the Senate and the Speaker of the House of Representatives his written declaration that he is unable to discharge the powers and duties of his office, and until he transmits to them a written declaration to the contrary, such powers and duties shall be discharged by the Vice President as Acting President.
4. Whenever the Vice President and a majority of either the principal officers of the executive departments or of such other body as Congress may by law provide, transmit to the President pro tempore of the Senate and the Speaker of the House of Representatives their written declaration that the President is unable to discharge the powers and duties of his office, the Vice President shall immediately assume the power and duties of the office as Acting President.

   Thereafter, when the President transmits to the President pro tempore of the Senate and the Speaker of the House of Representatives his written declaration that no inability exists, he shall resume the powers of his office until the Vice President and a majority of either the principal officers of the executive department or of such other body as Congress may by law provide, transmit within four days to the President pro tempore of the Senate and the Speaker of the House of Representatives their written declaration that the President is unable to discharge the duties and powers of his office. Thereupon, Congress shall decide the issue, assembling within forty-eight hours for that purpose if not in session. If the Congress, within twenty-one days after receipt of the latter written declaration, or, if Congress is not in session, within twenty-one days after Congress is required to assemble, determines by two-thirds vote of both Houses that the President is unable to discharge the powers and duties of his office, the Vice President shall continue to discharge the same as Acting President; otherwise, the President shall resume the powers and duties of his office.

Section 1 allows for the vice president to assume the office of president if the president steps down, dies, or is impeached. Since the Twenty-fifth

Amendment went into law, this section has been invoked once, when President Nixon resigned and was succeeded in the presidency by Vice President Ford. It would also have been invoked if, for example, Reagan had died in office following the assassination attempt, or if Congress had succeeded in convicting President Clinton after he was impeached, thereby rendering Vice President Gore president.

Section 2 allows for the president to replace the vice president when the office becomes vacant for whatever reason. Presidents could not avail themselves of this process until 1967. Prior to that, the vice president's office had become vacant eighteen times, for about thirty-seven years total, or about 20 percent of the nation's history. Each time the public had to wait for a new presidential election to fill the gap.[11] Since 1973, the vice presidency has been vacant only twice, for about six months total, or 2 percent of the years since.[12] This section has been used twice since its inception. The first time was after Vice President Spiro Agnew resigned amid accusations of scandal. President Nixon then nominated Congressman Gerald Ford, who was confirmed by Congress in less than two months. The existence of the Twenty-fifth Amendment proved very decisive in this case.[13] Without it, Democratic Speaker of the House Carl Albert would have assumed the presidency instead of Gerald Ford. Indeed, this threat of a shift in party was part of the reason that Congress had changed its succession law to favor the cabinet over Congress in 1886.[14]

The second time this section was invoked followed Ford's assumption to the presidency. Ford nominated Nelson Rockefeller as vice president.[15] Congress took much longer to confirm this nomination. Ford stands as the only president so far who was solely appointed to office. His tenure with Rockefeller remains the only time that the executive branch had no man in office who was elected for the post.

Section 3 provides for those situations of temporary disability where a president has the ability to recognize his real or potential impairment and can plan to turn over the reins of power to the vice president during his term of disability voluntarily. This can happen, for example, when a leader undergoes surgery that requires anesthesia, such as Reagan did when he had surgery for colon cancer in July 1985.

Section 3 has been invoked twice, in 1985 and 2002, and, depending on the perspective of the analyst, possibly a third time. It should have been invoked at least two additional times. First, as Herbert Abrams, M.D., carefully lays out in his book on the failed assassination attempt of Ronald Reagan, the president was much closer to death than any of his political advisers let on to the public at the time.[16] Abrams argues that the use of anesthesia alone during surgery should have prompted the invocation of the third or the fourth section of the Twenty-fifth Amendment at the time. Abrams suggests that the Twenty-fifth Amendment was not invoked at this time because of a combination of ignorance about its use by senior staff, caution on the part of Vice President Bush not to appear as if he was trying to seize power inappropriately, concern over the president's medical condition, and guile on the part of senior staffers who wanted to stay in charge.[17] Rather than appropriately invoking the Twenty-fifth Amendment after Reagan was shot, presidential staffers Counselor to the President Edwin Meese, White House Chief of Staff James Baker, and Deputy White House Chief of Staff Michael Deaver simply assumed and devolved authority onto themselves and wielded presidential power during Reagan's stay in the hospital and for some time afterward, just as surely as Edith Wilson did following Wilson's catastrophic stroke in October 1919.[18]

Depending on a given analyst's take, Section 3 actually was invoked in 1985 when Reagan underwent anesthesia for colon cancer surgery. At that time, White House Counsel Fred Fielding prepared two letters for Reagan to sign. One explicitly invoked the use of Section 3 of the Twenty-fifth Amendment. A second, "optional" one, did not. Reagan signed the "optional" letter on July 15, 1985, and sent it to the Speaker of the House of Representatives and the president pro tempore of the Senate. The letter reads as follows:

> I am about to undergo surgery during which time I will be briefly and temporarily incapable of discharging the constitutional powers and duties of the office of the President of the United States.
>
> After consultation with my counsel and the Attorney General, I am mindful of the provisions of Section 3 of the 25th Amendment to the Constitution and of the uncertainties of its application to such brief and temporary periods of incapacity. I do not believe that the drafters of this amendment intended its application to situations such as this instant one.
>
> Nevertheless, consistent with my longstanding arrangement with Vice President George Bush, and not intending to set a precedent binding anyone privileged to hold the office in the future, I have determined and it is my intention and direction, that Vice President George Bush shall discharge those powers and duties in my stead commencing with the administration of anesthesia to me in this instance.
>
> I shall advise you and the Vice President when I determine that I am able to resume the discharge of the constitutional powers and duties of this office.
>
> May God bless this nation and us all.
>
> Sincerely,
>
> RONALD REAGAN[19]

As Abrams notes in his careful reconstruction of Reagan's medical situation, the White House was sensitized to the issue of the Twenty-fifth Amendment as a result of criticism it had received for not invoking it after the attempted assassination of Reagan.[20] Nonetheless, Reagan did not want to create a precedent for the use of Section 3 because he believed it might weaken the office of the president. So, while declaring his awareness of it, he did not formally invoke it during his cancer surgery. In his autobiography, Reagan writes that he did do so: "Before they wheeled me into the operating room, I signed a letter invoking the 25th Amendment, making George Bush acting president during the time I was incapacitated under anesthesia."[21] George Bush remained in charge during this period, although he was not told he was in charge until some fifteen minutes after Reagan went under anesthesia.[22] Ironically, this kind of situation was precisely the sort of circumstance that the framers had in mind in developing Section 3. This type of use of the amendment, to cover short-term and temporary disability, as in the case of anesthesia during surgery, was what they were hoping to encourage as a result of its adoption.

After Reagan's surgeon told his aides that there was no sure way to determine if Reagan had returned to full cognitive functioning following surgery, White House Counsel Fred Fielding, in concert with White House Chief of Staff Donald Regan and White House Press Secretary Larry Speakes, decided that if Reagan could read and sign the note reclaiming his office, he was fit for duty. This occurred just after 7 p.m. the day of the surgery. The note read:

> Following up on my letter to you of this date, please be advised that I am able to resume the discharge of the constitutional powers and duties of the office of the President of the United States. I have informed the Vice President of my determination and my resumption of those powers and duties.

Vice President George Bush acted as president on that day for just under eight hours. The nuclear "football" remained close to Reagan in the recovery room following surgery.[23] As noted in the earlier chapter on the impact of aging on decision making, someone of Reagan's advanced age was highly unlikely to have recovered from the effects of anesthesia so quickly following major surgery.

The consequences of Reagan's aides' implicit transfer of power were almost as devastating as well. During this time, Reagan apparently agreed to the arms-for-hostages deal with Iran and Nicaragua. In this plan, the United States sold more than 1,500 missiles to Iran, and funds from the sale of these weapons were then diverted to help fund the Contra insurgency fighting against the Cuban-backed Sandinista army in Nicaragua. Reagan's primary interest was to secure the release of seven Americans held hostage in Lebanon by Hezbollah; he apparently hoped that selling arms to Iran would secure its help in pressuring the group to release the American hostages. By the time the deal became public, three Americans had been released only to be replaced by three others taken captive. Reagan later claimed that he could not remember approving the plan. Attorney General Edwin Meese testified before the congressional hearings into the Iran-Contra scandal that Reagan may have made those decisions while still infirm and that his judgment and memory may have been impaired by the medications he took in the wake of his illness. Lieutenant Colonel Oliver North, who worked for the National Security Council, testified that he had been diverting funds from the sale of weapons to Iran to fund the Contra insurgency in Nicaragua with the approval of National Security Advisor John Poindexter and, he assumed, of President Reagan. Poindexter resigned, North was fired, and Reagan appointed the Tower Commission to investigate. This commission found that Reagan's disengagement from the White House had allowed the funds from the sale of weapons to Iran to be diverted to the Contras but that there was no direct evidence linking Reagan to specific approval of these activities. Over the course of the next eight years, Independent Counsel Lawrence Walsh led an investigation into the affair. He charged fourteen people with crimes. North's conviction was overturned and President Bush issued six pardons, including ones given to Reagan's national security advisor, Robert McFarlane, and his secretary of defense, Caspar Weinberger, who was pardoned prior to coming to trial.[24]

Political judgment can be impaired by physical health problems. In President Wilson's case, Congress passed twenty-eight acts into law without presidential oversight, many of which ran contrary to Wilson's prior stated position.[25] During the same period, Wilson's literal fight to the death lost him his battle over U.S. entry into the League of Nations. Yet, as Jerrold Post and Robert Robins rightly note in the case of President Reagan, it was politically advantageous to declare the president competent as soon as possible following his injury and surgery, just as it later became politically advantageous to call attention to his being physically and psychologically compromised when decisions made at that time later proved controversial.[26] Even after the Irangate debacle, Reagan's mental state called into question his judgment and memory. When Senator Howard Baker took over from Donald Regan as White House Chief of Staff, he asked aide James Cannon to investigate White House decision-making procedures. Cannon interviewed the senior White House staff and reported to Baker that Reagan appeared detached from the presidency, preferring to spend most of his time watching movies. Cannon went so far as to recommend invoking Section 4 of the Twenty-fifth Amendment to declare Reagan unfit for office. Subsequent to this recommendation, Baker talked to Reagan himself and decided that Reagan was fit for office, without any additional formal medical evaluation.[27]

The second time that the amendment should have been invoked occurred during and following Reagan's prostate surgery in 1987. At this time, even though Reagan again underwent anesthesia and recovered very slowly, the Twenty-fifth Amendment was not invoked.[28]

The second time Section 3 was formally invoked involved a much more ordinary and mundane transfer of power. On June 29, 2002, President

George Bush invoked Section 3 to turn over the power of the presidency to Vice President Dick Cheney for about two hours while he underwent anesthesia for a routine colonoscopy. This event occurred without incident.

Section 4 has proved to be the most controversial of the amendment. This section deals with removing an impaired president who is either unwilling or unable to certify himself as disabled. Herbert Abrams, M.D., made recommendations, based on the lessons he had learned in his investigation of the assassination attempt on Ronald Reagan, that certain processes should be put in place to ensure that the Twenty-fifth Amendment be employed when it was most needed. He suggested that an "emergency book" containing contingency plans for how to address various scenarios of presidential disability be created and passed from one White House counsel to another during the presidential transition for review, modification, and adoption. Second, he advised that the succession procedures should be declassified and standardized. Further, he concluded that relevant personnel should participate in various simulations of presidential impairment scenarios so that people are familiar and comfortable with the appropriate procedures. Finally, he suggested that emergency communications should be strengthened.[29]

According to White House physician Lawrence Mohr, George Bush developed and implemented such a systematic plan for the first time during his presidency. This plan was developed during the transition following his election in November 1988; it was agreed upon in a meeting at the White House on April 18, 1989, in which the president, his wife, Vice President Dan Quayle, the presidential physician, Dr. Burton Lee, White House Counsel C. Boyden Gray, Chief of Staff John Sununu, Mrs. Bush's chief of staff, and several members of the Secret Service reviewed the plan for what to do in the case of Bush's disability.[30] It was then passed along to President Clinton when he came into office for revision and use.[31] This plan provides advance directives and informed consent by the president for specific actions to be taken under certain circumstances and for relevant medical information to be released to the vice president and other officials should the need arise. The process alleviates any legal or ethical concerns surrounding doctor-patient confidentiality.[32]

Foreign Rules of Succession

As is the case with the United States, in the rules governing succession in other advanced industrialized nations, definitions of what constitutes disability or who decides when a leader is disabled are not always clear.

French succession is governed by its 1958 Constitution. Article 7 holds that if the presidency becomes vacant for any reason, the duties fall temporarily to the president of the Senate or, if he is incapacitated, to the government writ large. The government can pronounce the president incapacitated by a vote of the absolute majority. If the vacancy or the incapacity of the president becomes permanent, as declared by the Constitutional Council, a new election for president is held not less than twenty days and not more than thirty-five days after the beginning of the vacancy or declaration of permanent incapacity. If a candidate dies before the first ballot, the Constitutional Council postpones the election. If either of the two lead candidates after the first ballot dies or becomes incapacitated, the Constitutional Council must repeat the election in full.[33]

Swedish succession law distinguishes between the head of state, the king, and the government, in the person of the prime minister, in its Constitution. If the king becomes ill or goes away on foreign travel and cannot perform his duties, "that member of the Royal House under the valid order of succession who is not prevented therefrom shall assume and perform the duties of Head of State in the capacity of Regent ad interim." If the royal house dies out, the Riksdag must appoint a regent to perform the duties of head of state. This applies if the king dies or abdicates and the heir has not yet reached the age of eighteen. If the king has not been able to perform his duties for six months for any reason, the government must notify the Riksdag and it will determine if the king shall be deemed to have abdicated. The Riksdag can appoint a person to serve as regent under a government order; the speaker or one of the deputy speakers may serve as regent if no other competent person is able. In the case of the government, if the prime minister is discharged or dies, the speaker discharges the other ministers, and standard procedures for the election of a new prime minister within the Riksdag take place.[34]

Germany also has rules concerning succession both for its president and its chancellor. It is important to remember that the German president does not hold the same responsibilities as the American president; such responsibilities fall to the German chancellor. Should the chancellor become incapacitated, the federal deputy chancellor assumes the position for forty-eight hours, at which point Parliament elects a new chancellor. Should the federal president become unable to perform his duties, or should the office become vacant, the president of the Bundesrat shall exercise his powers.[35]

There are no formal rules in Denmark concerning which minister succeeds a prime minister who becomes unable to fulfill his duties. Each administration can decide on a list of possible successors. However, in practice, certain criteria for succession have been developed. These include seniority – as a minister, as a member of parliament, as an elected official, as a public administrator – and chronological age. Prime Minister Anders Fogh Rasmussen, for instance, designated his successors, in order, as the ministers of economic and business affairs, foreign affairs, finance, employment, justice, and culture.[36]

The succession situation in Britain is quite complex. Because there is no official mention of a prime minister in the British constitution, everything is run as a matter of custom and convention. Technically, if the prime minister were to become incapacitated, the Queen of England, acting in her capacity as head of state and government, would assume the responsibilities of prime minister until the majority party in Parliament could elect another prime minister.[37]

As a former British colony, South Africa has adopted succession laws that in many ways most resemble the American. Under its 1996 Constitution, the National Assembly can remove the president, by a two-thirds vote, only on the grounds of a serious violation of the law or Constitution, serious misconduct, or the inability to perform the functions of his office. When the president is absent or unable to fulfill his duties, or when the office is vacant, succession falls, in order, to the deputy president, a minister designated by the president, a minister designated by other members of the cabinet, and finally the speaker, until the National Assembly designates one of its members. The acting president assumes the responsibilities, powers, and functions of the president, but not the job itself.[38]

The Swiss laws are governed by the Constitution as amended in 2000. The president of the Confederation is elected for only one year by the Federal Parliament, and the term is not renewable, nor is the president eligible for election as vice president the following term. The Constitution does not appear to have any explicit provisions for succession in the case of presidential death or disability.[39]

MILLER COMMISSION

Responding to various concerns about limitations in the Twenty-fifth Amendment or its implementation, the Miller Center Commission on Presidential Disability and the Twenty-fifth Amendment was convened. Cochaired by Eisenhower's attorney general Herbert Brownell and Senator Birch Bayh, one of the original framers of the amendment, the commission included former chief justice of the Supreme Court Warren Burger, as well as former U.S. senator William Spong of Virginia and former U.S. representative Caldwell Butler of Virginia. The commission met six times between 1985 and 1988 and issued its final report at the conclusion.

While supporting the amendment, the commission rendered several recommendations:

1. Problems of presidential disability and use of the Twenty-Fifth Amendment must be discussed and agreed upon through contingency planning by the new president, vice president, presidential physician and the White House chief of staff before the inauguration.

2. The presidential physician can and must play an increased role under provisions of the Twenty-Fifth Amendment.
3. No further constitutional changes should be made, but legislation should be considered by Congress and the president in order to bring current law into better harmony with the Twenty-Fifth Amendment and its intentions.
4. Any president receiving anesthesia should use Section 3 of the Amendment routinely so that appearance of crisis will be avoided.
5. The transfer of power under Section 3 should extend beyond the period of time in the operating room to perhaps twenty-four hours or more.
6. Even in borderline cases, the president should take the precaution of using Section 3.
7. Delegations by the president of his Section 3 authority under certain specified conditions to the vice president are incompatible with Section 4 of the Twenty-Fifth Amendment and should not be contemplated.
8. The creation by Congress of another statutory body to replace the cabinet in applications of Section 4 of the Twenty-Fifth Amendment is not warranted.
9. No set of rules or codes of conduct for future presidential spouses are recommended, but each spouse should be brought into the preparatory discussions.
10. To protect the belief of the American public in the dependability of the American presidency, White House staff members must not act to prevent use of the Twenty-Fifth Amendment in instances when it is called for.[40]

Abrams, for one, suggests that there are certain times and conditions that should call, almost automatically, for the invocation of Section 3 of the Twenty-fifth Amendment.[41] Specifically, concerning recommendations 4 and 5, Abrams argues that conditions that should require invocation of the Twenty-fifth Amendment include surgery involving anesthesia. For major surgery, Abrams recommends a transfer of power lasting from a minimum of a few days to three weeks. Another condition that should trigger the use of Section 3 would include the use of any psychoactive drugs in any reasonable amount. Other events that should spur the invocation of Section 3 include any illness, injury, or other condition, including emotional upset, that the president or his doctor believes might interfere with his ability to render reasonable judgments. Serious presidential illnesses, such as stroke, heart attack, or certain cancers, might require the use of Section 3 or 4, depending on the nature and severity of the incapacitation. Death or serious illness in the president's immediate family might render Section 3 useful. Had it been in place at the time, Wilson should have invoked this clause following the death of his first wife, Ellen Axson, as Calvin Coolidge should have done following the untimely death of his son Calvin Jr.[42]

At times, invoking the amendment might backfire; a president who is under impeachment might wish to be relieved of the distractions of presidential office, but in so doing might hurt his case by making himself appear weak.[43] Any diagnosis involving severe dementia or mental illness should preclude the president from remaining in power. Finally, any condition that would prevent the president from communicating with the government would constitute an appropriate use of this section. While it has not happened yet, it could be invoked, for example, if a president were to be kidnapped or captured. Because it might not be possible for the president to self-declare incapacity, the temporary transfer of power would need to take place under the procedures of Section 4, whereby others declared his inability to discharge the duties of his office until after his release from captivity, or until credible evidence of his death were received. The terrorist events of September 11 point to the serious nature of such considerations and the importance of planning for the possibility of the long-term inability of the president to contact or communicate with the other branches of the U.S. government.

Despite such recommendations for improvements in the provisions and application of the amendment, certain concerns regarding implementation of Section 4 of the Twenty-fifth Amendment continue to arise. Some concrete positive steps have been taken in response to the critiques provided by the Miller Commission. When President Bush came into power in 1989, many staff members and others began working on a careful plan for the circumstances under which the Twenty-fifth Amendment might be employed and how that would take place.

Yet various criticisms of the Twenty-fifth Amendment continued. The December 7, 1994, issue of the *Journal of the American Medical Association* dedicated substantial attention to this issue. In that volume, former president Carter issued a call for the revision of Section 4 of the Twenty-fifth Amendment as well.

> The great weakness of the Twenty-fifth Amendment is its provision for determining disability in the event that the president is unable or unwilling to certify to impairment or disability. In this case, the constitutional duty falls on the vice president and a majority of the Cabinet. In such an unhappy event, it is absolutely necessary for the vice president and Cabinet to obtain accurate and unbiased medical advice to determine whether the president is able to perform his or her duties. At this time, the determination is made by the president's personal physicians who must try to balance patient confidentiality and personal interest vis-à-vis the nation's interest. We must find a better way. This might be by creating a nonpartisan group of expert representatives of the medical community who are not directly involved in the care of the president. They could be given the responsibility for determining disability, thereby relieving the president's physicians for their potential conflict of interest and enabling the Twenty-fifth Amendment to work prudently and smoothly.[44]

In the same issue, Arthur Link and James Toole expressed their continuing concerns with the implementation of the Twenty-fifth Amendment. They argued that the Twenty-fifth Amendment had not sufficiently addressed the question of who should determine presidential disability and what Congress should do once it was discovered. They found major limitations in Section 4 in particular:

> There are several reasons why Section 4 of the Twenty-fifth Amendment does not provide a reliable method for rapid transfer of executive power in the event that the president is so incapacitated that he cannot perform his constitutional duties. It is unlikely that the Vice President and the Cabinet would resort to the complicated procedures of Section 4. First, the Vice President holds office only because the President chose him. Second, the Vice President might commit political suicide if he gave even the hint that he was masterminding a coup d'état. Third, the probability that the Cabinet would support a vice president's invocation of Section 4 is unlikely except in extreme cases. The Cabinet has long ceased to have a will of its own. Cabinet members, even more than the Vice President, hold office by virtue of their loyalty to the President.[45]

The question remains a bit more complicated than this passage indicates. The vice president, for instance, may have his own public and political constituency independent of the president; he may not be serving simply because the president chose him. More pragmatically, some cabinet members and others may evince loyalty to their country primarily or demonstrate actual concern for the president's health itself. Further, the Twenty-fifth Amendment does refer to "principal officers of the executive departments." This means, for example, that other officials who are not technically part of the cabinet might be included, such as the head of the Central Intelligence Agency. Additional language in the amendment refers to "such body as Congress may by law provide." Therefore, not all mechanisms for invoking Section 4 would be forced to rely exclusively on people solely dependent on the president for their political fortunes and futures.

An editorial in that issue of *JAMA* pointed out the importance of this question because presidents are powerful men who maintain stressful schedules involving a lot of jet lag, are often the target of assassins, and are least likely to be told by those close to them that they are becoming impaired. Finally, leaders tend to cluster in those age ranges which remain most susceptible to disabling illnesses, including depression, dementia, cancer, and cardiovascular disease. The first two conditions are especially problematic, because of the difficulties in recognizing the early stages of a mood disorder or a cognitive impairment in a typically highly stressed and intelligent person. And because one of the chief symptomatic characteristics of depression or dementia is loss of psychological insight, disabled individuals often remain unaware of the severity of their problem and react with great anger if disability is suggested to them.

Carter offered the use of his center in Atlanta to begin systematic discussions among scholars, doctors, politicians, and others about how to help close this gap in the amendment. In the wake of Carter's offer, and the 1994 meeting of the American Academy of Neurology on this topic, the Working Group on Disability in U.S. Presidents was born.

THE WORKING GROUP

The Working Group met three times over the course of two years to address the concerns raised by President Carter and others. They first met at the Carter Center on January 26–28, 1995. A second meeting was held at Wake Forest University, the home of one of the principal organizers and editors, James Toole, on November 10–12, 1995, in which former President Ford participated. A final meeting took place at the White House, organized by presidential physician Connie Mariano, on December 1–3, 1996. The final recommendations were then presented to President Clinton.

Senator Birch Bayh, in many ways the father of the Twenty-fifth Amendment, also entered the fray by writing his own op-ed piece on the issue in the *Minneapolis Star Tribune* in April 1995. At that time, he argued that the president's physician was capable of informing the relevant constitutional parties, should the need arise, and that the ultimate determination of presidential disability remained a political question that should be solved by political rather than medical officials. Like Abrams, he suggested that a contingency plan be developed and instituted by each administration prior to inauguration day. He encouraged closer daily contact between the president and his physician, who should be charged with remaining responsible to both his patient and the nation. He indicated that the physician's role in notifying the appropriate officials in the case of presidential disability should be more carefully delineated by Congress. Finally, he suggested passing a law prohibiting public officials, including physicians, from interfering with information about presidential disability.

This Working Group sought to address many of the concerns that had been raised in connection with the implementation of Section 4 of the Twenty-fifth Amendment, particularly in the years since the Miller Commission report had been issued in 1988. Although the group recognized that in many cases presidential impairment will appear in obvious ways, including instances of major stroke or blunt-force head trauma, many impairments such as depression and dementia can appear in more subtle, intermittent, hidden ways, while still managing to wreak substantial havoc on a leader's decision-making abilities. Several of these concerns had been raised in letters to the editor after the special issue on presidential disability appeared in the *Journal of the American Medical Association* in 1994.

Many of these letters expressed anxiety about how best to handle the appearance of psychiatric illness in particular. Such illnesses can readily lead to severe cognitive impairments. Depression can compromise decision making, memory, motivation, and energy. In addition, the incidence of various dementias including Alzheimer's increases with age. They can bring profound, if intermittent in the early stages, cognitive impairments. Steven Miles, M.D., commented on speculation that Reagan may have suffered from the beginning stages of Alzheimer's while in office. He argued that the early stages of Alzheimer's compromise the skills most vital to political performance and leadership, including imagination, reasoning, attention, and memory.[46]

Richard Friedman, M.D., suggested that a psychiatrically ill president was unlikely to receive adequate treatment both because the societal stigma attached to mental illness would mean that an ill president would not seek the help he needed and also because a president's physician, like most nonpsychiatrists, would not be properly trained to recognize the early signs and symptoms of mental illness easily or readily as he would the symptoms of a physical disorder. This appears particularly important given the high prevalence of such illness in the general population. Evidence from one study, for example, indicated that 21 percent of patients reported symptoms of mental illness in a fourteen-country study of primary health care facilities.[47] Friedman suggested that all presidents be screened yearly as part of their physical examination for mental as well as physical illnesses.[48]

The Working Group created subgroups to handle particular issues. These included how to strengthen the position of the White House physician, how to identify medical criteria for impairment, how to balance the public's right to know versus doctor-patient confidentiality, how to handle the role of the spouse in assessing presidential disability, and whether formal contingency plans for disability were advantageous or not.[49]

The Working Group, comprising more than fifty people with expertise in various areas associated with presidential disability, issued its findings in October 1997. Former White House physicians included James Young, Burton Lee, Lawrence Mohr, and Daniel Ruge; then current White House physician Connie Mariano, contributed as well. Important politicians included Senator Birch Bayh and Lloyd Cutler. Presidents Carter, Ford, and Clinton participated. Major scholars on the topic were also involved, including physicians such as James Toole, M.D., Herbert Abrams,

M.D., Jerrold Post, M.D., Kenneth Crispell, M.D., Robert Joynt, M.D., and Bert Park, M.D., and academics such as historian Stephen Ambrose, Fordham law school professor and dean John Feerick, Robert Gilbert, Arthur Link, and Robert Robins. Several journalists, Lawrence Altman, M.D. and Tom Wicker of the *New York Times,* and Edwin Yoder of the *Washington Post* were present at various sessions as well. Their nine recommendations were based on five assumptions. First, the committee believed that many presidents had suffered from debilitating illnesses in the past. Second, the Twenty-fifth Amendment gives Congress enough power to deal with a disabled president, even if he remains unable or unwilling to certify to that impairment on this own. Third, there should be a contingency plan that is familiar to all involved on who should do what when in the case of presidential injury or impairment. Fourth, medical advice should be sought from specialists when needed. And last, there should be a clear identification of the president's physician, who will also be responsible for notifying the relevant constitutional officers if necessary.

The Working Group recommendations were as follows:

1. The Twenty-fifth Amendment is a powerful instrument that delineates the circumstances and methods for succession and transfer of the power of the presidency. It does not require revision or augmentations by other constitutional amendment. However, guidelines are needed to ensure its effective implementation.
2. The Twenty-fifth Amendment has not been invoked in some circumstances envisioned by its founders. When substantial concern about the ability of the president to discharge the powers and duties of office arise, transfer of power under the provisions of the Twenty-fifth Amendment should be considered.
3. A formal contingency plan for the implementation of the amendment should be in place before the inauguration of every president.
4. Determination of presidential impairment is a medical judgment based on evaluation and tests. Close associates, family, and consultants can provide valuable information that contributes to this medical judgment.
5. The determination of presidential inability is a political judgment to be made by constitutional officials.
6. The president should appoint a physician, civil or military, to be senior physician in the White House and to assume responsibility for his or her medical care, direct the military medical unit, and be the source of medical disclosure when considering imminent or existing impairment according to the provisions of the Twenty-fifth Amendment.
7. In evaluating the medical condition of the president, the senior physician in the White House should make use of the best consultants in the field.
8. Balancing the right of the public to be informed regarding presidential illness with the president's right to confidentiality presents dilemmas. While

the senior physician to the president is the best source of information about the medical condition of the president, it is the responsibility of the president or designees to make accurate disclosure to the public.

9. The Twenty-fifth Amendment provides a remarkably flexible framework for the determination of presidential inability and the implementation of the transfer of powers. Its provisions should be more widely publicized and its use destigmatized.[50]

Several minority reports were issued about certain recommendations by those who opposed the majority consensus. Those who participated in the minority report on recommendation 4 included John Feerick, a noted historian of presidential succession issues and the Twenty-fifth Amendment, and Birch Bayh, the Senate father of the resolution leading to it. They argued that the distinction between presidential impairment and inability will not resonate with the public, and they objected to setting up a two-tier system of determining presidential disability. They seemed to prefer recommendation 5 over 4 and did not feel the need for both to exist. As Gilbert wrote, the power to remove the president involuntarily should remain in political hands because these officials are constitutional officers. In other words, he argued that removing the president involuntarily is a political judgment, not a medical one. As such, this decision should be made by political officials, not doctors. Such an arrangement works to protect the presidency as an institution while still providing for the possibility of a disabled leader. As Gilbert writes, "these political facts of life reflect a *strength* of the amendment rather than a weakness. It *should* be extraordinarily difficult for the president of the United States to be separated from the powers and duties of office and such action should be contemplated only under the most serious of circumstances."[51]

An appendix to recommendation 6 was issued by former and current military physicians. This statement argued that the president should be able to pick his own doctor and that he should appoint a senior physician to this role. This person should then be held accountable for implementing the Twenty-fifth Amendment if need arose. This person should be given appropriate rank and title and should maintain an office separate from the White House military office. A civilian doctor should still be given military support.

Finally, a minority report was issued by Herbert Abrams, M.D., Bert Park, M.D., Robert Robins, Ph.D., and others with regard to recommendation 7. These members advocated for the creation of a consulting commission to provide advice and guidance to the president's physician should the need arise. They argued that this sort of commission would not be subject to the same political or personal pressures as the White House physician and yet could provide objective and high-quality medical information that would assure public confidence and lower the risk of cover-up.[52]

Subcommittee on Criteria for Disability and Impairment

An additional important subcommittee report of the Working Group discussed the most appropriate criteria for disability and impairment. This subcommittee argued that specific medical guidelines for the application of the Twenty-fifth Amendment could help in several ways. First, they could provide boundary conditions to identify those circumstances, situations, and illnesses under which no leader could be expected to carry out his duty adequately. Second, they could help identify proper tests and procedures to determine the level and range of disability. Third, they could provide information on future prognosis. And finally, medical guidelines might help delineate those areas where a leader might prove least likely to recognize his own disability.

They argued that physical or mental incapacitation could be described in a variety of ways. First, disabilities can occur for physical or mental reasons or both. Second, incapacitation can happen in ways that are either sudden and transient, sudden and lasting, or intermittent. Conditions can appear gradually with progressive deterioration, gradually with gradual recovery, or gradually and then remain static. Impairment can range from the trivial to the complete. It can be anticipated or unexpected. Finally, the person may be able to recognize the problem, remain unaware of the problem, or deny the existence of the problem.

Most importantly, this group outlined those medical conditions which can cause impairment and disability and thus might prevent a leader from adequately exercising his duties and responsibilities as president. Development of these conditions should lead doctors and relevant political actors to consider invoking the Twenty-fifth Amendment to remove the impaired leader at least temporarily. These conditions comprise those which almost always result in complete incapacitation. They include: events that alter consciousness, like head trauma or anesthesia; severe physical trauma, especially that involving major blood loss; organic brain disorders, which severely compromise mental functions, such as dementia or stroke; major psychiatric disorders; severe medical conditions requiring intensive care, such as might be required in the event of an assassination attempt or serious accident; severe cardiopulmonary disease, such as heart attack; terminal cancer; and certain drug regimens, especially large doses of narcotics for pain.

This subcommittee recommended that impairments in a leader that can produce total incapacitation, such as those they outlined, should give rise to consideration of the use of the Twenty-fifth Amendment. They also argue that no specific set of rules can fully define every situation that might arise but that medical guidance can help determine the extent to which impairment results in occupational disability in a given leader. Finally, they note that the most problematic circumstances that might arise relate to the development and manifestation of severe neurological or psychiatric conditions that go unrecognized by the leader himself. These conditions warrant careful medical guidance and political action to remove a severely impaired leader who cannot recognize his own limitations.

DEFINING AND DETERMINING PRESIDENTIAL IMPAIRMENT

The most detailed and prominent proposal on how to handle the issues of physician involvement in determining presidential impairment comes from Dr. Bert Park, a neurosurgeon and historian. Park notes that leader illness involving impaired neurological functioning has emerged fairly frequently over the course of history.[53] Yet the question of how the public and president should respond to this reality remains unanswered. How the public reacts to issues of leadership impairment depends, in large part, on the political context in which it occurs. In a democracy, opposition forces, the media, and public opinion can call for an accounting of presidential behavior that seems odd or problematic, thus encouraging, though by no means assuring, the discovery or investigation of leadership impairment. However, in a more dictatorial or totalitarian society, there may be little recourse for defective leadership of whatever kind. When the public cannot remove the leader through elections, there remain few ways to insure the disposition of a disabled leader. Particularly if the leader stays in power through mechanisms involving repression, torture, and violence, even domestic opponents may prove loath to try to unseat the leader. Such a leader's associates may also consider their lives at risk should a repressive leader be overthrown.

In assessing presidential impairment, Bert Park, M.D., and Herbert Abrams, M.D., remain concerned about how best to define disability and how to establish a formal and professional mechanism for the appropriate transfer of power if such need arises. Park expresses particular concern about those cases where a leader is either unable or unwilling to recognize the degree of his own impairment because of neurological illnesses or injuries. This might happen, for example, in the wake of a major stroke, a blunt-force head trauma, an assassination attempt, or in the case of the insidious onset of Alzheimer's disease or other forms of dementia, among other causes.

Park, followed by Abrams and later President Carter, has called for the creation of a Presidential Disability Panel.[54] He argues that such a commission should be appointed before a new administration comes into office. He suggests that nominees should testify before Congress in order to determine their suitability for the job. Park advocates a panel composed of doctors skilled in the determination of disability assessment; he believes that this panel should be equally divided along party lines to assure that their recommendations do not fall prey to political infighting. He proposes that such a panel should examine the president's health on a yearly basis and report its findings to the vice president. This group itself would have no power to initiate disability proceedings against the president; rather, it would serve only to provide proper medical advice and support to the vice president on the question of the president's health.

Park posits that physicians remain the best interpreters of presidential impairment. He suggests that a Presidential Disability Panel could rely on the American Medical Association's *Guides to the Evaluation of Permanent Impairment*, which have been in widespread use since 1971. These guidelines carefully distinguish between impairment, which relates to the health of the person, and disability, which can be determined only in an occupational context. They produce an impairment rating, or a way to quantitatively compare and assess the extent to which impairment may produce disability. One of the questions on the test asks who is the president of the United States; obviously, if the president himself got this one wrong, the diagnosis would be apparent. In Park's view, any Disability Commission would conduct a physical examination of the president with appropriate tests. Next, they would determine the extent and nature of the president's physical functioning and limitations. Finally, the panel could compare its results with the criteria in the *Guides*. These criteria include categories along such dimensions as language, brain function, emotions, and neurological problems. This strategy would allow for a disability rating. The *Guides* could also help to determine if deficits are temporary or likely to remain permanent. Such a rating might then be used by the vice president or others to support a political case for establishing and determining whether the impairment remains so serious, so enduring, or of such a compromising nature as to necessitate invoking the Twenty-fifth Amendment for succession.

The members of the Working Group, however, voted 83–17 percent against the notion of establishing a standing Medical Advisory Board or Impairment Panel.[55] The arguments against such a panel included the belief that it might unconstitutionally violate separation of powers between branches of the government. Penalties that might accrue to a president who refused to submit to the examination by a panel remained unclear; such a refusal did not seem sufficient to warrant impeachment without additional documentation of disability. Additional concern surrounded the recognition that such a medical panel would have no public mechanism of accountability, and thus might have a hard time garnering public support and credibility, especially in the event of a crisis. Finally, many members of the Working Group remained skeptical about the likelihood that any panel could reach a medical consensus, thus leaving open the possibility that any report could be used for personal political

advantage by rival groups of actors. The potential for leaking information to be politically damaging remains high under such conditions, even
if medical conditions have no bearing on decision-making capability, as
when a female candidate is found to have had an abortion.

CONCLUSIONS

In an age of weapons of mass destruction and renewed terrorist threats,
the issue of presidential succession rises to ever higher levels of complexity and concern. In the modern age of terrorism lawmakers must
contemplate the manner of succession in the case of wholesale assassination of the officials in Washington, D.C. including the president, vice
president, cabinet, and members of Congress. While obscure passages of
various constitutional law provide requirements for passing laws under
various quota and quorum rules, such regulations have thankfully never
had occasion to be implemented as yet. A full-scale nuclear assault on the
United States, such as was commonly feared from the Soviet Union during the Cold War, could render such succession meaningless and useless.
However, a more common scenario in the current world might include
a single attack by a rogue state on a major city, such as Washington. If
such an event occurred, the rest of the country would desperately need
immediately qualified, credible, and confident leadership in the absence
of the majority of elected federal officials.

Procedures should be instituted to plan for such a contingency. In particular, institutional plans should be developed that utilize a more networked
approach to national and regional governance. After all, the Internet was
created by the Pentagon in an attempt to establish a communication system that could survive, at least in part, following a decapitating nuclear
strike on American command, control, and communication centers by the
Soviets. A similar program should also be established for governance in
the case of a devastating attack on the Capitol. Such a directive might
rely more heavily on regional leaders such as governors and local officials, including mayors, than might previously have been considered. In
this way, elected democracy can survive and thrive in the case of decapi-
tation of the federal leadership.

EIGHT

PRESIDENTIAL CARE

The problem of presidential illness, disability, or succession raises serious concerns about leadership performance and the conduct of American foreign and domestic policy. Several concerns are posed by impaired leadership, including the public's right to know about a leader's health, especially in a democracy; the physician's dual role as doctor and citizen; and the implications that such limitations might pose for public policy. This problem is neither rare nor trivial.

Since 1789, forty-two men have been president of the United States. Four of them have been assassinated in office (James Garfield, William McKinley, Abraham Lincoln, and John Kennedy). Unsuccessful assassination attempts were made on several others, including Franklin Roosevelt, Harry Truman, Richard Nixon, Gerald Ford, and Ronald Reagan. Only the attempt on Reagan's life led to serious injury to the victim.[1] Four others have died in office from natural causes (William Harrison, Zachary Taylor, Warren Harding, and Franklin Roosevelt). Nixon resigned his office. In that time, vice presidents have hardly fared better. Seven died in office (George Clinton, Elbridge Gerry, William King, Henry Wilson, Thomas Hendricks, Garrett Hobart, and James Sherman). John Calhoun and Spiro Agnew resigned. And nine left the office to assume the presidency (John Tyler, Millard Fillmore, Andrew Johnson, Chester Arthur, Theodore Roosevelt, Calvin Coolidge, Harry Truman, Lyndon Johnson, and Gerald Ford).[2]

Dr. Herbert Abrams estimated that when George Bush was president, Vice President Dan Quayle had a 35 percent chance of becoming president, based on the twentieth-century probability of presidential mortality rates.[3] As Dr. Abrams has noted, "In a society in which mental illness abounds, in which drug and alcohol abuse are virtually insoluble social problems on a wide scale, and in which political fanaticism and terrorism exist in all nations, we must anticipate that the assassin will appear again."[4] In the age of terrorism, the assassin may strike not only at one person but at a whole group of people, as the 9/11 attack on the Pentagon demonstrated. In such an environment, the importance of succession becomes particularly pressing.

Aside from the most severe consequence of mortality, the majority of the remaining men who have been president have suffered from a wide variety of illnesses while in office as well. Robert Gilbert states that cardiovascular disease killed six of the seven presidents who died naturally but prematurely in the twentieth century.[5] A brief survey of American presidents demonstrates the frequency and severity of the illnesses they have suffered. Among those who completed their term, George Washington apparently suffered from dementia in his second term in office;[6] John Adams, like George Bush, contracted hyperthyroidism; James Madison fell into a delirium from a high fever, which lasted about a month in 1813; Andrew Jackson suffered from the effects of a bullet lodged in his body following his duel with Charles Dickinson; Grover Cleveland underwent surgery for cancer of the jaw while in office; Calvin Coolidge suffered from debilitating depression following the sudden death of his favorite son; Dwight Eisenhower survived a heart attack, a stroke, and surgery for ileitis; and Lyndon Johnson had gallbladder surgery.[7]

In making his argument regarding the physical and psychological dangers of the presidency, Robert Gilbert also notes that many presidents died prematurely, compared to statistical life expectancy data for similar men of their age and background.[8] He documents that of the thirty-seven deceased presidents, twenty-five died prematurely, as calculated by the life expectancy of white males during their historical age. Between 1841 and 1991, twenty-three of the twenty-nine deceased presidents who served during this time died prematurely. Excluding the assassinated presidents only strengthens the findings. In a similar comparison, eleven out of thirteen British prime ministers between 1908 and 1970 suffered from illnesses that at least partly disabled them in some way while in office.[9]

Gilbert's findings appear particularly compelling when they are compared with other white males of similar educational and occupational achievements. Specifically, members of Congress and the Supreme Court live, on average, much longer than white men in the general population, and this trend has continued to increase over time. Pictures alone confirm how quickly presidents seem to age on the job. These findings should be approached cautiously, however, because many of the most recent presidents of the twentieth century, including Nixon, Ford, Carter, Reagan, and Bush, have done well in terms of longevity. This may result from improved medical care, but then the first ten presidents were the longest-lived group. Any conclusions must necessarily remain tentative, of course, because of the small size of the sample.

Gilbert also examines the relationship between presidential longevity and performance. Relying on an assessment of presidential performance conducted by William Ridings and Stuart McIver, who polled 700 scholars,[10] Gilbert compared ratings of effectiveness with mortality. He found that presidents judged as most successful lived the longest, while those judged least effective died soonest, on average. Gilbert argues that "although both groups of presidents tended to die prematurely, the presidents who accomplished the most fared better in terms of both reputation and longevity of life than did their less successful counterparts." Gilbert proposes a hypothesis for why this may be true:

> Effectiveness, as measured by concrete accomplishments, may ease some of the emotional stresses of the office and give its occupant some sense of comfort and satisfaction. Thus, the successful presidents had occasional respites from the debilitating stresses of the presidency even though they could not escape them completely. On the other hand, their unsuccessful counterparts, recognizing their weakness and ineffectiveness and continually facing their inability to cope with the demands of office, may well have been subjected to greater mental anguish during their tenure in office than anyone may have imagined.[11]

Gilbert proposes that the mechanism by which this process occurs involves the negative impact of stress on cardiovascular disease risk. However, it may also be the case that certain medical or psychological conditions may predispose a person to heart disease while also making them relatively ineffective leaders – depression, for example. In addition, some leaders thrive on stress, and what one leader might find stressful another would find stimulating.[12] Gilbert's point regarding the mitigating impact of success on stress remains germane in this context.

Having witnessed and observed the frequency and severity of this problem in presidential history, many physicians, politicians, and scholars have attempted to redress it through a variety of mechanisms, including the Twenty-fifth Amendment. This chapter examines various ways to improve and enhance presidential health care, including the issues of physician selection. Finally, lessons concerning the political implications and ramifications of presidential illness are addressed, along with suggestions concerning presidential succession in this age of terrorism.

INSTITUTIONAL PRESIDENTIAL HEALTH CARE

The White House Medical Unit is charged with the comprehensive care of the president and is staffed by the White House physician and additional medical personnel, which in 1987 included three assistant physicians, two physician assistants, four nurses, two Navy medical corpsmen, and two secretaries.[13] By 2000 the office had grown to twenty-one active duty military personnel working in the White House Medical Unit, including five physicians, five physician assistants, five nurses, three corpsmen, and three administrative staff. These officers retain responsibility for twenty-four-hour on-site care for the president, acute care in an emergency, medical contingency planning for events such as planned travel, protective medical support, and medical training for White House medical personnel. This office also oversees medical care for the president's family and, occasionally, other members of the White House staff.[14]

In seeking to update this material, the author sent a written inquiry to the White House Medical Unit in July 2003. Rear Admiral Michael Miller, USN, deputy assistant to the president and director, White House Military Office, declined to answer the request, offering the following justification:

> On behalf of the White House Military Office and the White House Medical Unit, I must regrettably decline most of your request for information. . . . much of the data you requested should not and will not be released. If it were to release the capabilities, manning and specialties within the Medical Unit, that information could be used to discern potential vulnerabilities for those who might wish to harm the President.
>
> You are correct that Colonel (Dr.) Richard J. Tubb, U.S. Air Force is Physician to the President and Director of the White House Medical Unit. He is paid at the same rate as any other active duty military officer, considering his time in service and status as a physician.
>
> Again, I regret being able to be of further assistance regarding your inquiry.

The title of "president's doctor" differs from president to president. Each president has made his own individual medical arrangements. While things may have become more systematic over time, with more review of the qualifications of the particular physicians, personal taste has never been abandoned altogether. For example, George H. W. Bush's personal physician, Burton Lee, was a friend from prep school, but a military doctor, Lawrence Mohr, remained in charge of the administration and medical care of the White House Medical Unit. Different titles may be used for different physicians who have different roles. Historically, most White House physicians have been in the military, although several have been chosen from civilian arenas more recently. William McKinley's doctor, Newton Bates, was the first presidential physician to be so named in 1897.[15] Prior to that, most presidents availed themselves of free medical service under the auspices of army and navy physicians. James Polk appeared to be the first president to have employed this type of service. Some argue that military doctors may be particularly susceptible to pressures from their presidential patients to keep a medical condition secret, because these leaders also serve in a dual capacity as their commander in chief. On the other hand, these officers also take an oath to the Constitution, not the president, and therefore may have no difficulty breaking personal medical privilege in order to safeguard the country. From this perspective, a military physician may retain more freedom than a medical doctor in private practice who does not swear such an oath.[16]

While a doctor's responsibility to the nation is a worthy topic for debate, it is not clear that even the best of doctors in the early 1900s, for example, could have provided much more than palliative care for most of the medical concerns that plagued leaders such as Wilson and Roosevelt. And the quality of care must be judged according to the standards of the time, not by current standards once more advanced care has become available. This lack of knowledge, however, does not provide an excuse for not being honest with the patient, and the country, about the president's condition, something that appeared to happen on more than an infrequent occasion with Roosevelt's doctor, McIntire, for example.

The current role of the White House physician involves many different responsibilities. This doctor should be able to function competently in the areas of outpatient medical care for minor injuries and illnesses, medical emergencies, especially cardiopulmonary resuscitation and life support, inpatient medical care including transport, dental care, and preventive care, including immunizations for travel. This physician is also responsible for anticipating potential medical emergencies and planning accordingly, not only in forecasting and responding to assassination attempts at home but in planning for medical or terrorist emergencies abroad as well.

The most potentially challenging and complex aspect of the White House physician's job involves the Twenty-fifth Amendment and possible determination of any presidential impairment or disability. The White House physician necessarily serves in a dual-role relationship with the president: first, as his doctor, with all that implies for issues of doctor-patient confidentiality; and, second, as the physician, responsible to the nation, charged with making sure that the president receives quality medical care but is not allowed to continue in his capacity as leader if he becomes sufficiently medically or psychologically impaired.[17]

PHYSICIAN SELECTION

Proposed Modes of Selection

Much discussion surrounds the issue of physician selection, and the justifications for this concern are evident. As MacMahon and Curry write,

American history is filled with instances in which presidential politics became entangled in presidential medical care. The mixture usually led to secrecy – and often disastrous consequences. Secrecy has produced poor medicine and poor medicine has produced cover-ups. Out of political considerations, presidents anxious to hide their health problems have accepted less than satisfactory care. Secrecy can prevent a competent physician from administering to the president the full range of tests and treatments that he would order for an ordinary patient. Secrecy also allows an incompetent physician to mistreat a president because he is not subjected to realistic review by his peers. Changes in the structure of presidential health are sorely needed, starting with the method of selecting the government-paid physician who attends him.[18]

Because many past presidential physicians have demonstrated notable incompetence in their professional roles, MacMahon and Curry argue that a panel should help pick the president's doctor in the future.[19] The problem with this strategy is that physician-patient rapport is key to open and honest communication, and this may be difficult for a president to establish with someone who is chosen for him, rather than with someone he chooses himself. These authors suggest that the role of presidential physician should be upgraded and formalized. They argue that the physician should at least be subject to congressional confirmation to make sure that the candidate holds suitable medical qualifications. They hope that these suggestions might help overcome some of the past problems inherent in the physician-president relationship, most notably those surrounding loyalty and secrecy. In the past, Congress has turned to the White House physician for help in determining presidential disability but, in so doing, often received heavily biased and misleading information in return. For example, Secretary of State Robert Lansing went to Dr. Cary Grayson to get information about President Wilson's condition after his October 1919 stroke, but Grayson honored Mrs. Wilson's desire for confidentiality and did not disclose the full extent of Wilson's impairment to his cabinet. MacMahon and Curry advocate for full medical disclosure, in the cases of infirmity, when necessary; careful and expert consideration in choosing a presidential physician; and a clear, stable method for removing a disabled leader.[20]

Different scholars have suggested various ways to improve the process of selecting a presidential physician. Robins and Rothschild offer two suggestions for ways to provide better health screening for candidates in order to reduce the chance that an impaired leader becomes elected while increasing the likelihood that such a truly sick man could be removed from office quickly and easily.[21] Their first proposal would be to screen the health of candidates for the presidency. A panel of three physicians would be appointed by a bipartisan committee of Congress or some other committee of high judicial officers. These physicians would thoroughly review each candidate's medical history and carefully examine the person. Their evaluation would be given to the nominee. This process would ensure competent medical review and reduce the likelihood that the person could bully the physicians into complying with his personal wishes. The report would not be made public except in the case of a hidden illness that could cause a severe impairment in the candidate's ability to govern. The possibility for political bias to intrude on this process remains problematic. Leaks of irrelevant but damaging information on candidate or presidential health pose serious consequences for politicians, who might thus prove understandably averse to submitting to such procedures.

One of the benefits of such a panel would be that, with the performance of regular exams, it might at least be able to assure that potential medical problems were discovered early and that the best treatment was found quickly. Second, the burden of confrontation, compromised confidentiality, or the public's right to know if a leader is disabled would then fall not solely on the president's physician but rather on the panel. This does not mean that noncritical medical information should be revealed or that information needs to be revealed if the president certifies to his own inability under the terms of Section 3 of the Twenty-fifth Amendment. However, to the extent that the president is unable or unwilling to certify to his own inability, and his impairment poses a threat to his decision-making abilities, then a panel might relieve a personal physician from having to undertake a task that might more easily be hidden than disclosed.

Milton Greenblatt has suggested the establishment of a Presidential Health Commission composed of specialists in various fields including mental health.[22] This group would be charged with advising on the medical and emotional screening of candidates, selecting the president's doctor, deciding when to employ other specialists or consultants, reviewing questions of hospitalization, determining what information should be released to the public, and educating the public on relevant medical matters. The group would also serve to help advise when the president might become too impaired to continue to serve in office.

Crispell and Gomez's examination of physician selection expands on Barber's notion of presidential character. However, rather than predicting presidential behavior from an understanding of a president's character, world view, and style, Crispell and Gomez view illness as a source of unpredictability in leadership.[23] Illness can occur randomly, without warning, and can disappear just as quickly, or leave permanent disability in its wake. Sometimes the difference in outcome can be determined by a skilled doctor, or special equipment, or simple luck. For example, Reagan's life was no doubt saved in 1981 by the short distance between his attack and a first-rate trauma team and emergency center at George Washington Hospital.

Because of the increasing importance of high-quality medical care as medicine becomes more complicated, specialized, and filled with sophisticated technology, Crispell and Gomez also argue that the position and status of the president's physician should be increased, although they do not advocate for a cabinet-level post.[24] They too endorse the notion of Senate confirmation for physician appointments.

Drawing on the results of the Miller Commission report and the earlier work by Crispell and Gomez, Dr. Herbert Abrams has also put forth a list of procedures for strengthening the position of the president's physician. Although in some ways these suggestions come out of larger discussions concerning the scope of the Twenty-fifth Amendment, these guidelines deserve discussion here because they most closely relate to the role of the president's physician. In this view, the physician should be well acquainted with the constitutional provisions for succession, including the Twenty-fifth Amendment. First, he notes that the president's physician

> should be fully aware of the cognitive, emotional and psychological effects of illnesses such as heart disease, stroke, trauma, hypertension, cancer, prolonged infection, and metabolic disorders; of drugs and medications used or likely to be used by the president; and of common medical procedures, especially as they may relate to the President's current state of health. He should also be alert to the symptoms of common emotional psychological and personality disorders.[25]

Second, the physician should always carry unsigned, undated letters to invoke the Twenty-fifth Amendment in an emergency if necessary. Third, the president's doctor should inform him in person and in writing about the nature and potential consequences of any medical procedure he is about to undergo. If any mind-altering drugs are planned, such as anesthesia, the doctor should recommend that the president invoke the Twenty-fifth Amendment as a routine matter of course. If there is a medical emergency, the doctor should tell the president if he is, or is likely to become, incapacitated and encourage the use of the Twenty-fifth Amendment as well. Next, if the doctor thinks that the president has become impaired for any other reason, he should recommend the use of the Twenty-fifth Amendment. If the president does not take action, the doctor should consult outside medical experts. If they agree with the doctor's assessment, the doctor should tell the president that he plans to notify the appropriate persons in writing, including the vice president, the cabinet, and the chief of staff, about his medical opinion of the president's condition. If the president is unable to recognize his own impairment, the physician should inform the relevant officials. If the president still does not come into compliance with appropriate procedures following this notification, the physician should notify the leaders of both houses of Congress, in writing. When and if the president returns to good health, the physician should inform the president that he can return to work and should inform the vice president and other officials as well.

Despite the development of careful institutional procedures, it can still prove emotionally difficult and challenging for a physician to go against the will of his patient, even if it is in the patient's, and the country's, best interest, in order to certify disability. As has been evident throughout history, this kind of personal and political confrontation proved insurmountable for many physicians who were genuinely attached to their patients and wanted to give them what they wanted and tell them what they wanted to hear about their health.

Some suggestions for improvement in physician selection and presidential disability certification seem relatively easy to implement, as long as sufficient political will exists to execute them. For example, garnering congressional approval for a presidential physician's nomination, as suggested by Ferrell among others, should not prove especially difficult, especially because Congress is used to engaging in this process of approval for a wide variety of other government appointments, such as cabinet officials, judges, and ambassadors to foreign countries.[26] At the very least, such procedures should ensure that truly incompetent physicians do not ascend to the rank of presidential physician.

The importance of adequate physician selection for the president grows out of two independent pressures. First, past presidential physicians like Cary Grayson, Ross McIntire, and Janet Travell present cases of presidential physicians whose political loyalty appeared to exceed either their medical skills and qualifications, their sense of larger political responsibility, or both. Most would agree that at the very least, the president's physician should be a highly skilled medical professional. Second, because so many scholars and politicians have discussed the difficult structural position of the White House physician, many observers remain concerned about the president's doctor's ability to walk the tightrope between offering high-quality and confidential care to the president and remaining alert and receptive to indications that the president may no longer remain competent to discharge the duties of his office, either physically or psychologically.

Many authors have argued that the dual role imposed on a leader's physician has led in the past to inadequate medical care in at least some cases, as with the shah of Iran.[27] In addition, such incompetent care has on occasion also led to public cover-ups of the severity of presidential illness.[28] The divided duties placed on a leader's physician make it challenging for a doctor to retain confidentiality with a patient he recognizes as impaired. First, a physician needs his patient to be honest about all his symptoms if the doctor is going to be able to offer the best care possible. It is not in the patient's best medical interest to lie, even if there remain political incentives to do so. The physician does not want to inadvertently encourage a patient to go elsewhere to receive alternative and possibly suboptimal care, because he or she cannot assure the patient complete confidentiality. Yet the doctor must also realize that he or she retains a duty to the nation that the leader serves to notify the appropriate figures if the leader becomes too impaired to function adequately in his office.

Second, in many cases a physician may be confronted with the ethical dilemma of believing that the best care for the patient involves allowing the president to continue in his job. Physicians over the course of history have made the argument that displacing a certain leader whose life and identity remained closely tied with his political stature would hasten his death. Edith Wilson claimed that Wilson's eminent neurologist Francis Dercum argued that if he were forced from office, his physical condition would rapidly deteriorate in the wake of his inevitable depression.[29] However, because Mrs. Wilson did not make this claim until after Dercum's death, it is impossible to know if this is true, or whether she used his prestige to validate her own strong preferences. Lord Moran allowed Winston Churchill to stay on in office after his major stroke in 1953 at least partly because he believed that the alternative would kill him. This came years after Lord Moran had noted to others at Yalta that Roosevelt looked so bad that he did not have long to live and should not be allowed to remain in office.[30] Vice President Cheney's physicians have shared this belief. When asked whether stress would increase Cheney's risk for additional heart trouble, his main doctor argued, against the majority of extant research, that new studies did not demonstrate an association between stress and heart disease. Rather, he argued that forcing Cheney to leave office would be worse for his health, because it would deprive him of meaning, purpose, and status.[31] What seems striking about all these comments is the emphasis they place on the welfare of the patient, which is certainly a natural medical predilection. It seems in this instance, however, that the focus should be on the country these leaders are in charge of governing and on their decision-making abilities that could affect millions, and not primarily on their own personal preferences.

Last, a physician, like a politician, may honestly believe that the sick leader remains capable of fulfilling his constitutional role or that he continues to present a better option than the putative alternative, and the doctor might be correct in that determination. Would the voters have rejected Roosevelt in 1944 if he had told the nation he had congestive heart failure? The war was still on, and Roosevelt was a larger-than-life figure for many Americans, who may have seen him as the most qualified to bring the war to a successful end. They might well have voted him back into office regardless of his health problems. Given the importance of his personal relationships with Churchill and Stalin, many voters could easily have preferred Roosevelt working at half capacity to any other fully able alternative.

Finally, any given presidential physician may simply be interested in retaining his job. If his patient were to be declared incompetent to serve, all benefits that accrue to the physician might be lost. While such losses may seem trivial for a presidential physician in a democracy, especially one who can return to a profitable civilian practice, physicians in more authoritarian political systems may even lose their lives if they prove incapable of keeping their leader both fit and in charge.

The point of this study is not that all impaired leaders should not govern. Many of them remain effective and may prove much more enlightened than their potential successors or opponents. In a democratic system, however, the public should have a right to know any potentially compromising medical information before making a decision about how to vote. They can then still choose to elect a leader with a known illness over another candidate whom they judge to be inadequate on some other, presumably more important, dimension. In this way, the public can assess how serious the impairment is, as with any other individual characteristic on which they base their votes, such as policy positions. But, as with financial disclosures, the public in a democracy should be informed of these factors before going to the polls.

Qualifications

The qualifications of the White House physician have come under scrutiny in the past few decades. Many presidential doctors throughout history appear to have been chosen as much for their charm and social connections as for their medical skills. Others have argued that presidential physicians accept the largely tedious, time-consuming job because of their desire to obtain a better, more prestigious post later.

Lawrence Mohr, a former White House physician, suggests that all presidential physicians should share several specific qualifications.[32] They should be board-certified in a patient care specialty. They should possess competence and experience in outpatient treatment, emergency care, and advanced cardiac and trauma life support. They should continue to practice medicine outside the White House, preferably at a major medical center, in order to stay fresh and up-to-date on the latest medical developments. Mohr concurs with Crispell and Gomez, Abrams, and the Miller Center recommendations that White House physicians should have achieved the highest degree of professional respect and accomplishment.[33] They should be well-known, well-respected, expert clinicians with well-regarded academic publications capable of landing them a senior faculty position at a major academic medical center. A president's doctor should also possess sufficient experience to be comfortable with the role of White House physician and confident enough to stand up to the president when medically necessary. In addition, the president and his family should like and trust the person.

These requirements seem very demanding for someone who may not want to interrupt an academic career to move to Washington to work around the clock for a single major patient, although other benefits would accrue with such a position. These qualifications are particularly unlikely in combination with a military career, which would have required a different career trajectory, placing less emphasis on publications, for example. Yet the president, as commander in chief, chief of state, and chief executive of the United States, should receive exemplary care.

Several commentators have suggested that a panel be created to nominate or appoint an appropriate presidential physician. Robins and Rothschild offer two suggestions for ensuring the proper health screening of candidates.[34] First, they propose a bipartisan panel of three physicians, appointed by Congress or the Supreme Court, who would conduct a full examination of each candidate. These reports would then be given to the candidates' doctors. Public disclosure would occur only in the wake of a discovery of a hidden illness that might substantively affect the decision-making abilities of the candidate. Their second proposal, related to the monitoring of presidential health, similarly suggests a three-doctor panel appointed by Congress. This special President's Official Physicians Panel would meet with the president once a quarter and participate in a yearly physical examination. It would also have the right to be consulted during any question regarding presidential illness. Its results would be secret unless they felt it incumbent upon them to reveal compromising information to the vice president or Congress. They suggest that physicians who are one step removed from the personal closeness that typically characterizes a long-term doctor-patient relationship would be a good thing in this situation; such distance would introduce a double check on a primary-care physician who may not see, acknowledge, or inform the president about the severe nature of a particular illness or disability.

Dr. Herbert Abrams, who undertook an extensive investigation into the assassination attempt on Ronald Reagan, strongly advocates that all candidates fully reveal their medical history.[35] He makes this argument in part based on his investigation of the cover-ups of Paul Tsongas's non-Hodgkin's lymphoma and President Bush's Graves' disease (hyperthyroidism) during the 1992 presidential primary.

William Safire suggested that the Democratic and Republican National Committees should appoint a Candidate Medical Review Board to review the medical histories, conduct physical examinations of all candidates, and interview their doctors.[36] This board would then make a short statement about the overall health of the candidates. Safire argues that good health should be a requirement for such a demanding and important job as president and that the public has a right to know the life expectancy of each candidate prior to the election.

Yet determining adequate qualifications for a White House physician remains an important and complex task. More importantly, Robins and Post discuss the complexity of choosing a healthy president.[37] They base their suggestions on several interesting and important assumptions. First, they argue that presidents do not need to be completely healthy in order to function well in office. Lawrence Altman, who has covered presidential health issues for several decades, agrees with this point. He believes that no candidate for president should be disqualified on the basis of health reasons, as long as any potentially compromising information is fully disclosed to the public prior to the election.[38] Robins and Post proceed to argue that the public is capable of understanding and evaluating medical information about candidates and that more information will lead to a better choice. They suggest that the candidate's right to privacy is conditional on the nature of the job.[39] Thus, if someone wants to run for the presidency, he needs to understand that this process will involve disclosing certain medical facts as a consequence of the job application. If a candidate is not willing to publicly disclose such health information, then he or she should not run for office. Voters in a democracy have the right to make an informed choice, for example, concerning whether they would rather have a good leader who does not have optimal health or a corrupt, ineffectual one who is nonetheless physically fit. This choice is extreme and dichotomous, but the example remains illustrative. The key is that the choice be informed. Russian voters made this choice when they elected Yeltsin president for a second term, although he was too sick to be seen in public in the last few days of the campaign, over the retrogressive Communist Gennady Zyuganov. Certainly voters may have made that choice in electing Roosevelt in 1944 over a more physically fit opponent while the war was still ongoing.

However, some screens do exist. First, the rigors of the campaign itself help demonstrate the endurance of each candidate. Second, political insiders such as party leaders often screen candidates prior to nominating them for office, although this process can be deeply flawed if the candidate does not disclose certain information to the party leaders. Thomas Eagleton did not reveal his history of depression to relevant party leaders in the 1972 presidential campaign, and when his electroshock therapy was revealed, he was removed from the ticket. Finally, the media serves as a screening device through their investigative work. However, this process also remains flawed. If a candidate goes to great lengths to hide particular health information, as Tsongas did in the 1992 campaign concerning the recurrence of his lymphoma, the media may not always find out in time to ensure appropriate disclosure. Had he won the election, he would have died in office.

A world of difference exists between treatable and nontreatable ill-nesses, and the need to cover up the latter remains much weaker. The kinds of medical problems that are most likely to affect the quality of presidential decision making and performance, such as addiction or men-tal illness, are often those that leaders try hardest to conceal because of associated stigma. They also can be the most difficult conditions for oth-ers to discover.[40] Robins and Post argue that undisclosed medical prob-lems have caused problems with campaigns, divided party politics, and compromised associated leaders, as the Eagleton example demonstrates. Such problems can also cause the quality and credibility of the presi-dency itself to decline should such problems emerge once the leader is in office.

Robins and Post present a very sophisticated argument about the dif-ficulties of resolving some of the issues surrounding disclosure of medi-cal information.[41] If the public requires too much information, a patient might not reveal everything to his doctor, thus potentially compromising the quality of his own care. This dynamic can lead to a bad outcome for everyone, including increased risk for serious illness or death on the part of the candidate. When leaders fail to reveal their problems even to their doctors for fear of public exposure, they subsequently risk the loss of not only their political power but their lives as well. But if too little informa-tion is required, then medical cover-ups can compromise the quality of leadership.

Robins and Post suggest that partial disclosure offers the best solution.[42] The president's physician, with the permission of his patient, would reveal only certain predetermined information about particular health problems, treatments, and medications. George Annas argues, for instance, that cer-tain specific information should never be revealed.[43] These areas include visits to psychiatrists, HIV/AIDS status, and the outcome of certain poten-tially prejudicial genetic tests, such as those for terminal illnesses such as Huntington's chorea, a progressive neurological disease leading to demen-tia and death. He also argues that if a woman ever ran for office, she should not be forced to reveal if she has ever had an abortion. This would not affect her medical ability to serve but could nonetheless compromise her political viability. Some of these categories appear ill-considered, because Huntington's, for example, might compromise an individual's ability to lead effectively. However, the point that some medical history remains irrelevant to effective leadership, even if politically explosive like abor-tion, is well taken.

The most important of these suggestions concerns psychiatric care. Annas argues that leaders should be able to get the help they need and that they will never do so unless they are assured of complete confidentiality of care. Gilbert for one suggests that the Office of the White House Medical Unit should contain a psychiatrist who remains available to the president twenty-four hours a day and travels with him.[44] By making such care automatic, the institutional bureaucracy can begin to destigmatize the role of mental illness and mental health care in society. This often happens when well-known people become afflicted with a particular illness and even turn it into a cause; Betty Ford's addiction served this purpose, for example. It may also provide genuine help to a stressed leader, who may be completely mentally healthy but may nonetheless suffer from the strains of office. Having a confidential, skilled medical professional who is trained to observe, recognize, and treat cases of mental strain and illness could prove beneficial for leader and country.

Ethics

The ethics of the presidential physician have also prompted some discussion. The three most influential statements in this regard have come from Anastasia Kucharski, Robins and Rothschild, and Post and Robins.[45] Kucharski writes about some of the ways in which the medical treatment of leaders and other important people may differ from that of others in ways that can present ethical dilemmas.[46] First, she notes that referral channels for the doctor, or specialists, are often indirect, or unusual. This means the best doctors may not be the ones most likely to be chosen. Second, there are either too many or too few people involved in the care of the patient. The shah's medical care provides an example of medical warfare that compromised the quality of his care. Tancredo Neves of Brazil offers another example of a powerful leader who, after many doctors treated him with differing protocols, died of diverticulitis, a condition that seldom causes the death of normal people afflicted with it. Third, clinical attention becomes misdirected and focuses on irrelevant details. Fourth, clinicians disagree more than usual about diagnosis and treatment. This happened repeatedly with the shah of Iran, as well. Fifth, professional role strain becomes exacerbated by the close nature of the relationship with the patient and the close association of self-esteem and professional acclaim with clinical success. Finally, the physician's own attitudes about money, fame, or power are often scrutinized in terms of his attachment to his patient.

Robins and Rothschild explore the doctor's obligation to his or her patient.[47] Arguing that the traditional Hippocratic Oath is "obsolete and unrealistic,"[48] they suggest a new code of ethics based in part on the following characteristics: minimize harm; do what is medically best; tell the truth; be candid; encourage patient autonomy; maintain or improve quality of life; maintain confidentiality and respect for patient privacy; be economical; consider family wishes if the patient can't make his or her own decisions; keep current in medical knowledge; know your limitations; and consider the implications of your actions and decisions for society.

They note six particular ethical dilemmas that attend to presidents' physicians. First, the status of the patient may be higher than that of the doctor, which can cause problems if the patient pressures the doctor for illegal drugs, for example. This can also cause problems when a president chooses a doctor based partly on social graces, engaging conversation, loyalty, fame, or some other factor that has little or nothing to do with substantive clinical accomplishments or skills. Second, the doctor will lose status and rewards if he or she is fired by the president. This creates pressures to do what the leader wants in order to hold onto valued personal benefits. Third, the influence of those around the president may be so great as to affect the medical treatment of the patient. For instance, Cary Grayson was decisively affected by President Wilson's wife, Edith, in helping to keep the extent of the president's impairment secret. Fourth, the doctor's treatment may have major historical or social consequences and may be scrutinized by future generations. Roosevelt's main physician, Ross McIntire, has come under great attack for concealing the extent of Roosevelt's cardiovascular disease, for example. Some physicians may choose to play it too safe, or take unnecessary risks, in order to make medical history, or remain blameless in the eyes of history. Fifth, it remains very hard to maintain secrecy regarding an important patient, and yet the consequences of leaks can prove more dangerous than with others. Finally, the relationship between the doctor and the president is likely to be especially close. This may blind the doctor to changes over time in the condition of the president that others quickly see, and it might also make it more difficult for the doctor to give bad news to his or her patient. The doctor may also have a genuine and natural human desire to protect his or her patient from bad news, especially if the doctor believes that it might compromise the physical or psychological health of the patient. The doctor may want to protect the patient from political outcomes resulting from the disclosure of a compromising medical condition like alcoholism, for example.

Robins and Rothschild note that these ethical dilemmas challenge the twin commitments to patient confidentiality on the one hand and implications for society on the other. They suggest that a physician should breach confidentiality if the president becomes incompetent or is about to commit an illegal or an immoral act. These conditions appear to overreach the physician's duty in the last and possibly in the second case. For example, while any physician is required to notify a potential victim if his patient intends to try to kill that person, in line with the 1976 Tarasoff ruling, it is not clear that all illegal or immoral acts should remain under the physician's purview to report. The Tarasoff ruling followed the case in California in which a University of California student, Prosenjat

Poddar, told his UC student health care therapist that he planned to kill a young woman, Tatiana Tarasoff, because she had spurned his affections. The therapist told the police, who interviewed the young man and found him sane. Two months later, Poddar killed Tarasoff. Her parents sued the UC regents, arguing that she should have been warned of the threat he posed. The court finding in their favor found an affirmative duty on the part of therapists to warn potential victims if their patients threaten harm. Should the physician be required to report a sexually transmitted disease in a president if it does not compromise his decision making or ability to serve? Such illness might reflect an immoral act in a married man but, depending on the disease, need not necessarily require the doctor to compromise nonmedical confidentiality. Should a physician who caught Nixon erasing tapes be required to divulge that "illegal" activity? What if a doctor knew his patient had robbed a bank but was perfectly healthy and sane? Would he have a duty to report such unethical but not physically or psychologically impaired behavior? It seems best to keep the physician's role clearly circumscribed to the medical arena.

Building on earlier work done by Kucharski and Robins and Rothschild about the difficulties and challenges a doctor faces in treating important patients, Post and Robins mention several special conditions that affect the issue of doctor-patient confidentiality and the balance between patient privacy and the public's right to know about compromised leadership.[49] Some of the following points may seem redundant but nonetheless serve to illustrate the consensus around which medical ethicists converge in their judgment concerning the treatment of powerful individuals. First, they note that typically those around the president display an inordinate amount of influence on medical decision making. This may make it particularly difficult for a doctor to provide the best *medical* care for the patient, especially if advisers judge that the lack of medical treatment may provide the best *political* outcome. Second, because the status of the patient can be so much higher than that of the doctor, the doctor might easily be bullied by the patient into providing inappropriate care, including the dispensing of illicit medication. Or, the patient may not need to bully a particular physician. He can simply fire the doctor, or go behind one doctor's back to seek the treatment he wants from another. Kennedy's medical record, for example, is rife with such occurrences. Third, because the physician may lose status, rewards, or even his life in certain totalitarian societies as a result of being fired by the leader, his or her medical treatment of the patient might be compromised by his or her high level of personal involvement with the patient and his health. Fourth, the doctor's decisions and treatments can have major societal implications. This can be particularly problematic when a doctor helps to cover up a leader's increasing incapacity, including abuse of drugs or alcohol, especially in a crisis, or aids in hiding increasing manifestations of mental illness or neurological impairment. Last, because the relationship between doctor and patient is very close in this kind of situation, the doctor's objectivity might come to be compromised over time as he or she becomes emotionally close to the leader.

Public Right to Know versus Privacy: Doctor-Patient Confidentiality

The presidential doctor serves two roles: he must respect his or her patient's confidentiality, and keep in mind a larger responsibility to society to assure competent leadership. The Hippocratic Oath and more recent revisions of ethical standards stress the importance of maintaining doctor-patient confidentiality.[50] One of the main reasons this factor remains critical in patient care is because it encourages the patient to be completely honest with his doctor about any medical issues that may arise, without having to worry unduly about the political consequences that such revelation might induce. Only when the patient can be completely honest with his doctor can the physician offer the best care possible.

Two important points deserve mention in this context. First, just because a leader may have some particular infirmity does not necessarily mean that he is unable to discharge the functions of his office effectively. Particular medical or psychological diagnoses should rest with qualified medical personnel. But decisions concerning fitness for office also demand a *political* evaluation, which, while taking into account a leader's limitations, also considers his strengths and resources in compensating for them as well as available realistic substitutes. Similarly, just because a leader's actions and decisions can affect history in some meaningful and decisive way does not mean that this will occur. The leader's limitations, both medical and political, interact within a particular political context with specific goals and demands. An impaired leader in a time of peace and tranquillity, for example, may not have as negative an effect on policy outcomes as such a leader in a time of war might.

In this way, disclosing medical information presents a double-edged sword. Such information might be released by men of integrity for the good of the country. It might also be leaked by a political opponent who wishes to discredit the leader for some unrelated political reason. Thus, any institutional procedures put in place concerning the disclosure of medical information deserve systematic attention so that the motives for the release of medical information remain transparent. And penalties for falsifying information should be severe.

Second, as Post and Robins noted, a real disparity in goals can exist between medical and political imperatives.[51] Medical treatment may demand immediate surgery for cancer or some other procedure for the treatment of heart disease or another major medical concern, for example. However, political exigencies might encourage delays in treatment to allow time for an election to take place, a policy to be pushed through legislation, or for some other political reason. If a leader and his entourage believe that public disclosure of infirmity on the part of the leader might compromise some other important political goal, incentives for delays in disclosure may exist. Secret treatment outside the country may improve the prospects for the quality of care, while decreasing the likelihood of success in achieving a political cover-up. The style of leadership can prove decidedly consequential as well, because leaders with a more hands-on style can cause greater difficulty if they fall ill than a leader who tended to delegate more authority from the start. There have been many instances of leaders refusing timely or appropriate medical care for political motives, only to lose their lives as a result. Governor Earl Long of Louisiana did just that in 1960, when he put off going to the hospital on the day of a closely contested election for fear of losing and died of a heart attack despite winning the congressional election.[52] This trade-off should not become necessary, but is often perceived as such by a leader and his aides.

Presidential Health

The question of doctor-patient confidentiality versus the public's right to know has generated considerable discussion among those concerned with presidential disability issues. Many physicians, such as Dr. Herbert Abrams, firmly fall on the side of the physician's responsibility to reveal information about a president's severely compromised health to the appropriate officials, or even to the public. Abrams argues that a person who runs for president must understand that some of his personal privacy, including health information, must be revealed for the safety of the nation.[53] If the candidate is not willing to go along with such a constraint, then he should not run for office.

In addition, Abrams argues that the "Principles of Medical Ethics" adopted by the American Medical Association in 1957 allow for such proposed violations of confidentiality when "necessary in order to protect the welfare of the individual or the community."[54] In this way, the president becomes like any other employee charged with public health and safety, such as an airline pilot, bus driver, or member of the Joint Chiefs of Staff, who must submit to periodic drug testing in order to keep his or her job. In those situations, as in cases where community health officials try to trace sexual and other contacts in order to limit the spread of communicable diseases like HIV, doctors may violate confidentiality in order to preserve the larger public health. The difference, of course, is that the president must protect his political power if he is to govern effectively in ways quite unlike other jobs, even those with great responsibility like airline pilots'.

AGE LIMITS

One of the most striking and fascinating aspects of the literature on presidential disability lies in some of its inherent contradictions. On the one hand, almost everyone expresses serious concern about age-related problems in leadership, from cardiovascular disease to dementia. Yet almost no one proposes imposing age limitations on the presidency itself. Only one physician's letter in *JAMA* even raises the issue in passing and then quickly dismisses it as unreasonable in light of how such a limit might squander the wisdom, experience, and intelligence of those past a certain age.[55]

And yet the framers of the original Constitution had no problem placing lower-end age limits on who could be president. If those under thirty-five are judged to be too brash, if more likely to be healthy and energetic than those above thirty-five, who is to say that the age-related health risks of those over a certain age might not outweigh their contributions as well? Why did the original framers not include this in their original document? Probably because the vast majority of men in the late 1700s did not live long enough for this issue to present a serious broad-scale concern.

So why are such age limits beyond contemplation now? Some of the reticence results from concern about precluding potentially gifted leaders on arbitrary grounds. While, in general, mandatory retirement age is permissible only where it can be shown that the job at issue cannot be performed effectively by a person over a specified age, several notable exceptions exist. For example, state and local police and firefighters must retire between the ages of fifty-five and sixty, while federal firefighters and law enforcement and corrections officers must retire at fifty-seven. Air traffic controllers are forced into retirement at fifty-seven and commercial airline pilots at sixty.[56] Yet the president experiences the most extreme effects of stress and aging as a result of being in office. Perhaps some of the reason analysts shy away from age limits is because most of those examining the issue identify with the leaders they investigate; after all, no one would want to propose an age limit too close to his own.

And yet the base rates of compromise in the general population remain clear. Take, for example, the case of driving, which became salient after an eighty-six-year-old man plowed into a crowded Santa Monica farmer's market on a Saturday morning, killing ten and injuring more than forty-five, fifteen critically. No drugs or alcohol were found in his system.

But it turned out that he had previously crashed his car into his garage at least twice in the days before the accident and may have been running from the scene of another accident when he ran into the market. He told investigators he mistook the gas pedal for the brake, apparently a not uncommon occurrence in elderly drivers.

The overall statistics support the frequency of such events among the elderly. A 1997 study by the National Safety Administration found the while older drivers (over eighty-five) make up about 9 percent of the population, they account for more than 14 percent of all traffic fatalities and more than 17 percent of all pedestrian fatalities. Drivers over eighty hit more pedestrians per 100,000 people than any other age group, including the youngest cohort. Drivers over sixty-five join those under twenty-five as the most dangerous on the road, producing the highest number of accidents per mile driven. Controlling for miles driven, the fatality rate for drivers over eighty-five is nine times as high as for those between twenty-five and sixty-nine years old. The two main reasons cited for such poor driving among older drivers include "poor judgment" and "decreased ability to change behavior in response to an unexpected or rapidly changing situation."[57] Such problems with older drivers prompted California state senator Tom Hayden to propose that drivers over seventy-five be required to take vision tests and written and road tests when renewing their licenses.

If such problems exist among those over sixty-five in overlearned behaviors such as driving, imagine the impact of similar cognitive deficits in a world leader. If older leaders are loath to impose age restrictions on their comrades, they should at least be willing to mandate that a president over the age of sixty-five be required to pass certain cognitive and neurological tests at least once a year.

POLITICAL RAMIFICATIONS AND IMPLICATIONS

Several commonalities emerge from an examination of the impaired leaders undertaken in the present study. A perverse kind of self-selection exists in all these leaders, both foreign and domestic, to pursue and maintain their public political careers no matter what the personal or physical costs of power. Perhaps, in part, this reflects the kind of personalities and temperaments that predominate in those who obtain powerful political positions in the first place. Not only does a bit of grandiosity help a leader to gain power, but a healthy dose of determination and courage can help him maintain it as well. Of these commonalities, four in particular are worth mentioning.

First, most of the leaders examined in this study felt a strong sense of temporal urgency about their work as a result of their illnesses. In other words, leaders who believe that their time is limited, and yet retain strong agendas for the work they would like to complete before they lose power or die, often push harder to accomplish things faster than their healthy counterparts. These leaders may feel a much stronger urgency in completing their own legacy; they often feel history creeping up on them in the daylight of their power, trying to steal their potential from the hands of time. This adds to the sense of time pressure even normal individuals feel under times of crisis and stress. Sometimes this can lead to amazing accomplishments, as the enormity, quickness, and breadth of Wilson's early legislative triumphs illustrate. But sometimes this attempt to speed things ahead of a more natural schedule can backfire, as the shah's attempts to bring westernization to his country too rapidly resulted in a fundamentalist Islamic backlash, helping to precipitate his own downfall.

Second, many of these leaders demonstrated a certain degree of detachment, even stoicism, in the face of their often tremendous pain and illness. Any serious examination of the lives of the American presidents examined here indicates that these men could have chosen to lead much easier and less painful lives in more reserved occupations if they preferred to do so. While they may have enjoyed the public limelight, they nonetheless paid a price for it in the enormously stressful and painful personal physical consequences of their occupations. Kennedy's quiet courage and Roosevelt's relentless endurance represent examples of resolve for the sake not only of personal power but of public service as well. Indeed, no one can read their medical records without emerging with tremendous respect and admiration for the long-standing courage and endurance manifested by these men.

In addition, in each case of impairment, leaders appear to learn the identical lesson: they all come to believe that because they had mastered their physical weaknesses and limitations, they could accomplish anything in the political arena. Nothing seemed as difficult as controlling their physical or psychological bodies. This appears to be especially true in Roosevelt's case. His incredible political comeback after polio all but killed him but also led him to view many personal and political problems from a similar vantage point. He believed that if he worked hard and ignored negative feedback, he could achieve anything. This characterized the way he approached the cognitive and physical limitations imposed on him by his cardiovascular disease, as well as how he handled American involvement in the Second World War. He is not alone among leaders who come to believe that failure is not an option or that it is worse than to die trying.

Third, in all the cases presented here, impaired leaders not only demonstrated remarkable compassion for others who shared similar physical or mental limitations but also worked hard politically to pass legislation to aid those who were similarly affected. Late in his first term, Wilson passed progressive welfare legislation. Kennedy passed major reforms in health care, especially for the elderly. Roosevelt, of course, was responsible for all the New Deal legislation that provided public assistance on a broad variety of fronts, including Social Security. Eleanor Roosevelt stated directly that her husband's own suffering facilitated his political compassion and concerns for the less fortunate; others implied that without it, Roosevelt might have been too arrogant and patrician to have succeeded in politics. Although he ultimately failed in his attempts, even Richard Nixon fought for the Family Assistance Plan, a program designed to provide support for needy families with children; it even included job training programs for those without work. The coincidence of personal pain and illness with widespread support for legislation designed to help those in similar straits seems more than accidental. Perhaps it takes those who have personally experienced the cost, difficulty, and pain of personal illness to realize how isolating and challenging such impairments can be.

Fourth, as noted from the outset, medical and psychological illness present only one of many inputs that help determine presidential judgment, decision making, and action. Some illnesses and conditions can prove more devastating and thus more influential than others. Analysis of disabled leaders indicates that subtle and fluctuant illnesses have the worst impact on leadership. Obvious disabilities, such as those that followed Reagan's assassination attempt, for example, do not require the leader to pretend to be acting at full capacity. Interested and influential actors can then step in and try to exert inappropriate control over the situation, but the public does not expect the leader to remain unaffected by the experience. However, subtle disabilities, those in which the leader can perform adequately enough for short periods of time sufficient to fool others into thinking everything is fine, appear to pose a more detrimental effect. In Roosevelt's case, the effects of his coronary artery disease emerged slowly and manifested intermittently. No one knew about Kennedy's Addison's disease because his medication controlled its most obvious ill effects. But these very treatments, in turn, exerted an independent impairment on his psychological state. Cases such as these can be hard to distinguish from the effects of ordinary stress on leaders in times of crisis.

In the end, leaders, like anyone else, get sick and die. What remains important is how they choose to allocate the time they have available to them. An ill leader who can marshal his resources to overcome his physical or psychological adversities can benefit from the experience in unexpected ways. With insight, a disabled leader can use his struggle with illness as a model for overcoming and facing other challenges successfully throughout politics and life. But a leader who is only able to turn his pain outward can prove destructive for many; such men can wreak unnecessary havoc on the world at large.

APPENDIX

FOREIGN LEADERSHIP AND MEDICAL INTELLIGENCE: THE SHAH OF IRAN AND THE CARTER ADMINISTRATION

Although the bulk of this study concerns the impact of medical and psychological impairment on the foreign policy decision making of U.S. presidents, another major way in which illness can impact American foreign policy occurs when leaders of foreign countries fall prey to illnesses. Their subsequent incapacitation can hold profound implications and consequences for American national and international security. Obtaining timely and accurate information on the health and welfare of critical allies and enemy leaders alike can prove helpful in inoculating American leaders from the often shocking virus of unanticipated revolution, leadership crisis, or state collapse.

In the interest of investigating the impact of foreign leader illness on American foreign policy, this appendix examines the notable case of the shah of Iran's illness and how the American government's ignorance of its severity produced a cascade of events that culminated in the holding of American hostages in the U.S. Embassy in Tehran. It proved a watershed in American-Iranian relations, from which the two countries have arguably still not recovered. This example serves to demonstrate the critical importance that medical intelligence can have in determining the direction of American foreign policy and points to the significance that such information can have in future threats and challenges.

MEDICAL INTELLIGENCE

Examples of governments going to great lengths to obtain medical information on foreign leaders abound. For example, the Israeli government obtained a urine sample from President Assad of Syria. What possible use might Israeli intelligence make of Assad's urine? Obviously, the Mossad considered this information important enough to undertake risks in order to obtain it. More recently, after the first wave of major fighting in Afghanistan, American and British intelligence officers were sent into various caves in the Hindu Kush area bordering Pakistan, which had recently been heavily bombed, to find or kill Osama bin Laden. These officers took tissue samples from dead bodies in order to test DNA samples to see whether bin Laden had been one of the people killed in the bombing. They were not successful in finding a match.

Medical information can also be used to manipulate the public's image of a leader. For example, when Yasser Arafat died after a mysterious ailment in November 2004, French laws allowed the widow to keep his medical records private. Very little was known of his condition, other than the fact that he had a low platelet count and a high white blood cell count, symptoms consistent with any number of illnesses. In the wake of such uncertainty, various speculations arose, including the concern among Palestinians that Arafat had somehow been poisoned by Israel. In the Western and Israeli press, a great deal of speculation arose as to whether the Palestinian leader had died of AIDS. John Loftus reported on ABC radio on October 26, 2004, that the CIA knew that Arafat had AIDS for quite some time. Loftus claimed that this information was used by the United States to urge Ariel Sharon, Israel's leader, not to try to kill Arafat because he would die soon anyway. They assumed that widespread knowledge of Arafat's presumed homosexuality would discredit him in ways that were preferable to simply killing him outright. David Frum, a former White House speechwriter, speculated that Arafat had contracted AIDS as a result of his homosexual liaisons with his bodyguards. He suspected that Arafat was being treated by French, and not Arab, doctors, to keep his illness secret.[1] He based his speculation on the 1987 memoirs of Lieutenant General Ion Pacepa, the deputy chief of Rumania's intelligence services under former communist leader Nicolae Ceausescu. In this book, *Red Horizons*, Pacepa relates a story of his conversation with Constantin Munteaunu, the general charged with teaching Arafat how to get the West to recognize the PLO. Munteaunu used a variety of surveillance techniques to monitor Arafat and reportedly caught Arafat's homosexual activities on tape.[2]

Le Monde, the French newspaper, early on cited sources claiming that Arafat had died of cirrhosis of the liver, which can be caused by many kinds of liver disease, including hepatitis, as well as alcoholism. But on Wednesday, November 17, 2004, *Le Monde* reported that Arafat had died of disseminated intravascular coagulation, which causes the blood not to clot properly, a disease typically secondary to another infection or cancer. Arafat's nephew Nasser al-Kidwa claimed, after seeing the medical record, that while poisoning and leukemia had been ruled out, no definitive cause of death was revealed.

The cause of Arafat's death would have political implications, and people close to him might want to suppress this information. Had Arafat been poisoned, such action would have undoubtedly produced near hysteria among the Palestinian population, blaming Israel for the assassination. But if Arafat died of AIDS, his memory might be tainted in a culture that views homosexuality as a sin. In this case, as in similar others, medical information on important leaders can have profound effects on political decisions in other countries, public perceptions, and leaders' historical legacy.

These examples raise a whole host of questions and issues related to the use of medical information and intelligence concerning foreign leaders for purposes of improving American national and international security. Is it important to obtain and retain medical information on foreign leaders in order to properly assess them? Is such information important and necessary for predicting future government stability or succession? Is this kind of intelligence gathering anomalous or should it become standard operating procedure? Does medical intelligence represent the wave of the future in intelligence gathering? Is this kind of intelligence gathering ethical?

Sometimes there will be indications in the signs and symptoms displayed by leaders that can help observers determine from a distance the conditions that might be affecting them. One of the most sophisticated examples of this is the "leadership at a distance" project that psychiatrist Jerrold Post helped develop for the Central Intelligence Agency to assess the mental status and personality characteristics of foreign leaders based on biographies, speeches and writings, profiles, behavior, and interviews with people who have known them. The Center for the Analysis of Personality and Political Behavior uses this input to investigate the leader's family and educational background, his ideological training and mentorship, and his personal drives and coping mechanisms.[3]

Once intelligence officials become aware of particular illnesses that a foreign leader might suffer from, the American government might prove more able to devise effective responses. The U.S. government has offered assistance to ailing foreign leaders in the past. For example, the American government can offer specific forms of medical care or other aid to help compensate for whatever specific limitations might be imposed by an illness; such strategies may help friendly leaders to avoid losing power or, conversely, hasten the downfall of hostile regimes. This kind of medical information can prove especially important when impaired leaders teeter on the brink of losing control over their mechanisms of power, such as the military. The most important potential problems revolve around debilitating physical or psychological illness in leaders who have control over nuclear weapons. In one of the most troubling examples of this kind of problem, French premier Georges Pompidou struggled with numerous health problems, including the disease that killed him, multiple myeloma, toward the end of his life. In the days before he died on April 2, 1974, he was not able to remember the six-number code for the release of French nuclear weapons. The numbers were then stamped on a medallion he wore around his neck, which others might have been able to read as well.[4] In addition, the control over nuclear weapons remained a serious concern during the many years when Boris Yeltsin was president of Russia and suffering from a variety of illnesses, including heart disease, stomach ulcers, various respiratory conditions, and alcoholism.

Knowing the particular medical strengths and weaknesses of foreign leaders can help the American intelligence community to understand and interpret the behavior of these leaders and make better policy choices based on full information. Such knowledge can also help the United States to predict and prepare for leadership failures and transitions in these countries. Finally, obtaining such medical information and intelligence in a systematic fashion can allow the American government to create institutional procedures, probable scenarios, and reasonable responses to foreign leaders' medical impairments. Such procedures might include encouraging elderly or ill leaders to designate a successor or to develop clear procedures for a peaceful transition process. In addition, good medical care may forestall the need for such procedures until an adequate successor is in place. In this way, the United States can make more informed decisions and avoid backing a leader who cannot stay in power due to a potentially disabling or fatal illness. In addition, helping newly democratic nations develop careful institutional procedures for succession as well as the peaceful removal of disabled leaders might also prevent violent overthrows upon the death of a personalistic leader. Cultivating careful succession rules or principles, particularly in the case of long-serving leaders, may prove crucial in ensuring the continuation of democratic rule, or at least governmental stability.

When a leader suffers from a diminished ability to formulate high-quality judgments and decisions, international peace and security may be compromised. Systematic use of medical intelligence and information concerning foreign leaders can provide an early warning system to inform American leaders about the potential for destabilization in regimes where leaders are found to be gravely ill. For example, the former president of France, François Mitterrand, managed to keep his prostate cancer diagnosis secret for more than eleven years.[5] This information appears particularly important in less democratic governments, where power and decision making remain concentrated in the hands of very few leaders or perhaps even one man. Where likely succession has not been established, or where local political responses to transitions may not always be peaceful, such early warning can help preserve American policy options, encourage prospects for a peaceful transition, or allow more suitable conditions for possible or necessary humanitarian intervention. It is imperative in a challenging international environment that the United States not be caught unawares by an ostensibly predictable leadership crisis, as the Carter administration was with the Iranian revolution.

Obtaining reliable medical information and intelligence on foreign leaders from a distance can be difficult. This does not mean the payoff does not warrant the effort. Sometimes intelligence on the ground can find some relevant information. Oftentimes, especially in poorer and less developed nations, leaders who are ill seek out more skilled foreign doctors for their diagnosis and treatment, and useful information can be gleaned by exploiting these channels. The shah of Iran, for example, consistently employed French doctors during his treatment for various cancers at the end of his life. Boris Yeltsin's heart surgery, while conducted by a Russian physician, was overseen by an American specialist, Dr. Michael DeBakey. Establishing and maintaining dedicated intelligence assets whose job is to cover major medical centers and leading physicians could provide critical information in obtaining accurate and important medical intelligence concerning foreign leaders, their illnesses, and their care. Members of a foreign leader's entourage may leak information inadvertently in making plans for future travel, for example.

The question of the ethics involved in obtaining personal medical information on foreign leaders presents a separate, and potentially troubling, concern. But we can be certain that foreign countries try to collect such intelligence on American leaders; part of the reason the Bush administration argues that more complete medical information concerning Vice President Dick Cheney is not released to the public is the concern that such information could be exploited by elements hostile to the United States. At the very least, when the U.S. collects such intelligence, it needs to be confined to the highest levels and given only to those who really require such intelligence in order to formulate policy. If such information were to become more widely known among the public of the leader's country, it could lead to premature revolt or overthrow. In addition, prolonged or violent succession struggles needlessly divert valuable energy and resources from the more important tasks of governing.

This kind of information can prove crucial, and when such information is unavailable, or inaccurate, can prove disastrous for future plans, as the case of the shah of Iran demonstrates. This appendix outlines an instance when the medical condition of a particular foreign leader exerted a decisive influence on policy outcomes of great importance to the U.S. government. In this case, medical intelligence on the shah was either lacking altogether or severely limited in scope and accuracy. And yet the shah's ultimate weakness caused problems for his rule, his country, and American national interests in the region. Relations between these countries have never recovered from this legacy. In this case, at least, it appears that greater knowledge at an earlier stage about the type and severity of the shah's illness would have aided American planning in structuring more advantageous outcomes for critical U.S. interests in the Persian Gulf area.

THE SHAH OF IRAN

The shah had been ill with a slow-growing type of cancer for some time before the hostage crisis in 1979 began.[6] The U.S. government remained unaware of this fact, although the French government apparently knew some broad outlines of the shah's illness because his physicians were French. As Marvin Zonis writes,

> [T]he government of France apparently learned of the Shah's illness from his physicians, and it is plausible that the United States was not informed. It is less plausible that the British could have learned of his cancer and kept that secret from its principal ally. Nevertheless, there are assertions that Shahpour Reporter, a confidant of the Shah and a British subject, knew of the illness and informed Sir Douglas Home during the mid-1970's. Yet until dangerously late in the revolution, the U.S. government had no knowledge of the Shah's cancer.[7]

The illness took an increasing amount of the shah's time and energy, and he began to put less attention into his tasks of state. At the same time, local religious leaders became increasingly frustrated with the rapid pace of westernization, modernization, and secularization. Noticing such increasing vulnerability, the Ayatollah Khomeini planned a return to Iran from his exile in France. When the U.S. government was informed of the shah's illness, a great deal of pressure was put on President Carter by prominent conservative Republicans to allow the shah into the country for medical treatment. Initially Carter refused the shah's entry for a variety of reasons, including his personal opposition to the shah's human rights record, his concern for American citizens in Iran, and his desire to establish good relations with a new regime in Iran. However, once Carter was told that the shah's condition was serious and could only be adequately treated in the United States, he relented on humanitarian grounds and allowed the shah into the country. Within days, American hostages were seized in the Tehran embassy and were then held by Iranian student captors, with the Ayatollah's support, for more than a year. As soon as the shah was able to travel, Carter ordered him removed from the United States in a futile attempt to resolve the hostage crisis.

Events Leading Up to the Shah's Exile

The specifics of the shah's illness were complicated.[8] He first became ill in late 1973, when he was in his forties. At first, he suffered from vague gastrointestinal disturbance, but later he developed a swollen spleen. In 1974 the shah was seen by a world-renowned French hematologist, Dr. Jean Bernard, and his younger protégé and colleague, Dr. Georges Flandrin.[9] Dr. Flandrin became the shah's primary doctor and consultant from this time until his death; he made more than thirty-five trips between Tehran and Paris alone after the shah's diagnosis but before his departure from Iran in January 1979. Because the shah was terrified of public exposure of his illness, he would not allow the doctors to conduct definitive tests. As William Shawcross explained,

> The Shah had chosen French doctors for a particular reason. He had confidence in their discretion. His distrust of the British was such that he was sure that somehow they would profit from whatever illness he might have. And he thought that if he saw a top American specialist, then there would be a memo on the desk of the Secretary of State or the director of Central Intelligence within days. If Washington knew he was ill, he would no longer expect the same unqualified American support he now enjoyed. He would be deserted by his allies. The Great Civilization would crumble. (When his cancer was finally revealed in 1979, American officials did indeed say that had it been known before, American support for him would have been much less absolute.)[10]

The shah would not even go to a hospital for fear of the rumors that might circulate. This placed the French doctors at a severe disadvantage. They were unable to conduct the necessary tests to make a proper diagnosis. The shah insisted that they would have to do their best without a firm diagnosis.[11] The French doctors suspected that the shah had chronic lymphocytic leukemia, but the shah's personal doctor, Abdol Karim Ayadi, asked that the French doctors not use the words "cancer" or "leukemia" in telling the shah about his condition.[12] As a result, the doctors were left telling the shah that he suffered from Waldenstrom's macroglobulinemia, a disease that resembles chronic lymphocytic leukemia but does not carry the actual name. When the French doctors talked to the shah about his illness, they told him that as long as he took his medication, he would have many years to live. They were trying, in part, to keep his morale high.[13] Dr. Abbas Safavian, a local Iranian physician, monitored the shah's condition on a daily or weekly basis and reported his findings to the French doctors. Dr. Safavian, first in his medical school at National University and later chancellor of the University, would go to see the shah as though he were visiting, just like any other minister. Dr. Ayadi, the Iranian medical director, gave the shah his medication. Beginning in September 1974,

Dr. Flandrin prescribed the drug Chlorambucil for the shah's condition. At the time, this was both the preferred and the least aggressive anti-cancer treatment available. Adverse reactions to this drug can include confusion and agitation.[14] But this treatment succeeded in bringing down the swelling in the shah's spleen and lymph nodes.

Dr. Benjamin Kean, the American doctor who took charge of the case just before the shah came into the United States, claimed that later diagnosis of a lymph node in the shah's neck in New York Hospital showed that the shah had been suffering from lymphatic lymphoma, a more serious condition than the one the French doctors, who were unable to conduct definitive tests at the time, had diagnosed.[15] This would not be unusual, because such illnesses can often shift and worsen over time. Some doctors argue that had the shah allowed himself to be properly treated from the time his condition was first discovered, by having his spleen removed and undergoing intense chemotherapy, he could have been cured. Others claim that, at the time of shah's death, the average life-span from diagnosis to death was about six to eight years, regardless of treatment protocol, and this was about how long the shah lasted after his initial diagnosis. Regardless, the shah was unwilling to undergo any treatment that might expose his illness or which would impose long absences from his country or other inconveniences that he believed might hamper the speed of his White Revolution political program. In fact, the shah told Dr. Bernard that if he insisted on removing his spleen, he would simply go to another doctor. Beginning around February 1975, the shah also reportedly began to take psychiatric medication as well to treat depression and anxiety; particularly in combination with powerful chemotherapy, these psychiatric drugs would have affected his mood, judgment, and mental abilities.[16]

The shah's illness can take an intermittent course, but with proper therapy the patient can live many years after diagnosis. Disease progression occurs slowly, and because the main observable symptoms are fatigue and weight loss, the true nature of a person's condition can be hidden for a long time. In the shah's case, this was particularly easy because the political conditions and demands were such that his symptoms could readily and plausibly be attributed to stress. As a result, the shah and his advisers were able to keep his condition secret until 1979; even his wife was not informed of his illness until 1977. Even then, the queen was informed by the French doctors, not by the shah himself.[17] When the shah eventually talked to her about his illness, he told her that there was a good chance that he would survive.[18]

While it is not clear that the shah knew he had "cancer" at this point in time, he nonetheless knew he had a serious illness. Beginning in March 1975, he began to refer to his own death in speeches.[19] While he remained reluctant to discuss his illness with others in private, he remained consumed by his legacy and the state of the country he would leave to his

son. About this time, he called his prime minister and other ministers of
the court and generals together to talk about what they should do if something happened to him. At this point the shah was still a relatively young
man, in his forties. While he did not mention his illness in this meeting,
he informed the officials that if something were to happen to him, they
should follow the dictates of the queen as his heir if his son, the crown
prince, had not yet reached twenty years of age. He named her as his
successor and commander of the armed forces. Subsequently, he revised
the Constitution to provide for her to be his successor.[20] At this point, the
shah knew the severity, if not the actual diagnosis, of his illness.

Politically, the shah became concerned about his modernization effort.
The original plan for his so-called White Revolution called for slow
decades of change. Once the shah got sick, however, he increased the
speed of his reform program dramatically.[21] The shah broke from OPEC
the year he got sick; as a result, oil prices catapulted from $5 to $20
a barrel.[22] By 1975 Iran's oil revenues surpassed $25 billion a year.[23]
The shah was in a hurry to complete his efforts. Everything was being
imported. Goods sat at the ports out in the open for want of warehouses,
trucks, drivers, and roads. The shah drafted a plan of development and
then multiplied it by four times. Soon there were more than 1 million
foreign workers in the country helping with building and development.[24]
When Seyyed Nasr, president of Aryamehr University, met with the shah
to ask for a major investment in a new campus, he was shocked when
the shah replied, "You may have all of it, and even more. But spend it as
quickly as you can."[25] Because the shah knew that he had so little time left,
he pushed all his programs to completion faster than originally intended;
he wanted to leave the country better by the time of his death.[26] Such rapid
modernization served only to increase the alienation and dislocation that
many traditional Iranians felt at the time.

The shah also experienced another severe loss in his ability to govern
about this time. His minister of the court, Assadollah Alam, the shah's
closest friend and confidant, came down with and died of the same illness
in 1977. Ironically, he died in New York Hospital, after being treated
by the same French doctors at the American Hospital in Paris. In 1962–
1963, when Alam had been prime minister, he had saved the shah from
an earlier uprising instigated by the Ayatollah Khomeini, leading to the
Imam's exile to France. Apparently, while the shah pretended to be tough,
he proved especially weak and indecisive in crises.[27] Alam claimed that if
it had been up to the shah in 1962, the revolutionaries would have won.[28]
By 1978 Alam was dead, and the shah was surrounded by people who
were similarly weak in their political actions and intentions; and by this
time, the shah himself had become more physically compromised by his
illness and medication. The shah's political weakness and indecisiveness
confirmed Alam's prediction in the crisis of 1978–1979 in several ways;

Zonis, for one, notes that "what appears remarkable are the relatively small number of deaths which occurred in the fourteen months of violence preceding the return to Iran of Ayatollah Khomeini."[29]

Revolutionary violence did begin, however, in Qum in January 1978. By June 1978 Pierre Salinger overheard a famous French doctor tell a French government official at a reception that "the Shah is very, very ill. Not only is he ill, but his illness renders him incapable of making decisions."[30] In October, 16,000 teachers from 56,000 schools came to Tehran for Teacher's Day, a two-day function involving a big rally in an indoor stadium. At 6:00 p.m., the shah, doing something he had never done before, called his ministers together for a late-night meeting. All top-level military, SAVAK (intelligence), and cabinet ministers met with the shah and his wife to discuss what to do about the revolutionaries taking over the country. In particular, the shah wanted to know if the government should take decisive measures or resign, or if he should declare a state of emergency. The shah's advisers could not agree on an appropriate course of action. Some thought that the shah could not take decisive action because it would cause bad press; others felt it was essential for the shah to reassert control. The meeting lasted until one o'clock in the morning without a firm decision being reached.

The shah appeared quite politically indecisive during this entire time period. Between September 1978 and the following February, the shah changed governments five times, instituting a new government essentially every two months. The penultimate government, before Shapour Bakhtier, the shah's last prime minister, was a military government led by General Azhari, which failed to gain control over the revolutionaries and resigned in December 1978.

By December 11–12, 1978, Iranian political turmoil had worsened. By this time, the illness and the medicine had made the shah noticeably weaker. These days represent important mourning days in Iran where processions take place. The Muslim clerics intended to take political advantage of this situation. Education Minister Ganji recalls going to talk to the shah at the time. The shah had a very large office, about fifty to sixty feet long, where he was accustomed to walking back and forth alongside visitors as a form of exercise; he only sat in the presence of foreign dignitaries. He would also sip tea in very small glass cups. But on this day, Ganji reports, everything was different. The shah sat and drank several bottles of mineral water. Ganji went to talk to the shah about the uprisings going on in the streets, where the shah had ordered that the military should shoot into the air, over the heads of the protesters. The shah refused to cut the phone lines to Paris to stop messages from Khomeini or to jam the nightly BBC broadcasts to Iran in support of Khomeini. The French government even sent the Comte de Maranch, who was in charge of the French version of the CIA, to ask the shah if he wanted the French government to eliminate Khomeini, and the shah said no. They also offered to nullify Khomeini's passport, which would have forced him to go to Libya, the only country that would take him under that circumstance. Again, the shah refused. By this time, the queen was running the country. She was surrounded by friends and advisers who realized that power was in her hands. The queen was led to believe that she was working to crush the revolutionaries by at least some of her advisers who reportedly secretly supported the revolutionaries.[31]

American Responses

As the shah's illness began to contribute to his loss of control over the reins of power, the U.S. government was similarly undergoing a shift in priorities toward Iran. During most of the postwar period, the United States had been a staunch supporter of the shah. The CIA helped engineer the overthrow of the Iranian nationalist leader Mohammed Mossadegh in 1953, returning the shah to power from his exile in Italy.[32] But the Carter administration demonstrated markedly different policies and an increasing concern with human rights issues, and the State Department in particular sought to force the shah to begin power sharing with his Regency Council. Many State Department officials even supported the shah leaving the country so that National Front coalition leader Prime Minister Bakhtier could take over. However, National Security Advisor Zbigniew Brzezinski opposed this move and encouraged the shah to take a firmer hand to reassert his former control of Iran. As a result, the shah imposed the military government under General Azhari in November 1978. This attempt to regain control failed and the shah eventually left Iran in desperation and disgrace on January 16, 1979. By the time the shah left, only Brzezinski supported admitting him into the United States. Along with Henry Kissinger and other prominent conservatives, Brzezinski continued to agitate for the shah's admittance until he was finally allowed in for humanitarian reasons. At first, however, when the shah left Iran, he made brief stopovers in Egypt and Morocco before he landed in exile in the Bahamas.

While he was in exile, the shah's physical condition deteriorated further. Dr. Flandrin flew to the Bahamas in April 1974 and discovered that the shah's chronic condition had become acute. He again advocated that the shah have his spleen removed, which is the standard treatment. However, the shah refused this form of treatment, being frightened of sabotage on the operating table, and also believing he could still affect the outcome of the political situation in Iran. Instead, the shah chose to undergo chemotherapy. The specific regimen instituted was a combination of four drugs called MOPP for short (nitrogen mustard, oncovin, procarbazine, and prednisone); this treatment remains a standard one for Hodgkin's disease, where it is known to be more effective. MOPP combines two very powerful anticancer drugs with an antibiotic containing anticancer properties and a steroid. All these drugs compromise the immune system and render the patient much more vulnerable to infections of various sorts. Thus began the shah's treatment with steroids (prednisone), with all their concomitant mood sequelae, ranging from euphoria at first to depression in later stages.[33] After a time, the Bahamian government refused to extend the shah's visa. The shah moved to Mexico in early June.

By the time the shah arrived in Mexico, he was suffering from severe jaundice, resulting from his cancer. The Mexican doctors, who were not informed of the shah's underlying medical problems, diagnosed malaria and were treating the shah with cholorquine. As a result, at this point, one of the shah's advisers, Robert Armao, who had been put in place to help the shah by David Rockefeller, contacted Joseph Reed, David Rockefeller's assistant, to ask for some medical help. Reed and his family had been patients of Dr. Benjamin Kean for more than twenty years. In at least one prior instance, Reed had called Kean to treat a seriously ill Swedish banking tycoon. More recently, Kean, a specialist in tropical diseases such as malaria, had treated Armao for Mexican turista. Thus began Dr. Kean's involvement in the shah's medical care. Kean had actually met the shah previously, examining him for tropical diseases in 1949 in New York, and met him again in Iran while Kean was working for the Ford Foundation. Kean went to Mexico, saw the shah, and concluded that the shah's jaundice was most likely the result of a blocked major bile duct, by either a stone or cancer of the pancreas; jaundice rarely accompanies malaria. At this point, Joseph Reed called David Newsom in the State Department to inform him of the shah's condition and to request the shah's admittance to the United States for purposes of proper medical diagnosis. At this time, no independent medical determination was made by the U.S. government. Newsom asked Kean to contact the State Department medical officer, Dr. Eben Dustin, to tell him of the shah's condition. Kean claims he told Dustin that he could treat the shah in Mexico but that he would prefer to bring the shah to New York.

At this time, no one in the U.S. government had previously been informed about the nature of the shah's illness, despite the fact that he had known he had cancer for more than five years. The U.S. government was not informed of the shah's medical condition until David Rockefeller reported it in September 1979.[34] Dr. Kean swears that at no time did he tell Dr. Dustin that the shah had to be treated in the United States in general or in New York in particular. Kean told Dustin that the shah was very ill with a variety of complex illnesses and that his treatment would require complicated care. He insisted that the shah needed to be treated like "Peter Smith," an ordinary patient who could avail himself of the all-out care available in major teaching medical hospitals and not restrict himself to the suboptimal boutique care which all too often compromises the health of dignitaries and celebrities. Kean did tell Dustin that he preferred his medical team at New York Hospital, but the shah could be properly treated elsewhere. He encouraged Dustin to come see the shah for himself or send another physician for a second opinion; Dustin never availed himself of either opportunity. Kean believes that Dustin faithfully forwarded this information up the chain of command.[35]

The Secret White Paper that Dustin prepared for the State Department belies Kean's confidence, or Kean was more categorical at the time than he was willing to admit later. This paper said, in part, that "These studies cannot be carried out in any of the medical facilities in Mexico.... Each day of worsening jaundice and physiological deterioration lessens the chances of recovery from surgical relief which may well be necessary."[36] Thus, by the time this information reached Carter, he was told that the shah had to be treated in New York Hospital or he would likely die; Carter had been led to believe that this hospital was one of the very few in the world that would be able to properly diagnose and treat his various illnesses. On October 19 Carter met for breakfast with Secretary of State Cyrus Vance, White House Chief of Staff Hamilton Jordan, and National Security Advisor Brzezinski. Vance had now shifted position and advocated admitting the shah on humanitarian grounds. Jordan thought the political fallout should the shah be allowed to die in Mexico could prove politically catastrophic among conservative voters and their representatives. Carter remained alone in his opposition to the shah's entry. At the end of the meeting, Carter presciently asked the others, "What are you guys going to advise me to do if they overrun our embassy and take our people hostage?"[37] Carter requested more information on the shah's condition. The memo he received the following day from the State Department said, "Dr. Kean... has advised us that these diagnostic studies cannot be carried out in Mexico, and he recommends that the examination take place in the United States. David Rockefeller has asked that we admit the Shah.... The State Department's Medical Director supports Dr. Kean's recommendation."[38] The State Department later noted, "The great urgency of the request when it came and when its true nature became apparent effectively prevented a U.S. search for alternative facilities in other countries."[39] Under these pressing conditions, Carter decided to let the shah into the country, rather than delay matters by consulting others first.

Following this political turmoil, the shah was admitted to New York Hospital on October 23, into the same rooms in which Dr. Kean had examined him in 1949 for tropical diseases, where it was quickly determined that his jaundice was caused by a stone in the common bile duct, which was removed a few days later.[40] But the situation was complicated by uncoordinated medical care. For one thing, the shah's oncologist was not told the shah was to undergo surgery on his gallbladder; when he found out, he rushed to ask the surgeon to also remove the spleen, which he refused to do, claiming the shah was too weak. Moreover, the surgeons left one of the gallstones in the shah, which continued to block his bile duct. This forced the shah's medical teams to wait for a Canadian specialist to come clear the gallstone with a noninvasive method. In the meantime, they gave the shah radiation on the lymph nodes in his neck, considering him too weak to endure either a second surgery on his spleen or systemic chemotherapy. Subsequent diagnostics revealed that the shah was now in Stage III or Stage IV histiocytic lymphosarcoma.

Twelve days after the shah was admitted, the American Embassy in Tehran was seized by Islamic fundamentalist students under the control of the Ayatollah Khomeini. Thus began 444 days of captivity for fifty-three Americans and a sharp decline in domestic political support for President Carter. While he was not a political expert, Kean's knowledge of the circumstances surrounding the shah's admittance led him to firmly believe that the shah's entrance into the United States had nothing whatever to do with the seizing of the American Embassy in Tehran. He argued that the seizure occurred because the Ayatollah had been threatened by recent political progress between Brzezinski and moderate leaders in Iran, Mehdi Bazargan and Ibrahim Yazdi, and he sought to confirm his power by authorizing the students to seize the embassy.[41]

When Carter tried to return the shah to Mexico to help defuse the hostage situation, it refused to take him. Eventually, the shah moved to Panama, where his medical condition continued to deteriorate. He desperately needed to have his spleen removed, but he was again afraid of being intentionally killed on the operating table. Treatment battles between the shah's American physicians led by Kean, now including Dr. Michael DeBakey, and the local Panamanian doctors and authorities ensued. Kean remained adamant that the shah be treated at the American military hospital in Panama, Gorgas, consistent with the Lackland agreements that the American government had reached with the shah when he left the country. French doctors attributed Kean's position to American elitism and arrogance, believing that the local Panamanian hospital provided more than adequate facilities for the shah's proper care. The Panamanian leader, General Torrijos, wanted the surgery conducted at his hospital, Paitilla, by his physician, Dr. Carlos Garcia. The shah was understandably concerned about all the fights going on over who would administer his care. In addition, the Iranian government was seeking extradition of the shah from Panama to stand trial for war crimes against humanity. Even worse, General Torrijos began to pursue the shah's wife, sending her flowers and inviting her to go on outings without the shah.

But the shah's wife would have none of it. By this point, she distrusted both the Americans and the Panamanians. Throughout her exile, she had remained in close contact with Jehan Sadat, wife of President Anwar Sadat, in Egypt. When Mrs. Sadat heard about the shah's difficulties, she asked her husband to offer the shah asylum, and he quickly agreed. He offered a bill to the Egyptian parliament to invite the shah to Egypt, and it passed unanimously. For their part, the American government would not pressure Torrijos to conduct the shah's surgery at Gorgas, nor would it allow the shah back into the United States for surgery. The U.S. government worked hard to prevent the shah from going to Egypt; Carter in particular believed that sheltering the shah would be hard for Sadat's public approval in the Arab world, particularly after he had signed the Camp David accords, making peace with Israel. President Carter even called Sadat to express his concern. Sadat told Carter not to worry about Egypt, but to do what he could to facilitate the release of the hostages. Nonetheless, Hamilton Jordan flew to Panama in March 1980 to try to stop the shah from leaving. He even contacted Dr. DeBakey to ask if he would operate on the shah in Panama; DeBakey refused, being unwilling to operate under the control of Panamanian doctors, as would be required under Torrijos's command. DeBakey, a cardiothoracic surgeon, might seem an odd choice of surgeon, but his high-profile reputation made many of the shah's advisers believe he would be impervious to any blackmail attempts to kill the shah.

But all of Jordan's efforts proved futile, and the shah flew to Egypt on March 23, 1980, one day before the legal deadline for Iran to file extradition papers in Panama. On the way, the plane stopped in the Azores for refueling. Jordan, acting through Secretary of Defense Harold Brown, still trying to secure the release of the hostages, ordered the plane to be held for more than two hours in the freezing cold, while the shah suffered on board with a high fever. Jordan still believed he could work a deal to free the hostages if the shah was returned to prison in Panama. The plan fell through, and the plane was released. When Carter found out what Jordan had done, he was furious. Torrijos ordered that the queen's room not be touched, saying, "I didn't sleep with her, but at least I'll sleep in her sheets."[42]

Five days later, the shah was operated on in Egypt by an American surgical team led by Dr. DeBakey. The shah's spleen was twenty times normal size. Worse still, the shah's cancer had metastasized to his liver. Kean recommended no further treatment. But the family could not accept the shah's fate peacefully, and the shah decided to undergo a harsh course of chemotherapy. In his weakened state, he developed sepsis and hemorrhaged. He died there on July 27, 1980. To the very end, American and French doctors fought over his condition and treatment, Dr. Flandrin arguing that the shah's death had been precipitated by a subphrenic abscess caused in surgery, and Dr. DeBakey claiming that the shah's weakened immune system, which prevented strong chemotherapy, allowed a return of the cancer.[43] As Dr. Kean noted afterward, "the tragedy is that a man who should have had the best and easiest medical care had, in many respects, the worst."[44]

Three points from this case deserve special attention. First, had the Carter administration had prior knowledge of the severity of the shah's illness, it might have been forewarned, and thus better prepared for his imminent loss of power and control over Iran. In particular, it is unlikely that American policy toward the shah would have been so divided; Brzezinski would not have been so enthusiastic about encouraging the shah to remain strong and reassert power if he had known how ill he was and that a succession crisis was only a matter of time. Perhaps the United States would have been able to reach out to some political moderates who might have constituted an alternative to the shah, while being less radical than Khomeini. The French had provided asylum to Khomeini, when they alone knew the severity of the shah's illness to some degree. Such diplomatic responsiveness placed the French in a much better situation relative to the new Iranian government than the Americans. Such prior knowledge might have helped the U.S. government to have a more systematic response in place prior to the critical events leading up to the taking of the hostages, rather than the chaotic, crisis-mode decision-making style that prevailed at the time. And yet the consequences of these ill-considered decisions have carried an enduring legacy in American-Iranian relations.

Second, the information that Carter received about the shah's condition from the outset was flawed. The shah had coerced the American government early on in his tenure into relying solely on his internal intelligence unit, the SAVAK, for all its internal information about Iran, including its information about the shah himself. This gave the shah unique control over the dissemination of important information to his allies. The American government had no independent source of intelligence corroboration outside its minimal embassy staff. Thus, the American government was dependent on the shah's inner circle for information not only about the shah and his illness but also about the internal political state of the country. In this way, the Americans were almost totally caught by surprise by the depth of support for the Islamic fundamentalist leader Khomeini.

In addition, Carter's intelligence prior to admitting the shah into the country was incorrect, and there was no check on this information to ascertain its authenticity. If Kean is telling the truth, he told the State Department doctor, Dr. Dustin, that the shah could be treated in Mexico or in New York. Kean believed that Dustin passed this information along faithfully. But, as noted, the report that Dustin passed along to his State Department supervisors told a much more categorical story about the shah's medical condition requiring treatment in New York. Somewhere between Kean's assessment and Carter's intelligence, some information was either miscommunicated or deliberately manipulated, so as to maximize the shah's chances for admittance. Given the large number of conservative Americans who believed that the United States owed the shah a great historical debt, there are many individuals who might have been motivated to highlight information about the importance of the shah's treatment in the United States over other possible but more medically difficult options. As it turned out, all the equipment and personnel necessary for the shah's surgery were available in Mexico, as Kean originally indicated. The equipment may not have been all in one place, but it would have been possible to bring it all together. The shah, however, was paranoid by this time and did not trust any but his French doctors, who by then had been pushed aside by Dr. Kean.

It was not the case, however, that the shah's medical treatment in the United States was required for humanitarian purposes. Had Carter known this fact, given how reluctant he was to admit the shah to begin with, and given the warnings he had received from the Iranian government regarding its concern about being able to secure the safety of Americans in Iran if the shah were admitted into the United States, even on humanitarian grounds Carter probably would not have allowed the shah to enter the country. Having the shah receive medical treatment in Mexico would have been more consistent with overall American foreign policy during the Carter administration. This action, in turn, would probably have averted the proximal cause of the hostage taking in Tehran.

Third, the psychological effect of his diagnosis may have ultimately proved more destructive politically for the shah than his physical disabilities. The shah was a monarch who had taken control of his country from his father and wished to pass it along to his son. He worked hard early on to bring modernization, secularization, and westernization, including a decrease in religious influence and better treatment of women, to Iran. He knew that his so-called White Revolution would take time, but he appeared to be succeeding. But because his diagnosis brought a clear and close sense of mortality, he sought to accomplish his goals quickly. Once he broke with OPEC the year of his diagnosis, the rapid influx of oil money into the underindustrialized country brought about rapid social and economic dislocations that were easily exploited by fundamentalist clerics. Such attempts on the shah's part to ensure his place in history instead assured his political demise.[45]

CONCLUSIONS

This example demonstrates the way in which medical information and intelligence on foreign leaders can prove crucial in the formulation of

American foreign policy, both toward other nations and with regard to U.S. domestic policies. Having accurate information about foreign leaders, their conditions, and their prognosis can provide crucial insight into cases of failing leadership, succession crises, incipient local pressures toward revolution or government overthrow, and leadership transition. All these events remain important for being able to predict future threats to American lives and American homeland security. In addition, forewarning of such events allows for greater time and consideration in developing possible response options to help structure a better outcome for American values and interests at home and abroad.

This study suggests that the frequency and severity of leader impairment demands that greater attention be paid to the medical status of foreign leaders, especially in unstable or strategically important areas, in the case of authoritarian or totalitarian leadership, or in situations of obvious leadership disability. The systematic acquisition and use of medical information and intelligence can benefit future American foreign policy decision making. It remains important to obtain and update medical intelligence about foreign leaders in order to fully understand the complete background of their decisions and behavior. Odd decisions and behavior can oftentimes reflect unknown developments that can potentially lead to catastrophic outcomes if not planned for in advance. Once problematic medical information comes to light and provides appropriate context, seemingly odd judgments and actions can rapidly make sense. Medical information often manifests in such a way. People want to keep their ill health secret so as not to appear vulnerable. But illness by itself can shift the quality of decision making and action in decisive and derogatory ways. Knowing the real source for seemingly atypical behaviors can help prevent misunderstanding and reduce the likelihood of preventable conflict. For instance, in the case of the shah, the speed with which he instituted his modernization program appeared counterproductive; while Iran's oil money could support extensive development, the rapidity with which he pressed his plans generated serious countereffects. Rapidly increasing secularization of society, in particular, caused severe antagonism in a society still composed of many more culturally conservative citizens.

Medical signs and symptoms convey important information about the health and performance of individual leaders. Such factors can hold tremendous importance for the people under their control. While not the only or even the most important piece, the use of medical intelligence or information to predict or explain seemingly irrational behavior on the part of a foreign leader can provide additional information in the intelligence puzzle. Such intelligence can then help American leaders anticipate, plan, and more appropriately respond to leadership crisis, failure, or transition in foreign countries. This may prove particularly critical in unstable regions, or areas where leadership remains highly personalistic or hereditary. Instituting systematic procedures to uncover and analyze medical information concerning foreign leaders can help the U.S. government to better predict particular outcomes in foreign countries. As noted, this can be accomplished in part through simple processes designed to monitor leading physicians in various countries, among other activities. Having longer warning periods allows a more careful examination of future options and possible responses. And such warning also allows greater time to implement the necessary procedures to protect American lives and interests both at home and abroad.

In addition, as America confronts a situation where nonstate actors play an increasingly important role on the global stage, it may be of use to consider how the United States might be able to obtain medical information to exploit weaknesses in vulnerable foreign leaders.

Astute American leaders should monitor the health of foreign leaders and strategize ways to take advantage of, or compensate for, various medical vulnerabilities. Being caught unaware, as the Carter administration was in the case of the shah's illness, can only limit available options. In that case, two issues determined the fate of American-Iranian relations. First, the shah's terminal illness forced him to accelerate his modernization program in a way that created a cultural backlash. Second, the U.S. government proved unable to detect the cover-up engineered by the shah and his advisers to keep his illness secret. Thus, when an administration does not possess adequate or accurate information, it remains vulnerable to the manipulations of those who desire a particular outcome. Careful attempts to plan for predictable transfers of power in the wake of leader illness or incapacity can help prepare American leaders for planning responses that serve to further U.S. national interests.

NOTES

Chapter 1. Introduction

1. For a brief overview of this history, see Steven Hook and John Spanier, *American Foreign Policy since World War II*, 17th ed. (Washington, DC: CQ Press, 2007).
2. For an excellent discussion, see Robert Gilbert, *The Mortal Presidency: Illness and Anguish in the White House* (New York: Fordham University Press, 1998).
3. For excellent coverage, see Walter LaFeber, *America, Russia and the Cold War, 1945–2001*, 10th ed. (Boston: McGraw-Hill, 2008).
4. See Clarence Lasby, *Eisenhower's Heart Attack* (Lawrence: University Press of Kansas, 1997), and Jerrold Post and Jerome Robins, *When Illness Strikes the Leader* (New Haven, CT: Yale University Press, 1993).
5. See Gilbert, *The Mortal Presidency*, chap. 4, and Post and Robins, *When Illness Strikes the Leader*, 14–17.
6. Gilbert, *The Mortal Presidency*, 127.
7. Kenneth Waltz, *Theory of International Relations* (Reading, MA: Addison Wesley, 1979); and Bruce Bueno de Mesquita, *Principles of International Politics: People's Power, Preferences and Perceptions* (Washington, DC: CQ Press, 2000).
8. Kenneth Crispell and Carlos Gomez, *Hidden Illness in the White House* (Durham, NC: Duke University Press, 1988).
9. Post and Robins, *When Illness Strikes the Leader*, XIII.
10. Hugh L'Etang, *The Pathology of Leadership: A History of the Effects of Disease on 20th Century Leaders* (New York: Hawthorn, 1970); Hugh L'Etang, *Fit to Lead?* (London: William Heineman Medical Books, 1980); Post and Robins, *When Illness Strikes the Leader*; Gilbert, *The Mortal Presidency*; Bert Park, *The Impact of Illness on World Leaders* (Philadelphia: University of

Pennsylvania Press, 1988); and Bert Park, *Aging, Ailing and Addicted: Studies in Compromised Leadership* (Lexington: University Press of Kentucky, 1993).

11. Post and Robins, *When Illness Strikes the Leader.*

12. Leda Cosmides and John Tooby, "Evolutionary Psychology and the Emotions," in M. Lewis and J. Haviland-Jones (Eds.), *Handbook of Emotions*, 2nd ed. (New York: Guilford Press, 2000), 92.

13. D. Swanson, "Clinical Psychiatric Problems Associated with General Surgery," in H. Abrams (Ed.), *Psychologic Aspects of Surgery, International Psychiatry Clinics* (Boston: Little, Brown, 1967), 105–113.

14. A great deal of work in psychology has focused on time perspective, mostly under the direction of Philip Zimbardo. See Illona Boniwell and Philip Zimbardo, "Time to Find the Right Balance," *Psychologist* 16, 3 (2003): 129–131, and "Balancing Time Perspective in Pursuit of Optimal Functioning," in Alex Linley and Stephen Joseph (Eds.), *Positive Psychology in Practice* (New York: John Wiley & Sons, 2004), 165–178; for the measure, see Philip Zimbardo and John Boyd, "Putting Time in Perspective: A Valid, Reliable Individual-Difference Metric," *Journal of Personality and Social Psychology* 77, 6 (December 1999): 1271–1288.

15. Post and Robins, *When Illness Strikes the Leader.*

16. Samuel McLure, David Laibson, George Loewenstein, and Jonathan Cohen, "Separate Neural Systems Value Immediate and Delayed Monetary Rewards," *Science* 306, 5695 (October 2004): 503–507. For a presentation of the discounted utility model and an interesting and important critique of it, see Shane Frederick, George Loewenstein, and Ted O'Donoghue, "Time Discounting and Time Preference: A Critical Review," in George Loewenstein, Daniel Read, et al. (Eds.), *Time and Decision: Economic and Psychological Perspectives on Intertemporal Choice* (New York: Russell Sage, 2003), 13–86.

17. Irving Janis, "Decision Making under Stress," in L. Goldberger and S. Breznitz (Eds.), *Handbook of Stress: Theoretical and Clinical Aspects* (New York: Free Press, 1982), 69–87.

18. See H. H. Goldman, *Review of General Psychiatry*, 2nd ed. (Norwalk, CT: Appleton & Lange, 1988), chap. 30, for diagnostic criteria and discussion.

19. Several previous works that provide examples of such analysis include James David Barber, *The Presidential Difference* (Englewood Cliffs, NJ: Prentice-Hall, 1972); Fred Greenstein, "The Impact of Personality and Politics: An Attempt to Clear Away the Underbrush," *American Political Science Review* 61 (1967): 629–641; Stanley Renshon, *The Psychological Assessment of Presidential Candidates* (New York: Routledge, 1998); and Jerrold Post, *The Psychological Assessment of Political Leaders* (Ann Arbor: University of Michigan Press, 2003).

20. I am grateful to Stephen Biddle for helpful discussion on this point.

21. Jerrold Post and Robert Robins, "The Captive King and His Captive Court: The Psychopolitical Dynamics of the Disabled Leader and His Inner Circle," *Political Psychology* 11, 2 (1990): 346.

22. Post and Robins, *When Illness Strikes the Leader.*

CHAPTER 2. AGING, ILLNESS, AND ADDICTION

1. On Eagleton, see Jerrold Post and Robert Robins, *When Illness Strikes the Leader: The Dilemma of the Captive King* (New Haven, CT: Yale University Press, 1993), 33. On the refractory nature of severe depression, see H. H. Goldman, *Review of General Psychiatry*, 2nd ed. (Norwalk, CT: Appleton & Lange, 1988), 344. In fact, electroshock therapy appears successful in about 70 percent of those treated, who are in fact the most severely depressed. The main side effect is anterograde amnesia. Ibid., 504. It remains the treatment of choice for those with refractory depression or for patients who need rapid improvement because of anorexia or other complicating factors. See Lawrence Tierney, Sanjay Saint, Mary Whooley, *Essentials of Diagnosis and Treatment*, 2nd ed. (New York: Lange Medical Books/McGraw-Hill, 2002), 342.

2. Post and Robins, *When Illness Strikes the Leader.*

3. Kenneth Walker, "Medical Condition of Leaders Often Hushed Up," *Chicago Sun-Times*, February 15, 1998, 44.

4. Robert Robins, "Recruitment of Pathological Deviants into Political Leadership," in Robert Robins (Ed.), *Psychopathology and Political Leadership* (New Orleans: Tulane University, 1977), 53–78.

5. For more on this issue, see Ian Kershaw, *The Hitler Myth* (New York: Oxford University Press, 2001); Daniel Jonah Goldhagen, *Hitler's Willing Executioners* (New York: Vintage, 1997); and Fritz Redlich, *Hitler: Diagnosis of a Destructive Prophet* (New York: Oxford University Press, 2000).

6. On Hitler, see Redlich, *Hitler*, and Post and Robins, *When Illness Strikes the Leader*. For a review of Redlich's book, *Hitler*, see Jerrold Post, *New England Journal of Medicine*, May 27, 1999, 1692.

7. Robins, *Psychopathology and Political Leadership*, 14.

8. Thomas Schelling, *The Strategy of Conflict* (Cambridge, MA: Harvard University Press, 1980).

9. For more on this fascinating case, see the superb book by Robert Gilbert, *The Tormented President: Calvin Coolidge, Death and Clinical Depression* (Westport, CT: Praeger, 2003).

10. The first author to systematically address the effects of age on leadership was Jerrold Post, "On Aging Leaders: Possible Effects of the Aging Process on the Conduct of Leadership," *Journal of Geriatric Psychiatry* 6 (1973): 109–116.

11. Post and Robins, *When Illness Strikes the Leader.*

12. See Robert Robins and Robert Dorn, "Stress and Political Leadership," *Politics and Life Sciences* 12 (1993): 3–17.

13. Robert Sapolsky, *Why Zebras Don't Get Ulcers: A Guide to Stress, Stress-Related Disease and Coping* (New York: Freeman, 1994).

14. For an excellent discussion of this distinction, see Stephen Peter Rosen, *War and Human Nature* (Princeton, NJ: Princeton University Press, 2005), chap. 4.

15. See Post and Robins, *When Illness Strikes the Leader*, chap. 5.

16. Bert Park, "Presidential Disability: Past Experiences and Future Implications," *Politics and the Life Sciences* 7 (August 1988): 55.

17. A. Becker and E. Weeks, "Post Operative Cognitive Dysfunction," *Best Practice* 17, 2 (June 2003): 259–272.
18. J. R. Flatt et al., "Effects of Anesthesia on Some Aspects of Mental Functioning of Surgical Patients," *Anesthesia and Intensive Care* 12 (1984): 315–324; Bert Park, *The Impact of Illness on World Leaders* (Philadelphia: University of Pennsylvania Press, 1986).
19. J. Riis, B. Lomholt, et al., "Immediate and Long Term Mental Recovery from General vs. Epidural Anesthesia in Elderly Patients," *Acta Anaesthesiologica Scandinavica* 27 (1983): 44–49; Bert Park, *Ailing, Aging, Addicted: Studies of Compromised Leadership* (Lexington: University Press of Kentucky, 1993).
20. Post and Robins, *When Illness Strikes the Leader*, 174.
21. J. Heaver, "Toxicity of Anesthetics," *Clinical Anesthesiology* 17, 1 (2003): 1–3.
22. J. T. Moller et al., "Long Term Postoperative Cognitive Dysfunction in the Elderly," *Lancet* 351, 9106 (March 21, 1998): 857–861.
23. R. Gorna et al., "Assessment of Short Term Neuropsychological Change after Monothermic vs. Hypothermic Coronary Artery Bypass Grafting," *Psychiatric Politics* 35, 5 (2001): 781–795.
24. Jerrold Post, "The Seasons of a Leader's Life," *Political Psychology* 2 (1980): 35–49.
25. Ibid., 45.
26. David Wang, Schott Koehler, and Cary Mariash, "Detecting Graves' Disease," *Physician and Sportsmedicine* 24, 12 (1996): 35.
27. Hugh L'Etang, *Fit to Lead?* (London: William Heinemann Medical Books, 1980).
28. Herbert Abrams, "Sudden Incapacitation," in James Toole and Robert Joynt (Eds.), *Presidential Disability: Papers, Discussions and Recommendations on the 25th Amendment and Issues of Inability and Disability in Presidents of the United States* (Rochester, NY: University of Rochester Press, 2001): 39–44.
29. Ibid.
30. Ibid.
31. Jerrold Post, "Behavioral Disorders" in Toole and Joynt, *Presidential Disability*, 52–60.
32. Ibid., 52.
33. Herbert Abrams, "Disabled Leaders, Cognition and Crisis Decision Making in Accidental Nuclear War," in *Proceedings of the Eighteenth Pugwash Workshop on Nuclear Forces* (Toronto: Science for Peace 1990).
34. For a wonderfully rich and textured account of Coolidge's depression, see Gilbert, *The Tormented President*.
35. *Diagnostic and Statistical Manual of Mental Disorders*, 4th ed. (Washington, DC: APA Press, 1994), 322.
36. Robert Robins and Jerrold Post, *Political Paranoia: The Psychopolitics of Hatred* (New Haven, CT: Yale University Press, 1997), 5.
37. See Jerrold Post, "Saddam Hussein of Iraq: A Political Psychological Profile," *Political Psychology* 12 (1991): 279–289. Also see Jerrold Post, *Leaders and Their Followers in a Dangerous World* (Ithaca, NY: Cornell University Press, 2004).

38. Robins and Post, *Political Paranoia.*
39. Robins, "Recruitment of Pathological Deviants into Political Leadership."
40. C. H. Owen, "Diseased, Demented, Depressed: Serious Illness in Heads of State," *Quarterly Journal of Medicine* 96, 5 (2003): 325–336.
41. Post, "Saddam Hussein of Iraq: A Political Psychology Profile."
42. Post and Robins, *When Illness Strikes the Leader.*
43. For a wonderful psychobiography of Pittman, see Betty Glad, *Key Pittman: The Tragedy of a Senate Insider* (New York: Columbia University Press, 1986).
44. Post and Robins, *When Illness Strikes the Leader.*
45. Ibid.
46. William McKim, *Drugs and Behavior: An Introduction to Behavioral Pharmacology*, 4th ed. (Upper Saddle River, NJ: Prentice-Hall, 2000).
47. Roy Lubit and Bruce Russett, "The Effects of Drugs on Decision Making," *Journal of Conflict Resolution* 28, 1 (1984): 85–102.
48. McKim, *Drugs and Behavior*, 134.
49. Ibid., 161–162.
50. Ibid., 168–169.
51. Ibid., 259.
52. L. Judd et al., "Effects of Psychotropic Drugs on Cognition and Memory in Normal Humans and Animals," in H. Y. Meltzwer (Ed.), *Psychopharmacology: A Third Generation of Progress* (New York: Raven Press, 1987), 1467–1475.
53. M. D. Majewska, "Cocaine Addiction as a Neurological Disorder: Implications for Treatment," *NIDA Research Monograph* 163 (1996): 1–26.
54. McKim, *Drugs and Behavior*, 233.
55. Ibid.
56. Post and Robins, *When Illness Strikes the Leader*; L'Etang, *Fit to Lead?*; Park, *The Impact of Illness on World Leaders*; and Park, *Aging, Ailing and Addicted.*
57. This point is made by Post and Robins, *When Illness Strikes the Leader*; Park, *The Impact of Illness on World Leaders*; and A. Kucharski, "On Being Sick and Famous," *Political Psychology* 5 (1981): 69–82, as well.
58. Post and Robins, *When Illness Strikes the Leader*, 66.
59. Ibid., 66.
60. Ibid., 63.
61. Ibid., 65.
62. Elizabeth Attree, Christine Dancey, Deborah Keeling, and Christine Wilson, "Cognitive Function in People with Chronic Illness," *Applied Neuropsychology* 10, 2 (2003): 96–104.

CHAPTER 3. THE EXACERBATION OF PERSONALITY: WOODROW WILSON

1. For more on psychobiographies in general, see Rose McDermott, *Political Psychology in International Relations* (Ann Arbor: University of Michigan Press, 2004), 189–213.

2. Judith Weaver, "Edith Bolling Wilson as First Lady: A Study in the Power of Personality, 1919–1920," *Presidential Studies Quarterly* 15 (1985): 51–52, 55.

3. Cary Grayson, *Woodrow Wilson: An Intimate Memoir* (New York: Holt, Rinehart & Winston, 1960), 53.

4. Edith Wilson, *My Memoir* (New York: Bobbs-Merrill, 1939), 290. It should be noted that modern medical science indicates that there are few things worse than social isolation for the recovery prospects of any serious illness.

5. Hugh L'Etang, *The Pathology of Leadership: A History of the Effects of Disease on 20th Century Leaders* (New York: Hawthorn, 1970), 52.

6. Arthur Link, "Woodrow Wilson and the Constitutional Crisis," in Kenneth Thompson (Ed.), *Papers on Presidential Disability and the 25th Amendment by Medical, Historical and Political Authorities* (Lanham, MD: Miller Center, University of Virginia and University Press of America, 1996), 53–80. This argument is also presented in Edwin Weinstein, *Woodrow Wilson: A Medical and Psychological Biography* (Princeton, NJ: Princeton University Press, 1981), and Edwin Weinstein, James Anderson, and Arthur Link, "Woodrow Wilson's Political Personality: A Reappraisal," *Political Science Quarterly* 93 (1978): 585–598.

7. See Alexander George and Juliette George, *Woodrow Wilson and Colonel House* (New York: Dover Press, 1956). Also Juliette George and Alexander George, "Woodrow Wilson and Colonel House: A Reply to Weinstein, Anderson and Link," *Political Science Quarterly* 96 (Winter 1981–1982): 641–665. See also Alexander George and Juliette George, *Presidential Personality and Performance* (Boulder, CO: Westview, 1998), chap. 4. This chapter is an extension of the article in this note.

8. See Weinstein, *Woodrow Wilson*; George and George, "A Reply," especially 88–90, with references to the commentary on dyslexia by Dr. Critchley, president of the World Federation of Neurology.

9. Sigmund Freud and William Bullitt, *Woodrow Wilson: A Psychological Study* (New Brunswick, NJ: Transaction Publishers, 1967).

10. Both Freud quotations are from Erik Erikson, "The Strange Case of Freud, Bullitt, and Woodrow Wilson I," *New York Review*, February 9, 1967, 3.

11. Ibid., 3–5.

12. George and George, *Woodrow Wilson and Colonel House.*

13. Ibid.

14. See George and George, *Presidential Personality and Performance*, especially 107–117.

15. Ibid., 121.

16. Harold Lasswell, *Psychopathology and Politics* (Chicago: University of Chicago Press, 1930), 75. See also Harold Lasswell, *World Politics and Personal Insecurity* (New York: Whittlesey House, McGraw-Hill, 1935).

17. George and George, *Presidential Personality and Performance*, 103–104.

18. Ibid., 113.

19. Weinstein, Anderson, and Link, "Woodrow Wilson's Political Personality."

20. Robert Tucker, "The George's Wilson Reexamined: An Essay on Psychobiography," *American Political Science Review* 71 (1977): 103–104; Edwin

Weinstein, "Comments on 'Woodrow Wilson Reexamined,'" *Political Psychology* 4 (1983), 313–324; Jerrold Post, "Reply to the Three Comments on 'Woodrow Wilson Reexamined': The Mind Body Controversy Redux and Other Disputations," *Political Psychology* 4 (1983): 329–331; and Michael Marmor, "Comments on 'Woodrow Wilson Reexamined,'" *Political Psychology* 4 (1983), 325–327.

21. Weinstein, *Woodrow Wilson*; Weinstein, Anderson, and Link, "Woodrow Wilson's Political Personality."

22. George and George, *Woodrow Wilson and Colonel House*; Post, "Reply to the Three Comments on 'Woodrow Wilson Reexamined'"; and Marmor, "Comments on 'Woodrow Wilson Reexamined.'"

23. Jerrold Post, "Woodrow Wilson Re-examined: The Mind-Body Controversy Redux and Other Disputations," *Political Psychology* 4 (June 1983): 289–306.

24. Arthur Link, David Hirst, John Wells Davidson, and John Little, "Communication," *Journal of American History* 70 (March 1984): 945–955.

25. Ibid.; also Weinstein, *Woodrow Wilson*.

26. Marmor, "Comments on 'Woodrow Wilson Reexamined,'" 325.

27. Woodrow Wilson, *Papers of Woodrow Wilson*, ed. Arthur Link (Princeton: Princeton University Press, 1987), 16: 412 (hereafter *PWW*); also see Edwin Weinstein, "Woodrow Wilson's Neuropsychological Impairment and the Paris Peace Conference," appendix, *PWW*, 16: 631.

28. *PWW*, 16: 445–446; Arthur Link et al., Communication to the Editor, *Journal of American History* 70 (1984): 945–955.

29. Bert Park, *The Impact of Illness on World Leaders* (Philadelphia: University of Pennsylvania Press, 1996), 64.

30. See Bert Park, "The Impact of Wilson's Neurologic Disease during the Paris Peace Conference," *PWW*, 58: 611–630.

31. Ibid.; Park, *The Impact of Illness on World Leaders*, 4.

32. Bert Park, *Ailing, Aging, Addicted: Studies of Compromised Leadership* (Lexington: University Press of Kentucky, 1993), 98.

33. See Weinstein, *Woodrow Wilson*, 297.

34. Grayson Papers, *PWW*, 64: 500–505.

35. This term is also used by Park in "The Impact of Wilson's Neurological Disease," *PWW*, 58: 621, 630.

36. Park, *The Impact of Illness on World Leaders*, 14.

37. This point is made by Post in "Reply to the Three Comments on 'Woodrow Wilson Reexamined.'" Here, Post notes that the scholarly debate between the Georges and Link represented dichotomous psychological and medical positions. If Wilson was developing cerebral arteriosclerosis, which was highly likely, one would expect such a development to exacerbate preexisting personality characteristics, in this case making a previously stubborn individual such as Wilson more likely to become intransigent, belligerent, unyielding, and unwilling to compromise.

38. Weinstein, *Woodrow Wilson*, 181–194.

39. WW to EAW, July 20, 1908, *PWW*, 18: 371–372.

40. Diary of Breckinridge Long, January 11, 1924, reporting a conversation he had with Cary Grayson about Ellen Wilson, cited in Weinstein, *Woodrow Wilson*, 189.
41. Weaver, "Edith Bolling Wilson as First Lady," 53.
42. WW to EBG, September 19, 1915, *PWW*, 34: 491.
43. *PWW*, 34: 39, 117.
44. Weinstein, *Woodrow Wilson*, 259.
45. Ibid.
46. *PWW*, 31: 274.
47. Weinstein, *Woodrow Wilson: A Medical and Psychological Biography*, 259.
48. Grayson Papers, *PWW*, 64: 490.
49. Kenneth Crispell and Carlos Gomez, *Hidden Illness in the White House* (Durham, NC: Duke University Press, 1988), and Walter LaFeber, *The American Age: U. S. Foreign Policy at Home and Abroad*, vol. 2, *Since 1896* (New York: W. W. Norton, 1994).
50. Irwin Hood Hoover, *Forty-two Years in the White House* (Boston: Houghton Mifflin, 1934), 103.
51. As cited in Weinstein, *Woodrow Wilson*, 256.
52. Weaver, "Edith Bolling Wilson as First Lady." Weaver notes the second Mrs. Wilson did not like Tumulty because of his lowbrow Irish background. She apparently regarded Lansing as disloyal not only for questioning the president's health following his stroke, but also for questioning the value of the League of Nations in the testimony made before Congress by Bullitt. The old saying in marriage counseling is that if you get the first marriage right, you marry someone completely different the second time, whereas if you don't, you just keep marrying the same person (albeit with a different name) until you get it right. Judging by this standard, Wilson definitely got his first marriage right, probably to his ultimate dismay in the second one.
53. Weinstein, *Woodrow Wilson*.
54. Robert Ferrell, *Ill-Advised: Presidential Health and Public Trust* (Columbia: University of Missouri Press, 1992), 167.
55. Grayson Papers, *PWW*, 64: 507.
56. Appendix I, *PWW*, 63: 638.
57. Jerrold Post and Robert Robins, *When Illness Strikes the Leader: The Dilemma of the Captive King* (New Haven, CT: Yale University Press, 1993); Edward MacMahon and Leonard Curry, *Medical Cover-Ups in the White House* (Washington, DC: Farragut, 1987); Ferrell, *Ill-Advised: Presidential Health and Public Trust*; and Park, *The Impact of Illness on World Leaders*.
58. Post and Robins, *When Illness Strikes the Leader*.
59. Link, "Woodrow Wilson and the Constitutional Crisis."
60. Desk Diary of Robert Lansing and Diary of Josephus Daniels, *PWW*, 63: 554–555. Also Memo from Dr. Grayson, October 6, 1919, Grayson Papers, *PWW*, 64: 496.
61. See untitled document dated September 17, 1919, *PWW*, 63: 339, n. 4, and Joseph Tumulty, *Woodrow Wilson as I Know Him* (Garden City, NY: Doubleday, 1921), 441–443.

62. Diary of Ray Stannard Baker, *PWW*, 64: 363, n. 1.
63. See Edith Bolling Wilson, *My Memoir* (Indianapolis: Bobbs-Merrill, 1938), 288–289.
64. See Henry Cabot Lodge, *The Senate and the League of Nations* (Chapel Hill: University of North Carolina Press, 1944), 212–219, 226.
65. Crispell and Gomez, *Hidden Illness in the White House*, and Park, *Ailing, Aging, Addicted: Studies of Compromised Leadership*.
66. See Bert Park, "Woodrow Wilson's Stroke of October 2, 1919," appendix II, *PWW*, 63: 639–646.
67. See a memorandum by Robert Lansing, "The President's Capacity to Perform His Duties," December 4, 1919, *PWW*, 64: 123–125.
68. Tumulty, *Woodrow Wilson as I Know Him*, 443–444.
69. See Diary of Josephus Daniels, December 4, 1919, *PWW*, 64: 122, n. 1, and a memorandum by Robert Lansing, December 4, 1919, *PWW*, 64: 122–125. On the incidents with Mexico, see C. Trow, "Woodrow Wilson and the Mexican Interventionist Movement of 1919," *Journal of American History* 58 (1971): 46–72.
70. On the impact of stress on men who have been president, see Robert Gilbert, *The Mortal Presidency: Illness and Anguish in the White House* (New York: Fordham University Press, 1998).
71. Park, "The Impact of Wilson's Neurological Illness during the Paris Peace Conference," *PWW*, 62: 628.
72. Ibid., and Park, "Woodrow Wilson's Stroke of October 2, 1919," *PWW*, 63: 639–646.
73. Crispell and Gomez, *Hidden Illness in the White House*, and Park, *Ailing, Aging, Addicted: Studies of Compromised Leadership*.
74. Park, *Ailing, Aging and Addicted: Studies of Compromised Leadership*.
75. Marmor, "Comments on 'Woodrow Wilson Reexamined.'"
76. George de Schweinitz, *Diseases of the Eye* (Philadelphia: W. B. Saunders, 1906), 571–575.
77. Weinstein, *Woodrow Wilson*, 287.
78. Ibid., 295.
79. Park, *The Impact of Illness on World Leaders*.
80. Park, "The Impact of Wilson's Neurologic Illness during the Paris Peace Conference," *PWW*, 62: 613.
81. For initial characterization, see Weinstein, *Woodrow Wilson*. For viral interpretation, see Edwin Weinstein, "Woodrow Wilson's Neuropsychological Impairment and the Paris Peace Conference," *PWW*, 62: 630–635.
82. Park, *The Impact of Illness on World Leaders*.
83. Park, "The Impact of Wilson's Neurologic Disease during the Paris Peace Conference," *PWW*, 58: 616–618.
84. Ibid.
85. Herbert Hoover, *The Memoirs of Herbert Hoover* (New York: Macmillan, 1951), 1: 468.
86. Ike Hoover, *Forty-two Years in the White House*, 98.
87. Cary Grayson, *Woodrow Wilson: An Intimate Memoir* (New York: Dell, 1960), 82.

88. Note to April 3, 1919, Grayson Diary, *PWW*, vol. 56, citing Dr. Samuel Pegram and others; Weinstein, Anderson, and Link, "Woodrow Wilson's Political Personality."

89. For some reason, this particular influenza epidemic was most likely to kill young men between the ages of twenty and twenty-nine. John Barry, *The Great Influenza: The Epic Story of the Deadliest Plague in History* (New York: Viking, 2004).

90. See Dr. Toole and Dr. Park on this issue, from the commentary on Dr. Dercum's report to Cary Grayson, Grayson Papers, *PWW*, 64: 505–507, n. 11.

91. Link, "Woodrow Wilson and the Constitutional Crisis," 54.

92. Ibid., 71.

93. LaFeber, *The American Age*, 2: 516.

94. Introduction, *PWW*, 56: ix–xi.

95. George and George, *Woodrow Wilson and Colonel House.*

96. Park, "The Impact of Wilson's Neurological Disease," *PWW*, 58: 623.

97. Ibid., 625.

98. Link, "Woodrow Wilson and the Constitutional Crisis."

99. Weaver, "Edith Bolling Wilson as First Lady."

100. See Random Notes, June 10, 1920, *PWW*, 68: 382.

101. Link, "Woodrow Wilson and the Constitutional Crisis," 68.

102. Ibid., 69.

103. George and George, "A Reply," 121–122.

104. L'Etang, *The Pathology of Leadership.*

105. Tumulty, *Woodrow Wilson as I Know Him*, 238.

Chapter 4. Leading While Dying: Franklin Delano Roosevelt, 1943–1945

1. David Calhoun and Susanne Oparil, "Hypertensive Crisis since FDR: A Partial Victory," *New England Journal of Medicine* 332, 15 (April 13, 1995): 1029.

2. N. Keith, H. Wagener, and N. Barker, "Some Different Types of Essential Hypertension: Their Courses and Prognosis," *American Journal of Medical Society* 197 (1939): 332–343.

3. J. Webster, J. Petrie, T. Jeffers, and H. Lovell, "Accelerated Hypertension: Patterns of Mortality and Clinical Factors Affecting Outcome in Treated Patients," *Quarterly Journal of Medicine* 86 (1993): 485–493.

4. Jan Kenneth Herman, "Interview with Dr. Howard Bruenn," *Navy Medicine*, March–April 1990, 7–13.

5. Robert Gilbert, *The Mortal Presidency: Illness and Anguish in the White House* (New York: Fordham University Press, 1998).

6. J. Gunther, *Roosevelt in Retrospect* (New York: Harper and Row, 1950).

7. Ibid.

8. Hugh Gallagher, *FDR's Splendid Deception* (Carlington, VA: Vandamere Press, 1994).

9. Ibid., and Gilbert, *The Mortal Presidency.*

10. In fact, Kennedy and Johnson administration secretary of defense Robert McNamara claims that he and his wife's contracting polio in the same week was the only confirmed case of marital infection. See *The Fog of War*, motion picture documentary by Errol Morris, 2004, Sony Pictures.
11. M. Grossman and M. Kumar, *Portraying the President* (Baltimore: Johns Hopkins University Press, 1981).
12. Gallagher, *FDR's Splendid Deception*, 94.
13. Robert Ferrell, *The Dying President: Franklin Roosevelt, 1944–1945* (Columbia: University of Missouri Press, 1998).
14. A. A. Baruch, "Franklin Roosevelt's Illness: Effect on Course of History," *New York State Journal of Medicine* 77 (1977): 21–54.
15. Frances Perkins, *The Roosevelt I Knew* (New York: Viking Press, 1946).
16. Jerrold Post and Robert Robins, *When Illness Strikes the Leader: The Dilemma of the Captive King* (New Haven, CT: Yale University Press, 1993).
17. Gallagher, *FDR's Splendid Deception*.
18. A. Schlesinger, *The Crisis of the Old Order* (New York: Houghton Mifflin, 1956), 406.
19. Post and Robins, *When Illness Strikes the Leader*, 25.
20. Robert Gilbert, "Disability, Illness and the Presidency: The Case of Franklin D. Roosevelt," *Politics and the Life Sciences* 7, 1 (1988): 37.
21. Bert Park, *The Impact of Illness on World Leaders* (Philadelphia: University of Pennsylvania Press, 1986), and Ferrell, *The Dying President: Franklin Roosevelt, 1944–1945*.
22. P. D. White, *Heart Disease*, 2nd ed. (New York: Macmillan Press, 1937); Franz Messerli, "This Day 50 Years Ago," *New England Journal of Medicine* 332, 15 (April 13, 1995): 1038–1039.
23. Russell Cecil, *Textbook of Medicine*, 6th ed. (Philadelphia: W. B. Saunders, 1944); Bert Park. *The Impact of Illness on World Leaders*.
24. Ferrell, *The Dying President: Franklin Roosevelt, 1944–1945*.
25. Ibid.
26. Ibid.
27. Howard Bruenn, "Clinical Notes on the Illness and Death of President Franklin D. Roosevelt," *Annals of Internal Medicine* 72, 4 (1970): 579–591.
28. Herman, "Interview with Dr. Howard Bruenn."
29. Kenneth Crispell and Carlos Gomez, *Hidden Illness in the White House* (Durham, NC: Duke University Press, 1988).
30. Bruenn, "Clinical Notes on the Illness and Death of President Franklin D. Roosevelt," 580.
31. Crispell and Gomez, *Hidden Illness in the White House*.
32. Ferrell, *The Dying President: Franklin Roosevelt, 1944–1945*, 41.
33. Ross McIntire, *White House Physician* (New York: G. P. Putnam's Sons, 1946), 183–184.
34. Anna Roosevelt Boettinger to John Boettinger, February 5, 1945, box 6, John and Anna Boettinger correspondence and financial matters, Franklin Roosevelt Presidential Library, Hyde Park, New York.
35. Herman, "Interview with Dr. Howard Bruenn," 13.

36. Bruenn, "Clinical Notes on the Illness and Death of President Franklin D. Roosevelt."

37. Ferrell, *The Dying President: Franklin Roosevelt, 1944–1945.*

38. Ibid., 71.

39. Ibid., 72.

40. Bruenn, "Clinical Notes on the Illness and Death of President Franklin D. Roosevelt."

41. Typed notes, pp. 6 and 7, April 12, 1945, in Small collections, papers of Dr. Howard Bruenn, Roosevelt Library.

42. Jim Bishop, *FDR's Last Year: April 1944-April 1945* (New York: William Morrow, 1974), xiii. The embalming took over five hours because of Roosevelt's arteriosclerosis.

43. Park, *The Impact of Illness on World Leaders*, 228.

44. Ibid., 222.

45. Grace Tully, *FDR: My Boss* (Chicago: People's Book Club, 1949).

46. Rexford Tugwell, *The Democratic Roosevelt* (Baltimore: Penguin Books, 1957); Bishop, *FDR's Last Year*; James MacGregor Burns, *Roosevelt: Soldier of Freedom* (New York: Harcourt Brace and World, 1956).

47. James Byrnes, *Speaking Frankly* (New York: Harper & Brothers, 1947), 22.

48. Lord Moran, *Churchill Taken from the Diaries of Lord Moran: The Struggle for Survival, 1940–1965* (Boston: Houghton Mifflin, 1966), 242–243.

49. William Rigdon with James Derieux, *White House Sailor* (Garden City, NY: Doubleday, 1962), 140.

50. Edward MacMahon and Leonard Curry, *Medical Cover-Ups in the White House* (Washington, DC: Farragut Press, 1987).

51. Park, *The Impact of Illness on World Leaders*, 242.

52. Ibid., 243. Mentation here refers to thinking processes.

53. Ibid., 251.

54. Michael Beschloss, *The Conquerors: Roosevelt, Truman and the Destruction of Hitler's Germany, 1941–1945* (New York: Simon & Schuster, 2002). While in Hawaii, Roosevelt stayed at the Homes estate, a house left to the United States government by an alcoholic millionaire who committed suicide.

55. E. B. Potter (Ed.), *Sea Power: A Naval History* (Englewood Cliffs, NJ: Prentice-Hall, 1960).

56. Ibid., 238.

57. Carol Morris Petillo, *Douglas MacArthur: The Philippine Years* (Indianapolis: Indiana University Press, 1981): 436.

58. Walter LaFeber, *The American Age: U.S. Foreign Policy at Home and Abroad*, vol. 2, *Since 1896*, 2nd ed. (New York: W. W. Norton, 1994), 436.

59. Ferrell, *The Dying President: Franklin Roosevelt, 1944–1945.*

60. John Flynn, *The Roosevelt Myth* (New York: Devin-Adair, 1948), 403.

61. Ferrell, *The Dying President: Franklin Roosevelt, 1944–1945.*

62. LaFeber, *The American Age*, 2: 416.

63. Ibid., 437.

64. Anthony Eden, *The Memoirs of Anthony Eden, Earl of Avon: The Reckoning* (Boston: Houghton Mifflin, 1965), 593.

65. H. Goldsmith, "Unanswered Mysteries in the Death of Franklin D. Roosevelt," *Surgery, Gynecology and Obstetrics* 149 (1979): 902.
66. Herman, "Interview with Dr. Howard Bruenn."
67. McIntire, *White House Physician*, 202.
68. LaFeber, *The American Age*, 2: 435.
69. Henry L. Stimpson and McGeorge Bundy, *On Active Duty in Peace and War* (New York: Harper, 1948), 581. Also quoted in Ferrell, *The Dying President*, 156.
70. As quoted in Bishop, *FDR's Last Year*, 153. Also quoted in Park, *The Impact of Illness on World Leaders*, 239.
71. Robert Sherwood, *The White House Papers of Harry L. Hopkins*, vol. 2 (London: Eyre and Spottiswoode, 1949), 812.
72. Bradley Smith, *Reaching Judgment at Nuremberg* (New York: Basic Books, 1977), 31. Also quoted in Park, *The Impact of Illness on World Leaders*, 239.
73. Tugwell, *The Democratic Roosevelt*, 657. Also quoted in Park, *The Impact of Illness on World Leaders*, 239.
74. Ibid.
75. William Bullitt, "How We Won the War and Lost the Peace," *Life Magazine*, September 6, 1948.
76. Gilbert, "Disability, Illness and the Presidency," 46.
77. Quoted in Bishop, *FDR's Last Year, April 1944–April 1945*, 270. Also cited in Park, *The Impact of Illness on World Leaders*, 258.
78. Herman, "Interview with Dr. Howard Bruenn."
79. Fleet Admiral William Leahy, *I Was There: The Personal Story of the Chief of Staff to Presidents Roosevelt and Truman Based on His Notes and Diaries Made at the Time* (New York: Whittlesey House, 1950), 290.
80. Moran, *Churchill Taken from the Diaries of Lord Moran*, 239.
81. Charles Bohlen, *Witness to History: 1929–1969* (New York: W. W. Norton, 1973), 171–172.
82. Edward Flynn, *You're the Boss* (New York: Viking Press, 1947), 188.
83. Eden, *The Reckoning*, 593–594.
84. W. Averill Harriman and Elie Abel, *Special Envoy to Churchill and Stalin, 1941–1946* (New York: Random House, 1975), 389.
85. Edward Stettinius, *Roosevelt and the Russians: The Yalta Conference* (Garden City, NY: Doubleday, 1949), 73, 203, 267.
86. Byrnes, *Speaking Frankly*, 23.
87. Robert Stuart memo, "Meeting President Roosevelt: Algiers," F. D. Roosevelt, Health folder, Roosevelt Library.
88. Mark Bloom, "Should the Health of Presidential Candidates Be a Campaign Issue?" *Medical World News*, February 9, 1976, 34–54; quote from 41–42.
89. Byrnes, *Speaking Frankly*, 59.
90. Herman, "Interview with Dr. Howard Bruenn."
91. Franklin Roosevelt, *The Public Papers and Addresses of Franklin D. Roosevelt* (New York: Russell and Russell, 1950), 570.
92. Herman, "Interview with Dr. Howard Bruenn," 9.
93. Ibid., 10.

94. Eleanor Roosevelt, *The Autobiography of Eleanor Roosevelt* (New York: Harper and Row, 1961), 269.

95. James Roosevelt and Sydney Shallett, *Affectionately, FDR* (New York: Harcourt and Brace, 1959), 313.

96. Ibid., 311.

97. Gallagher, *FDR's Splendid Deception*, 195.

98. Ferrell, *The Dying President: Franklin Roosevelt*, 103.

99. Perkins, *The Roosevelt I Knew*, 393.

100. Stettinius, *Roosevelt and the Russians*, 72–73.

101. John Gunther, *Roosevelt in Retrospect* (New York: Harper, 1950), 31.

102. Thomas Fleming, "Eight Days with Harry Truman," *American* Heritage 43 (July–August 1992), 56. Also cited in Ferrell, *The Dying President*, 174.

103. Ferrell, *The Dying President*, 151.

104. Nixon Oral History, 128, as cited in ibid., 169.

CHAPTER 5. ADDICTED TO POWER: JOHN F. KENNEDY

1. Robert Kennedy et al., *John F. Kennedy: As We Remember Him*, ed. Goddard Lieberson (New York: Macmillan, 1965).

2. Robert Gilbert, *The Mortal Presidency: Illness and Anguish in the White House* (New York: Fordham University Press, 1998), and Bert Park, *Ailing, Aging, Addicted: Studies of Compromised Leadership* (Lexington: University Press of Kentucky, 1993).

3. George Burkley shot record, 1962–1963, box 48, John F. Kennedy Presidential Library, Boston.

4. In order to access these files, scholars are required to bring a physician with them in order to properly understand and interpret the complex medical material contained therein. In this endeavor, I was generously assisted by Dr. Robert Hopkins, professor emeritus of medical science at Brown University School of Medicine. Dr. Hopkins's help was invaluable in making sense of these files. All errors remain my own.

5. Robert Dallek, "The Medical Ordeals of JFK," *Atlantic Monthly*, December 2002, 49–54.

6. Dr. William P. Herbst, 1953–1963 file, series 14, Medical Records, 1942–1964, subseries 14.1 Attending Physician's Records, 1950–1964, box 45, John F. Kennedy Presidential Library, Boston.

7. Rose Kennedy, *Times to Remember* (New York: Doubleday, 1974), 202.

8. Janet Travell Oral History, 1966, Kennedy Library.

9. See Robert Dallek, *An Unfinished Life: John F. Kennedy, 1971–1963* (Boston: Little Brown, 2003) on Joe Sr.'s attempts to hide Kennedy's medical records from the military physicians.

10. Herbst medical file.

11. Herbst medical file.

12. Series 8, Navy Records, 1941–1964, box 11A, Bureau of Medicine and Surgery folder, Kennedy Library.

13. Ibid., Oct 16. 44, file.
14. Dallek, *Unfinished Life.*
15. Ibid., 196.
16. Philip Wilson, "Example of a Patient with Adrenal Insufficiency Due to Addison's Disease Requiring Elective Surgery," *American Medical Association Archives of Surgery* 71 (November 1955): 739.
17. Travell Oral History.
18. Series 14, Medical Records, 1942–1964, subseries 14.1 Attending Physician's Records, 1950–1964, box 45, 9/13/57–10/13/57 file, Kennedy Library.
19. Dallek, *An Unfinished Life.*
20. Russell Cecil, *Cecil's Textbook of Medicine* (Philadelphia: W. B. Saunders, 1944), 1243.
21. This note refers to K for Kennedy, Dr. T for Dr. Travell, Dr. W for Dr. Wade and Dr. B for Dr. Burkley. Hans Kraus notes, box 48, Kennedy Library.
22. X is Burkley's designation for Kennedy. Hans Kraus notes, box 48, Kennedy Library.
23. George Burkley medical files, Burkley 1963, box 48, Kennedy Library.
24. George Burkley medical files, Medical files on Patient X, 1962, April–December, box 48, Kennedy Library.
25. George Burkley medical files, Burkley 1963, box 48, Kennedy Library.
26. George Burkley medical files, Dr. George Burkley, Medical notes, 1961, 1/10/63 file, box 48, Kennedy Library.
27. George Burkley medical files, Dr. George Burkley, Medical notes, 1961, box 48, Kennedy Library.
28. Robert Marion, *Was George Washington Really the Father of Our Country? A Clinical Geneticist Looks at World History* (Reading, MA: Addison-Wesley, 1994).
29. Kenneth Crispell, "John F. Kennedy and the Issue of Presidential Disability," in Kenneth Thompson (Ed.), *Papers on Presidential Disability and the 25th Amendment by Medical, Historical and Political Authorities* (Lanham, MD: University Press of America, 1997).
30. Cecil, *Cecil's Textbook of Medicine,* 1238; Robert Williams, *Textbook of Endocrinology,* 5th ed. (Philadelphia: W. B. Saunders, 1974), 271–272; and Crispell, "John F. Kennedy and the Issue of Presidential Disability," 181.
31. Marion, *Was George Washington Really the Father of Our Country? A Clinical Geneticist Looks at World History.*
32. Cecil, *Cecil's Textbook of Medicine,* 1240, 1242.
33. Paul Beeson and Walsh McDermott, *Cecil's Textbook of Medicine,* 12th ed. (Philadelphia: W. B. Saunders, 1967), 1317–1319.
34. Robert Williams, *Textbook of Endocrinology,* 5th ed. (Philadelphia: W. B. Saunders, 1974), 271–272, from the original description by Thomas Addison. Also cited in Kenneth Crispell and Carlos Gomez, *Hidden Illness in the White House* (Durham, NC: Duke University Press, 1988), 181.
35. Joan Blair and Clay Blair, *The Search for J.F.K.* (New York: Berkeley Publishing Group, 1976): 560.
36. Crispell and Gomez, *Hidden Illness in the White House.*

37. Blair and Blair, *The Search for J.F.K.*, 566.
38. John Lungren and John Lungren Jr., *Healing Richard Nixon* (Lexington: University Press of Kentucky, 2003), 62.
39. Dallek, "The Medical Ordeals of JFK."
40. Janet Travell, *Office Hours, Day and Night: The Autobiography of Janet Travell, M.D.* (New York: World Publications, 1968), 327.
41. Quoted in Blair and Blair, *The Search for J.F.K.*, 575.
42. Cecil, *Cecil's Textbook of Medicine*, 1238.
43. Theodore Sorensen, *Kennedy* (New York: Harper and Row, 1957). Also quoted in Edward MacMahon and Leonard Curry, *Medical Cover-Ups in the White House* (Washington, DC: Farragut, 1987): 120.
44. Travell Oral History.
45. Ibid.
46. George Burkley medical files, Burkley 1963, box 48, 4/19/61 folder, Kennedy Library.
47. Herbst medical file.
48. Cecil, *Cecil's Textbook of Medicine*, 1238.
49. Herbst medical file.
50. Hugh L'Etang, *The Pathology of Leadership: A History of the Effects of Disease on 20th Century Leaders* (New York: Hawthorn, 1970), 188.
51. Robert Ferrell, *Ill-Advised: Presidential Health and Public Trust* (Columbia: University of Missouri Press, 1992), 189; B. Rensberger, "Amphetamines Used by a Physician to Lift Moods of Famous Patients," *New York Times*, December 4, 1972, 34; and Thomas Reeves, *A Question of Character: A Life of John F. Kennedy* (New York: Free Press, 1991): 295–296.
52. Park, *Ailing, Aging, Addicted: Studies of Compromised Leadership*.
53. Jerrold Post and Robert Robins, *When Illness Strikes the Leader: The Dilemma of the Captive King* (New Haven, CT: Yale University Press, 1993).
54. Ibid, 69.
55. Park, *Ailing, Aging, Addicted: Studies of Compromised Leadership*.
56. Ferrell, *Ill-Advised: Presidential Health and Public Trust*, 156.
57. Ibid., 172.
58. Clayton Cowl, *Physician's Drug Handbook*, 10th ed. (Philadelphia: Lippincott Williams & Wilkins, 2003), 133.
59. Rensberger, "Amphetamines Used by a Physician to Lift Moods of Famous Patients."
60. Richard Reeves, *President Kennedy: Profile of Power* (New York: Simon & Schuster, 1993), 36.
61. George Burkley medical notes, 1961: April, 1961–March 1962: 3/21/62 folder, box 48, Kennedy Library.
62. Park, *Ailing, Aging, Addicted: Studies of Compromised Leadership*, 172.
63. H. H. Goldman, *Review of General Psychiatry* (Norwalk, CT: Appleton & Lange, 1988), 276.
64. W. Bowman and M. Rand, *Textbook of Pharmacology*, 2nd ed. (Oxford: Blackwell Scientific Publishers, 1980), 4283.
65. Dallek, *An Unfinished Life*, 576.

66. Park, *Ailing, Aging, Addicted: Studies of Compromised Leadership*.
67. *Newsweek*, December 18, 1972, 73.
68. George Kennan Oral History, 5, Kennedy Library.
69. Michael Beschloss, *The Crisis Years: Kennedy and Khrushchev, 1960–1963* (New York: HarperCollins, 1991): 223–224.
70. Quoted in ibid., 224–225, from interview in the *New York Times*, June 5, 1961.
71. James Reston, *Deadline: A Memoir* (New York: Random House, 1991).
72. Beschloss, *The Crisis* Years, 224.
73. Kennan Oral History.
74. Llewellyn Thompson Oral History, Kennedy Library.
75. Beschloss, *The Crisis Years*, 234.
76. William Taubman, *Khrushchev: The Man and His Era* (New York: W. W. Norton, 2003), 581.
77. Harold Macmillan, *Pointing the Way, 1959–1961* (New York: HarperCollins, 1972), 357. Also quoted in Beschloss, *The Crisis Years*, 226–227.
78. Park, *Ailing, Aging, Addicted: Studies of Compromised Leadership*.
79. Walter LaFeber, *The American Age: U.S. Foreign Policy at Home and Abroad*, vol. 2, *Since 1896* (New York: W. W. Norton, 1994): 595.
80. National Security Files, series 6, Meeting and Memorandum, box 317, Kennedy Library.
81. Presidential Office Files, series 3, Speech Files, box 35, Kennedy Library.
82. National Security Files, series 1 Countries, Union of Soviet Socialist Republics, box 189, Kennedy Library.
83. As quoted from press interview in Beschloss, *The Crisis Years*, 206.
84. Janet Travell medical files, June 1961, box 4, Kennedy Library.
85. As quoted in Beschloss, *The Crisis Years*, 228, from WGBH interview with Burlatsky.
86. Ibid., 187.
87. See Goldman, *Review of General Psychiatry*, 275.
88. Ibid.
89. William McKim, *Drugs and Behavior: An Introduction to Behavioral Pharmacology*, 4th ed. (Upper Saddle River, NJ: Prentice-Hall, 2000).
90. Kalyna Bezchlibnyk-Butler and Joel Jeffries, *Clinical Handbook of Psychotropic Drugs*, 11th rev. ed. (Seattle: Hogrefe & Huber Publishers, 2002), 161.
91. Janet Travell medical records, June 1961, box 45, Kennedy Library.
92. Janet Travell medical records, George Washington Hospital, 1950–1953, box 45, Kennedy Library.
93. Ibid.
94. For excellent descriptions and documentation of Eden's use of benzedrine during the Suez Crisis, see Hugh Thomas, *Suez* (New York: Harper and Row, 1967), and Terence Robertson, *Crisis: The Inside Story of the Suez Conspiracy* (New York: Atheneum, 1984).
95. Post and Robins, *When Illness Strikes the Leader*, were the first to use the term "terminal urgency."
96. L'Etang, *The Pathology of Leadership*, 188.

97. Gilbert, *The Mortal Presidency*; Dallek, *An Unfinished Life*.

98. Gilbert, *The Mortal Presidency*.

99. Crispell and Gomez, *Hidden Illness in the White House*.

CHAPTER 6. BORDERING ON SANITY: RICHARD NIXON

1. Hugh Sidey, "The Man and Foreign Policy," in Kenneth Thompson (Ed.), *Portraits of American Presidents*, vol. 6, *The Nixon Presidency* (Lanham, MD: University Press of America, 1987), 299–314, 301.

2. For more on this event, see Robert McElroy, *Morality in American Foreign Policy* (Princeton, NJ: Princeton University Press, 1993).

3. Richard Nixon, *RN: The Memoirs of Richard Nixon* (New York: Grosset & Dunlap, 1978), 1084.

4. Jeffrey Kimball, *The Vietnam War Files: Uncovering the Secret History of Nixon-Era Strategy* (Lawrence: University Press of Kansas, 2004), 39.

5. William Ridings and Stuart McIver, *Rating the Presidents: From the Great and Honorable to the Dishonest and Incompetent* (New York: Citadel Press, 1997); Arthur M. Schlesinger Jr. "Rating the Presidents: Washington to Clinton," *Political Science Quarterly* 11, 2 (Summer 1997): 179–190.

6. For an exception to this trend, see David Greenberg, *Nixon's Shadow: The History of an Image* (New York: W. W. Norton, 2003).

7. Nixon, *RN*, 245.

8. For an insightful critique of some of the methodological, empirical, and theoretical problems with this approach with regard to psychobiographies of Nixon, see Stanley Renshon, "Psychological Analysis of Presidential Personality: The Case of Richard Nixon," *History of Childhood Quarterly: The Journal of Psychohistory* 2, 3 (Winter 1975): 415–450.

9. Vamik Volkan, Norman Itzkowitz, and Andrew Dod, *Richard Nixon: A Psychobiography* (New York: Columbia, 1997), 25.

10. Melvin Small, *The Presidency of Richard Nixon* (Lawrence: University Press of Kansas, 1999).

11. Other family information largely from Volkan et al., *Richard Nixon*.

12. David Abrahamsen, *Nixon vs. Nixon: An Emotional Tragedy* (New York: Farrar, Straus & Giroux, 1977).

13. Stephen Ambrose, *Nixon: Education of a Politician, 1913–1962* (New York: Simon & Schuster, 1987).

14. James Hamilton, "Some Reflections on Richard Nixon in the Light of His Resignation and Farewell Speeches," *Journal of Psychohistory* 4, 4 (Spring 1977), 491–511, 503.

15. Fawn Brodie, *Richard Nixon: The Shaping of His Character* (Cambridge, MA: Harvard University Press, 1981), 502.

16. Reported in Blema Steinberg, *Shame and Humiliation: Presidential Decision Making on Vietnam* (Pittsburgh: University of Pittsburgh Press, 1996), 125.

17. Ibid.

18. Brodie, *Richard Nixon*, 40.

19. Nixon, *RN*, 6.
20. Bela Kornitzer, *The Real Nixon: An Intimate Biography* (Chicago: Rand McNally, 1960), 79.
21. Ibid., 78.
22. Steinberg, *Shame and Humiliation*, 133–134.
23. L. Lurie, *The Running of Richard Nixon* (New York: Coward, McCann and Geohagen, 1972), 18.
24. The term is from Donald Winnicott, *The Maturational Process and the Facilitating Environment* (New York: International Universities Press, 1965). The term refers to children whose mothers (or primary care-givers) are either not able or not willing to provide sufficient care for the child to feel safe and secure. The child remains unable to create a sense of inner security, and his mothering is considered not "good enough."
25. Kornitzer, *The Real Nixon*, 57.
26. See, for example, Frank DeHart, *Traumatic Nixon* (Self-published, 1979), as cited in Greenberg, *Nixon's Shadow*. Also Michael Rogin and John Lottier, "The Inner History of Richard Milhous Nixon," *Transaction* 9 (1971): 1–2.
27. Abrahamsen, *Nixon vs. Nixon*.
28. Brodie, *Richard Nixon*.
29. Hamilton, "Some Reflections on Richard Nixon," 492.
30. Kornitzer, *The Real Nixon*, 19.
31. In James Johnson, "Nixon's Use of Metaphor: The Real Nixon Tapes," *Psychoanalytic Review* 66 (1979): 263–274, 268.
32. Robert Lifton, *Death in Life: Survivors of Hiroshima* (New York: Vintage, 1969).
33. Sigmund Freud, "Some Character-Types Met with in Psychoanalytic Work" (1916), in *The Standard Edition of the Complete Psychological Works of Sigmund Freud*, vol. 15 (1915–1916), *Introductory Lectures on Psycho-Analysis*, parts I and II (London: Hogarth Press, 1957), 316–332.
34. Lurie, *The Running of Richard Nixon*, 22.
35. Hannah Nixon, told to Flora Rheta Schreiber, "Richard Nixon, a Mother's Story," *Good Housekeeping*, June 1960.
36. Greenberg, *Nixon's Shadow*.
37. Story in Kornitzer, *The Real Nixon*, 61–66. Obviously, alternative psychodynamic explanations for survivor guilt exist. It is possible that Nixon did not necessarily want his brothers to die so that he could spend more time with his mother; rather, he may simply have been grateful that they died instead of him, rendering his guilt more directly. Or he may have envied his brothers for their exclusive time with his mother, while blaming her for her failure to adequately take care of him, although fate had apparently smiled on him by allowing him to live where his brothers had died. This interpretation would allow a more direct comparison with Lifton's model, where the survivor models both the aggressor and the aggrieved, whom he simultaneously identifies with and rejects. Alternatively, he could have blamed her for his brothers' deaths, believing that her underlying emotional neglect had killed them physically as surely as it had assassinated him emotionally and psychologically.

38. For more on this theoretical tendency, see the psychobiography chapter in Rose McDermott, *Political Psychology in International Relations* (Ann Arbor: University of Michigan Press, 2004).
39. Greenberg, *Nixon's Shadow*, 234.
40. These works include, but are not limited to Bruce Mazlish, *In Search of Nixon: A Psychohistorical Inquiry* (New York: Basic Books, 1972). Also see Bruce Mazlish, "Psychohistory and Richard M. Nixon," *Psychology Today*, July 1972, 77–90; and Bruce Mazlish, "Towards a Psychohistorical Inquiry: The 'Real' Richard Nixon," *Journal of Interdisciplinary History* 1 (Autumn 1970): 49–105; Rogin and Lottier, "The Inner History of Richard Milhous Nixon"; Abrahamsen, *Nixon vs. Nixon*; Brodie, *Richard Nixon*; Johnson, "Nixon's Use of Metaphor"; and Alan Rothenberg, "Why Nixon Taped Himself: Infantile Fantasies behind Watergate," *Psychoanalytic Review* 62 (1975): 201–223.
41. Mazlish, "Psychohistory and Richard M. Nixon"; see also Blema Steinberg, preface to Volkan et al., *Richard Nixon*.
42. Johnson, "Nixon's Use of Metaphor," 274.
43. For an interesting and sympathetic discussion of these issues, see John Lungren and John Lungren Jr., *Healing Richard Nixon* (Lexington: University Press of Kentucky, 2003).
44. Nixon, *RN*, 452.
45. David Frost, *"I Gave Them a Sword": Behind the Scenes of the Nixon Interviews* (New York: William Morrow, 1978).
46. Brodie, *Richard Nixon*, 510–512.
47. Peter Loewenberg, "Nixon, Hitler and Power: An Ego Psychological Study," *Psychoanalytic Inquiry* 6 (1986): 27–48, 29.
48. Johnson, "Nixon's Use of Metaphor"; Abrahamsen, *Nixon vs. Nixon*.
49. Henry Kissinger, *White House Years* (Boston: Little Brown, 1979), 1471.
50. Greenberg, *Nixon's Shadow*, 245.
51. Loewenberg, "Nixon, Hitler and Power: An Ego Psychology Study," 29.
52. Greenberg, *Nixon's Shadow*, 266.
53. Volkan et al., *Richard Nixon*.
54. This is similar to Jerrold Post's notion of the reparative charismatic leader. Post categorizes Ataturk, Gandhi, and Martin Luther King as such leaders. See Jerrold Post, *Leaders and Their Followers in a Dangerous World* (Ithaca, NY: Cornell University Press, 2004).
55. Steinberg, *Shame and Humiliation*.
56. Ibid., 133; also H. Nixon, "Richard Nixon."
57. Steinberg, *Shame and Humiliation*, 133; Brodie, *Richard Nixon*, 60.
58. R. de Toledano, *One Man Alone: Richard Nixon* (New York: Funk and Wagnalls, 1969), 22.
59. Greenberg, *Nixon's Shadow*, 242.
60. Arnold Hutschnecker, "President Nixon's Former Doctor Writes about the Mental Health of Our Leaders," *Look*, July 15, 1969, 51–54, 54.
61. Ibid., 54.
62. Ibid., 51.
63. Ibid.

64. James David Barber, *The Presidential Character: Predicting Performance in the White House* (Englewood Cliffs, NJ: Prentice-Hall, 1985).

65. Hutschnecker, "President Nixon's Former Doctor Writes about the Mental Health of Our Leaders," 52.

66. Ibid., 54.

67. Arnold Hutschnecker, "The Stigma of Seeing a Psychiatrist," *New York Times*, November 20, 1973, 39.

68. Rick Perlstein, foreword to Lungren and Lungren, *Healing Richard Nixon*, ix–xv, ix.

69. Lungren and Lungren, *Healing Richard Nixon*, 37.

70. Ibid., 38–39.

71. Ibid., 48.

72. For an interesting discussion of this affair, see Dean Kotlowski, "The Knowles Affair: Nixon's Self-Inflicted Wound," *Presidential Studies Quarterly* 30, 3 (2000): 443–463.

73. Lungren and Lungren, *Healing Richard Nixon*, 57.

74. "Secret Rich Men's Trust Fund Keeps Nixon in Style Far Beyond His Salary," *New York Post*, September 18, 1952, 3, 26; "Mitchell Urges Nixon to Name Fund Donators," *New York Herald Tribune*, September 20, 1952, 6; "Nixon Fund Uncovered; 76 Gave $18, 235," *New York Herald Tribune*, September 21, 1952, 1.

75. Richard Nixon, *Six Crises* (New York: Pyramid, 1962), 99.

76. David Winter and Leslie Carlson, "Using Motive Scores in the Psychobiographical Study of an Individual: The Case of Richard Nixon," *Journal of Personality* 56 (1988): 75–103.

77. American Psychiatric Association, *Diagnostic and Statistical Manual of Mental Disorders*, 4th ed. (*DSM-IV*) (Washington, DC: APA, 1994), 629.

78. H. R. Haldeman, *The Ends of Power* (New York: Times Books, 1978), 674–675.

79. Brodie, *Richard Nixon*, 116.

80. Bela Kornitzer, "My Son: Two Exclusive and Candid Interviews with Mothers of the Presidential Candidates," *Los Angeles Times*, September 18, 1960.

81. Anthony Summers, *The Arrogance of Power: The Secret World of Richard Nixon* (New York: Penguin, 2000), 93.

82. Jane Beeson Oral History, as cited in Steinberg, *Shame and Humiliation*, 132.

83. Steinberg, *Shame and Humiliation*, 126 (emphasis added).

84. Ibid., 126.

85. Arthur Woodstone, *Nixon's Head* (New York: St. Martin's Press, 1972), 93.

86. Volkan et al., *Richard Nixon*, 147.

87. Kissinger, *White House Years*, 9.

88. Ibid., 11.

89. Ibid., 45.

90. Ibid., 47–48.

91. Haldeman, *The Ends of Power*, 289.

92. American Psychiatric Association, *DSM-IV*, 654.

93. David Halberstam, interviewed by Brian Lamb on C-Span program, *Booknotes*, July 11, 1993, as cited in Lungren and Lungren, *Healing Richard Nixon*, 164.

94. All the quotes from Hutschnecker from interview with Summers, *The Arrogance of Power*, 93.

95. Kissinger, *White House Years*, as cited in Steinberg, *Shame and Humiliation*, 337, n. 47.

96. Seymour Hersh, *The Price of Power: Kissinger in the Nixon White House* (New York: Summit Books, 1983), 88.

97. Walter Isaacson, *Kissinger* (New York: Simon & Schuster, 1992).

98. For an early work on this topic, see Lucille Iremonger, *The Fiery Chariot: A Study of British Prime Ministers and the Search for Love* (London: Secker & Warburg, 1970).

99. As quoted in Walter LaFeber, *The American Age: U.S. Foreign Policy at Home and Abroad*, vol. 2, *Since 1896*, 2nd ed. (New York: W. W. Norton, 1994), 634.

100. Haldeman, *The Ends of Power*, 83. Also Thomas Schelling, *The Strategy of Conflict* (Cambridge, MA: Harvard University Press, 1960).

101. Kimball, *The Vietnam War Files*, 286.

102. Ibid., 15.

103. The facts surrounding the various strategies considered are covered very well in ibid. See especially chap. 1. Much of the material in the following section draws on these documents and analysis.

104. Ibid., 641.

105. Ibid.

106. Greenberg, *Nixon's Shadow*, 233.

107. LaFeber, *The American Age*, 2: 640.

108. Ibid., 616.

109. Kimball, *The Vietnam War Files*, 217.

110. Kissinger, *White House Years*, 200.

111. Ibid., 665–666.

112. Kimball, *The Vietnam War Files*, 32.

113. Hamilton, "Some Reflections on Richard Nixon," 503–504.

114. Steinberg, *Shame and Humiliation*, 169.

115. Harold Lasswell, *Psychopathology and Politics* (Chicago: University of Chicago Press, 1930), 75.

116. Summers, *The Arrogance of Power*, 92–93.

117. Ibid., 92.

118. Eli Chesen, *President Nixon's Psychiatric Profile* (New York: Peter Wyden, 1973), 231.

119. Summers, *The Arrogance of Power*, 93.

120. Daniel Kahneman and Amos Tversky, "Choices, Values and Frames," *American Psychologist* 39 (1984): 341–350. For application of this theory to American foreign policy, see Rose McDermott, *Risk Taking in International Politics: Prospect Theory in American Foreign Policy* (Ann Arbor: University of Michigan Press, 1998).

121. LaFeber, *The American Age*, 2: 634.

122. In Volkan et al., *Richard Nixon*, 148.
123. Ibid.

Chapter 7. Twenty-fifth Amendment

1. John Feerick, "The Twenty-Fifth Amendment: Its Origins and History," in Robert Gilbert (Ed.), *Managing Crisis: Presidential Disability and the 25th Amendment* (New York: Fordham University Press, 2000).
2. Robert Gilbert, "The Contemporary Presidency: The Twenty-Fifth Amendment: Recommendations and Deliberations of the Working Group on Presidential Disability," *Presidential Studies Quarterly* 33 (2003): 877–888.
3. Edward MacMahon and Leonard Curry, *Medical Cover-Ups in the White House* (Washington, DC: Farragut, 1987).
4. Arthur Link, "Woodrow Wilson and the Constitutional Crisis," in Kenneth Thompson (Ed.), *Papers on Presidential Disability and the 25th Amendment by Medical, Historical, and Political Authorities*, vol. 3 (Lanham, MD: Miller Center, University of Virginia and University Press of America, 1996), 53–80.
5. Bert Park, "Presidential Disability: Past Experiences and Future Implications," *Politics and the Life Sciences* 1 (1988): 50–66.
6. Feerick, "The Twenty-Fifth Amendment."
7. Robert Gilbert, *The Mortal Presidency: Illness and Anguish in the White House* (New York: Fordham University Press, 1998).
8. Kenneth Crispell and Carlos Gomez, *Hidden Illness in the White House* (Durham, NC: Duke University Press, 1988), 228–229.
9. Herbert Abrams, "Shielding the President from the Constitution: Disability and the 25th Amendment," *Presidential Studies Quarterly* 3 (1993): 533–553, 535.
10. Feerick, "The Twenty-Fifth Amendment," and Robert Gilbert, "The Genius of the Twenty-Fifth Amendment: Guarding against Presidential Disability but Safeguarding the Presidency," in Robert Gilbert (Ed.), *Managing Crisis: Presidential Disability and the 25th Amendment* (New York: Fordham University Press, 2000).
11. Gilbert, *The Mortal Presidency*.
12. The statistics on the vice presidency in this sentence and two sentences prior from Joel Goldstein, "The Vice Presidency and the Twenty-Fifth Amendment: The Power of Reciprocal Relationships," in Gilbert, *Managing Crisis*, 165–214.
13. Ibid.
14. Feerick, "The Twenty-Fifth Amendment."
15. John Feerick, *The 25th Amendment: Its Complete History and Applications* (New York: Fordham University Press, 1992).
16. Herbert Abrams, *"The President Has Been Shot": Confusion, Disability, and the 25th Amendment* (Stanford, CA: Stanford University Press, 1992).
17. Abrams, "Shielding the President from the Constitution," 546.
18. Ibid., 542.

19. Abrams, *"The President Has Been Shot,"* 200.
20. Ibid.
21. Ronald Reagan, *An American Life* (New York: Simon & Schuster, 1990), 500.
22. Ibid., 201.
23. Ibid., 204.
24. For fascinating coverage of this issue, see the PBS *American Experience* documentary, "Iran-Contra Affair" (written by Julie Wolf).
25. R. D. Silva, *Presidential Succession* (New York: Greenwood Press, 1968).
26. Jerrold Post and Robert S. Robins, *When Illness Strikes the Leader: The Dilemma of the Captive King* (New Haven, CT: Yale University Press, 1993).
27. Jerrold Post, "Broken Minds, Broken Hearts and the Twenty-Fifth Amendment: Psychiatric Disorders and Presidential Disability," in Gilbert, *Managing Crisis*, 111–124.
28. Birch Bayh, "Reflections on the Twenty-Fifth Amendment as We Enter a New Century," in Gilbert, *Managing Crisis*, 55–68.
29. Abrams, "Shielding the President from the Constitution," 547.
30. Burton Lee, "Presidential Disability and the 25th Amendment," *Journal of the American Medical Association* 274 (September 13, 1995): 797.
31. Ann Devroy, "Clinton Team Follows Bush 'Road Map' on the Transfer of Presidential Power," *Washington Post*, June 14, 1993, A17.
32. Lawrence Mohr, "Medical Consideration in the Determination of Presidential Disability," in Gilbert, *Managing Crisis*, 97–110.
33. French Constitution, October 4, 1958, Article 7.
34. Sweden's Constitution/Instrument of Government: Chapter 5. The Head of State and Chapter 6. The Government.
35. Basic Law for the Federal Republic of Germany: V. The Federal President, Article 57 and VI. The Federal Government, Articles 62, 67 and 69. Information provided by Mr. Neuen in the German Information Center at the German Embassy, Washington, DC.
36. Email correspondence from Kristian Rasmussen, Political Section, Royal Danish Embassy, Washington, DC.
37. Telephone interview with Michael Bronstein, aide to Labour Whip, British Embassy Inquiry Service, Washington, DC.
38. Constitution of the Republic of South Africa as adopted on May 8, 1996, and amended on October 11, 1996, by the Constitutional Assembly: Chapter 5. The President & National Executive, Removal of the President, Article 89, and Acting President, Article 90.
39. Swiss Constitution as amended in 2000: Chapter 3. Federal Government and Federal Administration, Section 1: Organization and Procedure; Section 2: Powers, Articles 174–187.
40. Kenneth Thompson (Ed.), "Report of the Miller Center Commission on Presidential Disability and the Twenty-Fifth Amendment," in Gilbert, *Managing Crisis*, 241–260.
41. Abrams, *"The President Has Been Shot,"* 222.
42. For an account of Wilson, see Alexander George and Juliette George, *Woodrow Wilson and Colonel House* (New York: Dover, 1956). For a

fascinating account of Calvin Coolidge's depression following the death of his son, see Robert Gilbert, *The Tormented President: Calvin Coolidge, Death and Clinical Depression* (Westport, CT: Praeger, 2003).

43. Gilbert, "The Genius of the Twenty-Fifth Amendment."

44. Jimmy Carter, "Presidential Disability and the 25th Amendment: A President's Perspective," *Journal of the American Medical Association* 272, 21 (1994): 1698.

45. Arthur Link and James Toole, "Presidential Disability and the 25th Amendment: A President's Perspective," *Journal of the American Medical Association* 272, 21 (1994): 1694–1697, 1695.

46. Steven Miles, "Presidential Disability and the 25th Amendment," *Journal of the American Medical Association* 274, 10 (1995): 798–799.

47. J. Ormel, M. Von Korff, B. Ustun, et al., "Common Mental Disorders and Disabilities across Cultures," *Journal of the American Medical Association* 272 (1994): 1741–1748, as cited in George Gellert, "Presidential Disability and the 25th Amendment," *Journal of the American Medical Association* 274, 10 (1995): 798.

48. Richard Friedman, "Presidential Disability and the 25th Amendment," *Journal of the American Medical Association* 274, 10 (1995): 797–798.

49. P. B. Fontanarosa, "New Multidisciplinary Working Group Focuses on Presidential Disability," *Journal of the American Medical Association* 273, 12 (1995): 905–906.

50. J. Toole, A. Link, and J. Smith, "Disability in US Presidents Report: Recommendations and Commentaries by the Working Group," *Archives of Neurology* 54, 9 (1997): 1256–1264.

51. Gilbert, "The Contemporary Presidency," 883. Also Gilbert, "The Genius of the Twenty-Fifth Amendment."

52. James Toole and Robert Joynt (Eds.), *Presidential Disability: Papers, Discussions and Recommendations on the 25th Amendment and Issues of Inability and Disability in Presidents of the United States* (Rochester, NY: University of Rochester Press, 2001).

53. Bert Park, *The Impact of Illness on World Leaders* (Philadelphia: University of Pennsylvania Press, 1986).

54. Ibid.; Bert Park, "Resuscitating the 25th Amendment: A Second Opinion Regarding Presidential Disability," *Political Psychology* 16, 4 (1995): 821–839; Bert Park, *Ailing, Aging, Addicted: Studies of Compromised Leadership* (Lexington: University Press of Kentucky, 1993).

55. Gilbert, "The Genius of the Twenty-Fifth Amendment."

Chapter 8. Presidential Care

1. Herbert Abrams, *"The President Has Been Shot": Confusion, Disability, and the 25th Amendment* (Stanford, CA: Stanford University Press, 1992).

2. Robert Gilbert, *The Mortal Presidency: Illness and Anguish in the White House* (New York: Fordham University Press, 1998).

3. Abrams, *"The President Has Been Shot."*
4. Ibid.
5. Gilbert, *The Mortal Presidency.*
6. James Flexner, *Washington: The Indispensable Man* (Boston: Little Brown, 1974), 261.
7. Robert Gilbert, "Presidential Disability: Effects and Remedies in the Age of Terror," 40th Annual Robert D. Klein Lecture, February 12, 2004, Northeastern University, Boston.
8. Gilbert, *The Mortal Presidency.*
9. Hugh L'Etang, *The Pathology of Leadership: A History of the Effects of Disease on 20th Century Leaders* (New York: Hawthorn, 1970).
10. William Ridings and Stuart McIver, *Rating the Presidents: From the Great and Honorable to the Dishonest and Incompetent* (New York: Citadel Press, 1997).
11. Gilbert, *The Mortal Presidency.*
12. For an excellent systematic discussion of this topic, see Robert Robins and Robert Dorn, "Stress and Political Leadership," *Politics and the Life Sciences* 12, 1 (1993): 3–17.
13. Edward MacMahon and Leonard Curry, *Medical Cover-Ups in the White House* (Washington, DC: Farragut, 1987).
14. E. Connie Mariano, "In Sickness and in Health: Medical Care for the President of the United States," in Robert Gilbert (Ed.), *Managing Crisis: Presidential Disability and the 25th Amendment* (New York: Fordham University Press, 2000), 83–95.
15. Charles Roos, "Physician to the President," *Bulletin of the Medical Library Association* 49 (July 1961): 291–360.
16. I thank an anonymous reviewer for this helpful perspective.
17. Lawrence Mohr, "The White House Physician: Role, Responsibilities and Issues," *Political Psychology* 16, 4 (1995): 777–793.
18. MacMahon and Curry, *Medical Cover-Ups in the White House,* 6.
19. Ibid.
20. Ibid.
21. Robert Robins and Henry Rothschild, "Hidden Health Disabilities and the Presidency: Medical Management and Political Consideration," *Perspectives in Biology and Medicine* 24 (1981): 240–253.
22. Milton Greenblatt, "Power and Impairment of Great Leaders" (1983), as cited in Kenneth Crispell and Carlos Gomez, *Hidden Illness in the White House* (Durham, NC: Duke University Press, 1988), 231.
23. Ibid.
24. Ibid.
25. Abrams, *"The President Has Been Shot,"* 234.
26. Robert Ferrell, *Ill-Advised: Presidential Health and Public Trust* (Columbia: University of Missouri Press, 1992).
27. MacMahon and Curry, *Medical Cover-Ups in the White House.*
28. Crispell and Gomez, *Hidden Illness in the White House.*
29. See Edith Bolling Wilson, *My Memoir* (Indianapolis: Bobbs-Merrill, 1939), 288–289.

30. Lord Moran, *Churchill Taken from the Diaries of Lord Moran: The Struggle for Survival, 1940–1965* (Boston: Houghton Mifflin, 1966).
31. Lawrence Altman, "Doctors Discount Workload as Factor in Cheney Case," *New York Times*, March 7, 2001, A15.
32. Mohr, "The White House Physician: Role, Responsibilities and Issues."
33. Crispell and Gomez, *Hidden Illness in the White House*; Abrams, *"The President Has Been Shot"*; and Kenneth Thompson, *Report of the Miller Center Commission on Presidential Disability and the Twenty-fifth Amendment.* (Lanham, MD: White Burkett Miller Center of Public Affairs at the University of Virginia and University Press of America, 1988).
34. Robins and Rothschild, "Hidden Disabilities and the Presidency."
35. Herbert Abrams, "Presidential Health and the Public Interest – The Campaign of 1992," *Political Psychology* 16, 4 (1995): 795–820.
36. William Safire, "Glossing Over Illness Unhealthy for Voters," *St. Louis Post-Dispatch*, April 28, 1992, Editorial, 3C.
37. Robert Robins and Jerrold Post, "Choosing a Healthy President," *Political Psychology* 16, 4 (1995): 841–860.
38. Lawrence Altman, "The Doctor's World," *New York Times*, October 9, 2002, F5.
39. Post and Robins, "Choosing a Healthy President."
40. Ibid.
41. Ibid.
42. Ibid.
43. George Annas, "The Health of the President and Presidential Candidates," *New England Journal of Medicine* 333 (1995): 945–949.
44. Gilbert, *The Mortal Presidency.*
45. A. Kucharski, "On Being Sick and Famous," *Political Psychology* 5 (1981): 69–82; Robert Robins and Henry Rothschild, "Ethical Dilemmas of the President's Physician," *Politics and the Life Sciences* 7, 1 (1988): 3–11; and Post and Robins, *When Illness Strikes the Leader.*
46. Kucharski, "On Being Sick and Famous."
47. Robins and Rothschild, "Ethical Dilemmas of the President's Physician."
48. Ibid., 5.
49. Kucharski, "On Being Sick and Famous"; Post and Robins, *When Illness Strikes the Leader: The Dilemma of the Captive King.*
50. Robins and Rothschild, "Ethical Dilemmas of the President's Physician."
51. Post and Robins, *When Illness Strikes the Leader.*
52. Ibid., 98–99.
53. Abrams, "Presidential Health and the Public Interest – The Campaign of 1992."
54. Abrams, *"The President Has Been Shot,"* 230.
55. Robert Joynt, "Who Is Minding the World?" *Journal of the American Medical Association* 272, 21 (1994): 1699–1700.
56. See report on Cato Web site: http://www.cato.org/testimony/ct-jg040909.html.
57. Jorge Mancillas, "They Did Not Have to Die," *San Francisco Chronicle*, July 23, 2003.

Appendix. Foreign Leadership and Medical Intelligence: The Shah of Iran and the Carter Administration

1. David Frum, "Deathbed," *National Review Online*, November 8, 2004 (http://frum.nationalreview.com).
2. Ion Mihai Pacepa, *Red Horizons: The True Story of Nicolae and Elena Ceausescus' Crimes, Lifestyle, and Corruption* (Washington, DC: Regnery Publishing, 1990).
3. For a fuller description, see Jerrold Post, *Leaders and Followers in a Dangerous World: The Psychology of Political Behavior* (Ithaca, NY: Cornell University Press, 2004). See also Jerrold Post, *The Psychological Assessment of Political Leaders: With Profiles of Saddam Hussein and Bill Clinton* (Ann Arbor: University of Michigan Press, 2005) for a comprehensive history of political personality profiling in government, as well as a methodology for the political personality profiling technique.
4. Kenneth Walker, "Medical Conditions of Leaders Often Hushed Up," *Chicago Sun-Times*, February 15, 1998, 44.
5. Ibid.
6. The best general reference on the fall of the shah is Gary Sick, *All Fall Down* (New York: Penguin Books, 1986). The best medical information comes from William Shawcross, *The Shah's Last Ride: The Fate of an Ally* (New York: Simon & Schuster, 1988), who meticulously documents the internecine struggles that plagued the shah's various medical teams. See also D. L. Breo, "Shah's Physician Relates Story of Intrigue, Duplicity," *American Medical News*, August 7, 1981, 3–22, and Lawrence Altman, "The Shah's Health: A Political Gamble," *New York Times Magazine*, May 26, 1981, 48–52. For a good overview of how the shah's health impacted President Carter's decision to admit the shah into the country, leading to the American hostages being seized by Iranian students loyal to the Ayatollah Khomeini, see Terence Smith, "Why Carter admitted the Shah," *New York Times Magazine*, May 26, 1981, 36–37.
7. Marvin Zonis, *Majestic Failure: The Fall of the Shah* (Chicago: University of Chicago Press, 1991), 160.
8. This section is largely drawn from an author interview with Dr. Manouchehr Ganji, minister of education to the shah of Iran from 1976 to 1979. He was also professor of international law and dean of the Faculty of Law and Political Science of Tehran University before the revolution. Telephone interview January 17, 2005.
9. Jerrold Post and Robert Robins, *When Illness Strikes the Leader: The Dilemma of the Captive King* (New Haven, CT: Yale University Press, 1993) claim that the shah really suffered from lymphocytic leukemia but that his French doctors told him he had Waldenstrom's because the shah's advisers would not allow them to use the word cancer in telling the shah what was wrong with him (p. 3). These illnesses resemble one another and in fact represent differential diagnoses for one another (L. Tierney, S. Saint, and M. Whooley, *Essentials of Diagnosis and Treatment*, 2nd ed. [New York: Lange Medical Books/McGraw-Hill, 2002]). Both are relatively slow-growing cancers of the blood and lymph system that progress intermittently,

inevitably but slowly, allowing the victim to survive many years from diagnosis. However, later in the same volume, Post and Robins attribute the main diagnosis to Waldenstrom's (p. 134) as does Altman. The spectrum of myeloproliferative disorders, of which these are part, can begin in one form and shift over time into a more severe condition. At autopsy, the shah was found to have died of histiocytic leukemia, but this does not mean the initial diagnosis was wrong, necessarily, but rather that the milder form of the illness had metamorphosed into the more serious form by the time he died. The important point is that both illnesses require combined chemotherapy that can be physically taxing and often require steroids that can exert mental effects as well.

10. Shawcross, *The Shah's Last Ride*, 234.
11. Zonis, *Majestic Failure*, 155.
12. Ibid, 232.
13. Ganji interview.
14. Clayton Cowl, *Physician's Drug Handbook*, 10th ed. (Philadelphia: Lippincott Williams and Wilkins, 2003).
15. Breo, "Shah's Physician Relates Story of Intrigue, Duplicity," and Tierney, Saint, and Whooley, *Essentials of Diagnosis and Treatment*, 2nd ed.
16. Post and Robins, *When Illness Strikes the Leader*, 3.
17. Zonis, *Majestic Failure*, 158; Shawcross, *The Shah's Last Ride*, 237.
18. Ganji interview.
19. Zonis, *Majestic Failure*, 156.
20. Ganji interview.
21. The notion of terminal urgency is spelled out in detail in Post and Robins, *When Illness Strikes the Leader*. This concept is also discussed in Jerrold Post, "Dreams of Glory and the Life Cycle: Reflections on the Life Course of Narcissistic Leaders," *Journal of Political and Military Sociology* 12 (1984): 49–60.
22. Ganji interview.
23. Zonis, *Majestic Failure*, 156.
24. Ganji Interview.
25. From Post and Robins, *When Illness Strikes the Leader*, 134.
26. Ganji interview.
27. E. A. Bayne, *Persian Kingship in Transition* (New York: American Universities Field Staff, 1968).
28. Assadollah Alam, *The Diaries of Assadollah Alam* (New York: New World, 1992).
29. Zonis, *Majestic Failure*, 248.
30. Pierre Salinger, *America Held Hostage* (Garden City, NY: Doubleday, 1981), 31.
31. Ganji interview.
32. For more on this time, see Stephen Kinzer, *All the Shah's Men: An American Coup and the Roots of Middle East Terror* (New York: Wiley, 2003).
33. Breo, "Shah's Physician Relates Story of Intrigue, Duplicity."
34. The Rockefeller family had a long-standing relationship with the shah dating back to at least 1951. Much of the Rockefeller fortune derives from

oil interests. These interests were compromised in 1953 when Iranian premier Mohammed Mossadegh nationalized Iranian oil assets, among other things. While at the time this hurt British Petroleum more than other oil interests, American oil interests, including those represented by Nelson Rockefeller, helped pressure the Eisenhower administration into overthrowing Mossadegh and putting the shah back in power, under the ideological guise of confronting communist incursions. After the shah was put back in power, all subsequent oil sales were handled through Chase Manhattan Bank, whose chairman was none other than David Rockefeller. This amounted to about $2 billion in 1975 alone. Henry Kissinger was on the Chase's international advisory board, and it was Nelson Rockefeller who recommended Kissinger to Richard Nixon as national security advisor.

35. This section from Breo, "Shah's Physician Relates Story of Intrigue, Duplicity," and Shawcross, *The Shah's Last Ride.*
36. In Shawcross, *The Shah's Last Ride,* 250.
37. Hamilton Jordan, *Crisis: The Last Year of the Carter Presidency* (New York: Putnam, 1982), 24. Carter's question was based on the previous Valentine's Day capture of American hostages in the embassy in Tehran, a seizure that the local government had quickly vanquished. At the time of letting the shah into the country, Carter sought, and gained, guarantees from the Iranian government for additional protection of the embassy staff.
38. Jimmy Carter, *Keeping Faith* (New York: Bantam, 1983), 456.
39. Ibid. See also Shawcross, *The Shah's Last Ride,* 251.
40. For more on the political calculations associated with Carter's decision to admit the shah, see Rose McDermott, *Risk Taking in International Politics* (Ann Arbor: University of Michigan Press, 1998).
41. Breo, "Shah's Physician Relates Story of Intrigue, Duplicity."
42. Shawcross, *The Shah's Last Ride,* 390.
43. Ibid., 410.
44. Breo, "Shah's Physician Relates Story of Intrigue, Duplicity," 22. This experience is consistent with that described in Post and Robins, *When Illness Strikes the Leader,* as "the captive king."
45. Post and Robins, *When Illness Strikes the Leader,* 133–135 especially.

BIBLIOGRAPHY

ARCHIVAL DOCUMENTS

John F. Kennedy Presidential Library, Boston, Massachusetts
Franklin Roosevelt Presidential Library, Hyde Park, New York
Woodrow Wilson collection at Seely Mudd Library, Princeton University, Princeton, New Jersey

OTHER SOURCES

Abrahamsen, David. 1977. *Nixon vs. Nixon: An Emotional Tragedy* (New York: Farrar, Straus & Giroux).
Abrams, Herbert. 1990. "Disabled Leaders, Cognition and Crisis Decision Making in Accidental Nuclear War." In *Proceedings of the Eighteenth Pugwash Workshop on Nuclear Forces* (Toronto: Science for Peace).
Abrams, Herbert. 1992. *"The President Has Been Shot": Confusion, Disability, and the 25th Amendment* (Stanford, CA: Stanford University Press).
Abrams, Herbert. 1993. "Shielding the President from the Constitution: Disability and the 25th Amendment." *Presidential Studies Quarterly* 3: 533–553.
Abrams, Herbert. 1995. "Presidential Health and the Public Interest – The Campaign of 1992." *Political Psychology* 16: 795–820.
Abrams, Herbert. 2001. "Sudden Incapacitation." In James Toole and Robert Joynt (Eds.), *Presidential Disability: Papers, Discussions and Recommendations on the 25th Amendment and Issues of Inability and Disability in Presidents of the United States* (Rochester, NY: University of Rochester Press), 39–44.
Alam, Assadollah. 1992. *The Diaries of Assadollah Alam* (New York: New World).

Altman, Lawrence. 2001. "Doctors Discount Workload as Factor in Cheney Case." *New York Times*, March 7, A15.

Altman, Lawrence. 2002. "The Doctor's World." *New York Times*, October 9, F5.

Ambrose, Stephen. 1987. *Nixon: Education of a Politician, 1913–1962* (New York: Simon & Schuster).

American Psychological Association. 1994. *Diagnostic and Statistical Manual*, 4th ed. Washington, DC: APA Press.

Annas, George. 1995. "The Health of the President and Presidential Candidates." *New England Journal of Medicine* 333: 945–949.

Attree, Elizabeth, Dancey, Christine, Keeling, Deborah, and Wilson, Christine. 2003. "Cognitive Function in People with Chronic Illness." *Applied Neuropsychology* 10, 2: 96–104.

Barber, James David. 1985. *The Presidential Character: Predicting Performance in the White House* (Englewood Cliffs, NJ: Prentice-Hall).

Barry, John. 2004. *The Great Influenza: The Epic Story of the Deadliest Plague in History* (New York: Viking).

Baruch, A. A. 1977. "Franklin Roosevelt's Illness: Effect on Course of History." *New York State Journal of Medicine* 77: 2154.

Bayh, Birch. 2000. "Reflections on the Twenty-Fifth Amendment as We Enter a New Century." In Gilbert 2000b, 55–68.

Bayne, E. A. 1968. *Persian Kingship in Transition* (New York: American Universities Field Staff).

Becker, A., and Weeks, E. 2003. "Post Operative Cognitive Dysfunction." *Best Practice* 17, 2: 259–272.

Beeson, Paul, and McDermott, Walsh. 1967. *Cecil's Textbook of Medicine*, 12th ed. (Philadelphia: W. B. Saunders).

Beschloss, Michael. 1991. *The Crisis Years: Kennedy and Khrushchev, 1960–1963* (New York: HarperCollins).

Beschloss, Michael. 2002. *The Conquerors: Roosevelt, Truman and the Destruction of Hitler's Germany, 1941–1945* (New York: Simon & Schuster).

Bezchlibnyk-Butler, Kalyna, and Jeffries, Joel. 2001. *Clinical Handbook of Psychotropic Drugs* (Seattle, WA: Hogrefe & Huber).

Bishop, Jim. 1974. *FDR's Last Year: April 1944–April 1945* (New York: William Morrow).

Blair, Joan, and Blair, Clay. 1976. *The Search for J.F.K.* (New York: Berkeley Publishing Group).

Bloom, Mark. 1976. "Should the Health of Presidential Candidates Be a Campaign Issue?" *Medical World News*, February 9, 34–54.

Bohlen, Charles. 1973. *Witness to History: 1929–1969* (New York: W. W. Norton).

Boniwell, Ilona, and Zimbardo, Philip. 2003. "Time to Find the Right Balance." *Psychologist* 16, 3: 129–131.

Boniwell, Ilona, and Zimbardo, Philip. 2004. "Balancing Time Perspective in Pursuit of Optimal Functioning." In Alex Linley and Stephen Joseph (Eds.), *Positive Psychology in Practice* (New York: John Wiley & Sons), 165–178.

Bowman, W., and Rand, M. 1980. *Textbook of Pharmacology*, 2nd ed. (Oxford: Blackwell Scientific Publishers).

Breo, D. L. 1981. "Shah's Physician Relates Story of Intrigue, Duplicity." *American Medical News*, August 7, 3–22.

Bruenn, Howard. 1970. "Clinical Notes on the Illness and Death of President Franklin D. Roosevelt." *Annals of Internal Medicine* 72, 4: 579–591.

Brodie, Fawn. 1981. *Richard Nixon: The Shaping of His Character* (Cambridge, MA: Harvard University Press).

Bueno de Mesquita, Bruce. 2000. *Principles of International Politics: People's Power, Preferences and Perceptions* (Washington, DC: CQ Press).

Bullitt, William. 1948. "How We Won the War and Lost the Peace." *Life Magazine*, September 6.

Byrnes, James. 1947. *Speaking Frankly* (New York: Harper & Brothers).

Calhoun, David, and Oparil, Susanne. 1995. "Hypertensive Crisis since FDR: A Partial Victory." *New England Journal of Medicine* 332, 15 (April 13): 1029.

Carter, Jimmy. 1983. *Keeping Faith* (New York: Bantam).

Carter, Jimmy. 1994. "Presidential Disability and the 25th Amendment: A President's Perspective." *Journal of the American Medical Association* 272, 21: 1698.

Cecil, Russell. 1944. *Textbook of Medicine*, 6th ed. (Philadelphia: W. B. Saunders).

Chesen, Eli. 1973. *President Nixon's Psychiatric Profile* (New York: Peter Wyden).

Cosmides, Leda, and Tooby, John. 2000. "Evolutionary Psychology and the Emotions." In M. Lewis and J. Haviland-Jones (Eds.), *Handbook of Emotions*, 2nd ed. (New York: Guilford Press), 91–115.

Cowl, Clayton. 2003. *Physician's Drug Handbook*, 10th ed. (Philadelphia: Lippincott Williams & Wilkins).

Crispell, Kenneth. 1997. "John F. Kennedy and the Issue of Presidential Disability." In Kenneth Thompson (Ed.), *Papers on Presidential Disability and the 25th Amendment by Dr. Kenneth Crispell and Other Medical, Legal and Political Authorities*, vol. 3 (Lanham, MD: University Press of America).

Crispell, Kenneth, and Gomez, Carlos. 1988. *Hidden Illness in the White House* (Durham, NC: Duke University Press).

Dallek, Robert. 2002. "The Medical Ordeals of JFK." *Atlantic Monthly*, December, 49–54.

Dallek, Robert. 2003. *An Unfinished Life: John F. Kennedy, 1917–1963* (Boston: Little Brown).

Devroy, Ann. 1993. "Clinton Team Follows Bush 'Road Map' on the Transfer of Presidential Power." *Washington Post*, June 14, A17.

Eden, Anthony. 1965. *The Memoirs of Anthony Eden, Earl of Avon: The Reckoning* (Boston: Houghton Mifflin).

Erikson, Erik. 1967. "The Strange Case of Freud, Bullitt, and Woodrow Wilson I." *New York Review*, February 9, 3.

Feerick, John. 1992. *The 25th Amendment: Its Complete History and Applications* (New York: Fordham University Press).

Feerick, John. 2000. "The Twenty-Fifth Amendment: Its Origins and History." In Gilbert 2000b, 1–24.

Ferrell, Robert. 1992. *Ill-Advised: Presidential Health and Public Trust* (Columbia: University of Missouri Press).

Ferrell, Robert. 1998. *The Dying President: Franklin Roosevelt, 1944–1945* (Columbia: University of Missouri Press).

Flatt, J. R., et al. 1984. "Effects of Anesthesia on Some Aspects of Mental Functioning of Surgical Patients." *Anesthesia and Intensive Care* 12: 315–324.

Fleming, Thomas. 1992. "Presidents on Presidents." *American Heritage* 43, 7: 1–5.

Flexner, James. 1974. *Washington: The Indispensable Man* (Boston: Little Brown).

Flynn, Edward. 1947. *You're the Boss* (New York: Viking Press).

Flynn, John. 1948. *The Roosevelt Myth* (New York: Devin-Adair).

Fontanarosa, P. B. 1995. "New Multidisciplinary Working Group Focuses on Presidential Disability." *Journal of the American Medical Association* 273, 12: 905–906.

Frederick, Shane, Loewenstein, George, and O'Donoghue, Ted. 2003. "Time Discounting and Time Preference: A Critical Review." In George Loewenstein, Daniel Read, et al. (Eds.), *Time and Decision: Economic and Psychological Perspectives on Intertemporal Choice* (New York: Russell Sage), 13–86.

Freud, Sigmund. 1916/1957. "Some Character-Types Met with in Psychoanalytic Work" (1916). In *The Standard Edition of the Complete Psychological Works of Sigmund Freud*, vol. 15 (1915–1916), *Introductory Lectures on Psycho-Analysis*, parts 1 and 2 (London: Hogarth Press).

Freud, Sigmund, and Bullitt, William. 1967. *Woodrow Wilson: A Psychological Study* (New Brunswick, NJ: Transaction).

Friedman, Richard. 1995. "Presidential Disability and the 25th Amendment." *Journal of the American Medical Association* 274, 10: 797–798.

Frost, David. 1978. *"I Gave Them a Sword": Behind the Scenes of the Nixon Interviews* (New York: William Morrow).

Frum, David. 2004. "Deathbed." *National Review Online*, November 8 (http://frum.nationalreview.com).

Gallagher, Hugh. 1994. *FDR's Splendid Deception* (Carlington, VA: Vandamere Press).

Gellert, George. 1995. "Presidential Disability and the 25th Amendment." *Journal of the American Medical Association* 274, 10: 798.

George, Alexander, and George, Juliette. 1956. *Woodrow Wilson and Colonel House* (New York: Dover).

George, Alexander, and George, Juliette. 1998. *Presidential Personality and Performance* (Boulder, CO: Westview).

George, Juliette, and George, Alexander. 1981–1982. "Woodrow Wilson and Colonel House: A Reply to Weinstein, Anderson and Link." *Political Science Quarterly* 96 (Winter): 641–665.

Gilbert, Robert. 1988. "Disability, Illness and the Presidency: The Case of Franklin D. Roosevelt." *Politics and the Life Sciences* 7, 1: 37.

Gilbert, Robert. 1998. *The Mortal Presidency: Illness and Anguish in the White House* (New York: Fordham University Press).

Gilbert, Robert. 2000a. "The Genius of the Twenty-Fifth Amendment: Guarding against Presidential Disability but Safeguarding the Presidency." In Gilbert 2000b, 25–54.

Gilbert, Robert (Ed.). 2000b. *Managing Crisis: Presidential Disability and the 25th Amendment* (New York: Fordham University Press).

Gilbert, Robert. 2003a. "The Contemporary Presidency: The Twenty-Fifth Amendment: Recommendations and Deliberations of the Working Group on Presidential Disability." *Presidential Studies Quarterly* 33: 877–888.

Gilbert, Robert. 2003b. *The Tormented President: Calvin Coolidge, Death and Clinical Depression* (Westport, CT: Praeger).

Gilbert, Robert. 2004 "Presidential Disability: Effects and Remedies in the Age of Terror." 40th Annual Robert D. Klein Lecture, February 12, Northeastern University, Boston.

Glad, Betty. 1986. *Key Pittman: The Tragedy of a Senate Insider* (New York: Columbia University Press).

Goldhagen, Daniel Jonah. 1997. *Hitler's Willing Executioners* (New York: Vintage).

Goldman, H. H. 1988. *Review of General Psychiatry* (Norwalk, CT: Appleton & Lange).

Goldsmith, H. 1979. "Unanswered Mysteries in the Death of Franklin D. Roosevelt." *Surgery, Gynecology and Obstetrics* 149: 902.

Goldstein, Joel. 2000. "The Vice Presidency and the Twenty-Fifth Amendment: The Power of Reciprocal Relationships." In Gilbert 2000b, 165–214.

Gorna, R., Kustrzycki, W., Kiejna, A., and Rymaszewska, J. 2001. "Assessment of Short Term Neuropsychological Change after Monothermic vs. Hypothermic Coronary Artery Bypass Grafting." *Psychiatric Politics* 35, 5: 781–795.

Grayson, Cary. 1960. *Woodrow Wilson: An Intimate Memoir* (New York: Holt, Rinehart & Winston).

Greenberg, David. 2003. *Nixon's Shadow: The History of an Image* (New York: Norton).

Greenstein, Fred. 1967. "The Impact of Personality and Politics: An Attempt to Clear Away the Underbrush." *American Political Science Review* 61: 629–641.

Grossman, M., and Kumar, M. 1981. *Portraying the President* (Baltimore: Johns Hopkins University Press).

Gunther, J. 1950. *Roosevelt in Retrospect* (New York: Harper and Row).

Haldeman, H. R. 1978. *The Ends of Power* (New York: Times Books).

Hamilton, James. 1977. "Some Reflections on Richard Nixon in the Light of His Resignation and Farewell Speeches." *Journal of Psychohistory* 4, 4: 491–511.

Harriman, W. Averill, and Abel, Elie. 1975. *Special Envoy to Churchill and Stalin, 1941–1946* (New York: Random House).

Heaver, J. 2003. "Toxicity of Anesthetics." *Clinical Anesthesiology* 17, 1: 1–3.

Herman, Jan Kenneth. 1990. "Interview with Dr. Howard Bruenn." *Navy Medicine*, March–April, 7–13.

Hersh, Seymour. 1983. *The Price of Power: Kissinger in the Nixon White House* (New York: Summit Books).

Hook, Steven, and Spanier, John. 2007. *American Foreign Policy since World War II*, 17th ed. (Washington, DC: CQ Press).

Hoover, Herbert. 1951. *The Memoirs of Herbert Hoover* (New York: Macmillan).

Hoover, Irwin Hood (Ike). 1934. *Forty-two Years in the White House* (Boston: Houghton Mifflin, 1934).

Hutschnecker, Arnold. 1969. "President Nixon's Former Doctor Writes about the Mental Health of Our Leaders." *Look*, July 15, 51–54.

Hutschnecker, Arnold. 1973. "The Stigma of Seeing a Psychiatrist." *New York Times*, November 20, 39.

Iremonger, Lucille. 1970. *The Fiery Chariot: A Study of British Prime Ministers and the Search for Love* (London: Secker & Warburg).

Isaacson, Walter. 1992. *Kissinger* (New York: Simon & Schuster).

Janis, Irving. 1982. "Decision Making under Stress." In L. Goldberger and S. Breznitz (Eds.), *Handbook of Stress: Theoretical and Clinical Aspects* (New York: Free Press), 69–87.

Johnson, James. 1979. "Nixon's Use of Metaphor: The Real Nixon Tapes." *Psychoanalytic Review* 66: 263–274.

Jordan, Hamilton. 1982. *Crisis: The Last Year of the Carter Presidency* (New York: Putnam).

Joynt, Robert. 1994. "Who Is Minding the World?" *Journal of the American Medical Association* 272, 21: 1699–1700.

Judd, L., Squire, L., Butters, N., Salmon, D., and Paller, K. 1987. "Effects of Psychotropic Drugs on Cognition and Memory in Normal Humans and Animals." In H. Y. Meltzwer (Ed.), *Psychopharmacology: A Third Generation of Progress* (New York: Raven Press), 1467–1475.

Kahneman, Daniel, and Tversky, Amos. 1979. "Prospect Theory: An Analysis of Decision under Risk." *Econometrica* 47: 263–291.

Keith, D., Wagener, H., and Barker, N. 1939. "Some Different Types of Essential Hypertension: Their Courses and Prognosis." *American Journal of Medical Society* 197: 332–343.

Kennedy, Robert, et al. 1965. *John F. Kennedy: As We Remember Him*, ed. Goddard Lieberson (New York: Macmillan).

Kennedy, Rose. 1974. *Times to Remember* (New York: Doubleday).

Kershaw, Ian. 2001. *The Hitler Myth* (New York: Oxford University Press).

Kimball, Jeffrey. 2004. *The Vietnam War Files: Uncovering the Secret History of Nixon-Era Strategy* (Lawrence: University Press of Kansas).

Kinzer, Stephen. 2003. *All the Shah's Men: An American Coup and the Roots of Middle East Terror* (New York: Wiley).

Kissinger, Henry. 1979. *White House Years* (Boston: Little Brown).

Kornitzer, Bela. 1960a. *The Real Nixon: An Intimate Biography* (Chicago: Rand McNally).

Kornitzer, Bela. 1960b. "My Son: Two Exclusive and Candid Interviews with Mothers of the Presidential Candidates." *Los Angeles Times*, This Week Magazine, September 18, 8.

Kotlowski, Dean. 2000. "The Knowles Affair: Nixon's Self-Inflicted Wound." *Presidential Studies Quarterly* 30, 3: 443–463.

Kucharski, A. 1981. "On Being Sick and Famous." *Political Psychology* 5: 69–82.

LaFeber, Walter. 1994. *The American Age: U.S. Foreign Policy at Home and Abroad*, vol. 2, *Since 1896*, 2nd ed. (New York: W. W. Norton).

LaFeber, Walter. 2008. *America, Russia and the Cold War, 1945–2001*, 10th ed. (Boston: McGraw-Hill).

Lasby, Clarence. 1997. *Eisenhower's Heart Attack* (Lawrence: University Press of Kansas).

Lasswell, Harold. 1930. *Psychopathology and Politics* (Chicago: University of Chicago Press).

Lasswell, Harold. 1935. *World Politics and Personal Insecurity* (New York: Whittlesey House, McGraw-Hill).

Leahy, William. 1950. *I Was There: The Personal Story of the Chief of Staff to Presidents Roosevelt and Truman Based on His Notes and Diaries Made at the Time* (New York: Whittlesey House).

Lee, Burton. 1995. "Presidential Disability and the 25th Amendment." *Journal of the American Medical Association* 274, 10: 797.

L'Etang, Hugh. 1970. *The Pathology of Leadership: A History of the Effects of Disease on 20th Century Leaders* (New York: Hawthorn).

L'Etang, Hugh. 1980. *Fit to Lead?* (London: William Heinemann Medical Books).

Lifton, Robert. 1969. *Death in Life: Survivors of Hiroshima* (New York: Vintage).

Link, Arthur. 1996. "Woodrow Wilson and the Constitutional Crisis." In Kenneth Thompson (Ed.), *Papers on Presidential Disability and the 25th Amendment by Medical, Historical and Political Authorities* (Lanham, MD: Miller Center, University of Virginia and University Press of America), 53–80.

Link, Arthur, Davidson, John Wells, and Little, John. 1984. "Communication to the Editor." *Journal of American History* 70: 945–955.

Link, Arthur, and Toole, James. 1994. "Presidential Disability and the 25th Amendment." *Journal of the American Medical Association* 272, 21: 1694–1697.

Lodge, Henry Cabot. 1944. *The Senate and the League of Nations* (Chapel Hill: University of North Carolina Press).

Loewenberg, Peter. 1986. "Nixon, Hitler and Power: An Ego Psychological Study." *Psychoanalytic Inquiry* 6: 27–48.

Lubit, Roy, and Russett, Bruce. 1984. "The Effects of Drugs on Decision Making." *Journal of Conflict Resolution* 28, 1: 85–102.

Lungren, John, and Lungren, John, Jr. 2003. *Healing Richard Nixon* (Lexington: University Press of Kentucky).

Lurie, L. 1972. *The Running of Richard Nixon* (New York: Coward, McCann and Geohagen).

MacMahon, Edward, and Curry, Leonard. 1987. *Medical Cover-Ups in the White House* (Washington, DC: Farragut).

Macmillan, Harold. 1972. *Pointing the Way, 1959–1961* (New York: HarperCollins, 1972).

Majewska, M. D. 1996. "Cocaine Addition as a Neurological Disorder: Implications for Treatment." *NIDA Research Monograph* 163: 1–26.

Mancillas, Jorge. 2003. "They Did Not Have to Die." *San Francisco Chronicle*, July 23, A23.

Mariano, E. Connie. 2000. "In Sickness and in Health: Medical Care for the President of the United States." In Gilbert 2000b, 83–95.

Marion, Robert. 1994. *Was George Washington Really the Father of Our Country? A Clinical Geneticist Looks at World History* (Reading, MA: Addison-Wesley).

Marmor, Michael. 1983. "Comments on 'Woodrow Wilson Reexamined.'" *Political Psychology*, 4, 2: 325–327.

Mazlish, Bruce. 1970. "Towards a Psychohistorical Inquiry: The 'Real' Richard Nixon." *Journal of Interdisciplinary History* 1: 49–105.

Mazlish, Bruce. 1972a. *In Search of Nixon: A Psychohistorical Inquiry* (New York: Basic Books).

Mazlish, Bruce. 1972b. "Psychohistory and Richard M. Nixon." *Psychology Today*, July, 177–190.

McDermott, Rose. 1998. *Risk Taking in International Politics: Prospect Theory in American Foreign Policy* (Ann Arbor: University of Michigan Press).

McDermott, Rose. 2004. *Political Psychology in International Relations* (Ann Arbor: University of Michigan Press).

McElroy, Robert. 1993. *Morality in American Foreign Policy* (Princeton, NJ: Princeton University Press).

McIntire, Ross. 1946. *White House Physician* (New York: G. P. Putnam's Sons).

McKim, William. 2000. *Drugs and Behavior: An Introduction to Behavioral Pharmacology*, 4th ed. (Upper Saddle River, NJ: Prentice-Hall).

McLure, Samuel, Laibson, David, Loewenstein, George, and Cohen, Jonathan. 2004. "Separate Neural Systems Value Immediate and Delayed Monetary Rewards." *Science* 306, 5695: 503–507.

Messerli, Franz. 1995. "This Day 50 Years Ago." *New England Journal of Medicine* 32, 15 (April 13): 1038–1039.

Miles, Steven. 1995. "Presidential Disability and the 25th Amendment." *Journal of the American Medical Association* 274, 10: 798–799.

"Mitchell Urges Nixon to Name Fund Donators." 1952. *New York Herald Tribune*, September 20, 6.

Mohr, Lawrence. 1995. "The White House Physician: Role, Responsibilities and Issues." *Political Psychology* 16, 4: 777–793.

Moller, J. T., et al. 1998. "Long Term Postoperative Cognitive Dysfunction in the Elderly." *Lancet* 351, 9106, (March 21): 857–861.

Moran, Lord. 1966. *Churchill Taken from the Diaries of Lord Moran: The Struggle for Survival, 1940–1965* (Boston: Houghton Mifflin).

Morris, Errol. 2004. *The Fog of War*. Sony Pictures.

"Nixon Fund Uncovered; 76 Gave $18, 235." 1952. *New York Herald Tribune*, September 21, 1.

Nixon, Hannah. 1960. Told to Flora Rheta Schreiber, "Richard Nixon, a Mother's Story." *Good Housekeeping*, June.

Nixon, Richard. 1962. *Six Crises* (New York: Pyramid).

Nixon, Richard. 1978. *RN: The Memoirs of Richard Nixon* (New York: Grosset & Dunlap).

Ormel, J., Von Korff, M., Ustun, B., et al. 1994. "Common Mental Disorders and Disabilities across Cultures." *Journal of the American Medical Association* 272: 1741–1748.

Owen, C. H. 2003. "Diseased, Demented, Depressed: Serious Illness in Heads of State." *Quarterly Journal of Medicine* 96, 5: 325–336.

Pacepa, Ion Mihai. 1990. *Red Horizons: The True Story of Nicolae and Elena Ceausescus' Crimes, Lifestyle, and Corruption* (Washington, DC: Regnery Publishing).

Park, Bert. 1986. *The Impact of Illness on World Leaders* (Philadelphia: University of Pennsylvania Press).

Park, Bert. 1987. "The Impact of Wilson's Neurologic Disease during the Paris Peace Conference." In Wilson 1987, 58:611–630.

Park, Bert. 1988. "Presidential Disability: Past Experiences and Future Implications." *Politics and the Life Sciences* 7 (August): 55.

Park, Bert. 1993. *Ailing, Aging, Addicted: Studies of Compromised Leadership* (Lexington: University Press of Kentucky).

Park, Bert. 1995. "Resuscitating the 25th Amendment: A Second Opinion Regarding Presidential Disability." *Political Psychology* 16, 4: 821–839.

Perkins, Frances. 1946. *The Roosevelt I Knew* (New York: Viking).

Perlstein, Rick. 2003. Foreword to John C. Lungren and John C. Lungren Jr., *Healing Richard Nixon: A Doctor's Memoir* (Lexington: University Press of Kentucky).

Petillo, Carol Morris. 1981. *Douglas MacArthur, the Philippine Years* (Bloomington: University of Indiana Press).

Post, Jerrold. 1973. "On Aging Leaders: Possible Effects of the Aging Process on the Conduct of Leadership." *Journal of Geriatric Psychiatry* 6: 109–116.

Post, Jerrold. 1980. "The Seasons of a Leader's Life." *Political Psychology* 2: 35–49.

Post, Jerrold. 1983a. "'Woodrow Wilson Reexamined': The Mind Body Controversy Redux and Other Disputations." *Political Psychology* 4: 289–306.

Post, Jerrold. 1983b. "Reply to the Three Comments on 'Woodrow Wilson Reexamined': The Mind Body Controversy Redux and Other Disputations." *Political Psychology* 4: 329–331.

Post, Jerrold. 1991. "Saddam Hussein of Iraq: A Political Psychology Profile." *Political Psychology* 12: 279–290.

Post, Jerrold. 1999. Review of *Hitler: Diagnosis of a Destructive Prophet* by Fritz Redlich. *New England Journal of Medicine*, May 27, 1692.

Post, Jerrold. 2000. "Broken Minds, Broken Hearts and the Twenty-Fifth Amendment: Psychiatric Disorders and Presidential Disability." In Gilbert 2000b, 111–124.

Post, Jerrold. 2001. "Behavioral Disorders." In Toole and Joynt 2001, 52–60.

Post, Jerrold. 2003. *The Psychological Assessment of Political Leaders* (Ann Arbor: University of Michigan Press).

Post, Jerrold. 2004. *Leaders and Their Followers in a Dangerous World* (Ithaca, NY: Cornell University Press).

Post, Jerrold, and Robins, Robert. 1990. "The Captive King and His Captive Court: The Psychopolitical Dynamics of the Disabled Leader and His Inner Circle." *Political Psychology* 11, 2: 331–351.

Post, Jerrold, and Robins, Robert. 1993. *When Illness Strikes the Leader: The Dilemma of the Captive King* (New Haven, CT: Yale University Press).

Potter, E. B. (Ed.) 1960. *Sea Power: A Naval History* (Englewood Cliffs, NJ: Prentice-Hall).

Reagan, Ronald. 1990. *An American Life* (New York: Simon & Schuster).

Redlich, Fritz. 2000. *Hitler: Diagnosis of a Destructive Prophet* (New York: Oxford University Press).

Reeves, Richard. 1993. *President Kennedy: Profile of Power* (New York: Simon & Schuster).

Reeves, Thomas. 1991. *A Question of Character: A Life of John F. Kennedy* (New York: Free Press).

Rensberger, B. 1972. "Amphetamines Used by a Physician to Lift Moods of Famous Patients." *New York Times*, December 4, 34.

Renshon, Stanley. 1975. "Psychological Analysis of Presidential Personality: The Case of Richard Nixon." *History of Childhood Quarterly: The Journal of Psychohistory* 2, 3 (Winter): 415–450.

Renshon, Stanley. 1998. *The Psychological Assessment of Presidential Candidates* (New York: Routledge).

Reston, James. 1991. *Deadline: A Memoir* (New York: Random House).

Ridings, William, and McIver, Stuart. 1997. *Rating the Presidents: From the Great and Honorable to the Dishonest and Incompetent* (New York: Citadel Press).

Rigdon, William, with James Derieux. 1962. *White House Sailor* (Garden City, NY: Doubleday).

Riis, J., Lomholt, B., et al. 1983. "Immediate and Long Term Mental Recovery from General vs. Epidural Anesthesia in Elderly Patients." *Acta Anaesthesiologica Scandinavica* 27: 44–49.

Robertson, Terence. 1984. *Crisis: The Inside Story of the Suez Conspiracy* (New York: Atheneum).

Robins, Robert. 1977. "Recruitment of Pathological Deviants into Political Leadership." In R. S. Robins (Ed.), *Psychopathology and Political Leadership* (New Orleans: Tulane University), 53–78.

Robins, Robert, and Dorn, Robert. 1993. "Stress and Political Leadership." *Politics and the Life Sciences* 12, 1: 3–17.

Robins, Robert, and Post, Jerrold. 1995. "Choosing a Healthy President." *Political Psychology* 16, 4: 841–860.

Robins, Robert, and Post, Jerrold. 1997. *Political Paranoia: The Psychopolitics of Hatred* (New Haven, CT: Yale University Press).

Robins, Robert, and Rothschild, Henry. 1981. "Hidden Health Disabilities and the Presidency: Medical Management and Political Considerations." *Perspectives in Biology and Medicine* 24: 240–253.

Robins, Robert, and Rothschild, Henry. 1988. "Ethical Dilemmas of the President's Physician." *Politics and the Life Sciences* 7, 1: 3–11.

Rogin, Michael, and Lottier, John. 1971. "The Inner History of Richard Milhous Nixon." *Transaction* 9: 1–2.

Roos, Charles. 1961. "Physician to the President." *Bulletin of the Medical Library Association* 49: 291–360.

Roosevelt, Eleanor. 1961. *The Autobiography of Eleanor Roosevelt* (New York: Harper and Row).

Roosevelt, Franklin. 1950. *The Public Papers and Addresses of Franklin D. Roosevelt* (New York: Russell and Russell).

Roosevelt, James, and Shallett, Sidney. 1959. *Affectionately, FDR* (New York: Harcourt and Brace).

Rosen, Stephen Peter. 2005. *War and Human Nature* (Princeton, NJ: Princeton University Press).

Rothenberg, Alan. 1975. "Why Nixon Taped Himself: Infantile Fantasies behind Watergate." *Psychoanalytic Review* 62: 201–223.

Salinger, Pierre. 1981. *America Held Hostage* (Garden City, NY: Doubleday).

Sapolsky, Robert. 1994. *Why Zebras Don't Get Ulcers: A Guide to Stress, Stress-Related Disease and Coping* (New York: Freeman).

Schelling, Thomas. 1960. *The Strategy of Conflict* (Cambridge, Mass.: Harvard University Press).

Schlesinger, Arthur, Jr. 1956. *The Crisis of the Old Order* (New York: Houghton Mifflin).

Schlesinger, Arthur, Jr. 1997. "Rating the Presidents: Washington to Clinton." *Political Science Quarterly* 11, 2 (Summer): 179–190.

Schweinitz, George de. 1906. *Diseases of the Eye* (Philadelphia: W. B. Saunders).

"Secret Rich Men's Trust Fund Keeps Nixon in Style Far Beyond His Salary." 1952. *New York Post*, September 18, 3, 26.

Shawcross, William. 1988. *The Shah's Last Ride: The Fate of an Ally* (New York: Simon & Schuster).

Sherwood, Robert. 1949. *The White House Papers of Harry L. Hopkins*, vol. 2 (London: Eyre and Spottiswoode).

Sick, Gary. 1986. *All Fall Down* (New York: Penguin Books).

Sidey, Hugh. 1987. "The Man and Foreign Policy." In Kenneth Thompson (Ed.), *Portraits of American Presidents*, vol. 6, *The Nixon Presidency* (Lanham, MD: University Press of America).

Silva, R. D. 1968. *Presidential Succession* (New York: Greenwood Press).

Small, Melvin. 1999. *The Presidency of Richard Nixon* (Lawrence: University Press of Kansas).

Smith, Bradley. 1977. *Reaching Judgment at Nuremberg* (New York: Basic).

Smith, Terence. 1981. "Why Carter Admitted the Shah." *New York Times Magazine*, May 26, 36–37.

Sorensen, Theodore. 1957. *Kennedy* (New York: Harper and Row).

Steinberg, Blema. 1996. *Shame and Humiliation: Presidential Decision Making on Vietnam* (Pittsburgh: University of Pittsburgh Press).

Stettinius, Edward. 1949. *Roosevelt and the Russians: The Yalta Conference* (Garden City, NY: Doubleday).

Stimpson, Henry L., and Bundy, McGeorge. 1948. *On Active Duty in Peace and War* (New York: Harper).

Summers, Anthony. 2000. *The Arrogance of Power: The Secret World of Richard Nixon* (New York: Penguin).

Swanson, D. 1967. "Clinical Psychiatric Problems Associated with General Surgery." In H. Abrams (Ed.), *Psychologic Aspects of Surgery, International Psychiatry Clinics* (Boston: Little, Brown, 1967), 105–113.

Taubman, William. 2003. *Khrushchev: The Man and His Era* (New York: W. W. Norton).

Thomas, Hugh. 1967. *Suez* (New York: Harper and Row).

Thompson, Kenneth (Ed.). 1988. *Report of the Miller Center Commission on Presidential Disability and the Twenty-fifth Amendment* (Lanham, MD: White Burkett Miller Center of Public Affairs at the University of Virginia and University Press of America).

Tierney, Lawrence, Saint, Sanjay, and Whooley, Mary. 2002. *Essentials of Diagnosis and Treatment* (New York: Lange).

Toledano, R. de. 1969. *One Man Alone: Richard Nixon* (New York: Funk and Wagnalls).

Toole, James, and Joynt, Robert (Eds.). 2001. *Presidential Disability: Papers, Discussions and Recommendations on the 25th Amendment and Issues of Inability and Disability in Presidents of the United States* (Rochester, NY: University of Rochester Press).

Toole, J., Link, A., and Smith, J. 1997. "Disability in US Presidents Report: Recommendations and Commentaries by the Working Group." *Archives of Neurology* 54, 9: 1256–1264.

Travell, Janet. 1968. *Office Hours, Day and Night: The Autobiography of Janet Travell, M.D.* (New York: World Publications).

Trow, C. 1971. "Woodrow Wilson and the Mexican Interventionist Movement of 1919." *Journal of American History* 58: 46–72.

Tucker, Robert. 1977. "The George's Wilson Reexamined: An Essay on Psychobiography." *American Political Science Review* 71: 103–104.

Tugwell, Rexford. 1957. *The Democratic Roosevelt* (Baltimore: Penguin Books).

Tully, Grace. 1949. *FDR: My Boss* (Chicago: People's Book Club).

Tumulty, Joseph. 1921. *Woodrow Wilson as I Know Him* (Garden City, NY: Doubleday).

Volkan, Vamik, Itzkowitz, Norman, and Dod, Andrew. 1997. *Richard Nixon: A Psychobiography* (New York: Columbia).

Walker, Kenneth. 1998. "Medical Condition of Leaders Often Hushed Up." *Chicago Sun-Times*, February 15, 44.

Waltz, Kenneth. 1979. *Theory of International Relations* (Reading, MA: Addison Wesley).

Wang, David, Koehler, Schott, and Mariash, Cary. 1996. "Detecting Graves' Disease." *Physician and Sportsmedicine* 24, 12: 35.

Weaver, Judith. 1985. "Edith Bolling Wilson as First Lady: A Study in the Power of Personality, 1919–1920." *Presidential Studies Quarterly* 15: 51–52, 55.

Webster, J., Petrie, J., Jeffers, T., and Lovell, H. 1993. "Accelerated Hypertension: Patterns of Mortality and Clinical Factors Affecting Outcome in Treated Patients." *Quarterly Journal of Medicine* 86: 485–493.

Weinstein, Edwin. 1981. *Woodrow Wilson: A Medical and Psychological Biography* (Princeton, NJ: Princeton University Press).

Weinstein, Edwin. 1983. "Comments on 'Woodrow Wilson Reexamined.'" *Political Psychology* 4, 2: 313–324.

Weinstein, Edwin, Anderson, James, and Link, Arthur. 1978. "Woodrow Wilson's Political Personality: A Reappraisal." *Political Science Quarterly* 93: 585–598.

White, P. D. 1937. *Heart Disease*, 2nd ed. (New York: Macmillan).

Williams, Robert. 1974. *Textbook of Endocrinology*, 5th ed. (Philadelphia: W. B. Saunders).

Wilson, Edith. 1939. *My Memoir* (New York: Bobbs-Merrill).

Wilson, Philip. 1955. "Example of a Patient with Adrenal Insufficiency Due to Addison's Disease Requiring Elective Surgery." *American Medical Association Archives of Surgery* 71 (November): 739.

Wilson, Woodrow. 1987. *Papers of Woodrow Wilson*, ed. Arthur Link (Princeton: Princeton University Press).

Winnicott, Donald. 1965. *The Maturational Process and the Facilitating Environment* (New York: International Universities Press).

Winter, David, and Carlson, Leslie. 1988. "Using Motive Scores in the Psychobiographical Study of an Individual: The Case of Richard Nixon." *Journal of Personality* 56: 75–103.

Woodstone, Arthur. 1972. *Nixon's Head* (New York: St. Martin's Press).

Zimbardo, Philip, and Boyd, John. 1999. "Putting Time in Perspective: A Valid, Reliable Individual-Difference Metric." *Journal of Personality and Social Psychology* 77, 6: 1271–1288.

Zonis, Marvin. 1991. *Majestic Failure: The Fall of the Shah* (Chicago: University of Chicago Press).

INDEX